From Jesus to Christ

PAULA FREDRIKSEN

FROM JESUS TO CHRIST

The Origins of the New Testament Images of Jesus

SECOND EDITION

Yale University Press
New Haven and London

Printed in the United States of America.

Library of Congress Cataloging-in-Publication Data
Fredriksen, Paula, 1951–
From Jesus to Christ : the origins of the New Testament images of Jesus / Paula Fredriksen.—2nd ed.
    p.   cm.
Includes bibliographical references and index.
ISBN 0-300-08457-9 (pbk.)
1. Jesus Christ—Person and offices—Biblical teaching. 2. Bible. N.T.—Criticism, interpretation, etc. 3. Jesus Christ—History of doctrines—Early church, ca. 30–600. I. Title.

BT198.F82 2000
232'.09'015—dc21

00-025505

A catalogue record for this book is available from the British Library.

10 9 8 7 6 5

Contents

Preface

I had thought that this would be an easy book to write. To present to the nonspecialist a discussion of the New Testament's images of Jesus, I would simply put into prose the material on Christian origins that I had been teaching my undergraduates. The book would write itself.

That was more than six years ago. My initial plan was frustrated both by my students, who never hesitated to let me know when some doctrine of New Testament scholarship made no sense to them, and by my own dissatisfaction with the various approaches to the material that I attempted as the semesters came and went. The documents in the canon resisted any approach I tried. If I began with the earliest Christian source, Paul's letters, the figure of Jesus of Nazareth never emerged; if I began with the gospels, which do depict Jesus, I was already treating a self-conscious Christian tradition that deliberately distanced itself from the historical Jewish context in which Jesus had lived and died. My husband finally suggested that I acquiesce to what I could not change, and let the documents dictate the structure of the book: begin with the (probably) latest and most theologically sophisticated depiction, namely John's; work back to Paul's letters; and then retrace my steps so that the reader could have a sense of the historical and social forces behind the development of these various images of Jesus.

The ideas that emerged surprised me. Once organized in this way, the data suggested new answers to some of the hoariest questions of New Testament scholarship—the circumstances surrounding the execution of Jesus; the reasons Diaspora Jews, Paul included, resisted the early Christian mission to the synagogues; the origins of the Law-free mission to the Gentiles; when "Mark" wrote his gospel, and why; how the Johannine Christ relates to the figure in the synoptic tradition. What began as an introduction to the Jesus of the New Testament for the general reader thus became an interpretive essay on Christian origins for fellow historians as well. The book maintains a narrative style and avoids detailed bibliographical annotation and argument for the sake of the general reader; but for both audiences I include citations to relevant ancient texts, so both can know why I say what I say.

Colleagues in New Testament history and theology generously criticized, discussed and debated my arguments, thus helping me to strengthen and clarify them. In particular, John Gager and E. P. Sanders both read and commented on the entire penultimate draft. Friends in other fields of history or in other professions entirely graciously consented to serve as my "general readers" when I feared the creeping incursions of technical jargon or excessive detail: the book profited especially from the merciless editing of David Landes, Nicholas A. Ulanov, and Michael Werner. Conversations with A. H. Lapin and with Robert Tannenbaum clarified important issues in rabbinic and Hellenistic Judaism respectively. Mark Spero and An van Rompaey provided special assistance. To all, my deep thanks.

Finally, I would like to thank Guy Lobrichon of the Collège de France, whose invitation to contribute a volume to the series on Jesus published by the Editions du Cerf initiated my research; Bernard Lauret, my editor at Le Cerf, and Charles Grench, my editor at Yale, for their enthusiasm and support; and Richard Landes, my husband, without whose intelligent suggestions and ability to distract the children I never could have completed this work.

Introduction

In the beginning was the spoken word. Jesus of Nazareth announced the coming Kingdom of God; but he did not write of it. Nor, apparently, did the immediate circle of disciples who followed him from the Galilee to Jerusalem and after his death proclaimed the good news. Paul the Apostle, some twenty years later, preached the Gospel "from Jerusalem as far round as Illyricum"; but when he wrote to his communities, he spoke less of the Kingdom than of its divine emissary: the Risen Christ, not the human Jesus. By the end of the first century, Christian communities preserved the memory of this message in their various interpretations of its first messenger. The Gospel had become the gospels.[1]

These traditions from and about Jesus continued to be fluid even once they attained written form. Different writers felt free to rearrange and alter the information they inherited—a simple comparison of the first three canonical gospels reveals this—because they did not see themselves as writing scripture. Justin Martyr, a church father of the mid-second century, referred to the gospels as "memoires" (*Dialogue with Trypho* 105): for him, as for almost all early Christians, scripture was the Greek translation of the Jewish Bible known as the Septuagint. Only eventually did the church come to see its own literary products as scripture—as *New* Testament, completing and superseding the Old—and by that time, the documentary unity created by the canon actually preserved a diversity of traditions.

These New Testament documents declare the good news of Christ's coming, the Christs who were the focus of the faith, hopes, and commitments of the communities that produced and, later, collected them. They convey a rich variety of theological images of Christ, mingled in different ways with histor-

1. Throughout this book, I have capitalized *Gospel* to indicate oral traditions concerning the coming Kingdom of God. In this sense, both Jesus and Paul preached the Gospel. With a lower-case g, *gospel* refers to later literary interpretations of Jesus' ministry.

ical information about Jesus. Our question to them in this study is twofold. First, what are these different images? And, second, how can we account historically for their development and their diversity, especially when we have no independent access to our logical starting point, the Jesus of history?

I propose to approach these questions by placing the various canonical images of Jesus within their historical context, the religious world of first- and second-century Mediterranean civilization. The Christian communities, the living matrix of our documents, themselves expressed the interaction of two contemporary cultures, Hellenism and Judaism.[2] Both of these cultures, each in its own way, affirmed certain common religious principles: that absolute divinity was absolutely good; that it stood in some relation, whether distant or direct, to the world; and that man's experience of the world, once properly understood, affirmed divine goodness. Both, therefore, had to confront the challenge to these principles posed by the problem of evil.

The defining characteristics of each—the philosophical culture and evolved metaphysics of Hellenism; the strong sense of history, community, and revelation in Judaism—are thus implicit theodicies, strategies for affirming divine goodness in the face of the challenge of evil. By considering these two cultures from this perspective, we should be better able to perceive the creative tensions that underlie and inform the canonical images of Jesus. These, too, are motivated by theodicy. They invest with positive—indeed, redemptive—significance two otherwise discomfiting facts: the delay of God's Kingdom, and the crucifixion of his messiah.

To approach our twofold question, we shall read the New Testament texts in three cycles: descriptive, historical, and explanatory. Part I, the descriptive cycle, portrays the canonical images of Jesus against their Hellenistic background. After a brief methodological introduction (chapter 1), I shall present a broad overview of the religious world of late Hellenism (chapter 2). Here we shall trace the historical circumstances that contributed to Hellenistic views of God, man, and the universe and explore the ways that people within this cultural tradition conceived and attempted to resolve the problem of evil. Here too we shall consider the first great synthesis of Hellenism and the biblical heritage, Hellenistic Judaism.

In coming to the second great synthesis, Christianity, I shall address our question: What images of Jesus do we find in New Testament documents? I shall proceed by examining the various images of Jesus conveyed in our chief canonical texts in *reverse* chronological order—the Gospel of John, the synoptic gospels, and finally the letters of Paul (chapter 3).[3] This strategy has two

2. These are abstractions, of course: both cultures varied widely, and many Jews—even traditionally religious ones—were, as we shall see, culturally Greek.

3. Broad consensus on the relative dating of these writings coexists with lively debate. See Suggested Reading for discussion.

advantages. First, by moving backwards, we more easily avoid the impression of teleological development that a forward chronological survey might falsely give: these images, even where they naturally depended on inherited materials, were the independent creations of their respective communities. Their lack of pattern is as historically important as their pattern. Second, by tracing their backward trajectory, we move chronologically closer to their point of origin, that documentary vacuum inhabited by Jesus of Nazareth. We stop where our texts leave us, in the Gentile communities of the Mediterranean around the year 50 C.E., some twenty years after Jesus' execution.[4]

In Part II, the historical cycle, we enter the religious world of Jesus of Nazareth: Judaism. At once both ethnic and cultic, Judaism organized itself through religious reflection on historical events in the life of the Jewish people. Consequently, we shall examine Judaism through the idea of Israel (chapter 5), moving forward in time through scriptural perceptions of Creation, the patriarchs, and the covenant; through the formative experience of the Babylonian period, the Exile and Return; to the varieties of first-century Palestinian Judaism. The goal of our narrative survey is to understand the development of that singular Jewish response to the problem of evil, apocalyptic eschatology—the great hope that God would intervene in history *soon* to restore Israel, redeem the world, and establish forever his own kingdom of peace. This spiritual orientation accounts for many of the religious and political responses to Roman rule in Palestine, among which, as I shall argue, was Jesus' ministry. Our overview of Judaism ends with the period following the destruction of the Second Temple in 70 C.E.

Having followed our two trajectories backward through the New Testament texts and forward through Jewish history to the area where they overlap at the period between the lifetime of Jesus and the composition of the New Testament texts, we shall reexamine the evangelical images of Jesus in light of our knowledge of his historical context (chapter 6). Approaching Jesus from these two chronological and cultural directions highlights the dynamics behind the gospel traditions, enabling us to distinguish between the different sorts of information they convey. Through this critical reading of the gospels, we may perceive the lineaments of the Jesus of history (chapter 7). Of course, no matter how cautious, critical, and self-conscious our methods and modest our claims when attempting to recover him, this "historical Jesus" is but an image, at best a coherent set of inferences from historical knowledge.

Part III, the explanatory cycle, attempts to reconstruct Christian "prehistory," the growth of traditions about Jesus in the period between his execution and the composition of our documents. Here we address our second question:

---

4. Academic convention designates the period "Before Christ" as "Before the Common Era" (abbreviated B.C.E.), and the period "Anno Domini" as "Common Era" (C.E.). I use these designations throughout this study.

What accounts for the development and the diversity of these early images of Jesus? If the life and career of Jesus was the necessary but insufficient cause of Christianity, the sufficient cause was the original community's experience of his resurrection. Starting from our historical image of Jesus, we shall work forward once again through the New Testament texts in order to see how these different Christian communities responded to the disappointment of the Kingdom's continuing delay by variously combining apocalyptic eschatology and metaphysics—the respective responses of Jewish and Greek cultures to the problem of evil—to create around the memory of Jesus' message of the Kingdom a new symbol of redemption, the crucified Son of God. By so doing, the Christian communities separated themselves from their two antecedent religious cultures, forming a movement that was neither Jewish nor Greek, but a new creation. In the process, as we shall see, the messenger became the message.

Introduction to the Second Edition

Who was Jesus of Nazareth? How did he fit into his native religious context, Judaism of the Late Second Temple period (c. 200 B.C.E.–70 C.E.)? Why does such a manifestly Jewish religious figure end up dying a Roman political death? Some of his close disciples were convinced that God had raised Jesus from the dead. Does their conviction stand in any meaningful relation to the message he proclaimed during his lifetime? What does the itinerant mission of an Aramaic-speaking Galilean Jew have to do with the triumphant cosmic agent whose imminent apocalyptic return was so blazingly announced by his apostle Paul? And how does any of this account for the momentous shift in the makeup of the Christian movement from almost exclusively Jewish to increasingly Gentile, to which Paul's letters, mid-first century, already attest?

Over the past fifteen years a flood of works considering these questions has inundated scholars, students, and the nonspecialist reading public alike. Paperbacks proliferate as the range of portraits of Jesus broadens. In recent scholarship Jesus has been imagined and presented as a type of first-century shaman; as a wandering Cynic-style wise man; as a visionary radical and social reformer preaching egalitarian ethics to the destitute; as a Galilean regionalist alienated from the elitism of Judean religious conventions (like Temple and Torah); as a champion of national liberation; as, on the contrary, its opponent and critic, and so on and on.[1] All these figures are presented with rigorous academic argument and methodology; all are defended

1. On Jesus the shaman, Stevan L. Davies, *Jesus the Healer* (London 1995). On Jesus the Cynic, Gerald F. Downing, *Christ and the Cynics: Jesus and Other Radical Preachers in First-Century Tradition* (Sheffield 1988) and *Cynics and Christian Origins* (Edinburgh 1992); Burton Mack, *A Myth of Innocence: Mark and Christian Origins* (Philadelphia 1988). On Jesus the radical peasant reformer, esp. John Dominic Crossan, *The Historical Jesus* (San Francisco 1991) and *Jesus: A Revolutionary Biography* (San Francisco 1994). On Jesus the regionalist, specifically anti-Temple, anti-purity agitator, Marcus Borg, *Jesus in Contemporary Schol-*

with appeals to the ancient data. Debate continues at a roiling pitch, and consensus—even on such basic issues as what constitutes evidence and how to construe it—seems a distant hope.

Reconstructions of the historical figure of Jesus currently seem polarized around two basic interpretive options: Jesus as a teacher of (some sort of) ethics and Jesus as an apocalyptic prophet of God's coming Kingdom.[2] Advocates of the first tend to privilege the sayings in the gospels as premier evidence for understanding Jesus; advocates of the second, specifically those sayings about the coming Kingdom of God (attested not only by the evangelists but also by Paul), as well as the actions attributed to Jesus during his mission. Applying new methods from other fields (social and cultural anthropology, political science, comparative literature) to the early Christian material, scholars have widened the scope of the search; now the effort to understand Jesus involves efforts to understand his context. We see quests for the historical John the Baptist (prophetic? anti-Temple? for or against traditional construals of purity?), the historical Galilee (urbanized and Hellenized? Temple-oriented or cosmopolitan? with a thin crust of the wealthy exploiting huge masses of the destitute, or with a healthy mix of farming and marketing within a generally well-fed village culture?), and the historical Temple (object of peasant resentment? preserve of the priestly elites? hotbed of nationalism? home base of a quisling aristocracy?).[3]

---

arship (San Francisco 1994), and specifically an alienated Galilean regionalist, Richard Horsley, *Jesus and the Spiral of Violence* (San Francisco 1987). On Jesus as champion of a new post-Torah antinationalist Judaism, N. T. Wright, *Jesus and the Victory of God* (Minneapolis 1996). On Jesus' context, see Richard Horsley, *Galilee: History, Politics, People* (Valley Forge 1995).

2. The academic genealogy of the apocalyptic Jesus can be traced from Johannes Weiss and Albert Schweitzer in the 19th c. to E. P. Sanders, *Jesus and Judaism* (Philadelphia 1985) and *The Historical Figure of Jesus* (London 1993). I place myself within this stemma. John P. Meier's huge, comprehensive, and authoritative study *A Marginal Jew*—which weighs in at well over sixteen hundred pages distributed over his first two volumes (New York 1991 and 1994), with more on the way—also presents Jesus in apocalyptic mode. Two recent briefer studies in this vein are Dale Allison, *Jesus of Nazareth: Millenarian Prophet* (Minneapolis 1998), and Bart Ehrman, *Jesus: Apocalyptic Prophet of the New Millennium* (New York 1999). For a review of some of the major works on the historical Jesus to 1994, see my article "What You See Is What You Get: Context and Content in Current Work on the Historical Jesus," *Theology Today* 52.1 (1995), 75–97.

3. Two recent examinations of John the Baptist are by Joan Taylor, *The Immerser: John the Baptist within Second Temple Judaism* (Grand Rapids 1997), and John Meier, in *Marginal Jew*, II:19–233. On Jesus' Galilee: Horsley, *Galilee;* Sean Freyne, *Galilee from Alexander the Great to Hadrian, 323 BCE to 135 CE* (Wilmington 1980) and *Galilee, Jesus, and the Gospels* (Philadelphia 1988); and Eric Meyers, "Jesus in His 'Galilean Context,'" in *Archaeology in the Galilee*, ed. Douglas R. Edwards and C. Thomas McCollough (Atlanta 1997). The Temple looms large in the various reconstructions by Crossan, *Historical Jesus,* Borg, *Jesus in Contemporary Scholarship,* and Wright, *Jesus and the Victory of God,* because all three define Jesus' mission as anti-Temple. For a historical consideration of the Temple within late Second Temple Judaism, see E. P. Sanders, *Judaism: Practice and Belief, 63 BCE–66 CE* (Philadelphia 1992).

In *From Jesus to Christ,* I touched only lightly on many of these issues. I chose instead to focus on the different portrayals of Jesus in the New Testament. To account for their variety and growth, I attempted to reconstruct the varying adjustments that the Christian movement made to its unanticipated circumstances: time's continuation, the Kingdom's delay, decreasing success among Jews, increasing—indeed, surprising—success among former pagans. The formative context for the growth of the movement's different images of Jesus, traced in the evidence from Paul's letters through the gospels and Acts, was "too many Gentiles, too few Jews, and no End in sight" (p. 169; for the full reconstruction, see pp. 142–76). The historical Jesus himself, as a consequence, played almost a cameo role in my study. At the center of the book, like the slim neck of an hourglass, stood my sole chapter specifically on Jesus of Nazareth, a scant four pages long (pp. 127–30). All my sifting through the later Christian traditions had made him that much more elusive.

But the people who read my book, who took my classes or wrote me letters or invited me to speak, would not let me continue to evade the historical Jesus. The sweep of subsequent Christian tradition, important as it was for understanding the shape of the New Testament evidence, was finally not as important to them as the figure of Jesus himself. Time and again—in the classroom, before church or synagogue groups, with communities engaged in interfaith dialogue, in front of nonspecialist audiences either directly or via the television camera—I was driven back onto the effort to construct a historically coherent image of the figure whose Jewish life and Roman death stand at the source of Christianity.

Six years after Yale University Press brought out *From Jesus to Christ,* in 1994–95, I went to Jerusalem to teach in the Religion Department at the Hebrew University. I was well into a new project on Augustine and Judaism. I had managed, so I thought, to free myself intellectually from the tar baby of Jesus scholarship. Two events then proved me wrong. First, I received an invitation to deliver a plenary address on current work on the historical Jesus at the annual meeting of the American Academy of Religion / Society of Biblical Literature. This plunged me into an intensive spell of reading and rereading the works of colleagues that had appeared since I had written mine. My exclusive concentration allowed me to see patterns in their scholarship that, in turn, had me rethinking my own. Second, my friend Oded Irshai of the Department of Jewish History at the Hebrew University volunteered to take me on a walk through Herod's Jerusalem. He may have meant it as a onetime offer, but he did not protest my interpreting it as a standing invitation. No matter where in the old Jewish Quarter we started from, we always ended up at the south-side excavations, looking up at the massive stones circling the mount where once the Second Temple had stood. The physical experience of standing in that place got me rethinking my earlier work, too.

The result was perhaps inevitable: I added yet one more book to the growing pile on the historical Jesus. Working on *Jesus of Nazareth, King of the Jews* (1999) created a critical promontory from which I could survey recent scholarship, critique my own, and see afresh the problems of evidence and argument that shape the field. Consequently, I have changed my mind on several issues since publishing *From Jesus to Christ*. When Yale University Press decided to reprint the book, my editor, Charles Grench, generously offered me the chance to write a new introduction. What follows here are my thoughts on the field as I now see it, as well as my pentimento.

Who wrote the gospels, Jews or Gentiles? No one knows, although scholars, on the basis of internal evidence, will venture various "ethnic" identifications. In *From Jesus to Christ,* I worked with an assumption that at least Mark and Luke were Gentiles. The author of Matthew is universally regarded as Jewish; for the past thirty or so years, especially after the influential work of Louis Martyn,[4] so is the author of John. Arguments for Luke can go either way, and second-century ecclesiastical tradition holds that the author was a Gentile companion of Paul's. The author's fluency with the Septuagint, however, combined with the probable date of composition (late first century) incline me now to suppose that he, too, was a Jew. The Bible was a bulky collection of books—scrolls, actually—that would not have circulated or been easily accessible outside a synagogue context in this early period.

What about Mark? Again, any answer is speculative. Ancient church tradition identifies the author as a Gentile, a companion of Peter's in Rome. Many modern scholars likewise identify him as Gentile: he demonstrates little of the familiarity with Jewish traditions and scriptures that Luke and Matthew so conspicuously display, nor does he evince close (if hostile) relations with local synagogue communities the way John does. On this I have changed my mind. I said that Mark was a Gentile; I now think that he, too, was a Jew. If Mark was a Jew, one colleague has observed to me, he was an extremely ignorant one. True. Ignorance, of course, is no respecter of persons or ethnic groups, and not everyone in the early movement could have Paul's education. But the very early date of the Gospel's composition (sometime, I still think, shortly after 70 C.E.), its scriptural underpinnings (evident especially in the Passion narrative), and the stimulus to write given (again, I still think) by the Temple's recent destruction all incline me to suspect that its author, too, was Jewish.

Why does it matter? In part because the implied social and religious location of the author gives us a jumping-off point for speculations about his

---

4. J. Louis Martyn, *History and Theology in the Fourth Gospel* (New York 1968) and *The Gospel of John in Christian History: Essays, for Interpreters* (New York 1978).

community—whether it, too, was Jewish, Gentile, or some mix—and thus for speculations on what his hearers might have understood when listening to the gospel. And such considerations can help when evaluating recent arguments made by some scholars that Jesus rejected and taught against the biblical laws of purity. A Jewish audience, for example, would have had a more concrete understanding of Jesus' order to the cured leper to "go, show yourself to the priest, and offer for your cleansing what Moses command-ed" (Mk 1:44): the command as Mark reports it would have evoked for them the rituals of purification prescribed in Leviticus 14 and would also have conjured the (now destroyed) Temple in Jerusalem, where such offer-ings had been made.[5]

Any ancient audience, Jewish or Gentile, would have understood that by evoking a situation calling for offerings and a priest, Mark's Jesus alluded to an etiquette of purification.[6] Sacrifice requires proximity to an altar, and such proximity (that is, to *any* god's altar) universally required (some sort of) preparatory purification: a brief preceding period of sexual abstinence, for example, or immersion or another sort of ablution. Nobody in antiquity did the equivalent of park-the-car-and-run-into-the-sanctuary. But Jewish audiences—Matthew's certainly, Luke's and John's probably, and I now think also Mark's—would have had specific associations through their bib-lical culture with what such purification entailed, as would those Gentile hearers ("God-fearers") associated with the synagogue. Accordingly, the attitude of the author toward Jewish scripture generally and the biblical purity laws in particular, as well as the significance of his depiction of Jesus on these points, is more complex than a straightforward anti-purity inter-pretation will allow.

What was Jesus' Galilee like? On this point, current interpretive debate rages, not least because of the important role played by social theory, eco-nomics, and comparative methods in interpreting the literary and archaeo-logical data. The hope in using theory is that we can wring more informa-tion from our data. If we know from studies of millenarianism in other

5. There is no need to postulate a high level of education for the audience to be able to make these associations. Familiarity with the first five books of the Bible was the reason for the weekly convocations of Jews (the "synagogue") on the Sabbath both in the Land of Israel and in the Diaspora. "For from early generations Moses has had in every city those who preach him," says James, Jesus' brother, in Acts, "for he is read every Sabbath in the synagogues" (15:21). Especially in Diaspora synagogues, interested Gentiles would be present and could hear the Torah, too.

6. The universality of purification practices in ancient Mediterranean religions, not just Judaism, represents another huge complication if one wants to see Jesus as somehow opposing the biblical purity laws: he would be incoherent not only to his Jewish hearers but to any con-temporary. On Jewish purity laws see now Jonathan Klawans, *Impurity and Immorality in Ancient Judaism* (New York 2000); as these relate specifically to Jesus, see my discussion in *Jesus of Nazareth, King of the Jews* (New York 1999), pp. 197–214.

cultures, for example, that perceived economic deprivation contributes to the mentality of a movement, we could have an interpretive grid on which to map the social realities of ancient Galilee. On this view, Jesus' audience, to the degree that they received his message of the impending Kingdom, would have been or felt themselves to be economically or socially deprived—hence his particular appeal to the disenfranchised: the sinner, the toll collector, the prostitute, and the pauper. Or, if aristocratic empires run on the systematic and ruthless exploitation of peasants, and the Roman Empire had exactly this sort of class structure, then peasants within the empire—all peasants, not just Jewish ones—must have been exploited, too. In this reconstruction, when speaking to (Galilean) peasants Jesus would have addressed not just the poor but the powerless and destitute. Or, if the texts and institutions of a Great Tradition—in Jesus' culture and period, these included literacy, sacrifices, knowledge of Torah, and access to the Temple—rested with an identifiable elite (aristocratic priests, scribes, and Pharisees), those disempowered by this structure would have combated their oppression with subversive countertraditions naturally not as visible in our data, because texts and Temple are remnants from the elites. On this construction, Jesus as peasant teacher would have spoken and acted in ways subversive of the institutions of the Great Tradition. And his followers would have responded because they, too, felt alienated—by the Temple, for example, or the laws of purity, or literate scribal traditions, when their own, "Little Tradition" was popular and oral, and so on.[7]

In other words, the method we use, by organizing our sparse data according to its criteria, holds out the promise of helping us perceive motives or meanings or social dynamics that are disguised, only implied, or perhaps otherwise invisible in the record once our positive evidence runs out. The method provides a "plot" by which we can organize our data into a story: the attractions of Jesus' message or the reasons for his execution can accordingly be explained by appeal to the method's criteria of meaning: class antagonism, hostility between a subversive peasant teacher and the representatives of the Great Tradition (priests, Pharisees), and so on. Theory-informed history has explanatory elegance.

The danger is that, absent positive evidence, we have little way to test the conclusions that a method offers us. If theory organizes data to begin with, arguments for its validation can easily start running in circles. Before bringing on Melanesian cargo cults or nineteenth-century Sicilian bandits, then, we need to have a long, hard look at Josephus, whose writings provide us with both political and social descriptions of the Galilee. And, as E. P.

---

7. On Jesus' Galilean hearers as destitute, see esp. Crossan, *Historical Jesus; on Galileans as preserving the Israelite Little Tradition* and thus resenting and resisting the Judean Great Tradition, see esp. Horsley, *Galilee;* cf. my discussion of the historical Galilee and how to look for it, *Jesus of Nazareth,* pp. 159–84.

Sanders has tirelessly pointed out, what Josephus does *not* say matters as much as what he does.[8] The Galilee in Jesus' lifetime was ruled by Antipas, one of Herod's sons. Unlike his brother Archelaus, to the south, Antipas enjoyed a long and quiet reign, from 4 B.C.E. to 39 C.E.—virtually the whole period of Jesus' life. Jews, not Romans, ran the Galilee. Had the people been near starvation or oppressed by outrageous taxes, or had Antipas flagrantly violated Jewish Law, we would hear the rumble in Josephus. But he says nothing about riots, religious antagonisms, or discontent rising to active unrest. No Roman troops were called in from Syria to protect their client Antipas from turmoil at home. Josephus speaks instead of the fertility of the Galilee and of its numerous prosperous villages (*BJ* 3.43).

Without the lens of imported interdisciplinary methods, it is hard to see economic deprivation and political oppression as an operative context for Jesus' mission. A Roman presence was virtually nonexistent in Jesus' Galilee, which was administered by a Jewish ruler. And while, then as now, nobody much liked paying taxes, we have no evidence of Galileans feeling crushed under a heavy tax burden.

In light of all this, I repent of my summary paragraph on the political, economic, and religious environment of Jesus' Galilee on page 93. People may indeed have rebelled "time and time again" in the course of the first century, but in Jesus' neighborhood during his lifetime, they did not. Why, then, did I describe the Galilee as I did? In part because of what I turn to when looking for explanation. Like many modern people, I tend to see social and economic factors as more "real" than, and somehow fundamentally causative of, religious ideas. That millenarianism flourishes in situations of economic deprivation has been gospel at least since Friedrich Engels wrote his essay comparing early Christian gatherings to contemporary workers' cells.

Were I writing that paragraph now, I would be more cautious. We have many texts other than, for example, the gospels, Paul's letters, and the Dead Sea Scrolls that speak of the coming of God's kingdom but for which we have very little clue of social context. Must we presuppose a general sense of disempowerment for these anonymous communities? On what basis other than the assumption of relative deprivation? Any theory so universalized soon loses its explanatory value. Economic or political reductionism—like its first-century equivalent, allegorical interpretation—simply takes terms from one context and translates them into its own frame of reference, giving them a new, more congenial meaning, one that says more about the method of interpretation and the orientation of the interpreter than about the data it supposedly interprets.

8. See his review of the alternating periods of peace and domestic strife in Sanders, *Judaism*, pp. 36–42; on Antipas and Jesus' Galilee, see his *Historical Figure*, pp. 20–22.

"The historian meets the gap between himself and others at its most sharp and uncompromising," Peter Brown has observed. "The dead are irreducible."[9] Ancient people in general, ancient Jews in particular, lived in a world radically different from our own, a world where leprosy and death defiled, where ashes and water made clean, and where one drew near the altar of God with purifications, blood offerings, and awe. To approach them, we need to reimagine their universe, not project our categories of meaning onto it. The past that we construct from our theories is accessible and meaningful to us because our world is the source of the interpretive criteria. When drawing on theory, we run the risk of obscuring rather than interpreting the past of our long-dead subjects. It is better, then, to try to hear what they seemed to think was important, to acknowledge how different from us they were, than to reconfigure them to fit our categories of meaning. The fear of false familiarity is the beginning of historical wisdom.

I incline now to see the message of biblical redemption as the fundamental factor shaping Jesus' mission and his supporters' response to him. Both he and they exist as points along an arc that stretches roughly from the Maccabees to the Mishna, from the prophecies of Daniel through the letters of Paul, from the later books of the classical prophets in the Jewish canon (Isaiah, Jeremiah, Ezekiel) to the Book of Revelation, which concludes the New Testament. It is the arc of a biblical perspective on God and history that scholars have labeled *apocalyptic eschatology:* the belief that God is good, that he will not countenance evil indefinitely, that in the End he will act to restore and redeem. This is what binds Jesus to his predecessors (like the Baptizer), his supporters, and his later apostles (like Paul). No sketch of the economic conditions of the Galilee can have a sufficient or convincing explanatory effect on all the data—in Paul, in the Gospels, in Josephus, in the pseudepigrapha, in the archaeological record—in the way these biblical apocalyptic commitments do.

The coins of the money changers. Describing how the Temple operated in Jesus' day, I wrote, "These pilgrims, coming from all parts, brought vari-

9. Brown alludes here to the fourth and fifth centuries, but what he says is equally valuable for work in any historical period. The rest of this passage repays attention. Brown continues: "The men and women of the Late Roman Empire lived out their lives in their own way; they have left us stark evidence of this, without having given a thought to our delicate sensibilities, without having worried for a moment whether their hopes and fears ran counter to the common-sense of men of the twentieth century. In short, saved by the passing of fifteen hundred years from the need to reassure us, they could appear exactly as they were—every bit as odd as we are, as problematical, as difficult of access. To explore such people with sympathy, with trained insight, and with a large measure of common cunning, is to appreciate what one of the greatest of them [scil. Augustine] said: 'Grande profundum est ipse homo . . . Man is a vast deep . . . the hairs on his head are more easily numbered than are his feelings, and the movements of his heart'"; *Religion and Society in the Age of Saint Augustine* (New York 1972), p. 2of.

ous currency; and money changers, doubtless for a charge, converted these to the Temple's standard coinage, which bore no offensive images" (p. 112). This statement is true, but not in the way I intended when I wrote it. Like everyone else, I "knew" that the Temple's coins, like the Temple's worship, had to be aniconic, and this presumption stands behind my sentence. No offensive images marred the Temple's standard coinage, but this was because the image that the coins did display—the head of the god Melkart, a Tyrian deity, on one surface and a Ptolemaic eagle on the other—evidently gave no offense.[10] The Tyrian shekel was the Temple's coin of choice for centuries, in part for the eminently practical reason that its silver content was high and stable. Supposed aniconism was never at issue. This whole construction about imageless coins is a case of New Testament scholars, unfamiliar with the real estate of Second Temple Judaism but very familiar with the Ten Commandments, imagining what should have been the case.[11]

Markan chronology and the Temple tantrum. During my bout of intensive reading for my 1994 plenary address, I was startled to note a single area of scholarly consensus. No matter how at odds with one another's constructions of Jesus, my colleagues inclined to draw on the chronology of Mark, with its narrative of Jesus traveling from the Galilee to Judea on his way to Jerusalem for Passover on his first and only trip to the city during his mission. Shortly after arriving in Jerusalem, Jesus becomes the target of fatal priestly hostility, which ultimately leads him to Pilate and the cross. What happened? Here the consensus was clear, and it too drew directly on Mark: Jesus, by scattering the money changers and turning over the tables of "those who sold," had enacted a prophecy of the Temple's coming destruction. In so doing, he moved himself into the crosshairs of the priests.

I had held these views myself, and I present them in *From Jesus to Christ* (pp. 111–22, 129). While in Jerusalem, however, my confidence in this reconstruction began to erode. The first undermining evidence was internal to New Testament texts. Paul, who knew at least several of the original disciples of Jesus and who himself speaks with authority on the coming Kingdom and Christ's return, never mentions such a prophecy when he reviews the signs of the End. How could he not have known it? If he had, how could he not have used it?

Also, the Synoptic evangelists themselves, who otherwise unabashedly show Jesus predicting the Temple's destruction—"Do you see these great buildings? There will not be left here one stone upon another that will not

10. See Peter Richardson's discussion and review of the data in "Why Turn the Tables? Jesus' Protest in the Temple Precincts," *Society of Biblical Literature Seminar Papers* (1992), 507–23. Richardson argues that Melkart's image did offend Jesus.

11. Richardson points out as one example among the many available, Marcus Borg, *Jesus: The New Vision* (San Francisco 1987), p. 174.

be thrown down!" Mk 13:1 and parr.)—did not understand Jesus' gesture in the Temple as enacting such a prophecy. For them, as also for John, his action represents his repudiation of the way the Temple was run. If by this gesture (wrongly and anachronistically interpreted in church tradition as the "cleansing of the Temple") Jesus had intended to prophesy the Temple's coming destruction, why did the evangelists—and especially Mark, for whom the Temple's destruction is such a major theme—not understand it this way? And if the gesture was so opaque and confusing to them, how meaningful could it have been to contemporaries of Jesus at the Temple who saw him act? And if the meaning of the gesture and hence its effect on the crowd were so uncertain, how worried need the priests have been about Jesus, his message, and his action?[12]

Further, since 1988 I have learned more about the Temple, both from E. P. Sanders' *Judaism: Practice and Belief* and from my time in Israel. Sanders provides approximate measurements that give a sense of the sheer size of the place: the total circumference of the outermost wall ran to almost nine-tenths of a mile: twelve soccer fields, including stands, could be fit in, and when necessary (as during the pilgrimage festivals, especially Passover), it could accommodate as many as 400,000 worshippers.[13]

I have trouble visualizing space from numbers. Not until I started walking around the Temple Mount did I begin to understand how huge the Temple area must have been—specifically its outermost court, around the perimeter of which, beneath the protection from sun or storm offered by the stoa or the Royal Portico, those who sold could be found. Its very size shrank the significance of Jesus' putative action and prompted a question: If Jesus had made such a gesture, how many would have seen it? The answer: Those in his retinue and those standing immediately around him. But in the congestion and confusion of that holiday crowd, how many could have seen what was happening, say, twenty feet away? Fifty feet? The effect of Jesus' gesture would have been muffled by the sheer press of pilgrims. How worried, then, need the priests have been?

My confidence in the historicity of the scene in the Temple and its role in bringing Jesus to his death steadily diminished as I contemplated, further,

12. The Gospel of John presents what is recognizably the same scene, but within an entirely different narrative chronology. John's Jesus causes the scene in the Temple at the beginning of his mission. He criticizes "those who sold" for turning the Temple into a "house of trade" (2:16). Finally, John interprets the gesture as a disguised prediction of the Passion("'Destroy this Temple, and in three days I will raise it up,' . . . but he spoke of the temple of his body"; vv. 19, 21). John's Jesus is in Jerusalem more often than in the Galilee, and this incident does not serve, as it does in the Synoptics, as the trip-switch for the Passion.

13. Sanders, *Judaism,* pp. 47–145. See esp. his chart comparing the dimensions of the Temple with those of Salisbury Cathedral and Temple Emanuel in New York, p. 67.

two of the few virtually indisputable facts from the earliest movement. The first concerns his death. Jesus of Nazareth was crucified. His manner of death implies a context. Crucifixion was a mode of execution that Rome reserved particularly for political insurrectionists. If Jesus died on a cross, then Pilate must have been concerned about the effect that Jesus and his message might have on the crowds massed in Jerusalem that Passover. But this inference runs head-on into a second, equally undisputed fact about the earliest Christian movement: although Jesus died as an insurrectionist, none of his followers did.[14]

If Pilate, whether mistakenly or not, had truly considered Jesus guilty of spearheading a seditious movement, more people than Jesus would have died. That Jesus alone was killed suggests that Pilate knew perfectly well that he posed no political threat. But the suggestion raises a more fundamental question: If Pilate knew Jesus was politically innocent, why crucify him? If the prefect—or, as the gospels depict, the priests—simply wanted Jesus dead, no public execution was necessary. They could have killed him by easier means. And the insistence, in the same gospels, on Jesus' popularity that Passover (the priests resolve to have him killed, says Mark, "but not during the feast, lest there be a tumult of the people"; 14:2) makes the choice of a public execution that much more mysterious.

These two anomalous facts—Jesus was crucified; those closest to him were left alone—compelled me to reevaluate both the traditions preserved in the New Testament and the various portraits of Jesus offered by current scholarship. The sort of chronology implied in the Gospel of John—currently out of favor in most academic reconstructions—emerged (to my surprise) as the key to resolving the dilemma posed by the facts of Jesus' execution and his disciples' survival. Only multiple trips to Jerusalem, such as John portrays, could explain how Pilate knew with such certainty that Jesus was politically harmless: so the disciples survived. And only what the pilgrim crowd thought about Jesus—not what Jesus thought about himself—can explain Pilate's use of crucifixion. The necessary dependence on the gesture at the Temple to explain Jesus' death, which is hardwired into any reconstruction that keeps to the outlines of Mark's presentation of Jesus' mission, diminished accordingly.

Undoubtedly, such a story circulated about Jesus: it is attested in both Mark and John[15]—though, significantly, not in Paul.[16] But why would the

14. Sanders considers these questions in his closing discussion in Jesus and Judaism, pp. 294–340. They drive my reconstruction in *Jesus of Nazareth*; see pp. 8–11.

15. If John used Mark, this is no mystery. If his account is independent of Mark's, then we have an instance of multiple attestation, which usually enhances the probable historicity of a reported event. See my discussion in *Jesus of Nazareth*, pp. 225–34.

16. I note this problem in *From Jesus to Christ*, p. 172f.

story have sprung up if Jesus had not performed such an act? Without evidence, speculations abound. I offer mine, briefly, here. I now incline to see the story of Jesus' action in the Temple as a post-70 tradition that harnessed the shock of the Temple's destruction in such a way that it reinforced Christian belief. Jesus, the evangelists could now urge, had disapproved of the Temple anyway (Mk 11); he had predicted its destruction (Mk 13). What matters to Christians is Jesus' resurrection (Jn 2): the destruction of the Temple means that the Kingdom, coupled with Jesus' return, is at hand. When the community sees the Temple destroyed, Mark's Jesus confides, its members will know that God "has already shortened the days" and that "this generation"—the generation straddling both Jesus' lifetime and the Jewish War—"will not pass away before all these things take place" (Mk 13:29).

Much of what I said in *From Jesus to Christ* I still maintain: the connectedness of the movement throughout its different phases, from Jesus through Paul to the evangelists; the way Paul and the different evangelists deal with the delay of the Kingdom; the link that Mark forges between the Second Coming and the destruction of the Temple. If I had to name the most important contribution in my book to the debates about Jesus and earliest Christianity, I would single out my reconstruction of the mission in the Diaspora and why it accommodated Gentiles from the beginning without requiring their conversion to Judaism.

The Law-free mission to the Gentiles has long been viewed in New Testament scholarship as the singular, even revolutionary contribution of Paul to the early movement. Some scholars attribute the ultimate source of the idea to the Hellenists, those shadowy Greek-speaking Jews resident in Jerusalem, represented by Stephen, whose story fills the opening of Acts. Others see the Gentiles' reception into "the people of God" without the requirement of circumcision and Torah-observance (in brief, without conversion to Judaism) as the implicit but logical extension of Jesus' own message to love one's neighbor (even where he is presented as quoting Leviticus!): loving neighbors, even enemies, must mean loving Gentiles, too.

But the roots of the first-century Law-free mission are not Christian or even Jewish-Christian. They are Jewish. They grew in the soil of apocalyptic eschatology. The belief that, at the End of Days, when God reveals himself in glory, Gentiles will repudiate their idols and as Gentiles (that is, without converting to Judaism) acknowledge and worship the true God together with Israel is native to ancient Judaism itself. This theme of the inclusion of Gentiles in God's Kingdom—a theme sounded in the classical prophets, various pseudepigrapha, the New Testament, and later synagogue prayer (e.g., the *Alenu*)—coheres with the other data attesting to the apocalyptic commitments of the first Christian generation. These people *as Jews* believed that Gentiles should be included, not converted, because *as Christians* they believed that they already lived in an eschatological hour, in a brief, final caesura in history between Christ's resurrection and his return, when he would establish the Kingdom of his father. These first Christians were prepared to realize socially what other Jews (if they thought about the question at all) may have only dimly anticipated for an unknown future. Indeed, some members of the movement, such as Paul, took the inclusion of Gentiles in the *ekklesia* as their mandate. Christian Gentiles were incorporated not because they were like "righteous Gentiles"—a theoretical but quotidian rabbinic category for Gentiles who do not worship idols—but because they were, within these earliest, spirit-filled communities, eschatological Gentiles, Gentiles who had repudiated their native traditions (or who had better repudiate them! see Paul's remarks, I Cor 5:11) because they had been adopted into God's people through his Son (e.g., Rom 8, esp. v. 15).[17]

Gentiles qua Gentiles were included in the earliest movement, from the time devotees began encountering interested Gentiles, because the earliest movement was Jewish and apocalyptic. The Bible thinks big—it begins Genesis with the creation of the universe and does not reach the calling of Abraham until Genesis 12—and apocalyptic thought tends to make biblical Big Thoughts bigger. More than Israel would be redeemed. So would the Gentiles. So would the dead, even those who, despite Moses, had stayed in Egypt; even those who were lost in Assyria (Is 27:12–13). If God could and would redeem Israel from exile, he could likewise redeem the Gentiles from their idolatry. After all, they were his children, too. "Is God the God of the Jews only? Is he not also the God of the nations also? Yes, of the nations also, since God is one" (Rom 3:29–30)—this is the fundamental principle of Torah (cf. 3:31). The ultimate redemption of the nations along with Israel is inherent to this stratum of Jewish religious thinking. It is, as Paul urges, the application to salvation history of the foundational principle of the Jewish credo, the *Shema*.

How the field of historical Jesus research will develop in the future is hard to say. Just when all the reasonable (and even some unreasonable) interpretive options seem exhausted, another book comes along. Will all this work result in some net gain, some new insight, some improved understanding? I do not know, but I hope so, particularly with regard to two related issues: the Christian study of Judaism and the relation of theology to history.

---

17. I expanded this argument with full notes in "Judaism, the Circumcision of Gentiles, and Apocalyptic Hope: Another Look at Galatians 1 and 2," *Journal of Theological Studies* 42 (1991), 532–64. See also Scot McKnight, *A Light among the Gentiles: Jewish Missionary Activity in the Second Temple Period* (Minneapolis 1991), and Martin Goodman, *Mission and Conversion: Proselytizing in the Religious History of the Roman Empire* (Oxford 1994).

To the first issue first. A notable characteristic of the current phase of the quest for the historical Jesus is the degree to which it draws upon the accomplishments in history, historiography, and archaeology that have marked the past half-century of Jewish Studies. The more we know about Second Temple Judaism, the more we know, if not about Jesus directly, then about his native religious context. No serious work on Jesus places him outside that context. Yet displacing him continues to be the effect of many scholarly descriptions of the Judaism of Jesus' time. In too many "reconstructions," Judaism functions as Jesus' contrasting backdrop; his contemporaries, as some sort of moral inverse of Jesus himself. Thus: Jesus was egalitarian; his contemporaries affirmed hierarchy. Jesus was kind to women, the poor, and the ill; his contemporaries scorned them. Jesus focused on ethics; they, on ritual. He preached and lived a politics of compassion; they practiced and enforced a politics of purity. Jesus taught a love of neighbor that extended naturally across ethnic or racial or national boundaries; they were consumed with nationalism and a concern for racial purity. No wonder he taught against them; no wonder they wanted him dead.

Some scholars soften such descriptions of Jesus' Jewish contemporaries by insisting that they intend no value judgment by them. One group was simply hierarchical, oppressive, patriarchal, exclusionary, and sexist; the other, egalitarian, inclusive, and compassionate: Nothing pejorative intended! Or they insist that Jesus criticized these contemporaries as an insider, a committed Jew, so to see him as anti-Jewish when such criticism is intra-Jewish misconstrues his situation. By extension, these reconstructions of Jesus' contemporaries are not anti-Jewish, either: they merely clarify what Jesus meant to say.[18]

Such tendentious descriptions of the Judaism from which Jesus supposedly sought to deliver his compatriots sets up a familiar comparison. Jesus, and, by extension, Christianity, were "good"; Jesus' contemporaries, and, by extension, their Judaism—especially the Judaism of his opponents (the scribes, the Pharisees, the priests)—were "bad." In effect if not intent, such descriptions perpetuate the long Christian tradition of scholarly anti-Judaism. I suppose it is a mark of progress that most of the currently offered derogatory descriptions of Judaism are at least introduced with disclaimers of negative intent.

But surely it is past time to put such characterizations—caricatures, really—to rest. They are both anachronistic and invidious and, as such, untenable both historically and morally. Explaining Jesus, his mission, and the shape of subsequent Christianity by imagining Jews and Judaism as some-

18. See my discussion of Borg, Crossan, and Wright on these issues in "What You See Is What You Get," pp. 83f., 86–91, 94–97.

how their opposite usually provides a glimpse at nothing more than the idealized politics of the scholar writing. More to the point, such an approach fails to address the single most secure fact we have about Jesus' life: his death. No amount of intra-Jewish religious contention explains the crucifixion. The more the historical Jesus is *truly* seen as a Jew of his own time, the less this opposition of what he supposedly stood for to what the rest of his people supposedly valued will be able to pass as historical explanation.

This brings me to my second issue, the relationship of theology and history. Many of the nonspecialist Christian readers of *From Jesus to Christ* have expressed their unease to me about the theological consequences of the quest for the historical Jesus. They feel that a Jewish Jesus leaves the modern believer with no place, theologically, to go. It seems a high price to pay for the benefit of critical thinking.

Critical thought can make the familiar strange, or—to rephrase this observation in perhaps more appealing language—it refreshes one's reading of traditional material, making the old, the familiar, new. This intellectual exercise is the necessary first step toward encountering the historical Jesus. I repeat: the fear of false familiarity is the beginning of historical wisdom. If we insist that Jesus make immediate sense to us, the past hardens into a mirror, a reflecting surface that reveals only ourselves. Acknowledging—indeed, being unafraid of—the huge distance between us and Jesus, *as between us and any ancient person,* can make our texts into windows, not mirrors. We peer through them to glimpse, however imperfectly, the human realities that ultimately stand behind them.

What might we see? If we look for Jesus, we will see the human being that even the stilted metaphysics of ancient high theology insisted had to be there. The attempt calls for a certain kind of religious courage, because it means decoupling history from theology and allowing each with integrity to do its respective work. History requires the acknowledgment of difference and the priority of ancient context. This means that if we start in search of the historical Jesus of Nazareth, then the person whom we seek will stand with his back to us, his face toward the faces of his own generation. They, not we, were his concern, the audience for his message. He was obliged to be intelligible not to us, but to them.

But if modern believers require that Jesus be morally intelligible and religiously relevant to them, then it is to them that the necessary work of creative reinterpretation falls. Such a project is not historical—the critical construction of an ancient figure. It is *theological*—the generation of contemporary meaning within particular religious communities. Multiple and conflicting theological claims inevitably result, as various as the different churches that stand behind them. For all the fundamental identity in their details, nonetheless the Catholic Jesus will be different from the Methodist Jesus will be different from the Armenian Apostolic Jesus will be different from the Lutheran Jesus—not because the historical Jesus of Nazareth was likewise manifold but because different traditions of meaning stand behind and inform these different modern communities. Historical research can only strive to reconstruct what Jesus *meant* to his first-century contemporaries—sympathizers, admirers, opponents, enemies. Theological creativity must strive to construct what Jesus *means* now to those who gather in his name. The two enterprises are related but distinct.

In this sense, the modern Christian tolerance of doctrinal difference between churches, its principled ecumenicism, is a good emotional and ethical model for tolerating historical difference, too. Keeping the distinctions between ancients and moderns in view can prevent the use of false history as a kind of empirical prop for modern theological commitments (e.g., Jesus the anti-Temple agitator endorsing modern egalitarianism). History interprets the past. Theology reinterprets, not the past, but religious tradition. This theological reinterpretation should neither be mistaken for nor be presented as historical description. And the reverse also is true: historical description cannot provide theological meaning.

It was on a related point that I originally concluded *From Jesus to Christ*: "But bad history . . . results in bad theology, the subtle Docetism of anachronism" (p. 215). Might good history, then, result in good theology? (And what would that be?) Again, I do not know. But I hope so.

I
THE WORLD OF THE
NEW TESTAMENT

Chapter 1
The Nature of the Documents

Sometime around the year 30 C.E., Jesus, a Nazarene peasant and charismatic religious leader, was executed in Jerusalem as a political agitator by the Roman prefect Pontius Pilate.[1] (He was crucified, a form of capital punishment used by Rome particularly for political offenders.) Despite his death, however, his followers did not disband. They grouped together, preserving some of Jesus' teachings and some stories about him, which became part of the substance of their preaching as they continued his mission to prepare Israel for the coming Kingdom of God. At the same time or very shortly thereafter, these oral teachings began to circulate in Greek as well as in Jesus' native Aramaic.[2]

Eventually, some of Jesus' sayings, now in Greek, were collected and written down in a document, now lost, which scholars designate Q (from the German *Quelle,* "source"). Meanwhile, other oral traditions—miracle stories, parables, legends, and so on—grew, circulated, and were collected in different forms by various Christian communities. In the period around the destruction of the Second Temple (70 C.E.), an anonymous Gentile Christian wrote some of these down. This person was not an author—he did not compose de novo. Nor was he a historian—he did not deal directly and critically with his evidence. The writer was an evangelist, a sort of creative editor. He organized these stories into a sequence and shaped his inherited

1. The Roman titles *praefectus* and *procurator* were used interchangeably in the first century and thereafter: an inscription found in Caesarea in 1961 identifies Pilate as "prefect"; Tacitus, *Annals* XV.44.4, calls him "procurator." Schürer, *HJP* I:358–59 provides a detailed consideration.

2. This shift in language does not necessarily indicate a shift in the tradition's ethnic/religious group or geographical location: Acts 6:1ff., for example, mentions Greek-speaking Jews resident in Jerusalem.

material into something resembling a historical narrative. The result was the Gospel of Mark.

This gospel eventually circulated beyond its community of origin to others, acquainted with different traditions about Jesus. From surviving literary evidence we know of at least two other anonymous Christians who, independently but at roughly the same time (c. 90–100), combined Mark with other materials, both written and oral—the Greek sayings source, Q; extensive references to the Greek translation of the Hebrew Bible, the Septuagint (LXX); and other, perhaps local, traditions. The results were the gospels of Matthew and Luke.

This hypothetical pattern of literary dependency—the so-called two-source hypothesis—answers two questions: why Matthew, Mark, and Luke share a common narrative chronology while Matthew and Luke, each in his own way, verbally duplicate material not found in Mark.[3] These three gospels clearly did not exhaust the material on Jesus that existed in the latter part of the first century: the fourth canonical gospel, John, differs so markedly from the first three that scholars assume John drew largely on other traditions, written or oral, to construct his account. Nor did traditions about Jesus cease to evolve and new gospels cease to be composed once some of the tradition attained a written form. Justin Martyr's references to Jesus' birth in a cave (*Dial.* 78) and fire in the Jordan at Jesus' baptism (*Dial.* 88) suggest both that he was familiar with material about Jesus, whether written or oral, other than what we find in our gospels, and that he considered it equally authoritative.

What then must be borne in mind when reading the canonical gospels for historical information about Jesus of Nazareth? First, the impression of orderliness conveyed by their connected narratives should not deceive us about their true nature: these are composite documents, the final products of long and creative traditions in which old material was reworked and new material interpolated. As they now stand, they are witness first of all to the faith of their individual writers and their late first-century, largely Gentile communities. Only at a distance do they relate to the people and the period they purport to describe. This is not to suggest that the concept we designate the "historical Jesus" was of no interest to the evangelists: the fact that they chose to present their message through a life-story, rather than through contextless sayings (like Q), suggests otherwise.[4] But fundamentally, the gospels are theological proclamation, not historical biography; and to the degree that they do present us with an image of Jesus, it is first of all the Jesus who "founded" the particular community behind each gospel.

3. For example, both later evangelists have the sentence, "You cannot serve both God and mammon." In Matthew, it appears in the Sermon on the Mount (6:24); in Luke, as one of a series of statements concluding the parable of the unjust steward (16:13).

4. See on this point the observations of Geza Vermes, *Jesus and the World of Judaism*, pp. 20–21.

Second, we must remember that forty to seventy years stand between the public career and death of Jesus of Nazareth and the probable dates of composition of the gospels. Jesus spoke Aramaic; his original early first-century audience was, for the most part, Jewish, Palestinian, and rural. The evangelists' language was Greek, their communities predominantly if not exclusively Gentile, their location the cities of the Mediterranean Diaspora. Traditions from and about Jesus spanning this temporal, cultural, and linguistic gap circulated orally; and the reliability of oral traditions, in the absence of independent or convergent lines of evidence, is nearly impossible to assess. Further, as psychological and anthropological studies of oral materials show, even reports going back to eyewitnesses are far from historically secure.[5] Interpretation or distortion between an event and the report of an event occurs almost inevitably, first of all because the observer is human. If the report is communicated through different people over a period of time before it achieves written form (as is the case with the gospels), revision can occur at every human link in the chain of transmission. In brief, though the oral transmission of traditions about Jesus allows us to assume some relation between what the gospels report and what might actually have happened, it also requires that we acknowledge an inevitable—often incalculable—degree of distortion in those traditions as well.

Faced with these uncertainties, scholars have formulated several basic criteria for testing the authenticity of evangelical materials on Jesus: dissimilarity, coherence, multiple attestation, and linguistic suitability. The criterion of dissimilarity holds that if the earliest form of a saying or story differs in emphasis from a characteristic teaching or concern both of contemporary Judaism and of the early church, then it *may* be authentic. Consonance with either indicates that the source of the saying may be not Jesus but the later church or some judaizing strain within it. The second criterion, coherence, is contingent upon the first: if material from the earlier strata of tradition is consonant with other material already established as probably authentic, then it too is probably authentic. The concept of multiple attestation suggests that if material appears in a number of different sources and literary contexts (for example, both in Paul's letters and in the gospels; or in sayings, parables, and proclamations), then it may be authentic. Finally, linguistic suitability means that material with a claim to authenticity should be susceptible of Aramaic rendering, since Jesus did not teach in Greek, the language of the documents.

These various criteria all seek to establish some firm ground in otherwise shifting sand, and I shall invoke them when I draw on the gospels and Paul to reconstruct the ministry of Jesus of Nazareth. Nonetheless, they are not

5. G. W. Allport and L. Postman, *The Psychology of Rumor*; J. Vansina, *Oral Tradition*. See John Gager, "The Gospels and Jesus," for a provocative application of these two studies to the gospel material.

without logical problems. Multiple attestation may demonstrate only the early date of a given tradition, and say nothing of its relationship to the historical Jesus. Translatability implies only that the earliest recoverable level of a tradition points to an Aramaic origin. But many people other than Jesus spoke Aramaic in the early church, and the tradition may have arisen just as easily in a Semitic Christian context as a Hellenistic one. Finally, dissimilarity and its corollary, coherence, presuppose that "authentic" teaching must be "unique." But if we take seriously the proposition that Jesus of Nazareth was a Jew, would none of his teachings have touched on principles traditionally promi- nent in his native religion, Judaism (love of God and neighbor, concern for the poor, and so on)? And if the church grew up around the memory of his message, would none of its teachings have related to his?

In any case, we still know too little both about early first-century Judaism and about the church in the period of the gospels' composition to apply these last criteria rigorously. A modified criterion might speak more appropriately to historical reality. If something stands in the gospels that is clearly *not* in the interests of the late first-century church—disparaging remarks about Gentiles, for example, or explicit pronouncements about the imminent end of the world—then it has a stronger claim to authenticity than otherwise. Stated briefly, anything embarrassing is probably earlier.

The now-lost primitive oral traditions, which these criteria attempt to reconstruct and assess, were all variously affected by processes of selection, invention, and reinterpretation. Working at the level of written tradition, especially with the synoptic gospels, we can see these processes immediately expressed in the myriad editorial decisions of the individual evangelists. And at the macro-level of the canon, these processes have determined the shape of the New Testament collection itself. For the canon (the Greek word for "measure" or "standard") represents an attempt on the part of one branch of the second- through fourth-century church to produce order, to authorize only some of the growing quantity of Christian writings for its members. The canon thus reflects the political and theological controversies of this later period more than it reflects either the historical situation of those controversies or the period that the canonical texts purportedly describe. The four gospels collec- tively stand as the survivors of a process whose principles of selection had more to do with competition between different Christian groups than with a disinterested concern for history. And once the choice was made, it was perceived and defended in terms persuasive and meaningful to its ancient audience:

> The Gospels could not possibly be either more or less in number than they are. Since there are four zones of the world in which we live, and four principal winds, the church . . . fittingly has four pillars, everywhere breathing out incorruption and revivifying men. From this it is clear that the Logos, the artificer of all things, he who

sits upon the cherubim and sustains all things . . . gave us the gospel in four-fold form, but held together by one Spirit. . . . For the cherubim have four faces, and their faces are images of the activity of the Son of God . . . [and] the Gospels, in which Christ is enthroned, are like these. (Irenaeus, *adv. Haer.* XI, 8)

Just as the many different stories about Jesus preserved in a single gospel, once linked by continuous narrative, give the impression of unity and coherence, so too, on a larger scale, do the gospels. Once circulated as a collection, they tended to be interpreted in light of each other and thus in effect passively rewritten. The variety in the images of Jesus they convey is suppressed by the interpretive impression of overall harmony, much as the separate *taches* of a Seurat convey an impression of unity of form. In all such cases—the individual gospel, the four canonical gospels, Seurat—this impression of unity is maintained best by distance. The closer we come, the more clearly we perceive that the whole is really an assemblage.

Finally, the second-century ascription of authorship to these originally anonymous gospels signals more than the bare fact that, once collected, they had to be distinguished one from another. The choice of attribution either to eyewitnesses from the original circle of disciples ("Matthew," "John") or to their companions ("Mark" is Peter's, "Luke" is Paul's) attests to an evolving historical consciousness on the part of this particular branch of Christianity, and an effort to define an orthodoxy.

A multitude of Christianities flourished in the second century: Gnosticism, Montanism, the radical Paulinism of Marcion, the communities that formed around such men as Irenaeus in Lyons or Tertullian in North Africa. Each viewed the others as heretical and each authenticated its own views by an appeal to various criteria of legitimacy: possession of the true interpretation of the Septuagint; or of the true Christian scriptures, once they had come into existence; or of the authentic oral tradition; or of the Holy Spirit, evinced variously through prophetic visions, true apostolic succession, the charismatic inspiration of gnosis (divine knowledge) and/or the ability to heal. The church upon whose canon subsequent Christianity eventually depended, the "orthodox" church, was the survivor of these early power struggles, emerging indisputably as victor only in the fourth century, when Constantine became its patron and suppressed its rivals.[6] This particular church defined itself, and hence its concept of orthodoxy, by its rootedness in the apostolic past, in "the faith once for all delivered to the saints" (Jude v. 4), by its claim to apostolic succession, and by its possession of the true, "apostolic" scriptures.

Consonance with the past, in other words, was for the victorious church the ultimate criterion of legitimacy. But the past, if it must bear this burden, is not

---

6. Eusebius, *Life of Constantine* III.64–66, on the emperor's suppression of various Christian communities.

so much preserved as remade in the image of the present: it is too important to be allowed an independent existence. Hence the necessarily anachronistic quality of the historical consciousness of orthodoxy. By perceiving and presenting these four gospels, largely the products of late first-century Gentile communities with progressively diminishing eschatological expectations, as the work of the apostolic generation, the church dispelled the otherness of its own history. The past, as presented in these documents, revealed to the church its own familiar face: that of a Gentile community free of the religious and national constraints of Judaism, situated firmly *in* time, not on its edge.

From oral to written; from Aramaic to Greek; from the End of time to the middle of time; from Jewish to Gentile; from the Galilee and Judea to the Empire. How can we begin to recover this other past, the past which exists concealed in our documents? Perhaps by recovering therein the varieties of the images of Jesus.

Chapter 2
The Legacy of Alexander

To his Logos, his chief messenger, highest in age and honor, the Father of all has given the special prerogative to stand on the border and separate the creature from the Creator. This same Logos both pleads with the Immortal as suppliant for afflicted mortality and acts as ambassador of the ruler to the subject. He glories in this prerogative and proudly describes it in these words: "I stood between the Lord and you." (Philo, *quis rerum divinarum heres* 42.205)

The man who penned these words was no Christian theologian meditating on the Gospel of John. He was Philo Judaeus of Alexandria, and when he died in the mid-first century the movement that was to become Christianity was just finding its way into the households of Mediterranean port cities. Philo died never having heard of Christianity. How was it then that he, an observant Jew, wrote in Greek about the scriptures concerning the Logos of God?

In part because of the dissemination of Greek civilization that had followed in the wake of Alexander the Great. By 323 B.C.E., Alexander had conquered the lands from the Peloponnesus in the west to the northern regions of India. The political unity of this vast territory survived only as long as its master: when Alexander died, his conquests fractured into a dozen smaller empires, kingdoms, and city-states. But a greater underlying cultural unity, Hellenism, endured.

The matrix of Hellenism was the city. Wherever Alexander conquered, he established cities and left behind resident Macedonian populations of soldiers, officials, and merchants. The first practical consequence of this policy was that Greek became the language of trade and government—not the high Greek of classical literary convention, but a flexible spoken Greek, "common" Greek, *koine*. The degree to which the conquered participated in their new political situation and took advantage of the new international field for commerce was the degree to which they learned koine.

The conquerors also offered a second type of international horizon, that of their intellectual culture, *paideia*. The new foreign ruling class established its traditional institutions of education—the school (for primary education), the gymnasium (for athletics, literature, music, and philosophy), the public library—and so maintained its Greek identity. But native elites with access to the gymnasium could also, through paideia, take on a Greek identity and self-consciousness and so enter into the classical heritage of the conquerors. One could transcend the accident of birth through education.

The particular genius of cultural Hellenism lay in its ability to translate the mythical into the philosophical, to take the divinities of all cultures and, through allegory, translate them into the larger syncretistic religious system of Hellenistic philosophy. Such a highly evolved and ecumenical intellectual vision held enormous appeal: one need not renounce one's heritage, merely see through it. Indeed, in the fourth century B.C.E., the Greeks had done the same thing with their own heritage, allegorizing the ancient poetry of Hesiod and Homer, those singers of incest, rape, murder, cannibalism (and that was divine behavior!). Myth demanded allegory: the stories' surface meanings were too clearly an affront to common decency to take them literally. So, for example, Chronos' devouring his children is really an allegory for the division of time into subunits; Zeus' rape of Ganymede really an expression of the soul's rapture when seized by the power of the divine, and so on. So too, through allegory, could the mythology of other cultures be sublimated, their various gods made into particular manifestations of general philosophical truths. The Egyptian deity Ammon-Ra and the Greek Apollo both symbolized the Sun, the physical representation of the luminous unity of the True Being, the divine One. Hellenistic reinterpretation, by thus "modernizing" ancient religious texts, reconciled them intellectually to a new age, and so created from previous heterogeny a cultural unity.

HELLENISTIC PAGANISM

By the first century of the common era, popular Hellenistic philosophy was itself a kind of koine, a flexible and syncretistic blend of Stoic ethics and Platonic metaphysics. The Stoics held that the cosmos (the Greek word for both "world" and "order") was permeated by an immanent, divine, rational force, the *logos spermatikos,* which ordered the universe according to law (*nomos*). Man through his own logos could recognize in the beauty of the universe the effects of divine law. By conforming himself to the logos, man could lead a virtuous and therefore happy life. Platonists saw the material universe as the imperfect reflection or image of the divine world. This sensible cosmos, they held, was imperfect and unstable by nature given its mutable substratum, matter. The material lacked reality; the real was the eternal, the changeless, that which was perceived solely through the intellect. The intelligible realm ordered matter but did not interpenetrate it, as in Stoicism. Rather, the One, the Ultimate Being, was totally other than matter. Perfect, good, immutable, ineffable, impassive—these attributes defined the Platonic High God.

How then did the intelligible order the sensible? The fact of the physical universe, with its myriad imperfections, had always been something of an embarrassment to philosophy, given its definition of divinity as perfect and changeless. Plato himself had been reduced, in the *Timaeus,* to telling a "likely story," the myth of the demiurge. This was a divine craftsman who ordered the sensible realm, an enterprise that the High God could never be directly involved in. By the beginning of the common era, the Platonic demiurge and the Stoic logos had merged, because their function was identical: they organized the world according to divine forms or principles, while at the same time (for the Platonist) attenuating God's involvement with such a flawed enterprise. Thus the answer to the question, how does a perfect God relate to such an imperfect world? was, through an intermediary, at a distance.

How did man living in the material world relate to such a god? The imagined architecture of the cosmos, the mental picture of the universe inherited from Aristotle and the Hellenistic astronomers, both set the question and suggested various answers. For ancient man placed himself on a continuum of being prejudiced in favor of what was higher. Reality, be it material, moral, or metaphysical, was ordered on a vertical axis: the better something was, the higher it stood, ontologically and even spatially, in the order of things.

What did man behold when he looked up? The luminous realm of the fixed stars, infinitely removed, enveloped in the rarified matter of fiery ether. Below this, more substantial matter and motion: the five planets (often identified with the gods of the classical pantheon), the sun, and the moon. The moon marked the boundary of the permanence, stability, and harmony which characterized the astral spheres. In the sublunar realm, matter grew thick and sinister; the air between the moon and the earth held demons and various spirits; chance, change, and fate ruled life on earth. And when man turned his gaze inward, he saw recapitulated in microcosm the contrasts that described his universe: his spiritual self, drawn to reason and virtue, set in a body whose demeaning urges recalled him to his corporeality. Surely the body was not the natural home of the soul. The soul's point of origin must lie beyond the moon, in the spiritual realm, closer to the Divine for which it yearned. How then should the soul cope with its life in the body? And how could the soul, once free of the body, go home?

Astrology and magic, philosophy and religion all worked to provide answers to these questions. Astrologers were particularly concerned to know the position of the "heavenly elements" (*stoicheia*), the stars and planets, at the moment of the individual's birth, for celestial configurations marked the path that the soul had taken in its descent into the body. These same celestial forces had accordingly exerted and would continue to exert an influence on the soul, perhaps even determining its experiences. Furthermore—and here astrology coincided with magic—the soul must know the secret names of the cosmic forces and astral intelligences intervening between it and God in order to pass by them once again on its ascent after death.

Magicians attempted to deal with these powers, especially those in the realm below the moon, on a friendly basis. Named variously in ancient texts as *aiōnes* (beings), *archai* (principalities), and *dunameis* (forces),[1] these powers could communicate vitally important information about life outside the body and also might heal or sicken the body on earth. Initiation into a mystery cult might further protect the soul, as membership in a cult held out the promise of a happy afterlife, and a release from hostile powers in this one. The cult's ceremonies—baptism, communal meals, group worship—ritually recapitulated for the individual the foundational experience of the divine savior (Mithras, Serapis, Isis/Osiris) who had overcome cosmic adversity. So too, then, would the initiate.

Philosophers tended to scorn such beliefs, which were popular expressions of the same concerns, set by the same cosmic geography, that motivated philosophy. More austerely intellectual, philosophers held that access to the divine Father was available to everyone, not just the adept or the astrologer, provided he exercise virtue. Against the fears of certain forms and moods of Hellenistic religion, the sense that astral forces oppressed and imprisoned the soul, philosophers counterposed feelings of piety and a curious sort of fellowship with the stars, which they viewed as the sensible expression of the beauty of the intelligible realm.

But the nature of life beneath the moon put a fundamental challenge to philosophical monotheism, with its definition of a god that was both all-good and all-powerful. If God were such, then why was there evil in the world? The Stoics argued that evil was only apparent, a question of perspective. The divine Logos had organized the best of all possible worlds. If man could perceive the whole, he would see that what seems to him to be evil actually expressed divine providence. The Platonists also maintained that evil was only apparent, but in a different way. What truly exists is the Good; therefore evil, its opposite, does not truly exist: it lacks ontological status, since it is really the absence of Good. Only God, absolutely without change, is completely good. Accordingly, anything other than God—and the further from him, the more "other" it was—is contingent upon God for its existence. Correspondingly less real and more mutable, it is also less good.

Evil, by this definition, was built into physical existence, since the visible cosmos depended on inherently unstable matter. But the human soul, contingent and hence unstable, was also involved in moral evil. Through the exercise of his free will, however, man could train his soul to regard the higher things—this was the function of philosophy. Once the body was shed, the

1. For these definitions, see W. Bauer, *A Greek-English Lexicon of the New Testament and other Early Christian Literature.*

soul, liberated, could return to those higher realms, closer to the One. The organization of the physical cosmos, properly understood, thus expressed the goodness of God like a huge, animated allegory. Man, the lonely sublunar outpost of the spirit, tormented by the problem of evil and buffeted by circumstance, could read through the cosmos as through a text, and so see beyond its terrifying multiplicity and heartbreaking arbitrariness the serene, divine Unity that it actually expressed.

HELLENISTIC JUDAISM

Judaism both resisted and embraced the seductive reasonableness of syncretistic Hellenism. It too preserved an ancient authoritative text full of now-unacceptable descriptions of divinity, of a God who loved, or grew angry, or changed his mind; who concerned himself immediately with the affairs of men; and who, worse yet, seemed directly involved with the ordering of the physical universe, and hence implicated in the problem of evil. Such a God, in such an age, was no longer intellectually coherent. Could he too be made respectable, demythologized according to the universalist principles of paideia? And if he were, what warrant would there be for the existence of a particular people, Israel? This, in brief, was the cultural and religious quandary of Hellenistic Judaism.

Jews had encountered various Eastern cultures at other periods in their history, through conquest or by living abroad in the Diaspora, that is, outside of Palestine. At least since the sixth century B.C.E., a large community had thrived in Babylon, speaking Aramaic, the Semitic language of its captors, but preserving its national and religious identity. But in the Western Diaspora, the Jews of the Mediterranean territories—though eventually those in all the lands Alexander conquered, including Babylon and Palestine itself—faced a very different cultural situation. The first language of this Western Jewish community became an Indo-European tongue, Greek. By the early third century B.C.E. familiarity with Hebrew had faded to such a degree that anonymous Jewish translators in Alexandria produced a written Greek version of the five books of Moses, the Torah (Teaching), so that the scriptures would be accessible during public worship. The Greek version of the entire Bible, the Septuagint (Seventy, hence the academic shorthand LXX) was available by the end of the second century B.C.E. in a divinely authorized translation. Seventy-two sages had been appointed to render the Bible in Greek; when they emerged from their task, it was discovered that, working independently, they had all produced identical translations. A miracle![2]

2. See esp. A. Momigliano, *Alien Wisdom*, pp. 82–122. The Letter of Aristeas (mid-2d c. B.C.E.?) reports this legend with reference to the Pentateuch (the first five books of the Bible, from Genesis to Deuteronomy); later tradition expanded the work of these 72 translators to include the entire Hebrew Bible.

This translation of the Hebrew scriptures into Greek both echoed and facilitated a translation of ideas from one cultural system to the other. With the Greek language came paideia. When, for example, the Jewish God revealed his name to Moses at the burning bush (Ex 3:14), the Hebrew *ehyeh* (I am) became in the LXX *ho ōn* (the Being): anyone with even a rudimentary Hellenistic education would recognize in this designation the High God of philosophy.[3] Similarly, when the Lord established the heavens "by a word" (Ps 33:6), the Hebrew *davar* became the Greek *logos:* the Creator had suddenly acquired a very Hellenistic factotum. Greek concepts, in brief, did not need to be read into scripture. They were already there, by virtue of the new language of the text.

Hellenistic Judaism did not appreciate Greek culture so much as appropriate it. Jews praised paideia and the wisdom of the Greeks to the degree that they perceived them as Jewish. For Judaism began with the same intellectual premise as Hellenistic syncretism: that Truth is One, and there can be no contradiction between true things. Torah was true; philosophy was true; therefore any contradiction was only apparent. But in a world where ancient was better, Torah was superior, for (as Hellenistic Jews expended great energy and ingenuity arguing) Jewish wisdom was of much greater antiquity than Greek. The Greek world had hungered for this ancient Jewish wisdom: this was why Ptolemy Philadelphus (285–46 B.C.E.) had commissioned the LXX translation of the scriptures for his library at Alexandria.[4] Homer, Hesiod, Pythagoras, Socrates, and Plato had all known Torah from an earlier Greek translation predating the sixth-century Persian conquest of Egypt.[5] So effectively did Jewish apologetic make its case that one pagan, Numenius of Apamaea, finally asked, "What is Plato but Moses speaking Greek?"[6]

The work of Philo of Alexandria (c. 20 B.C.E.–50 C.E.) is a literary monument to Jewish-Hellenistic paideia. A man of extensive and impressive Greek learning and a committed and observant Jew, Philo dedicated himself to the exposition of the LXX. He saw therein the very best philosophical thought of his day—no small intellectual feat, given the nature of biblical narrative and its involved and active God. How can story become philosophy? Again, through allegory. Allegory preserved the dignity and vitality of the scriptures by making them relevant to the new cultural situation of Hellenistic Jews. It

3. This Greek rendering of YHWH was altered, in later Christian manuscripts of the LXX, to *kyrios* (Lord) and thus understood to refer to the pre-incarnate Lord, i.e., Christ. See G. Vermes, *Jesus the Jew,* pp. 108–11, and literature cited.

4. This fantasy provides the background for the Letter of Aristeas (above, n. 3), which purports to originate in Ptolemy's court as his invitation to the sages of Jerusalem to go down to Egypt to participate in this project.

5. So Aristobolus, another Hellenistic Jewish writer (3d–2d c. B.C.E.), preserved in Eusebius, *Praeparatio Evangeliae* 13:12, 1–16.

6. Reported in Clement of Alexandria, *Strom.* I.72,4.

freed the biblical text, as it had earlier the text of Homer, from the limitations of its original historical context and the affront of a literal reading. The literal, surface meaning of the narrative, which might give philosophical offense— God concerning himself about fruit trees, deceitful serpents, and expulsions—obviously was not its true, essential meaning. This was available only through the spiritual interpretation of allegory, whereby Adam was revealed to stand for Reason and Eve for the labile part of the soul and sensory component of the mind which, if distracted by lower things (the snake), will pull even Reason down with her.

A literal reading of the sacred text indicted the reader's ignorance, not the scriptures' validity and meaningfulness. Obviously, maintained Philo, the changeless, transcendent God did not directly involve himself in the ordering of the cosmos. Rather, he shaped it by his Word, the divine Logos, the first-born of God and Image of God who "stands on the border" between Creator and creation. The Logos thus represents the point of contact between the human and divine realms, the agent who ordered the world according to divine Law, nomos. And what is divine Law if not Torah? Through the Logos, too, the soul could return to God: "For if we have not yet become sons of God, yet we may be sons of his invisible Image, the most holy Logos" (*de confusione linguarum* 28.147).

Despite Philo's predisposition as a Hellenistic philosopher to prefer the spiritual interpretation of the text to the literal, however, he never abandoned the literal meaning of the prescriptions of Torah, what the rabbis called halakic observance. The Law, he argued, did not consist of arbitrary prohibitions: these symbolized more profound moral commitments. Circumcision portrayed the excision of sexual passion; avoidance of pork, repudiation of the unsavory moral characteristics attributed to swine, and so on. Living according to the Law thus meant practicing virtue, the goal of true philosophy. But, cautioned Philo, to think that one could attain such a level of virtue without literal observance of the Law was a proud self-deception. Such men lived as though they were alone in the wilderness, or as if they were disembodied souls. "We shall be ignoring the sanctity of the Temple and of a thousand other things if we are going to pay heed to nothing except what is shown us by the inner meaning of things." Outward observance is like the body, inner meanings like the soul. As the wise man cares for the body because it is the home of the soul, so will he care for the letter of the Law. "If we keep and observe these [laws], we shall gain a clearer concept of those things of which these are symbols" (*de migr. Abr.* 16.89–93).

Hence, despite the universalizing of its message by the transposition of biblical thought and religious practice into the categories of Hellenism, Judaism retained its sense of a unique and particular identity and mission. It claimed vis-à-vis Hellenism what Hellenism had claimed vis-à-vis all non-Greek, "barbarian" cultures: to represent the true religious destiny of humankind. Indeed, the huge body of Jewish apologetic in Greek and the extensive corpus of law concerning proselytism in the rabbinic writings attest to the fact that Judaism in both its branches was at this time an active religion of conversion.[7] According to Philo, the proselyte, like Abraham, goes out from his native land—the false idols of paganism—to his true homeland, the One God.[8] And the Matthean Jesus complains, "You Pharisees cross land and sea to make a single convert!" (Mt 23:15).

But Judaism did not need to be a missionary movement in order to be committed to conversion: its "missionaries" were the resident Diaspora communities themselves. The boundary between these communities and the outside world was a fluid one, and interested pagans could visit the synagogue as they would. Some, as the Greek magical papyri evince, came simply to acquire some knowledge of a powerful god in whose name they could command demons.[9] Others—like those Gentiles who annually joined Alexandria's Jews in celebrating the miracle of the Torah's translation into Greek—attached themselves as God-fearers, often remaining pagans while assuming as much of the Law as they cared to.[10] But many—including some of the most illustrious names of Hellenistic Judaism—apparently decided to take upon themselves full observance of the Law. They thus became proselytes and, according to

7. See M. Simon, *Verus Israel,* pp. 315–55; see also Suggested Reading for discussion of recent secondary literature.

8. For example, *de spec. leg.* 4.178; *de virt.* 20.102–04, where Philo repeatedly alludes to Lv 19:33–34 ("the stranger [*proselytos*] that comes to you shall be as the native, and you shall love him as yourself") to emphasize both the equality of converts within the Jewish community and the special esteem due them since they left their idolatrous homeland "and journeyed to a better home . . . to the worship of the one and truly existing God."

9. For example, the anonymous pagan author of the 3d c. C.E. Paris Magical Papyrus, 11.3007–85, instructs would-be exorcists to adjure demons "by the god of the Hebrews. . . . 'I adjure thee by him who appeared to Osrael in the pillar of light and the cloud by day' [cf. Ex 13:21–22]. . . . 'I adjure thee by the seal which Solomon laid upon the tongue of Jeremiah [!] and he spoke.'" This charm may have been copied from some Jewish magical handbook, but the confusions in biblical chronology incline me to suspect that the magician relied on impressions and memory. Translation by C. K. Barrett, *New Testament Background,* pp. 31–35. The full corpus of these texts is now available in English: H. D. Betz, *Greek Magical Papyri in Translation.*

10. "Therefore, even to the present day, there is held every year a feast and general assembly on the island of Pharos [the site of the 72 translators' labors], whither not only Jews but multitudes of others cross the water, both to do honor to the place in which the light of that version first shone out, and also to thank God for the good gift so old yet ever new" (Philo, *de vita Mosis* 2.41). An inscription from the 3d c. C.E. synagogue of Aphrodisias has recently been discovered which lists the names of some 54 *theosebeis*—pagan God-fearers—along with those of Jewish donors who had contributed to the soup kitchen that the community ran for the poor. Two of these pagans also participated in the synagogue's prayer and study group, while nine were members of the city council. This last is most intriguing, since it indicates that Gentiles who were publicly responsible for the performance of the (pagan) sacrifices incumbent upon holders of such office were also worshipers of the Jewish God and active members of the synagogue community. See Robert Tannenbaum's discussion in Reynolds and Tannenbaum, *Jews and God-Fearers at Aphrodisias,* pp. 25–67.

Jewish tradition, full Jews.[11] Jews by birth, such as Philo and later the rabbis, saw in Judaism's openness to sympathetic pagans, and especially in the successful proselytism of the synagogue, the answer to the question of Israel's continuing dispersion. God, by means of the Diaspora, was making good his promise to Abraham that "through him all the nations [Heb. *goyim*, LXX *ethnē*] of the earth will be blessed" (Gn 18:18). Israel was in exile in order to turn the Gentiles to God.[12]

Once the movement that formed around the memory of Jesus spread from rural Palestine to the cities of the Roman Empire, it did not leave Judaism behind. On the contrary, it followed the lead of the Hellenistic synagogue both sociologically and theologically. Early Christian communities adopted the Jewish practice of meeting regularly once a week for group worship. They too established philanthropies for the needy, offered group support in time of persecution, and took responsibility for the burial of their dead. Such social structures sustained and gave expression to the strong sense of community and solidarity that distinguished these groups within their pagan environment.[13]

But these social structures were the concrete expression of something even more fundamental, also assumed from Hellenistic Judaism: a strong sense of a distinct identity, religious mission, and divine destiny. And together with this—indeed, its literary and sacral expression—came the LXX, the divine warrant for and story of the history and purpose of the people of the Lord. For the new community, however, the Lord spoken of in the LXX was not always and only the High God, the Father. It could also be his Son, the Lord Jesus, who as a preexistent divine intermediary preserved the dignity of the perfect Father and separated him from imperfect creation.[14] Finally, Hellenistic Christianity adopted allegorical interpretation as well as the Greek scriptures themselves. By these means it could redeem the Bible from its Jewish past and disclose its "true" meaning as the revelation of the New Israel, the church.

The starting point for this reinterpretation of the Bible was the figure of Jesus. Early Christians shared the conviction that, in the life, death, and resurrection of Jesus, God had uniquely revealed his plan of salvation. But different communities understood this revelation differently at different times. Their common conviction found a multiplicity of expressions in their various images of Jesus, to which we now turn.

11. Philo, Josephus, and the rabbinic tradition are all but unanimous on this score, but cf. G. F. Moore, *Judaism in the First Centuries of the Christian Era*, p. 335. Justin Martyr, the 2d c. church father, complains both that converts to Judaism strive to live exactly like those born to it and that they are regarded as fully Jewish by "native" Jews (*Dial.* 122–23).

12. Such a tradition is a form of theodicy, since it makes positive an initially negative fact, i.e., exile and dispersion.

13. Some three centuries after this period, the emperor Julian, a convert from Christianity to traditional Hellenistic paganism, characterized both Jewish and Christian communities by their commitment to such social arrangements (Loeb Ep. 22).

14. See above, n. 3.

Chapter 3
Images of Jesus in the Gospels and Paul

The language of the gospels and their communities was Greek; their scripture was the Septuagint (LXX). Paul, the one indisputably Jewish New Testament source, was a citizen of the Diaspora, at home in the society of the Mediterranean cities where he preached his message of salvation in terms drawn from both the Jewish and non-Jewish Hellenistic world. In brief, the milieu of Christianity, and thus its interpretive context, is the world of Hellenism.

These New Testament texts are concerned to portray, and communicate the unique significance of, the figure of Jesus. They do so partly in language that would have been familiar, whether from pagan tradition or from the LXX, to their Hellenistic audiences: Jesus is "Lord," "Savior," "Son of God," and God's "Logos." But other, unfamiliar language also appears and, especially in the synoptic gospels, even predominates—"Son of David," "Son of Man," "Kingdom of God," "messiah" (or more often its Greek equivalent, "Christ"). This language, variously interpreted and deployed by these New Testament writers, is an inheritance from the earliest years of the Jesus movement in Palestine. Its provenance is Jewish restoration theology.[1] We shall explore this layer of the tradition when we examine, in Part II, the world of Judaism. Here I

1. Restoration theology is the anticipation of the redemption of Israel and the world at the establishment of God's Kingdom. The phrase is preferable to *eschatological expectation* or *apocalypticism* since, although some groups, such as the Essenes or the first generation of Christians, expected the imminent arrival of the Kingdom, hope in the Kingdom's coming as such is a religious commonplace from the prophets to the rabbis and beyond. See Part II for an examination of several important themes in this tradition—the resurrection of the dead, the coming of the Messiah, the destruction and rebuilding of the Temple, the gratuitous redemption of the Gentiles, etc.

simply note that in these Hellenistic Christian documents we begin to encounter the literary vestiges of the older, Aramaic, apocalyptic tradition.

A broader and equally prominent concern of these texts is the status of Jews and Judaism. It was a complicated issue. The central figure of the new movement had been a Jew, the original disciples had been Jews, and Christianity claimed to be the fulfillment of the revelation embodied in the Jewish Bible. The past of the movement was Jewish. Its future, however, was with the Gentiles. Paul could not have known this, but his work was crucial in bringing about this transformation; the later evangelists did know, and they incorporated their perceptions of Jews and Judaism into their interpretation and presentation of the figure of Jesus. To understand their views of Jesus, then, we must keep in mind the fact that the evangelists and (to a lesser extent) Paul sought to explain, through their portraits of Jesus, why and how the Gospel had passed to the Gentiles.

I analyze these texts in reverse chronological order, from latest to earliest, in order to combat the false impression that their images of Jesus evolved in some sort of ordered development. What interests us is their particularity and individuality. I follow the (not uncontested) consensus that John should be dated late, after the synoptics. Matthew and Luke are thought to be roughly contemporary; but since Acts, also ascribed to Luke, must be considered together with his gospel and is usually dated roughly to 100 C.E., I consider Luke/Acts before Matthew. In brief, the sequence of our study is first, John, then Luke/Acts, Matthew, Mark, and finally Paul.[2]

JOHN: THE STRANGER FROM HEAVEN

The Gospel of John begins not at the banks of the Jordan, nor in a manger in Bethlehem, but "In the Beginning" itself, at the creation of the universe. To introduce his subject, the evangelist essentially revises Genesis: "In the Beginning was the Logos, and the Logos was with God, and the Logos was God. He was in the beginning with God; through him were all things made" (1:1–3). This divine principle entered the cosmos that he had made, actually becoming flesh in order to bring the power to become children of God to those who received him (1:10–12, 14). The prologue ends having established all the major theological themes that will contour this gospel's singular presentation of the figure of Jesus: that he is from above and descends into human history; that he supersedes both John the Baptist and Moses; that he is rejected by his own people (i.e., the Jews); and that access to the Father is exclusively through him, since only he, the Son, has seen God.

---

2. J. A. T. Robinson, *Redating the New Testament*, argues for a very early date for the Gospel of John as well as for earlier dates for all the canonical documents. See W. R. Farmer, *Synoptic Problem*, for the chronological priority of Matthew over Mark.

The story immediately establishes a mood of nervous anticipation when sinister agents of the Pharisees interrogate John the Baptist. Their questions and his responses set the stage for Jesus' entrance. "Who are you?" "Not the Christ." "Elijah? The Prophet?" "No" (1:19–27). As soon as Jesus appears, John proclaims him the Lamb of God (an image that foreshadows the coming Passion) and the Son of God (1:29–34). As the chapter proceeds, the Christological titles accumulate: messiah, King of Israel, Son of Man (1:41, 49, 51). They are defined neither by an allusion to a traditional messianic prophecy (e.g., Davidic descent, birth in Bethlehem), nor by the performance of any act that would provoke recognition, but simply by their common ascription to Jesus. But who is Jesus? The reader (who has the benefit of the prologue) knows, the believer in the Johannine community knows, and sympathetic characters in the story know: he is the divine redeemer who has descended and who will ascend.[3]

Thus the gospel has a double context. The first is that of the narrative's ostensible historical setting, the dramatic situation of the characters in this world. But this is dwarfed by the gospel's "true" context, the divine realm of light beyond, whence Jesus came. Those who are of this cosmos, namely Jesus' opponents, cannot see past the context of this world. Limited to it and by it, they are blind to the meaning of the events before their eyes. But for those in the know, this cosmos becomes transparent: one can look through it to see Jesus' true point of origin with and in the Father, and this knowledge puts everything in a radically different perspective.

The evangelist's brilliant device of the double context thus enables him at once and with great economy to establish his Christology and to sustain a terrible, if occasionally comic, irony. His Christ is the great Stranger from Heaven whose mission on earth must run its preordained course. Again and again plots against Jesus fail because it is not yet time for them to succeed— "My hour is not yet come" repeats throughout the gospel (2:4; 7:6, 30; 8:20; cf. 12:23). And even in the flesh, Jesus is not quite human. He does not laugh; he does not appear to suffer; he remains impassive through all the confrontations that he provokes with both Jews and Romans, until he accomplishes his goal: the cross. He dies only when he knows that all has been fulfilled, expiring in complete control and saying only, "It is finished" (19:30).

The story unwinds as a series of long revelatory discourses, broken up by occasional dialogues and wondrous signs, all of which serve to reveal Jesus' divine nature as Son—but only to those who already know. His opponents are merely baffled. They constantly ask him, "where are you from?" and "where are you going?" and inevitably misunderstand the answer. They think he is

---

3. This theme is analyzed both literarily and sociologically in the seminal article by Wayne A. Meeks, "Stranger from Heaven in Johannine Sectarianism," to which this discussion is greatly indebted.

really from Nazareth (7:27, 40–42, 52) or admit with unwitting irony that they do not know where he is from ("we know that God has spoken to Moses, but as for this man, we do not know where he comes from," 9:29). They do not know because they cannot know: Jesus proceeds from a realm to which they have no access. If they knew, they would not need to ask; since they ask, they can never understand. "You [Jesus' opponents] are from below, I am from above; you are of this cosmos, I am not of this cosmos" (8:23).

Again and again the evangelist sets up an ironic dialogue where an interlocutor, having inadvertently posed a significant question, obtusely misinterprets Jesus' ambiguous or cryptic response because he understands it literally, not spiritually. To Nicodemus, a ruler of the Jews, Jesus confides that unless one is born *anōthen*—a word meaning both "again" and "from above"—he cannot see the Kingdom of God. Nicodemus of course seizes on the "lower" definition and is consequently baffled. "How can a man be born when he is old? Can he enter his mother's womb and be born?" (3:4). Even after Jesus explains what the reader knows is a reference to baptism, Nicodemus remains in the dark ("How can this be?"). The woman at the well to whom Jesus offers "living water," that is, himself through baptism, is likewise baffled. "I have nothing to draw with, and the well is deep. Where do you get that living water?" (4:11). And later, when Jesus refers to Abraham's knowledge of his coming, the Jews exclaim angrily, "you are not yet fifty years old, and you have seen Abraham?" They miss Jesus' allusion to his own preexistence: "Before Abraham was, I am" (8:58).

As revelatory discourse, this verges on parody. The true audience of these dialogues is the Johannine community, who like the reader has special prior information. To his interlocutors in the story, Jesus reveals little other than their ignorance. He leaves them baffled, confused, and angry while he moves on, serenely untroubled, through the highly charged atmosphere that he has created.

These confrontational dialogues reveal the central Christological message of this gospel: that Jesus is the Son. By *son* John means a divine entity who uniquely reveals the Father, because only the Son has known the Father, only the Son has been with the Father in the upper realms. "No one has ascended into heaven but he who has descended from heaven, the Son of Man" (3:13). In fact, they are radically identified: "The Logos was with God, and the Logos *was* God"; "I and the Father are one" (1:1; 10:30).[4] Therefore one can come to knowledge of the Father through the Son alone (e.g., 8:19; 14:6), and he who rejects the Son likewise rejects the Father and so earns "the wrath of God" (3:36). "He who hates me hates my Father also" (15:23). Christ's

---

4. This identification stops short of full equivalence, since the evangelist omits the definite article before both *theos* (God) and *hen* (one). See the lengthy discussion in Raymond E. Brown, *The Gospel according to John*, vol. 1, pp. 3–21, 519–24.

purpose in coming into the world is to precipitate a *krisis,* calling the world to judgment (9:39), distinguishing by their response to him the children of light from the children of darkness; those who are from above from those who are from below; those who know the Father from those whose father is the "ruler of this world," the *archōn* of this *kosmos,* the Devil (14:30; 8:44).

Those who do follow Jesus believe because they, like him, are not of this cosmos (17:14). But their status is conferred, not earned: God chooses them ("No one can come to me unless the Father who sent me draws him"; 6:44), Jesus chooses them ("you are not of the world, but I chose you out of the world"; 15:19), or God gives them to Jesus ("I have manifested thy name [the Father's] to the men whom you gave me out of the cosmos; they were yours, and you gave them to me"; 17:6; also 10:29). John offers no theology of predestination to account for the choice, no explanation for divine election other than tautology: "He who is of God hears the words of God; the reason why you do not hear them is that you are not of God" (9:47). Nor can any amount of sympathetic interest or individual initiative move a person from one category to the other. Poor Nicodemus attempts to understand Jesus, interviews him (ch. 3), and even attaches himself to his followers, all to no avail: there he is on the eve of the resurrection, reverently packing Jesus' body in a hundred pounds of embalming spices (19:40). He never grasps the meaning of Jesus' identity as Son of Man (3:13ff.; 9:35ff.), or the import of his being "lifted up" on the cross. Nicodemus is simply not "of God."[5]

The double context of this gospel, the Christological theme of descent/ ascent, and the absolute distinction between believers and unbelievers converge nowhere more tellingly and with greater irony than in John's presentation of the crucifixion. Lifting up/crucifixion in the earthly context simultaneously entails lifting up/exaltation in the cosmic context: Jesus' crucifixion *is* his exaltation, and through it he brings about the salvation of those who believe that by his crucifixion he returns to the heavenly realm. John puns untiringly on the double entendre of *hupsothenai,* which means both "to be lifted up" and "to be crucified." Explaining to Nicodemus that only the Son of Man descends and ascends, Jesus says, "As Moses lifted up the serpent in the wilderness, so must the Son of Man be lifted up, that whoever believes in him may have eternal life" (3:14–15). Nicodemus gains no insight from this exchange: one must already know the message to understand it.

In the same connection, Jesus later taunts those paradigmatic unbelievers, the Jews, with their lack of understanding. Seeking to learn where Jesus is going, they cannot understand his answer. When Jesus says that where he is going they cannot follow, they stupidly assume that he purposes to travel abroad. "Does he intend to go to the Diaspora among the Greeks and teach the Greeks?" (7:35). But Jesus is going back whence he came, to the Father, a fact the Jews cannot or will not acknowledge; hence they cannot follow him—that is the exclusive prerogative of the believer. Only once the Jews "lift him up"— crucify him—will they know who he is (8:28). That moment is indicated, significantly, when the Greeks (i.e., Gentiles) come to Jesus (12:20). Then he knows that his mission is drawing to its predestined close. "The hour has come for the Son of Man to be glorified . . . and when I am lifted up from the earth, I will draw all men to myself" (12:23, 32). Thus the cross is literally the sole intersection of the "horizontal" context of mundane history (the only one Nicodemus and the majority of Jews can ever know) and the "vertical" context of heavenly reality. At the cross, heaven and earth are joined; via the cross, Jesus can move between these two dimensions back to his true home and so draw those who are his own back with him, out of the lower realm to the upper.

Thus Johannine irony reaches its height in the Passion. The word *passion* is a misnomer, for this is a trial without anxiety or suspense, a crucifixion without suffering and without pathos. The Stranger, unnerving and imperturbable, remains unmoved by the mockery and sarcasm through which his tormentors unknowingly proclaim his true identity: he really is the King of the Jews, as the Romans sarcastically call him (18:33, 39; 19:3, 14, 15, 17–22); he really is the Son of God, as the Jews accuse him of claiming and Pilate dimly senses (19:7–9). Perverse and obdurate to the end, the Jews deny his kingship: "The chief priests of the Jews then said to Pilate, 'Do not write, The King of the Jews, but write, This man said, I am King of the Jews' " (19:21; cf. v. 7, where they claim that Jesus made himself the Son of God). But Pilate declines: he has a better sense than they who Jesus really is.

"He came to his own home, and his own people received him not" (1:11). Jesus really is their king, but the Jews are not really his people, because their father is the Devil, not God. Dragging him to judgment and condemnation before Pilate, they actually indict themselves, for they execute the wishes of their father, who "was a murderer from the beginning . . . a liar and the Father of lies" (8:44). Jesus turns the tables on them: by allowing himself to be judged, he brings them to judgment. Through Jesus' death, "the Archon of this cosmos is judged" and his children with him (16:11; 12:31).

But what is the reward of the children of God? On this point John's gospel is less than clear, perhaps because the text as it now stands is the final redaction of several different ideas.[6] Salvation, according to John, comes through the recognition of Jesus' true status: this proves that the individual is "of God." Jesus redeems not by suffering on the cross (he is not presented as suffering) but by providing an opportunity for recognition—for this reason the Father sent him into the cosmos. Hence the didactic episode of Doubting Thomas,

---

6. Brown, *John*, vol. 1, pp. xxiv–xl, reviews the scholarly opinions on the gospel's literary composition and redaction.

whose true audience is all the faithful in the period after the resurrection: "Have you believed because you have seen me? Blessed are those who have not seen and yet believe" (20:29).

Belief in Christ—specifically, belief that Christ is the Son of God—brings eternal life, but what John means by this is unclear. At times he speaks as though it were a present reality: "He who believes in the Son *has* eternal life" (3:36); "Truly, truly, I say to you, he who hears my word and believes him who sent me *has* eternal life; he does not come into judgment, but *has passed* from death to life" (5:25). At other times, eternal life follows this one: "The water that I shall give him [baptism] *will become* in him a spring of water welling up to eternal life" (4:14), perhaps not until the resurrection of the dead "in the last day" (5:28–29; 6:44, 54; 10:24).

Likewise, the time of Christ's Parousia, his manifestation after the resurrection, is unclear. Will it be on "the last day"? At times it seems so (21:22); at other times, his Parousia seems simply to mean the giving of the Spirit to believers after his death while they are still on earth, so that they will realize "that I am in my Father, and you in me, and I in you" (14:20). His post-resurrection manifestation will not be known to the cosmos; it will not mark the dramatic End of Days; rather, only those who believe will know of it, so that "my Father will love [them], and we will come to [them] and make our home with [them]" (14:22–23). In other words, neither the believer's eternal life nor Christ's presence to believers after his resurrection describes an event at the End. Rather, they signify present realities, the believers' spiritual condition because God dwells in them. In this sense they are already ascended to the Father (14:6–7). Hence Jesus can tell his apostles that they cannot come where he is going; that they can but only afterward; and that in fact they are already there (13:31–14:7).

The identity of those who follow Jesus is defined in no small measure by who they are not. They are not followers of John the Baptist, for example, whose inferiority to Jesus is established immediately in the prologue. He too was sent by God, but only to bear witness to Jesus (1:6–9); he knows that Jesus "outranks" him, because although Jesus comes after John, he was before John (1:15). John reiterates his own inferiority continuously: he is not the Christ; he is not worthy even to untie his sandal. It is John, not Jesus, who hears the voice from heaven revealing Jesus' true identity in a passage so convoluted that, were it not for Christian tradition, one would have no reason on the evidence of the Fourth Gospel to think that John had baptized Jesus at all (1:32–33). John claims that Christ "must increase, but I must decrease," and he bears no grudge as his followers desert him for Jesus (3:30). Jesus in turn calls John a "shining lamp"; nevertheless, "the testimony which I have is greater than that of John" (5:36). The gospel so emphasizes this point that scholars speculate the community for whom and in which it was produced had to distinguish itself over against the sect of John the Baptist; perhaps they were even in direct conflict or competition with it.[7] Nevertheless, the tone here is not so much hostile as condescending.

Toward "the Jews" it is otherwise. The Fourth Gospel's emphasis on the uniqueness of its revelation—that receiving the Son is the only way to know and honor the Father, the only way to pass from death to life—leads to exclusivity in its idea of salvation as well. Only those who follow Jesus are saved; "He who does not believe is condemned already" (3:18). But the Jews insist that they have independent access to the Father through their scriptures. Not so, says John. "The scriptures . . . bear witness to me; and yet you refuse to come to me that you may have eternal life. . . . It is Moses who accuses you, on whom you set your hope. If you believed Moses, you would believe me, for he wrote of me" (5:39, 46).

The Jews' refusal to follow proves that they are not "of God" (8:47). They admit that "when Christ comes, no one will know where he comes from" (7:27)—exactly Jesus' situation in this gospel—but the Christ can come from only one place, according to John: the upper realm, from which he descends and to which he ascends. Jesus does come from above, but the Jews know nothing of the upper world since their father, the Devil, is the ruler of this one (8:44). This radical divorce from Judaism—its people, its history, and in a more complicated way, its scripture—liberates the evangelist stylistically and theologically from composing his gospel around biblical testimonia. The Johannine Christ is not heralded in Jewish history: he is an utterly untraditional messiah. John can therefore acknowledge forthrightly that Jesus comes from Nazareth, not the messianically correct town of Bethlehem: "Others [of the people] said: 'This is the Christ.' But some said, 'Is the Christ to come from Galilee? Has not the scripture said that Christ is descended from David, and comes from Bethlehem, the village where David was? . . . Search and you will find that no prophet is to rise from Galilee'" (7:40–42, 52). Jesus' earthly point of origin is irrelevant, because his true point of origin is beyond this cosmos, with the Father.

John states that "salvation is from the Jews" (4:22) meaning, perhaps, that it was among Jews that Jesus appeared in the flesh—but their role in his gospel is for the most part demonic. And while Jesus may truly be their king, little in his speech or actions indicates that he thinks of himself as Jewish. The Law is *their* law (e.g., 10:34; 15:25). Jesus regards the Jews as a hostile group to such a degree that when he speaks to Pilate, they, not Rome, seem like the enemy nation: "If my kingship were of this world, my servants would fight, that I might not be handed over to the Jews" (18:36).

This gospel, in other words, is written by someone who consciously placed himself outside, if not against, Judaism. This fact does not necessarily mean the author was not Jewish. Some scholars have argued that the very intensity

7. Ibid., lxvii–lxx.

of his hostility, and his references to Christians being excluded from synagogue services (9:22; 12:42; 16:2), suggest that he and his community were expelled from the synagogue and that they incorporated their bitter experience of rejection into their story about Jesus.[8] This document, then, would have been primarily for internal consumption, a sort of identity-confirming tract for the excluded group.

Against this argument, however, it must be said that the gospel neither assumes nor evinces any great familiarity with Judaism. The objections made by the crowds or the Pharisees to the miracles that Jesus works on the Sabbath are very strained (e.g., 5:8–18; 9:1–16), and the prohibition against carrying or constructing on the Sabbath could be known by someone only superficially acquainted with Judaism from the LXX or personal observation. Further, the evangelist continually makes asides to explain Jewish terms or concepts to his audience—"rabbi (which means teacher)"; "messiah (which means Christ)"; stone jars to be filled with water "for the Jewish rites of purification" (1:38; 1:42; 2:6). And, finally, John's Jews seem curiously unacquainted with their own traditions. They say that no one knows where Christ will come from, despite a firm tradition (knowledge of which John also attributes to them) that he will come from Bethlehem (7:42, quoted above); they tell Jesus that they have never been in bondage to anyone, apparently unaware of the Exodus story or Babylonian Captivity (8:33. The remark may refer solely to the current audience, but they respond in terms of descent from Abraham). But no matter what the immediate background of the writer and his community, "the Jews" serve as the evangelist's foil, the negative extreme of one of a number of antitheses around which he constructs his gospel: Jews (children of the Devil)/Christians (children of God); darkness/light; flesh/spirit; ignorance/knowledge; blindness/sight; Below/Above. The Jews stand for those who reject the evangelist's message as much as they represent the historical community that, as John and his readers knew, had not received Jesus as Son.

John thus maps his scheme of redemption onto the Greco-Roman model of the universe, with its strong verticality and valuation of higher realities beyond this cosmos. His presentation of Christ as a divine Stranger, alienated from and antipathetic to his immediate environment, may articulate the social experience of the group that stands behind this document. This group sees itself as it sees Jesus: unique, misunderstood, under attack from the ignorant and demonic, isolated in this cosmos which belongs to ignorance, darkness, and the Devil. Yet they, like their Jesus, are intrinsically connected with the realm of the Father. They could thus see themselves as they saw their Savior: alone in the darkness, yet the light of the world.

---

8. See esp. J. Louis Martyn, *History and Theology in the Fourth Gospel* and *The Gospel of John in Christian History;* Wayne A. Meeks, "'Am I a Jew?'"; Raymond E. Brown, *The Community of the Beloved Disciple.*

LUKE/ACTS: THE MESSIAH OF THE GENTILES

Inasmuch as many have undertaken to compile a narrative of the things which have been accomplished among us, just as they were delivered to us by those who from the beginning were eyewitnesses and ministers of the word, it seemed good to me also, having followed all things closely for some time past, to write an orderly account for you, most excellent Theophilus, that you may know the truth concerning the things of which you have been informed. (Lk 1:1–4)

If the prologue to the Fourth Gospel evokes the timelessness of the upper realm, the prologue to the Third evokes exactly the opposite: a world of eyewitnesses to past events, chains of transmission, researched narrative—in brief, the horizontal plane of human history that John's double context devalues. Luke, conscious of standing in an extended tradition, writes like a historian: he has carefully considered the "many" other narratives written about Jesus, and he now intends to supersede them with his own more reliable report, a history in two volumes. Jesus is the focus of Part 1, the gospel; the career of the apostolic church, and especially Paul, of Part 2, the Book of Acts. Luke in fact presents a history not of Jesus' career itself but of salvation, of how the Holy Spirit came into human history definitively through Jesus, and thence passed from the Risen Christ to his (and Luke's) largely Gentile church.

Luke shapes the beginning of his story in a number of ways. First, he locates the action in secular chronography: "In the days of Herod, king of Judea" (1:5); "a decree went out from Caesar Augustus . . . when Quirinius was governor of Syria" (2:1–2); "in the fifteenth year of the reign of Tiberius Caesar, Pontius Pilate being governor of Judea, and Herod being tetrarch of Galilee . . ." (3:1). He announces impending events through angelic messengers: "And there appeared to him an angel of the Lord" (1:11f.); "the angel Gabriel was sent from God to a city of Galilee named Nazareth" (1:26). His characters burst out in poetic proclamations: 1:14–17, a canticle in honor of John the Baptist; 1:47–55, Mary's Magnificat; 1:68–79, the Benedictus; 2:29–35, the Nunc dimittis. Finally, Luke frames his story within a sacred geography: the good news (Luke uses the word *euangelion*) of John the Baptist's advent is announced from the altar of the Temple in Jerusalem (1:17–19); and it is from Jerusalem that the good news of the gospel will go forth to the world (Acts 1:1ff.)

Within this elaborate and beautiful literary scaffolding, Luke builds his presentation of the Baptist. He is Jesus' slightly elder kinsman, the product of a miraculous conception by a barren couple, Zechariah and Elizabeth, both advanced in years. This story recalls the biblical narratives of Abraham and Sarah's conception of Isaac, of Jacob and Rachel's conception of Joseph, and most particularly of Hannah's conception of the prophet Samuel. Like Samuel, who anointed Saul and, more important, David, the first kings of Israel, so too will John "go before the Lord," Jesus the Messiah, Son of David, to prepare the people. So thoroughly is John's mission in life subordinated to Jesus' that he acknowledges his cousin's presence in utero, prompting his mother Elizabeth, "filled with the Holy Spirit," to declare Mary "the mother of [the] Lord" (1:43).

Jesus' conception is even more miraculous. The angel Gabriel announces to Mary that she, though a virgin, will conceive a son by the Holy Spirit and the power of the Most High. The child will thus be "the Son of God" who will inherit the throne of David his father [sic] and reign over Israel forever (1:32–34). When the time comes for her to give birth, she must travel to Bethlehem because her husband, Joseph, "of the house and lineage of David," must be enrolled in the city of David. When the child is born, angels announce the nativity to nearby shepherds: "For to you is born this day in the city of David a Savior, who is Christ the Lord" (2:11). Later, Mary and Joseph go up to Jerusalem, where Jesus is acknowledged in the Temple by a holy man "filled with the Spirit," Simeon. The infant, he says, is the Lord's Christ (i.e., messiah), the consolation of Israel and a light of revelation to the Gentiles (2:26–32; cf. Is 49:6).

Thus, in his first two chapters, Luke does much to define his Jesus. He has attributed most of the important Christological titles—Savior, Lord, Christ, Son of David (another way of saying messiah), Son of God. (For reasons I will later explain, Luke avoids Son of Man.) And he has defined these titles, and so the figure of Jesus, as consonant with the history of Israel. Christianity thus is continuous with Israel; it is the fulfillment of God's promise of redemption. Hence both Mary and Zechariah can hymn their miraculous children in terms directly appropriated from the LXX and modeled on similar passages in the Jewish Bible. Mary praises God for his mercy in exalting the humble and scattering the proud, for remembering his servant Israel as he had promised "to Abraham and to his posterity forever" (1:47–55). Zechariah blesses "the Lord of Israel" for redeeming his people and raising up the horn of salvation "in the house of his servant David"—that is, for sending Jesus, "the Lord," before whom John will go to bring "the knowledge of salvation to his people," the Jews (1:67–80; cf. 3:2–6).

In chapter 3, with John the Baptist's ministry, the tone of the gospel suddenly changes. Gone is the lyrical quality of the pleasingly symmetrical birth narratives; gone too the message of peace, joy, and salvation. Rather, when preaching a baptism of repentance for the forgiveness of sins, John suddenly (and inexplicably) condemns those multitudes streaming out to him as a "brood of vipers": "Who warned you to flee from the wrath to come?" (3:7: the reader thinks, John!; v. 4). The passage bumps along with advice to be charitable, fair, and irenic, a denial that John is the Christ and a prediction of Jesus' coming—and then, just as suddenly, John is whisked off stage and imprisoned by Herod the tetrarch (3:15–17, 19–20). Luke mentions in a subordinate clause that Jesus had been baptized (he does not say by whom) and addressed by a voice from heaven as "beloved son." Luke then interrupts his story to relate a lengthy genealogy tracing Jesus' descent through Joseph (his "supposed" father, as the text notes) to David and ultimately back to Adam, "the son of God" (3:23, 38). Again at some length, Luke then describes Satan's attempts to seduce Jesus from his purpose. Jesus' ministry finally gets underway in 4:15.

Luke thus brackets Jesus' ministry in several ways. Having removed John (whose ministry might otherwise deflect attention from that of Jesus), Luke exiles Satan until the gospel's denouement (4:13; 22:3; cf. 10:18). Jesus' earthly ministry is thus a special interval in which Israel receives her redeemer. For, despite an inauspicious rejection at his home synagogue after he cites acts of past prophets that were of benefit to Gentiles (4:24–30), Jesus is for the most part well received by the Jewish people, who greet him enthusiastically, follow him in great numbers, and welcome him in Jerusalem. Not the Jews, but illness and infirmity represent the demonic forces against which Jesus conducts his mission. And the chief message of this mission, according to Luke, is that God forgives repentant sinners. Sinners thus can and should repent; further, since God forgives sinners, man can do no less. "Those who are well have no need of a physician, but those who are sick. I have not come to call the righteous, but sinners to repentance" (5:31–32).

But the Pharisees deplore Jesus' easy fellowship with tax collectors and sinners (e.g., 5:27ff.; 7:29; 15:1ff; 19:1–10). Their opposition to him stems not from demonic inspiration but a sort of spiritual ungenerosity: they resent his forgiveness of repentant sinners in the way the elder son resented his father's rejoicing at the return of the prodigal (15:11–32). The irony, of course, is that the Pharisees in their proud self-righteousness are sinners too. Though they scrupulously tithe even small things like herbs, they neglect justice and the love of God (11:37–44). Hence Jesus' mission is also to them, and Luke portrays him as dining with Pharisees at least as often as with tax collectors (7:36–50; 11:37; 14:1–6). The opportunity for repentance is held out to everyone.

Luke's Jesus is thus the patient teacher par excellence. His particular concern is the unfortunate—the poor, the hungry, the sorrowful, all of whom are blessed. He who would follow Jesus should give a beggar the shirt off his back and attend to the sick and the outcast (14:13). He too should forgive, loving his enemies, praying for his tormentors, and treating others as he would be treated. No one should judge or condemn his fellow but should forgive as often as the offender repents (6:20–46). Poverty is not required of a disciple, but wealth is clearly a liability, for possessions pose great spiritual dangers (12:15–21; 18:23–27): better to relinquish them and have greater riches in heaven. Besides, the future will bring reversals, when those who are now first will be last. The proud will be humbled and the humble exalted (14:11). He who is truly religious is truly humble, and the ultimate model of humility is Jesus himself:

> A dispute also arose among them [the disciples], which of them was to be regarded as the greatest. And he [Jesus] said to them, "The kings of the Gentiles exercise lordship over them, and those in authority over them are called benefactors. But not so with you; rather let the greatest among you become as the youngest, and the leader as one who serves. For which is the greater, one who sits at the table, or one who serves? Is it not one who sits at table? But I am among you as one who serves." (22:24–27)

Luke thus explicitly presents Jesus as the ethical model and teacher for his disciples and (future) followers. Jesus often withdraws to pray (e.g., 5:16, to a wilderness; 6:12, to a mountain; 9:18, 28–36; 22:42); he also teaches his disciples to pray (11:1ff.), so that in the face of adversity they will persevere (18:1ff.) and receive the Holy Spirit, who "will teach you in that hour what you ought to say" (12:12). As Jesus will take up his cross, so anyone who would follow him must "take up his cross daily" (9:23). As Jesus preaches the Kingdom of God, heals, and has authority over demons, so do his followers (9:1–2; 10:8–12, 17–20), who should not on that account grow proud, "but rejoice that your names are written in heaven" (10:20). And as Jesus in his commitment to his mission had distanced himself from his family (even as a child, 2:41–49), so the true follower must likewise be prepared for family contention and strife (12:51–53; cf. 21:16), even giving up family for Jesus' sake (not burying parents or even saying goodbye to them, 9:57–60). "If anyone comes to me and does not hate his own father and mother and wife and children and brothers and sisters, yes, and even his own life, he cannot be my disciple. . . . And whoever of you does not renounce all that he has cannot be my disciple" (14:26, 33).

Nowhere does Jesus shine more as a moral exemplar than in the final stages of his ministry, as he suffers abuse in silence and prays for his tormentors. Knowing that humiliation and death await him in Jerusalem, Jesus nonetheless weeps for the city that refuses to let him nurture it, and mourns its impending destruction, the consequence of rejecting him (19:41–44; cf. 13:34). Driving out those who sell in the Temple courtyard, he nonetheless teaches there daily, still trying to turn the people to himself (19:45–48; 20:1; 21:37–38). Knowing that Peter will deny him, Jesus prays for him; later, his gaze after the denial helps Peter to repent (22:32, 62–63). He fears the ordeal before him but submits to God's will (22:39–44). Refusing to allow his disciples to defend him with arms ("No more of this"), he heals an enemy whom his followers had wounded (22:51). Later, from the cross, he entreats God's forgiveness for his executioners (23:34).

Luke's Jesus is thus no isolated figure: to function as teacher and exemplar requires an attentive community, a community that, centered around Jesus, spreads out from the disciples and apostles to the people of Israel past and present, the Samaritans, and ultimately the Gentiles. The disciples, Jesus' immediate community, are particularly partners in his mission. Any failure to understand their master is part of a larger design, not some fault of theirs. "But they did not understand this saying, and *it was concealed from them,* that they should not perceive it" (9:45); "But they understood none of these things; *this saying was hid from them*" (18:34). Despite their fear and confusion, they stay with Jesus to the end and witness his crucifixion (23:49); and Peter, bitterly repenting of his inconstancy during Jesus' arrest, is accorded a special post-resurrection appearance (24:34). Even after death, Jesus continues his instruction to them and "clothes them with power from on high" (24:27–53, Acts 1:1–7; 2:1–4), so that they can bring his message of repentance and forgiveness of sin from Jerusalem to Judea and Samaria, and ultimately to all the people of the world (Lk 24:47; Acts 1:8).

Much of Luke's material for this presentation of Jesus and his first followers is, as he announced in his prologue, inherited. But he shapes it to his own special vision of things, particularly through his use of four schemata: secular time, sacred biblical time, the sacred time of the mission itself, and finally sacred geography. These schemata are coordinated literary strategies by which Luke makes his particular theological points.

Luke's specific references to secular historical events—the reign of Herod, the governorship of Quirinius, the tetrarchy of Herod, Philip, Lysanias, and so on—all serve to anchor his story concretely to the public past. Examined more closely, this chronography turns out to testify more to Luke's skills as a storyteller than as an historian, for his references are often muddled by anachronisms. For instance, Herod the Great, King of Judea, ruled until 4 B.C.E.; the census under Quirinius occurred around 6 C.E.; but the chronology of the birth narrative presupposes synchrony (cf. Lk 1:5, 26; 2:2). Likewise, when Gamaliel the Pharisee, pleading for tolerance for the new movement, recalls previous insurrections, his speech contains significant chronological gaffes (Acts 6:34–39).[9] Even if inaccurate, however, these allusions to the public past help concretize Luke's tale. It is as if he were saying, "These things really happened, and not so very long ago, when all these other things that everyone knows about also occurred." This sort of secular chronography, despite the errors of fact, contributes directly to the *vraisemblance* of Luke's story by grounding sacred events in secular time.

Luke also grounds his story in sacred biblical time, linking the life and

9. Luke places Theudas before Judah the Galilean; actually, Theudas was active c. 46–48 C.E., Judah, in 6 C.E. E. P. Sanders notes, "New Testament scholars all tell themselves, one another and their students that the Gospel writers were not historians in the modern sense, but we do not apply this fact rigorously enough." He considers the shortcomings of Luke in particular, "who made most of being an accurate historian" (*JJ*, p. 299–300).

ministry of Jesus to the history of all Israel. Luke's theological claim that in Jesus the promises to Abraham are realized gives to the new movement a respectability and prestige that otherwise its very newness would decisively compromise. Luke supports his claim through an appeal to the authority and antiquity of the LXX—and, concomitantly, of Jewish religious history—in various imaginative ways. In the double birth narrative that constitutes the prelude to Jesus' ministry, he makes his case through imitation of archetypical scriptural events: miraculous births, angelic visitations, prophetic utterances, and so on. His characters utter long pronouncements that derive from the prophets. Consonant with his theme of Jesus' appeal to outcasts, Luke also has those on the margins of human or spiritual society (Samaritans, Gentile God-fearers, the physically handicapped, on the one hand; Satan or his demons, on the other) declare Jesus' identity in biblical terms as Son of God (e.g., Lk 4:3, 9, 34, 40; 8:28) and Son of David (e.g., 18:35–39). Elsewhere, Luke simply asserts that Jesus is the true subject of the writings of Moses and all the prophets (e.g., 24:27, 44). Finally, and with great economy, Luke calls Jesus "Lord." This title enables him to use scriptural passages referring to God as references to Jesus (e.g., the double entendre of John the Baptist as "great before the Lord" 1:15; also 1:76; 3:1–2; 20:41ff., where he makes the argument explicitly; Acts 2:25ff.). Thus, while the immediate historical context is prefectorial Palestine, the extended context, which gives Luke's story its religious depth, is the entire course of biblical history.

But Jesus' time on earth is a unique sacred period in its own right. Luke presents it as such by dividing his history of salvation into three periods. The first is the time of Israel, from the promise to Abraham through the mission of John the Baptist (Lk 7:28; 16:16). The second is the time of the earthly Jesus, during which Satan is banished (4:14–22:3). The third period, the time of the church, begins at Pentecost, after Jesus' ascension (Acts 2:1ff.), and continues indefinitely. Thus time past and time present are both oriented around the central and unique event of Jesus' ministry.

Finally, Luke articulates the meaning of his story through the device of sacred geography—the Holy Land, the Holy City, and particularly the Temple. The good news of impending redemption comes forth from the Temple, where Gabriel announces the *euangelion* to Zechariah (Lk 1:19). Later, in the same place, the infant Jesus is acknowledged as the salvation of Jew and Gentile both (2:29–32). Just before he begins his ministry, Jesus resists the final temptation of Satan from the peak of the Temple mount (4:9). And, once his mission begins, Jesus moves from the Galilee through Samaria until, finally, he goes up to Jerusalem, where he preaches in the Temple daily (19:46; 20:1; 21:37–38).

Jerusalem continues to be the center of Jesus' activities even after his death. His first post-resurrection appearances occur in and around the city, where his disciples continue to worship in the Temple (24:34; cf. v. 13; 24:53). Jesus remains there for forty days, speaking to them about the Kingdom of God until just before the Jewish feast of Shavuot (Greek: Pentecost; Acts 1:3). This holiday commemorates the giving of the Law on Sinai seven weeks after the Exodus, itself commemorated by Passover. Luke has the holiday stand for the giving of the Holy Spirit to the church seven weeks after the Passover on which Christ was crucified (2:1ff.). Peter preaches for the first time in Jerusalem on that Pentecost, thereby adding some three thousand souls to the church, and shortly thereafter he works his first cure in Jesus' name at the gates of the Temple (3:1ff.). Eventually, the Gospel spreads to the major cities of the Empire, from Jerusalem to Antioch to Athens and ultimately to Rome. However, in whatever Diaspora city the apostles find themselves, they invariably begin their proclamation in the synagogue, turning from it only when they are rejected. The message thus continually proceeds from the sacred Jewish foundation out to the Gentile world.

Luke's concept of Christianity's relationship to Judaism, and consequently his presentation of Jesus' relationship to Judaism, are complicated. On the one hand, the two religions are viewed as continuous: Jesus fulfills the promise of salvation made to Israel long ago. Jesus' parents are faithful, observant Jews who yearly journey to Jerusalem for Passover (Lk 2:41); and Jesus is first acknowledged not by a marginal figure like John the Baptist, but by mainstream, pious Jews traditional in their observance: Elizabeth, Simeon, Anna (1:41–44; 2:25–38). Jesus treats the authorities respectfully (2:46), even "cleansing the Temple" (an episode Luke quickly glosses over) with so little disruption that he can forthwith preach there daily (19:45–47). The Jews in turn welcome Jesus, heed his message, and rejoice in his coming. Indeed, the chief priests, the true villains of the Passion, arrest Jesus surreptitiously, so afraid are they of popular reprisal (22:1–2).

Yet with a clumsy foreshadowing that borders on anachronism, Luke works into his narrative the later tensions between Christianity and its parent religion. For example, when Jesus is speaking to the Jewish multitudes blessing those who are poor, hungry, or sorrowful, he suddenly says: "Blessed are you when men hate you, when they exclude you and revile you and cast out your name as evil, on account of the Son of Man. Rejoice in that day . . . for so did *their* fathers to the prophets" (6:23). The Jews have suddenly been shifted from audience to enemy. Jesus warns his disciples that the Jews will drag them "before the synagogues and rulers and authorities," as they are about to do to Jesus (12:11). And in the parable of Lazarus and the rich man, he cautions that an unbreachable chasm separates those who have heeded the scriptures from those who have not. If the latter "do not hear Moses and the prophets, neither will they be convinced if someone should rise from the dead" (16:19–31). Later in the gospel, of course, Jesus does rise from the dead and the Jews continue to disbelieve. Finally, once Jesus stands before Pilate, "the people," who only a chapter before were a serious impediment to the chief priests' plots, suddenly demand that Barabbas be released and Christ be crucified. A reluctant Pilate delivers Jesus up "to *their* will"—one has the impression that the Jews, not the Romans, performed the execution (23:1–25).

This submerged theme of aggressive Jewish rejection of Jesus, and hence of Christianity, emerges more clearly in Luke's second volume, the Acts of the Apostles. Peter informs some three thousand Jews and proselytes (i.e., Jews by conversion) who have assembled for Shavuot/Pentecost that *they* have crucified Jesus (Acts 2:23, 36). This theme of universal and corporate Jewish guilt in the death of Jesus figures prominently in every summary of the early kerygma (3:13; 4:14; 7:52; 10:39, etc.). Sadducees, elders, and scribes constantly instigate trouble and persecute the new movement. But once the disciples take their message to the Diaspora, the Jews abroad make up a sort of ubiquitous lynch mob, murderously rejecting the good news of forgiveness and salvation, which always comes to them first. They repudiate the Gospel not so much out of religious conviction but because they do not want to share salvation with the Gentiles (e.g., 13:16–52; 26:20–22). This lack of generosity had characterized the Pharisees' response to Jesus' mission to outcasts. Now these Diaspora Jews, like the Pharisees before them, end by excluding not the outsiders but, ironically, themselves:

> And Paul and Barnabas spoke out boldly, saying, "It was necessary that the word of God should be spoken first to you. Since *you thrust it from you and judge yourselves unworthy of eternal life,* behold, we turn to the Gentiles. For the Lord has commanded us, saying, 'I have set you to be a light for the Gentiles, that you may bring salvation to the uttermost parts of the earth.' " (Is 49:6; Acts 13:47; cf. 18:6; 28:26–28)

Of course toward the end of the first century, when Luke composed these volumes, the church was largely Gentile, the Jewish nation utterly defeated by Rome, and Jerusalem in ruins. To have associated Jesus with contemporary Judaism would not have elevated him. Accordingly, the Judaism Luke most links Jesus to is the Judaism of the biblical past. But the idea of the messiah, or, to use the Greek term, the Christ, does not figure overmuch in biblical Judaism: it was a preoccupation of the politically and religiously turbulent Judaism of the intertestamental period, the Judaism of the Pharisees, Sadducees, and zealots—the Judaism, in other words, from which Luke has detached Jesus. How then does Luke define the term messiah when he so repudiates its original context?

Luke first of all divests the term of its political content. Jesus' radical message of peace at any price, indeed his entire demeanor, excludes any traditional Jewish understanding of the messiah as a king of battles. Instead, incidents in Jesus' life, and especially his death and resurrection, provide new content which, Luke asserts, corresponds to predictions in scripture. Thus after the resurrection, when two disciples are mourning the death of "Jesus of

Nazareth . . . [who] we had hoped . . . was the one to redeem Israel," the incognito Risen Christ asserts, " 'Was it not necessary that the Christ should suffer these things and enter into his glory?' And beginning with Moses and all the prophets, he interpreted to them in all the scriptures the things concerning himself" (Lk 24:21, 26–27). The redemption of Israel is spiritual, not political; the messiah triumphs not over armies, but over death.

Still, Luke's text also hints at an originally political understanding of Jesus' messiahship. Entering Jerusalem, Jesus is hailed as king by his disciples; when the Pharisees request that he disavow the title, he declines (19:38–40). Later, before Pilate, he stands accused of sedition—"We found this man perverting our nation, and forbidding us to give tribute to Caesar, and saying that he himself is Christ a king" (23:3). Shortly thereafter, he dies as an insurrectionist (23:38ff.).

But when Luke's Jesus speaks of a kingdom other than Rome's, it is the Kingdom of God, a reality that is not future and political but present and spiritual. True, the gospel also speaks of the resurrection of the dead and the promise of eternal life in the age to come (14:14; 18:30). But these things cannot fundamentally characterize the Kingdom, which in some sense, Luke argues, exists here and now. "For behold, the Kingdom of God is in the midst of you" (17:20), developing subtly *within* time, the way a mustard seed becomes a tree or yeast leavens flour (13:18–21). It does not appear suddenly at time's end (21:7ff.).

By so spiritualizing the concept of the Kingdom and dissociating it both from earthly politics and from the End, Luke accomplishes much that is important apologetically and theologically. His new definition severs any link between Jesus and traditional Jewish political messianism—no small boon in the wake of Rome's bitter war against the Jews in 66–73. Further, it allays many of the tensions inherent in preserving an initially apocalyptic tradition in the face of the empirical disconfirmation of its central prophecy, for the world had not ended. Finally, it indicates a particular consciousness of the future of the new community, a deeschatologized, this-worldly future. Hence Luke does not include Son of Man, a term with strong apocalyptic associations,[10] in the narrative catena of Christological titles at the beginning of his gospel. Christian apocalyptic hope had no place in Luke's theology, with or without Rome. The future that Luke envisions for his community rests *in* time, *on* earth, incarnate as the church.

For if God's Kingdom is established by his messiah, if it is characterized by peace and righteousness (the idealized portrait of apostolic cooperation in Acts), and if those within the Kingdom receive the Holy Spirit, then for Luke the Kingdom of God can be understood, at least functionally, as the church. Luke's Jesus is thus the Ecclesiastical Christ, God's special messenger who

10. See "The Expectation of Redemption" in chap. 5 for further discussion of this term.

came to found this unique instrument of salvation in his name (Acts 4:12). And until Jesus returns at whatever point in the very distant future, the church is his earthly surrogate, continuing his work of bringing the message of salvation through repentance to all peoples.

MATTHEW: THE CHRIST OF THE SCRIPTURES

Jesus' messianic lineage opens the Gospel of Matthew. This "genealogy of Jesus Christ, the son of David, the son of Abraham" (Mt 1:1), which Matthew traces without apology through Joseph (cf. Lk's disclaimer, 3:23), recalls the lengthy genealogies of the Old Testament and so both immediately establishes the scriptural tone of this gospel and anchors Jesus firmly in biblical history. This gospel's messianic lineage cannot be made compatible with Luke's, but this is no surprise: neither evangelist had access to actual historical information about Jesus' ancestry, or, probably, to each other's work. Though the genealogies are not identical, however, their purpose is: to provide Jesus with the correct messianic pedigree. Luke, in tracing it back to Adam and thence to God (Lk 3:38), makes both a Christological and a universalist claim; Matthew, for whom the terminal ancestor is Abraham, emphasizes Jesus' Jewishness.

But Matthew also knows the tradition that the messiah will be born "of a virgin"; and so, the patrilineal genealogy established, Matthew goes on effectively to vitiate it by creating a narrative around a prooftext from Isaiah 7:14 LXX. Again, the salient details of Matthew's narrative cannot be matched to Luke's. Here, Joseph and Mary's home town is Bethlehem, not Nazareth, so no device like Quirinius' census is needed to move the Holy Family to the messianically correct town in time for the birth. In a sense, Matthew has the opposite problem: how should he move Jesus from Bethlehem, which is in the south in Judea, back north to the Galilee, to Nazareth, where Jesus was known to have come from? To this end, Matthew introduces those episodes unique to his birth narrative: magi journeying from the East, who innocently tell Herod the Great of the birth of the King of the Jews; the family's flight into Egypt before Herod's slaughter of the male babies in Bethlehem; and, after Herod's death, the Holy Family's return from Egypt to settle in Nazareth.

Matthew's birth narrative not only presents, in story form, the claim that Jesus is the messiah; it also provides the key to Matthew's theology and his strategy of evangelical composition. Matthew, like most early Christians and certainly the evangelists, believed that the scriptures had foretold Jesus' coming. But to an extent matched by no one else in the Christian canon, Matthew demonstrates his case by presenting narrative episodes explicitly constructed from biblical testimonies. Again and again he introduces or concludes an episode with the words, "This took place to fulfill what the Lord had spoken through the prophet," quoting directly from the Bible over sixty times in the course of his gospel. Where Matthew inherits historical information about Jesus—for example, that he performed cures and exorcisms—he thus enhances it by appealing to scripture (in this instance, Is 53:4: "This was to fulfill what was spoken by the prophet Isaiah, 'He took our infirmities and bore our diseases'" [Mt 8:17]). At other times, inferences from scripture create events. We see this most clearly in Matthew's birth narrative.

1. Joseph, a descendent of King David and of Abraham, discovers that Mary his fiancée is with child (1:18ff.). An angel appears to him in a dream to inform him of the true status of events. "'Joseph, *son of David* [a messianic designation] . . . [Mary] will bear a son, and you shall call his name Jesus, for he will save his people from their sins.' All this took place to fulfill what the Lord had spoken by the prophet: 'Behold, a virgin shall conceive and bear a son, and his name shall be called Emmanuel' (which means, God with us)" (1:22–23; Is 7:14 LXX).

2. Journeying wise men (significantly, Gentiles) come to Jerusalem in search of the child "born king of the Jews" (Mt 2:2). They had seen a star in the sky, perhaps Matthew's allusion to Numbers 24:17, "A star will come forth out of Jacob, a sceptre shall rise out of Israel." Herod assembles the chief priests and scribes, whose eventual antagonism to Jesus is thereby foreshadowed. From them he learns that the child must be in Bethlehem, "for so it is written in the prophet: 'And you, O Bethlehem . . . from you shall come a ruler who will govern my people Israel'" (Mt 2:6; Mi 5:2).

3. An angel warns Joseph in a dream to flee with Mary and Jesus to Egypt, since Herod plans to destroy the child (Mt 2:13ff.). After the family's escape, Herod slaughters the male children in Bethlehem, thus fulfilling Jeremiah 31:15: "A voice was heard in Ramah, wailing and loud lamentation, Rachel weeping for her children" (Mt 1:16). Since no other source, Roman or Jewish, mentions such a heinous crime, we may safely assume that the "prophecy" (and perhaps a reminiscence of Pharaoh's edict against the male children of Moses' generation; Ex 1:16) created the episode. Meanwhile, with Herod's death, the Holy Family can return. This allows Matthew to turn Hosea 11:1, "Out of Egypt I have called my son," originally a historical reference to the Exodus from Egypt, into a Christological witness.

4. Finally, an angel warns the returning Joseph not to return to Bethlehem, which is now under the jurisdiction of Herod's son. He proceeds therefore to Nazareth (which was also under one of Herod's sons!), "that what was spoken by the prophets might be fulfilled, 'He shall be called a Nazarene'" (Mt 2:22–23). Scholars have failed to turn up any such text in extant scripture, however, and it is possible that Matthew created this "prophecy" to fit the facts.

Such a presentation has both synthetic and polemical value. Synthetically, Matthew uses the scriptures to generate a theologically sophisticated definition and characterization of Jesus of Nazareth as the long-awaited messiah of prophetic hope. Matthew chooses innumerable passages and verses that in their original context had nothing to do with a messiah, and by applying them to Jesus makes them seem to. For example, Isaiah 7:14 is not a messianic prophecy. In its original context, it represents God through the prophet assuring King Ahaz that evil days are fast approaching for his enemies. "Behold, an *aalmah* will conceive and bear a son, and shall call his name Immanuel. . . . And before the child knows how to refuse the evil and choose the good [i.e., before he has reached the age of reason], the land before whose two kings you are in dread will be deserted." Further, the Hebrew *aalmah* simply means "young girl." But it was translated in the LXX by the more ambiguous *parthenos,* which means either "young girl" or "virgin" (Heb. *betulah*). Thus this relatively unexceptional event—a young girl bearing a child—becomes a prediction of a miraculous birth. Similarly, "God with us" (*emmanu-El*) would mean one thing to its original Jewish audience, and something quite different to a Christian when applied to the figure of Jesus.[11]

Further, by viewing scripture primarily as a collection of prophecies awaiting fulfillment, Matthew could implicitly expose the incompleteness of Judaism. Only Jesus fulfilled these prophecies, and therefore only Christianity could complete Judaism. Such a reading grants importance only to those Jewish scriptures that seem to speak to Christianity. Hence Matthew builds his story largely around selected quotations from Isaiah, Jeremiah, the minor prophets, and Psalms, books whose texts are monuments of metaphor and ambiguity. Other books, which bend less easily to such narrative remodeling (e.g., the bulk of Torah, or the historical books) do not receive as much of Matthew's attention. And since the texts so remodeled are significant chiefly or uniquely because they refer to the Matthean Jesus, their original historical meaning is invalidated. The identity of the messiah as Jesus of Nazareth thus necessarily becomes the culminating revelation of all of scripture, as only those scriptures relevant to Jesus are valued.

Such a task of theological appropriation is by its very nature polemical. This is a combative gospel, and its main figure, the spokesman for Matthew's position, is a combative Christ. He constantly tangles with the representatives of "official Judaism," the scribes and Pharisees, who seem at times almost demonic. When, for example, Jesus is tempted just before he begins his ministry, Satan taunts him with his divine sonship: "If you are the Son of God, then . . ." (4:1–11). Later, at the crucifixion, this same taunt issues from the mouths of the passers-by, the chief priests, scribes and elders: "If you are the Son of God, come down from the cross" (27:39–43). These figureheads of Judaism and professional interpreters of scripture come in for special vitupera-

---

11. Already by the mid-second century, Gentile Christians were aware of this problem in the LXX translation: Trypho, the Jew in Justin's dialogue, objects that *aalmah* should be rendered in Greek as *neanis* (young girl) (*Dial.* 43). See the discussion in Raymond E. Brown, *The Birth of the Messiah,* pp. 145–63. Vermes, *Jesus the Jew,* pp. 213–22, reconstructs a possible Jewish Aramaic context for the tradition of the virgin birth.

tion. The Sadducees and Pharisees are a "brood of vipers" (cf. Lk 3:7), hopeless hypocrites, whitewashed tombs that house uncleanness (Mt 23:27), murderers and persecutors of prophets and wise men (Matthew clearly has in mind the later church, 23:34–36). So deep is their hypocrisy and their indifference to justice that when Judas Iscariot regrets his spilling of innocent blood, the chief priests and elders shrug, "What is that to us? See to it yourself." Compliant—indeed, complicit—in the crime of murder, they nonetheless fastidiously refuse as unlawful Judas' proffered refund of the thirty pieces of silver, "since they are blood money" (27:3–6).

In vain does Jesus make Israel the sole focus of his and his disciples' mission, even to the point of turning away Gentiles who seek him out (15:24; cf. 10:5): Israel will not heed. Corrupt leaders corrupt their followers, and when Pilate, insisting on Jesus' innocence, leads him before the crowds in Jerusalem, the Jews roar "Let him be crucified. . . . His blood be upon us and upon our children!" (27:22–25). Even in the face of Jesus' divine vindication, the chief priests prefer a lie, bribing the soldiers guarding the tomb to say that the disciples have stolen the body (28:11–15). They will not acknowledge the resurrection.

The social reality behind Matthew's anti-Jewish polemic is difficult to establish. By the time he wrote, circa 90 C.E., at least one generation after the Roman destruction of the Temple and at least two since the execution of Jesus, the general nonresponse of Israel to the Christian message was a pervasive fact. This nonresponse, in light of the divine censure implied by the destruction of the Temple, might have struck Matthew as so unintelligent as to be perverse (see, for example, his expansion of the parable of the wedding feast, 22:1–14). Or, if he himself were a Jewish convert to Christianity, as some scholars have argued, his hostility might be the measure of his anger with his former community, whose continued nonconversion he viewed as a reproach and a challenge to his faith. Or perhaps his anger was an inevitable consequence of the battle for possession of the scriptures against a community with a different tradition of exegesis and a more widely recognized claim. We cannot know.

Beneath Matthew's occasionally baroque anti-Judaism, however, lies a subtler polemic against other Christians. Here we can gain more of a sense of his personal situation. Matthew's Christ warns continually against false insiders—presumably, Christians with opinions different from those of Matthew and his community. "Not everyone who says 'Lord, Lord' will enter the kingdom of heaven" (7:21), nor will everyone invited to the marriage feast remain, for "many are called, but few are chosen" (22:11–14). The false insiders are like the seed fallen on rocky ground: they hear the word joyfully but have no real root, and so they fall away in time of tribulation (13:20–21). False insiders, like the Jews, never really believe, despite the most overwhelming evidence that God stands behind Christian claims: when Christ, risen from his grave, presents himself to his disciples on a mountaintop in the Galilee, there are some, even in this inner circle, who doubt (28:17b).

Who then is of the true church? Those who really hear Jesus' words and do them (e.g., 7:21–24). Matthew's Jesus is preeminently a preacher—indeed, *the* Preacher—and the figure who addresses the crowds on the mountain and in the synagogues actually speaks across time to Matthew's church. Jesus exhorts his followers to let their good works shine and to follow the Law truly, not just conforming to the minutiae of observance like the hypocritical Pharisees. Prayers, fasts, and almsgiving without ostentation, trust in God without material anxiety, not judging others and forgiving their trespasses—these are the commandments that Jesus gives to his church.

In the Sermon on the Mount, one of Matthew's longest and most dramatic presentations of Christian moral teaching, Jesus radically extends and intensifies the demands of the Law, especially those touching on social relations, that is, community life. Anger at one's brother is the moral equivalent of murder; lust in the heart, of adultery (5:21ff., 27–28). "For unless your righteousness exceeds that of the scribes and the Pharisees, you will never enter the kingdom of heaven" (5:20).

Even more radical are the demands of Christian love. Jews had long been enjoined to love both their fellow Jews ("love your neighbor as yourself"); and even Gentiles ("the stranger who sojourns among you shall be to you as the native among you, and you shall love him as yourself"; Lv 19:18, 34). But Matthew, who often presents Jesus' extensions of Torah as contradistinctions ("You have heard it said . . . but I say . . ."), radicalizes this command too. Christians should love not only strangers but also enemies. "You have heard it said, 'You shall love your neighbor and hate your enemy' " (a teaching in fact not found in Jewish tradition), "but I say, Love your enemies and pray for those who persecute you" (5:43–44). For the church must "be perfect, even as your heavenly Father is perfect" (5:48; cf. Lk 6:36).

The disciples, and particularly Peter, figure prominently as examples and role models, both positive and negative, for Jesus' church. Jesus commissions them to preach, teach, heal, and even to raise the dead, proclaiming that the Kingdom is at hand. They should bear testimony (to the Gospel) before governors and Gentiles ("looking ahead" to Matthew's own situation, 10:18ff.; a few verses earlier, the disciples were charged to have nothing to do with Gentiles, 10:5). They were to expect bad treatment from Gentiles, Jews, and even their own families, but should be consoled by the greatness of their reward, for they had been given the secrets of the kingdom of heaven (13:11).

Peter is the spokesman for the group (15:15; 18:21; cf. Mk 7:17 or Lk 17:4, where the subject is all the disciples). When at Caesarea Philippi he discerns Jesus' true identity—"You are the Christ, the Son of the Living God"—Jesus responds with lavish praise:

> Blessed are you, Simon Bar-Jona! For flesh and blood has not revealed this to you, but my Father who is in heaven. And I tell you, you are Peter, and upon this

Rock I shall build my church, and the powers of death shall not prevail against it. I will give you the keys of the kingdom of heaven, and whatever you bind on earth shall be bound in heaven, and whatever you loose on earth shall be loosed in heaven. (Mt 16:13–19)

Yet ultimately Peter and the other disciples disappoint Jesus. They are greatly distressed by Jesus' predictions of his passion, and Peter, in the passage cited above, even attempts to dissuade him: "God forbid, Lord! This shall never happen to you!" (16:22; also, e.g., 17:22ff.) For this effort Jesus violently repudiates him: "Get thee behind me, Satan! You are a hindrance to me" (16:23). Once events begin to unwind in Jerusalem, the disciples act as if they had never been told what to expect. Jesus informs them that, as scripture had foretold, they will all fall away from him—a prediction that Peter (who a short time later becomes the worst offender) characteristically denies (26:30–35; cf. vv. 69–75). In Gethsemane, the disciples doze while Jesus, sorrowful and troubled, contemplates the prospect of his coming crucifixion alone (26:36–46); he catches them asleep three times during his vigil (vv. 40, 43, 45; cf. Lk 22:45 and his charitable gloss on the incident).

The disciples' inconstancy is nowhere more evident than at the actual moment of crisis, when Jesus is led away by the men sent by the chief priests and elders. All the disciples flee, and Peter in the High Priest's court three times denies knowing Jesus (Mt 26:56, 69–75). Only the women remain to the end, in the face of adversity; only they keep watch while Jesus suffers on the cross; only they witness the Risen Christ in Jerusalem (27:55–56; 28:9). But the disciples must wait until they reach Galilee, where some of them doubt even while worshipping him (28:10, 16, 17). On balance, it is not an inspiring performance, and Matthew's harsh presentation perhaps reflects his dim view of the faith of some of his fellow Christians.

To Matthew, and thus to his Jesus, constancy is important not only in the Christian's relationship to Jesus, but also in his relationship to ritual as well as moral obligations. Matthew makes this point in his use of that perennially embarrassing issue, Jesus' baptism by John. This episode implied to later Christians Jesus' subordination to John, a concern that Matthew has John voice: "I need to be baptized by you, and do you come to me?" Jesus reassures him by saying, "It is fitting for us to fulfill all righteousness" (3:13–15). That is, even I must fulfill ritual requirements; how much more those who would follow me.

This message is brought home repeatedly to the reader of Matthew's gospel. The Christian's righteousness must exceed that of the Pharisees and Sadducees; like them, he too must give alms, pray, and fast, but without display (5:20; 6:1–18, but cf. 9:14). Jesus comes not to abolish the Law, but to fulfill it (5:17). He even pays the voluntary half-shekel tax to the Temple (17:24–27; note Peter's role). When teaching the great commandment to love

God and neighbor, Jesus cites directly from Torah (Dt 6:5; Lv 19:18); but the Pharisees and scribes displace the Law with "the traditions of men" (Mt 15:1–9). They are blind guides and hypocrites who claim to do the will of the Father but in fact do not (15:7, 14). They are anything but righteous, responsible as they are for "all the righteous blood shed on earth," from Abel to the Christian prophets, wise men and scribes whom Jesus will send out (23:34–35; cf. Luke's characteristically milder phrasing, 11:49–50). Untrue to their own scripture because they fail to see Christ as its fulfillment, they are likewise, or consequently, untrue to their own principles and, in trying to keep the Law, they actually violate it. Therefore, sinners who repent their initial defiance and obey the Father will enter the kingdom of heaven before they do (the parable of the two sons, 21:28–32).

How long will such a situation endure? Until the "close of the age," when Christ the Son of Man will return to separate the wicked from the righteous. Many of Matthew's parables concern this final judgment. It is like the harvest, when the weeds are bundled together and burned but the wheat gathered into the barn (i.e., the good enter the kingdom of heaven; 13:24–30, 36–43). As fishermen sort through fish, so will the angels sort the good from the wicked "at the close of the age" (13:47–50), when, Jesus warns, men will have to render an account for every careless word they ever uttered (12:36). For then the Son of Man will return in glory to execute judgment, appointing all humankind either to eternal life or eternal punishment (25:31–46). Then the disciples will sit on twelve thrones next to the enthroned Son of Man, judging the tribes of Israel "in the new world" (19:28).

But when will Jesus assume his role of final judge? What, Matthew asks through the voice of the disciples, "will be the sign of your coming and of the close of the age?" (24:3). Jesus gives two different answers, which stand in some tension with each other. On the one hand, he asserts the nearness of the End: "Truly, I say to you, there are some standing here who will not taste death before they see the Son of Man coming in his kingdom" (16:28). "This generation will not pass away until all these things take place" (24:34). These are puzzling statements, since Matthew's community knew that Jesus' audience had already passed away. On the other hand, Jesus describes an elaborate eschatological scenario that must first occur before he comes again as the Son of Man, the Judge at the Parousia: the Temple must first be destroyed; false Christs, international contention, and natural disasters will befall humankind—and all this will be only the "onset of labor" (24:1, 4–8). Believers will apostatize and betray one another; false messiahs and false prophets will work signs and wonders; the sun and the moon will fail, the stars fall, and even the powers of the astral realms (*dunameis tōn ouranōn*) will be shaken (24:15–29). And even then the End will not come, because first the Gospel must be preached to the whole world (24:13). In the indefinite interim, the believer can only remain alert, aware that neither the angels nor even the Son himself knows the appointed hour, but only the Father (25:13; cf. 24:42–44). The parables of the wise and foolish virgins and of the talents caution that one should be prepared both for a long wait and for the final reckoning when it does come (25:1–12, 14–30).

Who then, finally, is Matthew's Jesus? He is first and foremost the one who fulfills all the prophecies of the scriptures. This emphasis is quite different from those of John and Luke, with appreciably different consequences. John in essence renounces Judaism as having nothing much to do with Christianity. He passes on a few pro forma remarks about Moses' witness to Jesus and once mentions that salvation comes from the Jews (Jn 4:22). But his attention and energies focus on the mystery of a cosmic Son of Man who comes down and goes up, not an apocalyptic Son of Man who goes away and will return. His Jews—and by extension, Judaism—provide an absolute contrast to Christianity rather than a preliminary stage. Luke, on the other hand, emphasizes the continuity of Judaism and Christianity. Christ is the central point around which both earlier biblical and current ecclesiastical witnesses are oriented, and from which everything both before and after derives its meaning. The church is the true Israel, hence even after Christ's resurrection Israel continues, though the Jews themselves might drop away.

Matthew says something different. His Christ is not the center, but the endpoint.[12] He is the ineluctable and unequivocal conclusion to the peculiar messianic teleology that Matthew's strategy of prophetic citation has created. If the traditions behind our gospels reflect the efforts of early communities to understand the career of their redeemer in terms of the scriptures, then Matthew's gospel seems to have reversed the process: now the scriptures are to be explained in terms of Jesus. Matthew brooks no alternative interpretation, whether Jewish or Christian, and he anticipates with confidence the vindication of his views when the Son of Man returns, as eventually he must, to divide the saved from the damned. Meanwhile, the evangelist and his community could take comfort in the face of the active competition which Matthew's combative tone suggests they faced. They had ahead of them the great work of a universal mission to bring about the second coming of their messiah (24:14). And they had the consolation that, as long as the community congregated, Christ was indeed together with them, until he should come again (28:20).

---

12. "The point of continuity between the old People of God and the new is thus Jesus himself. . . . No quotation is culled from the Scriptures to demonstrate that the Church is the fulfillment of the OT hope from Israel. With few exceptions the quotations are selected for the purpose of showing that *Jesus* is the fulfillment of the OT hope," Douglas R. A. Hare, *The Theme of Jewish Persecution of Christians in the Gospel according to St. Matthew*, p. 160; discussion of this point, pp. 156–62.

MARK: THE SECRET MESSIAH

Mark begins his gospel in medias res, with John baptizing multitudes in the Jordan, among whom, Mark states without editorial apology, is Jesus (1:9). Immediately (to use one of Mark's favorite words: it occurs forty times in his brief gospel) Jesus hears a voice from heaven declaring him God's beloved son; he is driven out to the wilderness by the Spirit, tempted by Satan, and ministered to by angels; and then, John having been arrested, he begins his own ministry in the Galilee. "The time is fulfilled; the Kingdom of God is at hand. Repent, and believe in the gospel" (1:15).

Mark presents all this in the first fifteen verses of his gospel, and he maintains this breathless pace throughout. " . . . Immediately . . . immediately . . . at once. . . ." Immediately Jesus calls his fishermen, and immediately they follow him; immediately he teaches in the synagogue on the Sabbath, and immediately a man with an unclean spirit appears (1:16–23). His fame as a healer spreads "at once"; immediately he leaves the synagogue and cures Simon's ill mother-in-law (1:28–31). Mark's Jesus is a man in a hurry, dashing throughout the Galilee in rapid, almost random motion, from synagogue to invalid, from shore to grain field to sea, casting out demons and amazing those who witness him. The spare prose and staccato cures create a mood of nervous anticipation. The times *must* be fulfilled. Who is this man, and what will he do next?

Mark's dashing, busy Jesus is first of all someone with great personal authority. When he calls, men follow (e.g., 1:16–20). He teaches without invoking any source for his instruction, thus "astonishing" his listeners (1:21–22). "With authority he commands even the unclean spirits, and they obey him" (1:27). He is master over sickness and hence sin (2:1–10, the healing of the paralytic). He commands even nature: at a word, the wind and sea grow calm and a fig tree withers (4:39; 11:14, 20).

When Mark presents Jesus as this commanding figure, it is usually in conjunction with the term, not otherwise explained, Son of Man. Jesus speaks of this figure in the third person, but the reader knows clearly from the context that the referent is Jesus himself. Thus the Son of Man has authority on earth to forgive sins (2:10), and the Son of Man is lord even over the Sabbath (2:28). But the Son of Man is also an example of humility; he is not served, but he serves, ultimately giving his life as a ransom for many (10:46). Suffering, ignominy, and death are his lot: rejected by the Jewish authorities, he is to be delivered to the Gentiles, mocked, scourged, and killed (the Passion predictions, 8:31ff.; 9:12, 31; 10:32), as the scriptures foretold. Still, vindication awaits: the Son of Man will come again in glory and power, with angels, to usher in the Kingdom of God (8:38–9:1; 13:26; 14:62).

Mark makes other claims for Jesus. God (1:11; 9:7), demons (e.g., 1:24; 3:11; 5:7), the High Priest (14:61) and a Roman centurion (15:39) all identify him as the divine Son. Peter, at a dramatic moment at Caesarea Philippi (8:27), and the blind beggar Bartimaeus (10:47) proclaim him the messiah, the Son of David, whose kingdom the crowds in Jerusalem mistakenly think Jesus has come to establish ("Blessed is the kingdom of our father David that is coming!"; 11:10). But Jesus is the Son of God, not of David, and Mark seems specifically to repudiate Davidic descent as a necessary precondition of messianic status. Jesus asks, "How can the scribes [his worst antagonists] say that the Christ is David's son?" and he cites Psalm 110.1 LXX against such an idea: "'the Lord [God] said to my Lord [the messiah], "Sit at my right hand"' . . . David [the author of the psalm] himself calls him [the messiah] 'Lord': so how is he David's son?" (12:35–37).[13]

Matthew and Luke both reproduce this passage, but since their respective birth narratives elaborately make the case that Jesus *is* of David's house (birth in Bethlehem; patrilineal genealogies), they cannot give it the same meaning. Perhaps in their gospels the passage argues simply for Jesus' superiority to David. The Fourth Evangelist feels free to dismiss the tradition of messianic descent through David out of hand (7:42), perhaps because his absolute separation between Judaism and Christianity makes such an idea superfluous. But Mark, unlike John, does place Jesus on some kind of historical continuum with Judaism. Perhaps, then, he dismisses Davidic descent because Jesus was known as "Jesus of Nazareth," and no tradition explaining how this Nazarene had been born in Bethlehem had yet developed. Or perhaps, as we shall see, Mark thought it politically prudent to do so.

At only one place in his story does Mark bring all three of his chief Christological designations together: the climax of the trial scene. The High Priest asks, "Are you the Christ, the son of the Blessed?" And Jesus, who up to now has been extremely reticent about his identity (a point we return to later), suddenly and surprisingly acknowledges the High Priest's question: "I am: and you will see the Son of Man seated at the right hand of power and coming with the clouds of heaven" (14:61–62).

Up to this point, only demons had known that Jesus was the Son of God; only humans through a special insight of faith had realized that he was the messiah. But here, spontaneously, the High Priest identifies him as both. Thus the awful events at the climax of the gospel—the interrogation before Pilate, the humiliation by the soldiers, the death on the cross: all of which, through Mark's device of the Passion predictions, serve to confirm Jesus' identity as Son of Man—are actually and ironically set in motion by the High Priest. He alone of all their contemporaries, including the apostles, has divined Jesus' full identity during his lifetime, and he alone receives direct confirmation from

13. This confusion, or conflation, is possible only in Greek, where *kyrios* is used both times for "Lord." Hebrew uses two different words; see "The Kerygma of the Early Mission," in chap. 8, for further discussion.

Jesus himself. Nonetheless, the High Priest repudiates Jesus as a blasphemer. The next person to understand Jesus' true status is, significantly, a Gentile, the Roman centurion at the foot of the cross: "Truly, this man was the Son of God" (15:39).

Much of Mark's gospel is structured around this paradox of hiddenness and recognition, and much of his story is about not understanding the story.[14] Thus, for example, while demons invariably recognize who Jesus really is, his own disciples often fail to comprehend—indeed, their obtuseness seems to be one of Mark's major themes. Despite Jesus' special attention, the disciples rarely understand his parables and must ask for further instruction: Jesus explains everything to them in private (4:10, 33). Having witnessed the stupendous feeding of five thousand men from only five loaves, "they did not understand . . . for their hearts were hardened" (6:52), so much so that later they are distressed when they have only one loaf for themselves (Jesus has to remind them of the miracle, 8:14–20). Fundamental instruction on cleanliness and defilement escapes them, as do unambiguous predictions, for which they fear to ask clarification (7:14–15; 9:32).

The vagaries of Peter's insights and actions symbolize the moral vacillation of the whole group. At the dramatic midpoint of the gospel, Peter realizes that Jesus is the Christ (8:29). But when Jesus then predicts his own passion, Peter rebukes him, and Peter is rebuked in turn as Satan, "not on the side of God but of men" (8:33). Peter, James, and John are privileged witnesses to a miraculous transfiguration in which a dazzling Jesus converses with Elijah (the prophetic forerunner of the messiah) and Moses (the giver of the Law). But Peter, at a loss, asks if they would like booths built, "for he did not know what to say, for they were exceedingly afraid" (9:6). The disciples so misunderstand Jesus' message and example of humility that they quarrel about precedence among themselves (9:33ff.; 10:35–46) and seek to prevent children from "bothering" Jesus (10:13–14). Finally, in Jerusalem, the disciples fall away. Judas betrays Jesus; the others slumber rather than watch at Gethsemane; in Jesus' hour of anguish before his trials, Peter denies him and all scatter—just as Jesus, and scripture, had predicted (14:27–50, 54–72). It is the women who keep watch at the crucifixion, the women who go first to the tomb, and consequently the women who first know that "he is risen; he is not here"; he has gone on to meet his disciples in the Galilee (16:1–7). Jesus has kept the faith, even if his disciples have not.

What is "faith" in Mark, and what part does it play in his story about Jesus? Faith seems to be the crucial element in responses to Jesus. He calls people to believe (*pisteuō*) that he is the authoritative messenger of the Kingdom, and he forgives the sins and cures the ills of those who have faith (*pistis*) in him: "And when Jesus saw their faith, he said to the paralytic, 'My son, your sins are

14. On this theme, Frank Kermode, *Genesis of Secrecy.*

forgiven'" (2:5); "Daughter [the woman with the issue of blood], your faith
has made you well" (5:34; so also to the blind Bartimaeus, 10:52). Faith, says
Jesus, can move mountains and ensure the response to prayer (he has just
successfully withered a fig tree with a malediction), providing that the believer
"does not doubt in his heart, but believes that what he says will come to pass"
(11:23).

Unbelief can thus cut one off from the benefits faith brings. When the
disciples, frightened by a storm, challenge Jesus to calm it, he rebukes them
with the question, "Have you no faith?" (4:40). When Jesus returns home to
his own country, he is rejected by his family as well as by his people. (This
rejection is symbolic of the Jewish community's reaction to Christian claims
about Jesus, evident by the time Mark wrote.) Jesus finds his own powers
compromised by their negative response—"he *could* do no mighty work
there"—and he marvels at their unbelief (3:21, 31–35; 6:1–6). His disciples
fail to cure a child afflicted with a demon; Jesus responds, "O faithless
generation! How long am I to be with you? How long am I to bear with you?"
(9:19). When the child's father intervenes, asking Jesus to help if he can, Jesus
apparently takes offense: "'*If* you can'! All things are possible to him who
believes." The father's anguished reply must have touched Mark's contemporaries as much as it does the modern reader: "I believe! Help thou my unbelief!" (9:24). Without faith, no cures, no signs, no divine response—the
situation particularly of the scribes, Pharisees, Sadducees, and priests.

But receive Jesus as what? Jesus' extreme reticence on the subject of his
identity both as Christ (he never, unlike Matthew's Jesus, acknowledges
Peter's response to his question at Caesarea Philippi; cf. Mk 8:29–30//Mt
16:16–17) and as Son of God (the demons who recognize him are always
charged to be silent) highlights his relative loquaciousness about the Son of
Man. This seems to be the Christological designation that Mark holds most
significant in his presentation of Jesus' demand for faith. Those who have faith
receive Jesus as the Son of Man, whose powers as an exorcist and healer evince
his authority to announce a "new teaching" (Mk 1:27).

This assertion has a polemical edge: the "old teaching" that cannot accommodate, countenance, or comprehend the new is, of course, Judaism. New
cloth cannot patch an old garment without doing further damage; new wine
bursts old wineskins—Mark's perception, perhaps, of what had occurred to
Judaism since Jesus' coming (3:21–22). Mark presents a Jesus whose instruction on fasting (or, rather, not fasting; 3:18–19), on breaking the Sabbath
when life is not at risk (2:23–28; 3:1–6), on forgiving sin (which Mark's
scribes deem blasphemous; 2:7), and on following the commands of God
rather than the traditions of men (a point he makes, and so somewhat compromises, by citing Jewish scriptures, 7:1–13, cf. Is 29:13 LXX) challenges and
upsets his Jewish audience, especially the Pharisees.

Further, Mark asserts, Jesus proclaimed that a man's interior state, if it be evil—that is, set on "fornication, theft, murder, adultery, coveting, wicked-ness, deceit, licentiousness, envy, slander, pride, foolishness"—defiles him, not what is exterior (7:14–23). This observation would be unexceptional in the context of actual (as opposed to evangelical) Judaism. But Mark's editorial gloss extends the passage to a repudiation of *kashrut,* the Jewish dietary laws ("Thus he declared all foods clean"; 7:19). Such a position would indeed offend the sensibilities of observant Jews, as we know from the example of Philo. But, as we again know from Philo's lament about spiritualized nonob-servance, even this argument was hardly "new."[15] Mark's polemic, however, requires that it *appear* new, for much of Jesus' significance as the authoritative and suffering Son of Man demands that his teaching stand in high contrast to Judaism.[16]

The only extended passage of Jesus' teaching that Mark relates (Mk lacks Q, the sayings source containing much of the teachings presented in Mt and Lk) comes in chapter 13, the core of the so-called Synoptic Apocalypse. There Jesus describes at some length the events that will precede the coming of the Kingdom of God—a catalogue, typical of Jewish apocalyptic writings, of wars, famine, natural and celestial disasters, social disintegration, and the defilement and destruction of the Temple. But within this most traditionally Jewish of passages comes a truly new teaching. Jesus here links the arrival of God's Kingdom to his own, *second* coming as the glorious Son of Man.

> But in those days, after that tribulation, the sun will be darkened, and the moon will not give its light, and the stars will be falling from heaven, and the powers in the heavens will be shaken. *And then they will see the Son of Man coming in clouds with great power and glory.* And then he will send out the angels, and gather his elect from the four winds, from the ends of the earth to the ends of heaven.   (13:24–27)

This is the new teaching that Jesus as the Son of Man is uniquely placed to present with authority: that he will come *again,* and that his Second Coming will herald the Kingdom. To number among his elect then, the hearer must believe now that the Son of Man has already come for the first time as Jesus of Nazareth, who suffered, died, and on the third day was (or, within the gospel's time frame, "will be") raised. According to Mark, in other words, *Jesus' identity as Son of Man is his message.*

This makes all the more puzzling Mark's portrayal of a Jesus who demands silence from those who do realize who he really is. Jesus routinely censures professions of his status as Christ and Son of God. And while no one calls him

---

15. *De migr. Ab.* 16.89–93.

16. S. G. F. Brandon speculates on why this should be so, *The Fall of Jerusalem and the Christian Church,* pp. 186–204.

the Son of Man but himself, his identity as such is demonstrated by his power to heal, and he usually forbids those he cures to speak of the miracle, even if the circumstances, as in the raising of Jairus' daughter, make such a request incredible (see, e.g., 1:44; 2:1–10; 5:35–43; 7:31–37, but cf. the Gerasene Demoniac, 5:1–20, esp. v. 19). Why a Jesus who apparently works at such cross-purposes?

Why? In part because the device has both great apologetic and theological value. Mark can thus explain, and give vital religious significance to, three uncomfortable facts that confronted his community: the lack of recognition that Jesus had apparently received among his own people in his lifetime; the continuing lack of Jewish recognition for Christian claims about Jesus; and the recent destruction of Judaism's holiest site by the same imperial power that had executed Jesus a generation earlier.

As we know from the evidence of Paul, whose letters predate Mark by some fifteen years, early Christians sought to interpret their recent past through an appeal to scripture (e.g., 1 Cor 15:3b; Rom 1:2; etc.). But the argument that Jesus' life and death conformed to a revealed design only heightened the problem of early and continuing Jewish nonresponse: why did those best placed both to know the scriptures and to see how Jesus had fulfilled them— that is, Jesus' Jewish contemporaries in Palestine—remain indifferent? Matthew solves the problem by claiming that the Jews' reaction was also predicted in scripture: in rejecting Jesus, the Jews thus actually confirmed his status, responding to God's Son and messiah as scripture had said they would. Luke pursues a different path. According to him, many Jews do join the movement; those who do not, decline not because they disbelieve Jesus' message but because they resent sharing it with any other people. John, seeing the Jews as the children of darkness and the Devil, does not address the issue; for him it is not a problem. The Jews, not of God, could never have followed Jesus.

Mark's answer is in its way as absolute, and as morally problematic, as John's. The Jews, he argues, did not respond because Jesus did not *want* them to. To this end Jesus hid his true identity and ordered others during his lifetime to do likewise. "He charged them to tell no one what they had seen [i.e., the Transfiguration] until the Son of Man should have risen from the dead" (9:2). But even after the resurrection, when Jesus' status had been made clear, the Jews, Mark knew, still did not understand. They could not, because Jesus during his ministry had prevented them, deliberately concealing from them the true meaning of his message, preaching in parables so obscure that even his own disciples could not understand:

And when he was alone, those who were about him with the twelve asked him concerning the parables. And he said to them, "To you has been given the secret of the Kingdom of God, but for those outside everything is in parables, *so that* they may indeed see but not perceive, and may indeed hear but not understand, *lest* they should turn again and be forgiven." (4:10–12)[17]

To understand and appreciate the force of Mark's argument, we must recall the context in which he made it: that of Gentile Christianity, perhaps in Rome itself, in the wake of the Jewish War of 66–73.[18] For Mark, the destruction of the Temple represented both the natural political outcome of the Jewish refusal to follow Christ and the divine censure of that refusal, the clearest signal imaginable that the Christian interpretation of scripture was right and the Jewish one wrong. Jewish religious intransigence had led directly to the rebellion against Rome, in which Gentile Christians, despite their belief in a messiah who had died as a rebel, had played no part. Mark in fact claims messianic status for Jesus by emptying the concept of any political content, even such as was implied by descent from that archetypal successful military leader of Israel, David. The entire gospel presents a Jesus who is consciously independent of Jewish tradition, whose worst enemies are the "leaders" of Judaism in Jerusalem (the same group who had figured prominently in the recent rebellion), and who was himself in a sense the victim of Jewish insurgency (15:7–15; cf. v. 32; Lk 23:39–43). The priests had engineered his death, claims Mark, and then only with Rome's unwilling acquiescence (14:55–15:15).

Thus, despite Jesus' death on the cross as a political insurrectionist, Mark argues that his concerns were far from political, as Pilate sensed and the Roman centurion realized (15:10, 39). Jesus did herald a new kingdom, but its import is religious and cosmic, not political. If the Jews do not understand, it is because they were never meant to; if the messiah suffered and died, that is what he had come for. Scripture had always said that he would, and the Jews, who always follow their own ways rather than God's, had naturally failed to perceive this. And if they who alone know the truth—that is, the true disciples of Christ—have met with adversity, hatred, and betrayal, this too confirms rather than disproves their beliefs. For true disciples are meant to suffer as the Son of Man suffered (e.g., 8:34; 10:29ff.; 13:12ff.). Their steadfastness will be rewarded, "for he who endures to the end will be saved" (13:13).

And when comes this hour of deliverance? When is the End? Soon, Mark argues; very, very soon. The Temple's recent destruction clearly marks the beginning of that period that will terminate with the Second Coming of the Son of Man. In fact, the Lord has *already* shortened the days before the consummation for the sake of his elect (13:14): the Parousia could occur at

17. On the moral unattractiveness of this saying, and the ways in which commentators have struggled with it, see Kermode, *Genesis of Secrecy,* p. 30.

18. Ecclesiastical tradition has long associated Mark with Rome (Eusebius, *EH* II.15, 2); modern scholarship is divided. See Brandon's imaginative reconstruction of events in Rome reflected in this gospel, *Jesus and the Zealots,* pp. 228–29.

any time, certainly within the lifetime of Mark's community. "Truly, I say to you, this generation will not pass away before all these things take place" (13:30; cf. 9:1).[19] Meanwhile, the faithful must remain vigilant: "And what I say to you I say to all: Watch" (13:37).

Matthew and Luke reproduce substantial sections of Mark's "apocalypse," including the prediction that the final events would occur within the lifetime of Jesus'—or Mark's—audience (Mk 9:1//Mt 16:28//Lk 9:27). But, writing at least a generation after Mark, their expectation that the End is imminent is diminished. Salvation has more to do with membership in the community of the church than with enduring as a community until the eschatological finale. If Mark sees the light at the end of the tunnel, then Matthew, more cautious, sees rather the darkness at its mouth; whereas in Mark the Lord has shortened the days, in Matthew even that lies in the future ("For the sake of the elect, those days *will be* shortened"; 24:22), and Luke drops the passage entirely. The reason, in both cases, seems clear. By the time Matthew and Luke write, the destruction of the Temple was well in the past, and things had continued much as before. It could not, therefore, have been the signal for the beginning of the End.

But Mark, writing shortly after 70, could not have known this, and for him the destruction of the Temple announced the nearness of the Parousia. Why this should have been so is a question we will examine when we consider what in the traditions inherited by the evangelist might go back to Jesus himself.[20] Here we should note simply that this link between the Temple's destruction and the Second Coming may help us to understand why Mark alone accords such prominence to the High Priest. During the trial, immediately after "false witnesses" impute to Jesus a threat to the Temple ("We heard him say, 'I will destroy this temple' "; 14:58), the High Priest, alone of all Jesus' interlocutors in Mark, identifies him both as messiah and divine Son. And to the High Priest alone does Jesus, suddenly abandoning his policy of concealment, confirm this identification while speaking of the glorious Son of Man (v. 62; cf. Jesus' evasiveness in Mt 26:64 and in Lk 22:67–70, where he is questioned by the entire Sanhedrin). Apparently the High Priest, like Mark and the members of his community, understood that the Temple's destruction was linked to the revelation of Jesus' true status. But unlike Mark's community, which must hold this conviction by faith, the High Priest received confirmation of this message directly from Jesus himself—but still did not believe. Therefore God had justly deprived the High Priest and his people of their Temple, as a prelude to the definitive vindication of his Son.

---

19. The Greek is ambiguous, however, since "this generation" (*genea autē*) might be interpreted to mean, "This generation, the one that will witness the things just described, will not pass away."

20. See "The Gospels: The Second Reading," in chap. 6.

The tension springing from this expectation of the impending Parousia informs Mark's entire gospel—its mood, its tone, its message, and most striking, its ending. For Mark never really concludes his gospel: rather, and quite abruptly, it just stops (16:8).[21] No theatrical miracles, no extended post-resurrection appearances, but simply the empty tomb, the promise of a reunion in the Galilee reaffirmed, and the trembling, frightened women.[22] Mark thus effectively recreates for his own audience the experience of the women at the tomb, leaving his reader in the same state that he had imagined for those first witnesses that first Easter morning: startled—indeed, frightened—but looking forward to the imminent manifestation of the glorious Son of Man.

PAUL: THE CHRIST OF THE PAROUSIA

When we turn from the gospels to Paul's letters, we encounter a paradox: we are at the same moment moving closer to the origins of the movement and further away. Paul was Jesus' contemporary. He personally knew the first followers of Jesus and his immediate disciples, Peter and John, as well as "the Lord's brother," James (Gal 1:18–19; 2:9). And Paul had come into contact with the movement very early, within a few years of Jesus' execution.[23] Yet, as Paul boasts, he was very independent of this original circle. The source of his Gospel (by which he means "message"), as distinct from theirs, was neither the earthly Jesus nor a human tradition passed from man to man, but the Risen Christ, who had been revealed to him through a special act of God (Gal 1:11–17; but cf. 1 Cor 11:23; 15:3a).

Paul thus places himself at some distance from those traditions, presumably emanating from the earthly ministry of Jesus, that the later evangelists eventually wrote down. Further, his surviving letters stand at a chronological remove both from Jesus' earthly ministry and from the early days of the post-resurrection community. They apparently date from mid-century, toward the end of Paul's own missionary career and some two to three decades after the lifetime of Jesus.[24]

Accordingly, Paul cannot take us as close to the historical origins of the Jesus movement as we might expect, and wish, he would. But his letters do come from someone irrefutably acquainted with the leaders of the original community. And they do come directly from Paul himself, without the vicissi-

21. "The conclusion is either intolerably clumsy; or it is incredibly subtle"; Kermode, *Genesis of Secrecy,* p. 68.

22. Galilee, some commentators have argued, may in the symbolic geography of this gospel stand for Gentile territory, and thus the Gentile mission. See Kümmel, *Introduction to the New Testament,* p. 88.

23. On the dating of Paul's call, see R. Jewett, *A Chronology of Paul's Life;* cf. G. Luedemann, *Paul, Apostle to the Gentiles.*

24. See E. P. Sanders, *PPJ,* pp. 432–33 and n.

tudes of oral transmission that make criticism of the gospels so complicated. In this sense, then, the Pauline letters are the primary sources for the Christian tradition par excellence.

Some necessary preliminary considerations before turning to the letters themselves:

First, the investigation here focuses solely on the information Paul provides in his own letters: I resist supplementing that information with the stories about Paul provided in Acts. Acts dates from a significantly later period, well after the Roman destruction of Jerusalem in 70. By that time, the original community gathered in Jerusalem, to which Paul had a complicated and highly charged relationship, had virtually disappeared. Further, as we shall see, the information that Acts relates about Paul—most specifically, on the event and circumstances of his call to be an apostle to the Gentiles, and on his later negotiations with the Jerusalem community—contradicts Paul's own statements in crucial ways.[25] Finally, Paul's speeches in Acts, according to the conventions of ancient historiography, are the free compositions of the author; they thus tell us more about Luke than about Paul. For all these reasons, then, Acts is not used here as a source for reconstructing Paul's reflections on the figure of Jesus.

Second, though the basis of our investigation is solely the letters of Paul, not all the letters attributed to him in the canon are his. Ancient Christian tradition ascribed fourteen of the twenty-seven writings comprising the New Testament to Paul. Modern scholarship accepts as definitely Pauline only half that number: 1 Thessalonians, 1 and 2 Corinthians, Philippians, Philemon, Galatians, and Romans (in probable order of composition). The Pauline authorship of all the others—2 Thessalonians, Ephesians, Colossians, 1 and 2 Timothy, and Titus—is disputed; that of Hebrews, dismissed. This second group originated most probably not from Paul himself, but from various early Christians in the generation following who saw themselves as standing in a tradition established by Paul and who accordingly wrote in his name.[26] The theologies of this second group vary much among themselves and differ markedly from that of Paul. That Paul was so widely interpreted by those who stood so close to him should caution us about the difficulties of his thought.

Third, questions also surround the literary integrity of the individual letters: we cannot be sure whether the text of the letters as we now have them is substantially the same as when Paul dictated them. Many scholars, for example, see several letters edited together in our present versions of Philippians, 2

25. Jewett, *Paul's Life,* and Luedemann, *Paul,* survey these problems; see also Paula Fredriksen, "Paul and Augustine," esp. pp. 3–20. Luke may be more reliable on the course of the mission in the Diaspora than he is about Paul's life or the early situation in Jerusalem. For a more optimistic assessment of Acts' historical reliability, the work of Martin Hengel, e.g., *Acts and the History of Earliest Christianity* and *Between Jesus and Paul.*

26. Tradition ascribes Pauline authorship to Hebrews, but the writing is in fact anonymous.

Corinthians, and Romans; others argue that a significantly anachronistic interpolation, post-70 C.E., follows 1 Thessalonians 2:13. I disregard here the various theories of partition and concentrate for the most part on the letters as they now appear. The reader concerned with this thorny problem—the Pauline analogue to the redaction hypotheses for the gospels—should consult the standard introductions to the Pauline literature.

Finally, there remains the consideration of the nature of Paul's writings as letters—real letters to particular communities occasioned by specific incidents within a mutually familiar context. Much of this context is now lost to us, and we can only partially reconstruct it from clues in the letters themselves. When Paul explicitly replies to questions raised by his communities, as when the Thessalonians require instruction on the status of the dead at the Parousia, or the Corinthians on sexual relations or meat sacrificed to idols, this task is relatively easy. But inferring a coherent picture of the beliefs of Paul's opponents from the heated charges of his polemic is nearly impossible. Try we must, for interpretation requires an understanding of context. But the letters provide only a small portion of an ongoing dialogue between Paul and his correspondents, and only half a dialogue at that. The silent half is in no small measure lost to us.

The fact that Paul's thought is preserved for us in letters means, further, that we cannot approach them directly to discern his image of Jesus, as we could the gospels. The gospels as gospels are concerned precisely to convey an image of Jesus: this is their raison d'être. Paul left no such formal, literarily self-conscious writing. With the arguable exception of Romans, his are true *lettres d'occasion,* and while his interpretation of the person and work of Christ is fundamental to his message, it is not as such his topic. Thus, whereas the gospels employ various polemics and theological arguments to develop and present their respective images of Jesus, Paul rather employs his interpretation of Christ to press an argument against opponents or to develop a particular teaching. We must attempt therefore to reconstruct his situation carefully, for only once we have done so can we distill from the letters Paul's image of Jesus.

Before we turn to Paul's image of Jesus, then, we should ask, who was Paul? We have little information about him—though more, and certainly more first-hand, than we do for any other figure of the early period, including Jesus. Acts tells us that Paul was a Jew of Tarsus, the son of a Roman citizen and hence a citizen himself. It further relates that Paul studied in Jerusalem under Gamaliel, the famous teacher of the late Second Temple period; that he enthusiastically participated in anti-Christian persecutions there; and that he personally sought to extend the persecution to Damascus. En route to Damascus, according to Luke, Paul was smitten by celestial light and converted by the voice of the Risen Christ, since "he is a chosen instrument of mine to carry my name before the Gentiles and kings and the sons of Israel" (9:15). Proclaiming

Jesus as Son of God and messiah in the Damascus synagogue, Paul aroused
Jewish hostility, and he fled forthwith back to Jerusalem, where he joined the
disciples and preached the Gospel (9:23–31). Always taking the Gospel first to
the Jews and only subsequently to other peoples, Paul pushed his mission ever
further west, to Athens and finally to Rome, as he continued Peter's work
among the Gentiles (15:7–10) to bring them to salvation in Christ.

One longs to avail oneself of this biographical information, for it fills in
many of the gaps in our knowledge both of Paul and of the developing church
in the crucial decades between Paul's call to join the Jesus movement (c. 33)
and our earliest extant Christian documents, his letters (c. 50–60). Unfortunately, what little biographical information Paul does give us seems to fatally
compromise, if not contradict, what we have from Luke. Paul himself never
states that he studied in Jerusalem under Gamaliel or anyone else (as we would
expect he would when he boasts of being a "Hebrew of Hebrews"; Phil 3:4–
6); nor that he participated in any way in persecutions there (as we would
expect when he speaks of his former life as a "persecutor"; e.g. Gal 1:13–14).
Further, he explicitly denies that he went up to Jerusalem immediately after his
call or sought to confer with the original disciples until some time later, after a
sojourn in Arabia and another trip to Damascus. At this point, "after three
years," Paul reports that he "was still not known by face"—either as a
persecutor (cf. Acts 8:1) or as an apostle (cf. Acts 9:28–29)—to the churches
of Judea (Gal 1:17–24). And while he alludes to having been punished several
times in his career by synagogue authorities (2 Cor 11:24), Paul claims to have
been explicitly and uniquely called to—indeed, created for—the mission to
the Gentiles. The Jewish mission he left to James and Peter, to whom he refers
with some sarcasm as "so-called pillars," later disparaging Peter as a hyp-
ocrite whom he opposed "to his face" (Gal 1:15; 2:9, 11).

If Acts did not exist and all we had were Paul's letters, we would have no
reason to think of him as other than a Jew of the Diaspora whose language was
Greek, whose original arena of activity was Damascus, and whose relations
with the original disciples were complicated and occasionally difficult. More
difficult still were Paul's relationships with fellow Christian missionaries in the
field, whom in his letters he variously describes as "dogs," "mutilators of the
flesh," "servants of Satan," and "false apostles" (Phil 3:2; 2 Cor 11:12–14; cf.
the "false brethren" of Gal 2:4). Such men were guilty, in Paul's eyes, of
preaching a "different gospel" and a "different Jesus"—different, that is, from
Paul's own.

Who then is Paul's Jesus? Paul identifies him only briefly in the ways that,
decades later, dominated the gospel narratives: as a human being (*anthrōpos*),
though "from heaven" (1 Cor 15:49; cf. Rom 5:12–17); a man born of
woman, under the Law, that is, a Jew (Gal 4:4; Rom 9:5); a descendent in fact
of King David (Rom 1:4), and thus the messiah. But Paul spends little time

either arguing or demonstrating from episodes in Jesus' life or from the LXX that Jesus is the messiah. He uses the Greek term, *Christos,* more as a name than as a messianic title: Jesus Christ, not Jesus *the* Christ.

The Jesus who is the focus of Paul's fierce commitment is the divine and preexistent Son of God, the agent of creation "through whom all things are" (1 Cor 8:6), who came to earth, died by crucifixion, was raised and exalted, and is about to return. This pattern of descent, ascent, and approaching return is the essential content of Paul's gospel—or, as he sees it, of *the* Gospel, the secret and hidden wisdom of God decreed before the *aiōnes* (ages) for the glorification of the believer (1 Cor 2:7). Before his life on earth, Jesus was "in the form of God" (i.e., divine), but he did not grasp at "equality with God." Instead, entering the plane of human existence, Christ "emptied himself," took on the "form of a slave," and was born in the "likeness of men," in "human form" (Phil 2:5–10), even taking on the "likeness of sinful flesh" (Rom 8:3), thereby "becoming sin" for the sake of humankind (2 Cor 5:20). Thus moving from the "riches" of his preincarnate state to the "poverty" of life in the body (2 Cor 8:9), Christ humbled himself even to the point of dying on a cross (Phil 2:8; also 1 Cor 2:8; Gal 2:20; 5:24, etc.). All this occurred "according to the scriptures" (1 Cor 15:3; Paul does not reveal what scriptural passage he has in mind). Therefore God raised Christ from the dead and exalted him, so that "every tongue should confess that Jesus is Lord, to the glory of God the Father" (Phil 2:11).

But how does Christ's crucifixion and resurrection glorify the believer, the Son, and the Father himself? And why did God seek to accomplish this end by such complicated means, having his Son come in the likeness of flesh and die? Before we can answer these questions, we must recall the nature of our sources and the temperament of their author. Paul wrote letters, not treatises; and while subsequent generations of Christians have naturally used Paul to write their systematic theologies, Paul himself did not leave us any. Thus, whereas Paul's communities were probably acquainted with a reasonably coherent view of his vision of redemption, we are not. We must try to piece one together, aided neither by the nature of the epistolary evidence, which is fragmentary and often allusive, nor by Paul's own temperament as a thinker and writer, for he was as often inconsistent and (as his own congregations found) as difficult to understand as he was creative and energetic.

According to Paul, Christ is God's special agent whose mission is nothing less than the redemption of humankind and, indeed, all creation, which has been "subjected to futility . . . [in] bondage to decay" (Rom 8:19ff.). How this situation came about Paul does not say, but presumably he sees it as linked to the Fall (Rom 5:12). Christ, entering fallen creation in the "likeness of sinful flesh," was crucified by the "rulers of this age," the *archontes* of this *aiōn,* who had failed to understand God's secret wisdom—cosmic powers, not human authorities, seem suggested, as we shall see (1 Cor 2:8). His death was an expiation in blood for human sin, and men who receive this news in faith are redeemed, for God has acquitted them through his son's sacrifice (Rom 3:24; also, e.g., 4:24; 5:9).

Though the believer has been released, in Christ, from his bondage to the elemental spirits of this cosmos (the *stoicheia* of Gal 4:3, 9; see also 5:1), these astral forces still exert tremendous influence as long as the believer dwells in this universe. The present *aiōn* is evil (Gal 1:4), ruled by Satan, who undermines the community (2 Cor 2:10), interferes with Paul's missions (1 Thes 2:18), tempts believers with apostasy (3:5) and lust (1 Cor 7:5), and dispatches rival Christian missionaries to Paul's communities (2 Cor 11:14). This cosmos lies under the dominion of "the god of this world" (Satan?), who blinds the minds of unbelievers (2 Cor 4:4); of pagan gods, which are demons (1 Cor 10:20; Gal 4:8–9); of hostile cosmic or astral forces (1 Cor 15:24; Gal 4:3–9; Rom 8:38–39); of bodily flesh (Rom 7 passim; 8:3); of sin (Rom 3:9; 5:21–6:23; 7:7–8:2), the Law (Gal 4:1–11), decay (Rom 8:3), and Death itself (Rom 8:38; 1 Cor 15:26), all of which Paul sees as personal, enslaving powers. Thus the believer finds himself engaged in no mere fleshly (*sarkika*) warfare, but a cosmic one. His afflictions unite him with those of the Apostle and of Christ himself (2 Cor 1:5; Phil 1:29; 3:10; Rom 8:17), who grants him "divine power to destroy strongholds" (2 Cor 10:3–4).

How has Christ triumphed over these powers, and how does the believer participate in this triumph? Had Christ only come in the flesh, or been born of Davidic lineage (Rom 1:3), or only died on the cross, the evil forces of this age would still reign unprovisionally supreme (1 Cor 15:12–19). But they have been defeated by the power of the *resurrection* of Christ, who is "the first fruits of those who have fallen asleep" (1 Cor 15:20). Henceforward the believer need not grieve like those who have no hope (1 Thes 4:13), for having been brought into Christ's body and consequently into his death through baptism, he may hope as well to be united with Christ in a resurrection like his (Rom 6:1–5).

Further, the believer already shares in Christ's victory in this life through the gift of the Spirit in baptism. This Spirit, which Paul calls variously the Spirit of God or of Christ, or the Holy Spirit, is the believer's aid and assurance of his hope in Christ (2 Cor 5:5). Through the Spirit, the Gentile is made a son of God through adoption (Gal 4:4–6; Rom 8:15, but cf. v. 23; Jews are already sons, 9:4). Through the Spirit, the spiritually mature or perfected individual (*teleios*) can receive the secret and hidden wisdom of God, namely, the good news about Christ (1 Cor 2:6ff.). The Spirit binds together Christ's new body, the church, bringing love, joy, and peace, gentleness and self-control, patience, kindness, faithfulness, and goodness (Gal 5:22ff.). It is manifested in power by mighty deeds—healings, prophecy, ecstatic glossolalia (1 Thes 1:4; 1 Cor 12). It sustains the faithful while they "groan," awaiting the redemption of their bodies (Rom 8:23ff.).

It is the Spirit that enables the believer's participation in the dying and rising of Christ. This dying and rising is Paul's root metaphor for viewing Christ, the world, and one's place in it.[27] As Christ suffered in this cosmos, so will the believer (1 Thes 3:4); as Christ died to the world, passing beyond its power, so should the believer, crucifying the flesh with its passions and desires (Gal 5:24; 6:14), dying to sin that he might be a slave to righteousness (Rom 6:10–11, 18). The believer should accordingly shun unchastity, adultery, and dissension as the works of the flesh. In putting on Christ, he has put off these things, remaining, if possible, completely chaste, in order to concentrate on the affairs of the Lord (1 Cor 7:32–33). Thus, though the believer still lives in this world, to the degree that he shares in Christ through the Spirit he has died to it, as he awaits final redemption on "the day of the Lord Jesus" (1 Cor 5:5).

But what exactly will happen on the Day of the Lord? And when will it occur? Here Paul's teaching is uncharacteristically clear and consistent throughout his letters. Believers whether living or dead will receive a new, glorious body, like Christ's at his resurrection—and this will happen very, very soon. Christ's resurrection itself proves the nearness of the End of all things: it is a sign, for Paul, that the final days are not merely "at hand," but have *already arrived.* It is upon *us,* he informs his Corinthian community, that the end of the ages *has come (ta telē tōn aiōnōn katentēken;* 1 Cor 10:11); "The form of this cosmos *is passing* away" (7:31).

Nor shall this final period extend indefinitely: Paul expects to live to see the Last Days. He speaks of his hope for the transformation of his present body before death (2 Cor 5:1–5), and in light of his conviction, he even feels it reasonable to urge his congregants to forswear sexual activity, "[for] the appointed time has grown very short" (1 Cor 7:26, 29). So near is the End that both Paul and his communities are troubled by the death of believers before Christ's Second Coming: they did not expect this and do not know what to make of it (1 Thes 4:13). So anomalous is a Christian's dying before Christ returns that Paul suggests such deaths may be punitive: because the Corinthians have celebrated the eucharist unworthily, he argues, many "are weak and ill, and some have died" (1 Cor 11:30). Paul's deep and fervent conviction that the End is upon him spurs him on his missions to the Gentiles, whom accordingly he exhorts to put away their former sinful ways; to be sons of light, not of darkness; of day, not night; to wake, not sleep; to walk according to the Spirit, not the flesh. These commonplace moralisms are charged with new meaning and urgency, for the fast approaching Day of the Lord will be a day of judgment and wrath (1 Thes 1:9; 4:6; Rom 1:18; 2:16, etc.). The Lord is at hand (Phil 4:5): *Marana tha!* Lord, come! (1 Cor 16:22).

This expectation marks all Paul's letters, and through them we can piece

27. For the function of such a metaphor in Paul's "master eschatological picture," see Wayne A. Meeks, *First Urban Christians,* pp. 174–80.

together his vision of what was about to happen. As suddenly as "a thief in the night," the glorified Lord will return to earth amidst the clamor of cosmic battle—the cry of command, the call of archangels, the sounding of the trumpet of God (1 Thes 4:13–14). With Christ's coming, the "dead in Christ" will then rise, to be joined by those still alive at the Parousia (among whom Paul expects to be, 4:15). They will join Christ and his saints "up in the air" and will be with him forever (4:16).

But the dead will not be raised with physical bodies, nor could the living faithful join Christ in the air if they still had theirs. No: the raised body will not be fleshly, but spiritual, as Christ's was at his resurrection. Thus the body of the living believer will also be transformed, "in the twinkling of an eye, at the last trumpet. For the trumpet shall sound, the dead will be raised imperishable, and we shall all be changed" (1 Cor 15:51; see 35–52 for his entire discussion). This transformation is necessary, because "flesh and blood cannot inherit the kingdom" (15:50), nor can flesh dwell in the heavens, wherein lies the true commonwealth of the Christian (Phil 3:20).

After this transformation, Christ will lead the apocalyptic battle against the forces of evil, destroying "every rule (*archē*), authority (*exousia*), and power (*dunamis*)" (1 Cor 15:24; Paul probably means hostile spirits and astral powers).[28] Christ will then subject all things to himself (Phil 3:20), crushing Satan (Rom 16:20), and finally defeating even Death (1 Cor 15:26). Then the saints, now fully revealed as sons of God with the glorious redemption of their bodies (Rom 8:19ff.), will join in judging the world and even the angels (1 Cor 6:1–2). The enemies of Christ will perish: "Their end is their destruction" (Phil 3:19). Then the Son will subject himself to the Father, delivering the Kingdom to him, "that God may be everything to everyone" (1 Cor 15:24–25).

This Gospel, Paul claims, was revealed to him at his call to be an apostle to the Gentiles (Gal 1:11–12 and passim); it was spoken of by the prophets in the scriptures (e.g., Rom 1:2); and it will be vindicated shortly on the Day of the Lord, when Paul will be shown to be a true apostle (1 Thes 2:19; Phil 2:14–16; 1 Cor 3:10–15; 4:5). In the last letter we have from him, addressed to the Romans, Paul reviews his Gospel, placing it within the framework of biblical salvation history. Indeed, he sees proclaimed in his Gospel God's ultimate and unexpected act of redemption—Christ's coming and, more crucially, his resurrection—before he brings all history to a glorious close.

Paul opens Romans by observing that the level of ethical achievement by both Gentile and Jew has been rather low, despite the Gentile's knowledge of God through creation (1:20ff.) and the Jew's privileged possession of the Law and the prophets (chap. 2), which reveal God's righteousness. Now, however,

28. For the definitions of these terms, Bauer, *Greek-English Lexicon;* H. Conzelmann, *1 Corinthians,* pp. 269–73, takes them to refer to demonic powers; Sanders, *PPJ,* pp. 497–502, argues that they apply to cosmic bondage. On this view of the organization of the universe, see "Hellenistic Paganism" in chap. 2.

God has manifested his righteousness apart from the Law, in Christ. Christ died for the ungodly "at the right time" so that, through faith in his resurrection, they should sin no more. The Law, weakened because of the flesh, could not prevent sin. But God, by sending his Son "in the likeness of sinful flesh," accomplished what the Law could not and condemned sin in the flesh (6–7). All creation still groans in its bondage to decay—the mutability of physical reality—but it will be redeemed at Christ's second coming, when he will prevail against all the cosmic and astral powers now separating the believer from God (8).

> What then shall we say to this? If God is for us, who is against us? He who did not spare his own Son, but gave him up for us all, will he not also give us all things with him? . . . Who shall separate us from the love of Christ? Shall tribulation, or distress, or famine, or nakedness, or peril, or sword? . . . No, in all these things we are more than conquerors through him who loved us. For I am sure that neither death, nor life, nor angels, nor principalities, nor things present, nor things to come, nor powers, nor height, nor depth, nor anything else in all creation, will be able to separate us from the love of God in Christ Jesus our Lord.   (8:31–39)

But Paul must stop himself mid-flight in his praise of this universal redemption, because of an obvious problem: the majority of his "kinsmen by race" do not believe in Paul's Christocentric message of eschatological salvation. Will they then not be saved? *Will history end with God breaking his promises to Israel?* Impossible. So how is God's salvation working? Paul turns to biblical history for his answer (9–11). In the past, God had at significant moments elected the younger, making the elder serve him. Thus as Esau once served Jacob, so now Israel serves the Gentiles. And as God once hardened Pharaoh's heart so that God's name might be proclaimed in all the earth, so now, and to that same end, does he harden Israel.

Thus God has not rejected his people or broken his promise: on the contrary, his people are instrumental in his master plan of salvation. God hardens their hearts until the full number of the Gentiles can be grafted on to the tree of Israel. In the very fact of the Jews' rejection of the Gospel, Paul perceives the crucial role they still play in the drama of salvation—for the Gentiles, for themselves, and ultimately for the cosmos. For, shortly, the Jews will be reconciled to God's unexpected justification of the Gentiles apart from the Law in Christ. And their reconciliation will bring about "life from the dead," that is, the Parousia and its attendant redemption (11:15).

What Paul sees, in fact, is a divine comedy. By God's will Israel had "stumbled" against the Gospel, on account of which the Gentiles entered into the eschatological community of the redeemed. But then Israel too will join, for God's promises are irrevocable: Israel *never* could have stumbled so as to fall (11:24, 29). Overwhelmed by this vision of universal redemption brought about by God in such an ingenious and unexpected way, Paul once again breaks out in praise. "O the depth of the riches of the wisdom and knowledge of God! How unsearchable are his judgments and how inscrutable his ways!" (11:33). He then concludes with ethical exhortation, urging the Romans to remember the extremity of the hour, "For salvation is nearer to us than when we first believed" (13:11). The community should build itself up, maintain peace both within and without, and prepare for the fast-approaching redemption. For, as Christ's resurrection unambiguously announced, the End of all things is upon humankind, and "the God of peace will soon crush Satan under your feet" (16:20).

Thus, while being "in Christ" entails membership in "Christ's body," the community, and while membership in the community requires conformation to a high standard of morality, the Christ in whom believers hope is finally neither the founder of a church nor a moral exemplar per se. Paul's Christ is the eschatological Deliverer (11:26). With his resurrection, he signaled the beginning of the End; with his return, he will shortly sum up the ages. The rescue mission for which God had commissioned his Son (Phil 2:5–11) is now all but complete, Paul urges. Soon, with Christ's defeat of the hostile cosmic powers and his final victory over Death, the sons of God both adopted (Gentiles, Rom 8:23) and "natural" (Jews, 9:4) will join with the divine Son in rejoicing in God's kingdom.

Chapter 4
Hellenism and Christianity

Of course, history did not come to the glorious end that Paul so fervently believed it would. Time went on; Jews for the most part declined to follow the message of a divine, crucified messiah; and Christianity, as it spread in an increasingly Gentile Hellenistic milieu, had to accommodate these facts.

The texts just surveyed represent various results of this accommodation, and we have seen that most cannot be explained as simple linear developments. For example, John, probably the latest text reviewed, had a "high Christology" (i.e., a very developed theology of Jesus as the divine Son); but so did Paul, our earliest source. The term *Son of Man* had a similarly unpredictable career. Originating historically in Jewish prophecy and apocalypticism, Son of Man has a good claim to entering Christian tradition through the preaching of Jesus himself (see Part III). The term figures prominently in John, where it is utterly reinterpreted and given cosmic rather than apocalyptic significance. It appears variously in the synoptic tradition to express the paradox of present suffering and coming vindication; and in Paul, the most unabashedly apocalyptic of all our sources, it fails to appear at all. Similarly, antipathy toward Jews and Judaism is fierce both in the (Gentile?) Johannine gospel and in the (Jewish?) Gospel of Matthew, but relatively mild in the equally late, Gentile Gospel of Luke. Repentance for sin is a prevailing principle in the religion of Judaism and hence part of the spiritual context of the Jesus movement in Palestine. It is a major theme in the Gospel of Luke but seems explicitly denied as a possibility for Jews in Mark, the earliest evangelical source (4:10–12). And in our only indisputably Jewish source, the letters of Paul, it scarcely comes into play at all (e.g., 2 Cor 12:20). It seems safe to say that no general pattern emerges clearly in this stage of Christianity's development in the Hellenistic world.

This is not to suggest that when Christianity "encountered" Hellenism, what it saw was something radically other, from which it could consciously choose and reject. Gentiles entering the new movement brought their culture with them, and Hellenism had already significantly affected Jewish culture both at home and abroad. Paul's Gospel, as we have seen, was at home in this milieu; and his universe, despite the foreshortened perspective he sees it in, is still very much the universe of late Hellenistic science. He sees the world as the material expression of hostile forces—so hostile, in fact, that they have even crucified God's divine intermediary, his Son; and he views man himself as summing up in his own constitution this cosmic struggle of spirit and flesh. In order to understand this, the believer must know how to interpret the sacred writings that reveal reality, namely the Septuagint, by reading not "according to the flesh" (that is, literally, or indeed in any way other than Paul's), but "according to the spirit." Thus may the believer receive "the revelation of the mystery which was kept secret for long ages but is now disclosed and through the prophetic writings is made known to all nations" (Rom 16:25–26). Astral forces and the elements of the universe may threaten to enslave man and separate him from God, but for the believer, in Christ these powers have already been overthrown, and shortly they will be subjected to God once for all.

It is this note of expectation that God was soon to defeat evil once for all that diminishes in our sources as time goes on. Paul, seeing the final days announced by the fact of Christ's resurrection, expected the Parousia in his own lifetime, in the first (and as far as he knew, only) generation of believers. Mark in turn expected it in his generation, the second, after the fall of the Temple. Matthew saw it vaguely off in the future; Luke, for whom Christ's resurrection implied not his Second Coming but the founding of his church, even further. And John seems to think in different terms entirely: the distinction between the realms of light and darkness are absolute and static, and if one is Christ's he has already passed from death to life (Jn 5:25). A Last Judgment is not necessary, because the selection has already taken place and is always taking place. Paul's incomplete cycle of the Son who has descended, ascended, and will shortly come again gives way in John 14 to an already completed cycle of coming down and going up. John, even more than Luke, resolves the problem of evil less through an eschatological view of history than through an idea that God through Christ established his kingdom as a community within time, liberating believers from the evils of this aeon through membership in the church.

Yet Christianity did not become simply another Hellenistic mystery cult whose dying and rising savior secured the well-being of the initiate after death; nor did redemption come to be seen simply as the safe ascent of the soul through the astral realms to its true abode. True, these elements are in Christianity; and to the degree that its theology presupposed a metaphysics, that metaphysics was Greek. But it was neither to metaphysics nor to cosmology that Christian writers turned as they sought an answer to the problem of evil. The death of the Christ and the persecution endured by those who followed him raised the question of theodicy most pointedly: why would a good God have it so? Some believers saw an answer in a past event, God's sending his Son among men as man to be crucified and raised; others, in a future event, the glorious Parousia. But in either case, Christians looked to history for a resolution to the problem of evil.

To the degree that they did so, Christian writers retreated from the great intellectual triumph of Hellenistic syncretism, its ability always to see the general in the particular, to transform the mythological into the philosophical. Christians insisted on historical particularity; they pressed the unreasonable claim that the divine had manifested itself uniquely through a specific person at a specific moment, and that not so long ago. They in fact *re*mythologized their message of universal salvation in an unabashedly particularistic way. It was intellectually embarrassing; it was at once parochial and presumptuous; it was irreducibly odd.

It was, in fact, Jewish. To see how this was so, we must now remove ourselves from our first-century Hellenistic cosmos and transpose ourselves to another world: that of the descendents of Abraham, Isaac, and Jacob, of the Pharisees and Sadducees; the world of both Paul and Philo, and of Jesus himself. We must place ourselves within the history of Israel.

II
THE WORLD OF JUDAISM

For much of the discussion that follows, we are dependent on the evidence of the Hebrew Bible. A collection of texts of varying antiquity—the earliest strata of written tradition might date to the first millennium; the latest, to the Hellenistic period—the Bible, though a history of the Jewish people, is of course not a history in the modern sense. It preserves, rather, the religious reflections of various ancient writers and later redactors on events in the life of their people. These reflections, and not modern critical analyses of them, are what concern us here. My goal is twofold: to elucidate the broad lines of the history of the Jewish people up to the wars with Rome, and to describe how most Jews in the early first century would have interpreted both current events and their proper role in them in light of their understanding of this history.

I begin with a brief overview of the political career of the people of Israel down to the second century of the Common Era—the "outside" story. Then, beginning over again with Genesis, I shall explore the "inside" story, to show how Jews constructed and regarded their own past and how they saw that past as informing the choices, political and religious, that confronted them as they confronted Rome.

The origins of the nation of Israel are obscure. It was in the beginning a confederation of semitic tribes, some of whom had for some period lived in Egypt. By the end of the thirteenth century B.C.E., they had settled in the land of Canaan, roughly the area between the coastal plain of the eastern Mediterranean and the Jordan River. The need to resist the military ambitions of their immediate neighbors, the Philistines and Ammonites, along with the temporary impotence of more distant imperial powers, especially Egypt, provoked these tribes to unite under a monarchy. First under Saul (c. 1020–1000), and later under David (c. 1000–961) and Solomon (c. 961–922), the kingdom consolidated and extended its power in the region. It also consolidated its religious cultus, erecting a temple to the one God the tribes worshiped in the "city of David," Jerusalem.

This period of unity and autonomy was brief. After Solomon, the kingdom divided into two often antagonistic domains, Israel in the north and Judah in the south. Israel succumbed to the westward expansion of the Assyrian Empire in 722. Its population (the so-called "ten lost tribes") was deported and its territory resettled by other peoples from the Babylonian borderlands (2 Kgs 17). Less than a century and a half later, Judah fell to the political heirs of the Assyrians. In the summer of 586 B.C.E., Nebuchadnezzar's armies stormed Jerusalem, destroyed the Temple, and led many of the conquered away to captivity in Babylon.

When the Chaldean Empire capitulated in its turn to the Persians, this captive population was permitted to return home (in 538 B.C.E.; Ezr 1:2–4;

6:2—5). A significant number remained in Babylon. Those who did return set about rebuilding the Temple, reordering national (and hence) religious life, and restoring Jerusalem. True political autonomy as in the days of David and Solomon, however, never returned. In the centuries that followed, the territories of the Eastern Mediterranean changed hands repeatedly—from Darius the Persian to Alexander the Great, and later from the Hellenistic Ptolemies to the Hellenistic Seleucids. The Jews revolted successfully against Seleucid dominion and established self-rule under the Hasmonean family from about 160 to about 40 B.C.E., but the tiny state had to rely on an alliance with Rome to protect itself against its powerful neighbors.

Rome's military expansion into the area in the mid-first century B.C.E. further restricted Jewish political independence. Provoked by imperial taxes and insensitive government, the Jews revolted repeatedly during this period and were repeatedly repressed. The situation reached a crisis point in 66 C.E. with the successful occupation of Jerusalem by rebel Jewish forces. After three years of terrible fighting, Rome retook and destroyed the city and its temple. Two later major insurrections—circa 115–17 in the Diaspora and circa 132–35 in Palestine under Bar Kochba—only further reduced the cause of Jewish independence. By the mid-second century, Jerusalem had "disappeared." In its place stood a pagan city, Aelia Capitolina, and in its temple area, a shrine to the god Zeus and the emperor Hadrian.

Thus, viewed from the outside, Jewish history to the mid-second century C.E. is one more unhappy tale of the rise and fall of a polity too small to survive in an age of empire. Nothing unique or uniquely interesting here. But Jews viewed their history from the inside. For them it was charged with infinite importance, for they saw it as revealing to man the will of his Creator. The Jewish commitment to this point of view explains, or at least accounts for, the structure and content of that collection of writings that came to stand at the center of Judaism, the Bible. For the Hebrew Bible is a witness both to the history of the Jewish people and to their own view of that history—a history that they came to see as universally significant; a history that they both perceived and experienced through the dialectic of Exile and Return.

The Exile, the traumatic result of the Babylonian victory in 586 B.C.E., marked not only all subsequent Jewish history, but also, with the post-exilic redaction of the Torah, all *previous* Jewish history as well. For it was only after the Exile, according to modern textual critics, that the Torah, the first five books of the Bible, received its final form. Earlier traditions about the Creation, the patriarchs, the liberation from Egypt, the giving of God's Torah (teaching) on Sinai—all originating variously and at now indeterminate periods in the northern and southern Kingdoms—were now redacted by anonymous editors who incorporated their religious reflections on the Babylonian Captivity into the history of their people's ancient origins. And from this documentary montage emerged a narrative unity, the story of a universal deity's election of a people and of their role in his plans for all people.

The Jews of the first century C.E. shaped their beliefs and actions according to their understanding of this story and their place in it. From their encounter with the political realities of this period emerged a new messianic movement that came, eventually and after many changes, to dominate the culture of the West. In our trajectory backward, we have reviewed the various interpretations of the central figure of this new movement as they stand in the New Testament texts. Now, moving forward through canonical and noncanonical Jewish documents, we will review the social and religious world of first-century Judaism. Somewhere at the place where these two trajectories overlap is the ambit of that most enigmatic figure who left us no texts at all, Jesus of Nazareth.

Chapter 5
The Idea of Israel

THE BIBLICAL VIEW OF THE PAST

The Covenant

The starting point of Genesis, and of the biblical story as a whole, is universal monotheism. God is Lord of the whole universe and of all people; he is the only God, and there is none beside him. His existence is revealed in and through the universe itself, which the Bible regards as God's willed creation. His attributes—mercy, kindness, justice—are echoed in his expectation of moral behavior on the part of the creature whom he made uniquely in his image, man; and most particularly in his calling of a people whose election entailed its conscious acknowledgement of revealed ethical and spiritual responsibilities. The relationship between God and man, and especially between God and his people, Israel, is thus fundamentally a moral one.

Hence, although the Bible begins with the divine ordering of the physical universe, it moves swiftly to the creation of humanity and to humanity's moral failure. Adam and Eve violate God's command not to eat the fruit of the tree of the knowledge of good and evil (Gn 3:1–7); Cain murders Abel in a jealous rage (4:8ff.); and with the passage of generations man so fixes on evil that God repents having created him at all (6:1ff.). Beginning all over with the family of Noah, God destroys all else by releasing the waters of chaos. But after the flood, God acknowledges that "the imagination of man is evil from his youth" (8:21). Were creation to be contingent upon the level of man's ethical performance, it would cease to exist. Vowing never again to annihilate his creation on account of man's sins, God sets in the sky a rainbow as a sign of the covenant between himself and the family of man, to remind both himself and them of his promise (6:8–18).

Human behavior, despite this chastening episode, continues much as before, marked by indecent self-indulgence (Noah's drunkenness, 9:20–21), filial impiety (his son's reaction to it, 9:22–27), and presumptuousness (the Tower of Babel, 11:1–9). God finally embarks upon a third effort at moral human society; but rather than attempt to have all humanity conform to his expectations, he concentrates on the family of one man, Abraham.

> Now the Lord said to Abram, "Go out from your country and your kindred and your father's house to the land that I will show you. And I will make of you a great nation, and I will bless you and make your name great, so that you will be a blessing. I will bless those that bless you, and curse him who curses you; and through you shall all the families of the earth be blessed." (12:1–3)

The story of Abraham—and thus of Israel—begins with exile, with God's promise that the land he intends for Abraham and his family awaits, and with the vision that ultimately their unique relationship will benefit all mankind. God makes clear to Abraham that their special covenant will entail suffering, most especially exile and servitude for Abraham's descendents in a foreign land. But God will redeem them from slavery and bring them to the land of the promise, for God's covenant with Abraham and his family is eternal and the Land itself is its pledge. In return, they must walk before God and be blameless (17:1), sealing the covenant in their flesh by circumcision (17:10–13), keeping to God's way by doing righteousness and justice (18:19). Thus will they be his people and he their God.

This promise to Abraham reverberates throughout the patriarchal narratives, repeated in turn to and by Isaac, Jacob, and Joseph. When Israel toils and suffers in bondage to Pharaoh, God "remembers" his covenant and calls Moses to redeem his people from slavery (Ex 1–12). Leading these refugees through the wilderness and forging them into a nation, God finally reveals his will directly to Israel, by giving them the Torah (12:3–31:18).

At this point, as the people receive the Torah on Sinai and prepare to take possession of the Land, the style of the biblical narrative changes abruptly. Story gives way to the direct and detailed instruction—moral, social, and cultic—which occupies the greater part of the Pentateuch from the second half of Exodus through Leviticus and Numbers to the end of Deuteronomy. God, through Moses, instructs Israel on their obligations in light of their election, specifying both how they should worship him and how they should structure society: God will view man's transgressions against each other as sins against himself (e.g., Ex 22:22–24). Every imaginable aspect of the community's life is touched upon, from the proportions and materials for the ark of the covenant to the types and requirements of animal sacrifices (legislation later applied to, or in the modern critical view derived from, eventual Temple ritual) to their responsibility toward their fields and their animals, toward each other, strangers, and captives; toward children and spouses, toward the helpless and the poor. And toward the Land itself: they have obligations to the Land, for the Land is holy.

Implied in this text (by the stories of the Golden Calf, Korach's rebellion, and the ceaseless complaints of the children of Israel longing for the comforts of Egypt), and made explicit in later prophetic and rabbinic commentary, is the view that Israel was not awarded the covenant because of previous sinlessness or special merit. Neither is subsequent sinlessness a condition of the covenant. God is constant where man is not, and though he demands perfection, he does not expect it: much of his Torah teaches ways to repent, atone, and make restitution after sin. The election of Israel is a mystery, something God did graciously, "for his name's sake."[1] Israel's responsibility, since God dwells with his people, is to tolerate nothing that is unclean or abhorrent to God. The people both individually (the Ten Commandments are given in the second person singular) and corporately assume this responsibility by agreeing to "do" the Torah, "writing" it on their hearts and loving the God who gave his teaching to them.

> This command which I command you this day is not too hard for you, neither is it far off. It is not in heaven, that you should say, "Who will go up for us to heaven, and bring it to us, that we may hear it and do it?" Neither is it beyond the sea, that you should say, "Who will go over the sea for us, and bring it to us, that we may hear it and do it?" But the word is very near you; it is in your mouth and in your heart, so that you can do it. . . . I have set before you life and death, blessing and curse: therefore choose life, that you and your descendents may live, loving the Lord your God, obeying his voice, and cleaving to him . . . that you may dwell in the land which the Lord swore to your fathers, to Abraham, to Isaac, and to Jacob, to give them.   (Dt 30:11–14, 19–20)

The Monarchy

The period of the Exodus was followed by the period of the Judges, whose religious and social responsibility was to regulate the life of the tribes according to the precepts of Torah. Inasmuch as the tribes had one ruler, it was God (e.g., 1 Sm 12:12). But with settlement and territory came the desire for monarchy, a development the tradition regarded with considerable ambivalence.

The Book of Samuel views Israel's demand for a king as a desire to be like other nations, a rejection of God's kingship in favor of a human ruler (1 Sm 8; 10:18–19). But Israel is not like the other nations, nor can it ever be. Samuel thus "reiterates" to the Israelites the warning against monarchy "already" given in Deuteronomy: a king will raise armies, confiscate property, and take foreign wives who bring with them their gods. With misgivings and much

---

1. See esp. Sanders, *PPJ*, pp. 84–101, on the Tannaitic and later rabbinic development of this theme of the gratuity of Israel's election.

scolding, Samuel anoints Saul King of Israel, cautioning both monarch and people to follow "the Lord your God." Asking for a king was "great wickedness" (12:17), but the Lord would abide with them anyway, "For the Lord will not cast away his people, for his great name's sake, because it has pleased the Lord to make you a people for himself" (12:22).

Against this gloomy prognosis, however, stands the whole of the biblical messianic tradition that crystallized around the figure of Saul's successor, David. David united the tribes under his leadership, defeated Israel's enemies, and consolidated political power and national worship at Jerusalem, to which he brought the ark of the covenant, and where his son Solomon later established the "house of the Lord," the Temple. The tradition viewed David's success as the measure of his love for God (many of the Psalms are attributed to him) and of God's love for him and those of his house: "I [God] will be his father, and he shall be my son. When he commits iniquity [as Saul had done], I will chasten him with the rod of men. . . . But I will not take my steadfast love from him" (2 Sm 7:14–15). Consequently David, God's chosen vessel, and his house are promised eternal dominion, reigning from Jerusalem in justice and peace, "[for] your house and your kingdom shall be made sure forever before me; your throne shall be established forever" (7:16).

But the Davidic kingdom did not abide. Dividing after Solomon's death, the north eventually fell to Assyrian expansion, and by the early sixth century Jerusalem itself lay wasted, its Temple destroyed, and the people driven into exile from the land promised them in perpetuity by God. Viewed objectively, these events would seem an unambiguous repudiation of the promises of the covenant. But the tradition viewed these events religiously, as revealing in fact God's continuing commitment to his people. Thus what might have spelled the end of Israel was instead profoundly incorporated into its spiritual life. This religious reinterpretation of traumatic events was the accomplishment of the prophets.

Prophecy and Diaspora

Prophecy as a historical phenomenon appears to have developed with the monarchy. As a *nav'i* (Heb. "one who has been called"), the prophet was the chosen spokesman of God, charged with delivering his message to Israel. While prophets might heal the sick, work miracles and mighty signs, or foretell the course of future events to demonstrate the divine authority of their mandate, they were above all social and political gadflies.[2] Rebuking both kings and commoners for lapses from the Torah, they called those party to the covenant back to their agreement—most frequently the human parties, but on occasion God himself (e.g., Jer 14:9; 15:8).

---

2. Elijah, for example, raises a widow's son, 1 Kgs 17:17–24; Elisha blesses a widow's jar of oil, so that it fills many vessels, 2 Kgs 4:1–7.

In the face of the threat of the loss of the Northern Kingdom and, with the realization of that loss, the danger to the South, prophets assumed a major role in religiously interpreting political events. God's election of Israel, they argued, did not mean privilege, but responsibility; and if the nation neglected that responsibility, it would be punished. "Only you [Israel] have I chosen from among all the nations, and therefore I will punish you for your sins" (Am 3:2; also Is 1:1–2). Since Israel had turned from God, God would punish by turning from Israel. Israel had broken off their dialogue ("I called you, and no one answered; I spoke, and no one listened"; Is 66:4), and therefore God would not answer when called ("Why do You forget us forever, why do you forsake us so long?" Lam 5:20). But this calamity, the prophets argued, is punishment, not rejection. God's promises to Israel are irrevocable. He will always redeem, because of the nature of his covenant.[3]

And so, with the vision before them of the Temple destroyed and the people exiled, the prophets employed images of constancy and consolation to interpret Israel's suffering. God is Israel's *shepherd:* he allows his flock to scatter, but he will surely gather them in again (Jer 31:10–11). Israel has rebelled against God like an *unbroken calf* that protests at the yoke, but God will train her (31:18–19). Israel is a defective *servant,* both deaf and blind; nonetheless, God will be glorified in him. Through his *suffering,* which is also on behalf of the iniquities of the nations, the servant will bring them to the knowledge of God, so that they too will be counted as righteous (Is 49:1–6; 53). God is a *father* and Israel is his *son,* whom he has fed, carried, and taught to walk (Hos 11:1–3); "As often as I speak against him, I do remember him still. Therefore my heart yearns for him: I will surely have mercy on him, says the Lord" (Jer 31:9). And if God is Israel's father, Jerusalem is his *mother,* whom God has not divorced (Is 50:1–2). Likewise, God is Israel's *husband,* and she is his *bride.* "Fear not . . . for your maker is your husband, the Lord of Hosts is his name . . . the Lord has called you like a wife forsaken and grieved in spirit. . . . For a brief moment I forsook you, but with great compassion I will gather you. In overflowing wrath for a moment I hid my face from you, but with everlasting love I will have compassion on you, says the Lord your Redeemer" (54:5–8).

Thus, say the prophets, God and Israel are covenanted together in a permanently binding relationship of love and reciprocal obligation, a prototype of the marriage covenant. With the erring human partner returned to the Torah, Israel will also be returned to the Land, and to Jerusalem. And with the exiles returned, the Temple would be rebuilt and the house of David restored (Am 9:11). On that day, "a shoot will come forth from the stump of Jesse, and a branch shall grow out of its roots; and the spirit of the Lord will rest upon him . . . and his delight will be in the fear of the Lord" (Is 11:1). The repentant

3. Paul affirms the same belief, Rom 9–11, esp. 11:28–32.

and redeemed nation, under a righteous ruler, would rededicate itself to Torah, for God will have turned aside from his anger and ceased his punitive destruction, swearing to Israel as he had once sworn to all mankind in the distant days of an earlier covenant:

> For this is like the days of Noah to me:
>> as I swore that the waters of Noah
>> should no more go over the earth
> so have I sworn that I will not be angry with you
>> and will not rebuke you.
> For the mountains may depart
>> and the hills be removed,
> but my steadfast love shall not depart from you,
>> and my covenant of peace shall not be removed,
>> says the Lord, who has compassion on you. (Is 54:9–10)

Israel need not fear, for she rests on the foundation of God's promise to Abraham, Isaac, and Jacob:

> Look to the rock from which you were hewn,
>> and to the quarry from which you were digged.
> Look to Abraham your father
>> and to Sarah who bore you;
> for when he was but one I called him . . .
>
> . . . .
> For the Lord will comfort Zion . . .
>
> . . . .
> Listen to me, my people,
>> and give ear to me, my nation;
> for a teaching [Heb. *torah*] will go forth from me,
>> and my justice for a light to the nations.
>
> . . . .
> Hearken to me, you who know righteousness,
>> the people in whose heart is my torah;
> fear not the reproach of men . . .
>
> . . . .
> . . . my deliverance will be for ever,
>> and my salvation to all generations. (Is 51:1–8)

Repentance would meet mercy and forgiveness, as God had vowed to Moses when he gave the Torah to Israel: "If they confess their iniquity . . . then I will remember my covenant with Jacob, and I will remember my covenant with Isaac and with Abraham, and I will remember the Land" (Lv 26:41–42).

When the exiles return to Zion, God will renew his covenant. It will be a new covenant, because the people will not need to hear or read or study it. It will be in their hearts: "This is the covenant which I will make with the house of Israel in those days, says the Lord: I will put my torah within them, and I will write it upon their hearts. I will be their God, and they shall be my people . . . and I will remember their sin no more" (Jer 31:31–32).

Israel's suffering has redemptive meaning, the prophets urged. Dispersion does not disconfirm God's promise, but expresses it: his punishments are born of a steady love. Through chastisement, Israel will come to repent her iniquity and will learn to do justice and righteousness. Thus the historical dialectic of exile and return rearticulates the spiritual dialectic of straying and returning (in the later Hebrew idiom, to "do *tshuvah*'," i.e., repent), of turning from the Torah and turning toward the Torah, of sin and righteousness, of God's absence and presence. Through exile and tshuvah Israel would realize the promise to Abraham and bring blessings to the nations. Through Israel's faithfulness to Torah, peace would come to the whole world.

> Zion will be redeemed by justice,
>   and those in her who repent, by righteousness.
>
> And it shall come to pass in the latter days
>   that the mountain of the house of the Lord
> shall be established as the highest of the mountains,
>   and shall be raised above the hills.
> And all the nations shall flow to it,
>   and many people will come and say,
> "Come, let us go up to the mountain of the Lord
>   to the house of the God of Jacob
> that he may teach us his ways
>   and that we may walk in his paths."
> For out of Zion shall come forth the torah
>   and the word of the Lord from Jerusalem.
>
> . . . .
> Nation shall not lift up sword against nation,
>   neither shall they learn war any more.   (Is 1:27; 2:2–4)

In the wake of the terrible war with Rome, the late first-century Jewish community reaffirmed the prophetic answer to the problem of evil. It looked through the Roman destruction of Jerusalem and the ruin of the Second Temple to the literature produced by ancestors who had suffered in like wise at the hands of Assyrians and Babylonians—just as that generation, also driven into exile and slavery, had looked in its distress to the covenant at Sinai and, behind that, to the exile and slavery in Egypt, when God had brought his people out "with a strong arm and a mighty hand," keeping the promise he had made to the ancestor of his people, the first exile, Abraham.

Thus the Jewish response to the problem of evil was to turn to the very phenomenon that put the question: human history. And the pain and the puzzle of that history was interpreted and given meaning in light of the Torah, the promise of redemption, the certitude of the covenant: a bond between God, the people, and the Land going back through David to Moses to Abraham. And as a surety of their covenant, sanctified by the Sabbath that God shared through his Torah with Israel alone, stood Creation itself (Gn 2:1–3; Ex 31:12–17):

Thus says the Lord,
who gives the sun for light by day
    and the fixed order of the moon and the stars for light by night;
who stirs up the sea so that its waves roar—
    The Lord of Hosts is his name:
If this fixed order departs
    from before me, says the Lord,
Then shall the descendents of Israel cease
    from being a people before me forever.

. . . .
If the heavens above can be measured
    and the foundations of the earth below be explored,
then will I cast off all the descendents of Israel
    for all that they have done,
                              says the Lord. (Jer 31:35–37)

THE EXPECTATION OF REDEMPTION: RESTORATION THEOLOGY

The Exile ended in 538 B.C.E., following Babylon's capitulation to Persia. Cyrus the Great permitted the Jews to return home where, under Ezra and Nehemiah, they rebuilt the Temple and organized their observance of Torah around Temple obligations (2 Chr 36:22–23). During this period as well, according to modern criticism, the text of Torah was redacted in light of the recent Babylonian Captivity. This trauma, infused with religious meaning, served ultimately to affirm the tradition's view of the inviolability of the covenant.

But in the period beginning with Alexander and ending with Rome (late fourth century B.C.E. to mid-second century C.E.), Jews faced a new and different trauma. The experience of Exile had been well incorporated into their religious consciousness and their theology, but nothing in their tradition prepared them to cope with the crisis of continuing occupation. Instead of exile in an idolatrous kingdom, Jews now faced the situation of living in an alienated land. This was their land, God's land, pledged to holiness and seen as holy, and now ruled by idolators whose policies could at any time affect the operation of the Temple itself and the populace's ability to observe the ordinances of the Torah. Jews still living in the Diaspora experienced this problem less acutely than those for whom the presence and power of such a government was a daily reality. For this population, crisis followed crisis; and the first, which set a pattern for all the others, was under Antiochus Epiphanes, the Seleucid ruler of territorial Palestine.

Military Initiatives

In the eyes of the writer of I Maccabees, the trouble really began when certain Jews, desirous of adopting the culture of Hellenism, violated the covenant.

> In those days lawless men came forth from Israel and misled many, saying "Let us go and make a covenant with the Gentiles round about us, for since we have separated from them, many evils have come upon us." This proposal pleased them, and some of the people eagerly went to the king [Antiochus]. He authorized them to observe the ordinances of the Gentiles. So they built a gymnasium in Jerusalem . . . and removed the marks of circumcision, and abandoned the holy covenant. They joined with the Gentiles, and sold themselves to doing evil.   (1 Mc 1:11–15)

Among these "lawless men" was one Jason, a priest who attempted to buy the High Priesthood, in part by promising Antiochus to turn Jerusalem into a Hellenistic city. The similar aspirations of his rival, Menelaus, soon occasioned a clash between their respective factions, which Antiochus interpreted as a revolt against himself (*AJ* 12.5, 1–4). He attacked and subdued Jerusalem and undertook to enforce a policy of Hellenization, forbidding his subjects to observe their peculiar ordinances and directing "them to follow customs *strange to the land*" (1 Mc 1:41–42). Finally, he went so far as to erect an altar to Zeus in the Temple itself (forever after regarded in Jewish tradition as "the abomination of desolation"; 1 Mc 1:54,59; Dn 11:31; 12:11; cf. Mk 13:14, perhaps with reference to a similar action contemplated by Caligula in 40–41 C.E.).[4] Many in Israel apostatized. Many resisted passively, preferring death to apostasy. But many also joined the revolt led by the family of Mattathias, a priest. Ultimately his sons threw off the Seleucids, purified and rededicated the Temple, and reestablished Jewish rule in Palestine under their family, the Hasmoneans (c. 165).

At the root of the Maccabees' victory, in the eyes of the tradition, was their spiritual motivation and zeal for the Torah (e.g., 1 Mc 2:23ff.; Mattathias' death speech, 2:51–68). They thus served as a model of piety to later generations oppressed by the power of Rome. The great hope, in light of Maccabean success, was that the restoration of Israel could be inaugurated or achieved

---

4. Brandon explores the interplay between this incident from the Seleucid period and the ways that first-century Jews would have regarded Caligula's effort, *Jesus and the Zealots,* pp. 87–91.

militarily by warriors whose piety matched their prowess—a combination of attributes that characterized no less a person than Israel's first king and God's messiah, David. I will examine messianic speculation in this period shortly. Here I should note that, in analyzing Jewish responses to foreign occupation in this period, I make an anachronistic distinction between the political and religious sphere. The people who lived these events drew no such distinction: armed insurrection was an expression of religious hope.

Such rebellions continually marked the regimes of the Idumaean rulers installed by Rome after 63 B.C.E., when Hasmonean rule effectively came to an end. They were ruthlessly put down. Herod the Great (at the end of whose reign, according to the evangelists Matthew and Luke, Jesus was born) summarily executed one Ezekias the Galilean and "a great number" of his followers (to the protests of the Jewish court, the Sanhedrin; Josephus, *AJ* 14.9,2–3; *BJ* 1.10,5); later he had two religious leaders, Judas and Matthias, burned to death for having incited crowds in Jerusalem to tear down offending aquiline insignia that he had placed over the Temple gate (*AJ* 17.6,2; *BJ* 1.33,2). In 6 C.E., Varus, the Roman legate to Syria, had to put down a tax revolt in Judea led by Judah the Galilean, the son of the executed Ezekias. The revolt had been spurred by Rome's assumption of direct administrative power over Judea; eventually, Varus crucified some 2,000 rebels in order to pacify the countryside (*AJ* 17.10,9–10; *BJ* 2.5,2). Josephus' disapproving description of this rebellion relates the religious convictions which stood behind it: the insurgents, refusing to cooperate with the Roman census under Quirinius (Luke's device for getting the Holy Family from Nazareth to Bethlehem), urged that God would certainly join with them against Rome, for God and God alone was their king (*AJ* 18.1,1 and 6). The strength and success of their insurrection are the measure of their confidence in divine assistance.

Roman insensitivity to Jewish religious feeling in this period, particularly on the issue of introducing images into Jerusalem, seems to have bordered on deliberate provocation, and popular protest was always quickly subdued. One official of special interest, of whom descriptions survive in several sources, is Pontius Pilate, governor of Judea from 26 to 36 C.E. Josephus reports that he gratuitously provoked popular outrage when, contrary to usual Roman practice, he brought standards bearing imperial images into Jerusalem (*BJ* 2.9,2–3; *AJ* 18.3,1). Later a bloody riot ensued when he sought to appropriate Temple funds for the construction of a new aqueduct (*BJ* 2.9,4; *AJ* 18.3,2). Philo describes him as a man of "inflexible, stubborn, and cruel disposition," whose administration was marked by his "venality, thefts, assaults, abusive behavior, and his frequent murders of untried prisoners," among whom probably Jesus of Nazareth.[5]

5. Reported by Philo in *ad Gaium* 38.302; for discussion, see Schürer, *HJP* 1:383ff; E. Mary Smallwood, *Jews under Roman Rule*, esp. pp. 144–80. The second-century Roman historian Tacitus, himself no Judeophile, implicitly acknowledges the misgovernment of Judea, *Hist.* V.9,3–10,1.

The worse the perceived oppression, the more desperate, and hence stronger, the rebellion. Caligula's death in 41 C.E. averted the major convulsion that surely would have followed his order to have his own statue placed in the Temple.[6] Shortly thereafter, during the procuratorship of Fadus (c. 44–46), a significant multitude gathered around a prophet named Theudas in anticipation of his parting of the waters of the Jordan River—an act certain to recall both Israel's taking possession of the land under Joshua and that archetypical miraculous liberation, the Exodus from Egypt (Jos 3:13–14; Ex 14:16ff.). Roman cavalry cut him and his followers down (AJ 20.5,1). A few years later, around 46–48 C.E., two sons of Judah the Galilean, James and Simon, were crucified. Presumably they, like their father, had been instigating rebellion (AJ 20.5,2).

So it continued. Under Cumanus (48–c. 52), Jerusalem, swollen with pilgrims at Passover, broke into riot when antagonized by the insulting gesture of a Roman soldier. Many rioters were killed (BJ 2.12,1; AJ 20.5,3). Later, a murderous skirmish between Jews and Samaritans resulted in a further round of crucifixions (BJ 2.12,3–7; AJ 20.6,1–3). The country sank into a constant state of agitation under Antonius Felix (c. 52–60?), whose notorious misgovernment strengthened popular support for armed political "robbers" and assassins (BJ 2.12,8–13,2; AJ 20.7,1–8,5). Crowds continued to flock to manifestly apocalyptic activists. One, a Jew from Egypt, proclaimed himself a prophet and assembled a huge following in the desert (four thousand according to Acts 21:38; thirty thousand according to BJ 2.13,5), planning to march on Jerusalem. Its walls would collapse, he promised, at his command—a wonder that would have recalled the conquest of the land under Joshua (Jos 6:20). Felix attacked and scattered this crowd before the miracle could occur.

This volatile juxtaposition of official provocation or ineptitude and popular agitation finally ignited in open revolt in 66, in the Diaspora and especially in Jerusalem, where sacrifices on behalf of the emperor and the Gentiles were suspended and Roman troops slaughtered. The rebels held the imperial army at bay outside the city for some three years until, in 70, Titus finally breached its defenses and burned down the Temple.[7] Even in the face of this catastrophe, prophets within Jerusalem were predicting God's imminent intervention, urging people to assemble by the burning Temple, "that there they should receive miraculous signs of their deliverance . . . from God" (BJ 6.5,2). Indeed, Josephus claims, the chief inducement to insurrection had been an "ambiguous oracle" in scripture announcing "that a man from their country

6. On this plan of Caligula's see Philo, ad Gaium 30.203–42.337; BJ 2.10,2–5; AJ 18.8,2–9; Schürer, HJP 1:394–98; Smallwood, Jews under Roman Rule, pp. 174–80.
7. On the war of 66–73, Schürer, HJP 1:484–513; Smallwood, Jews under Roman Rule, pp. 293–388; Brandon, Fall of Jerusalem, esp. pp. 154–66, and Jesus and the Zealots, pp. 65–145.

would become monarch of the whole world" (*BJ* 6.5,4).[8] Considering these things ex post, Josephus knew the oracle to have been fulfilled in Vespasian, who was declared emperor while in Judea. But for the Jews who had placed their faith in it, this prophecy had foretold the coming of the messiah.

The destruction of Jerusalem and of the Second Temple was a major blow both to the political aspirations and to the religious institutions of Judaism. The supreme Jewish court, the Sanhedrin, ceased to exist; the sacrifices required by the Torah and restricted to the Temple could no longer be performed.

The blow should have been devastating. But Jewish history was familiar with precisely this disaster: the worst had already happened once before. In the meantime, religious scholars dedicated themselves to preserving, in minute detail, a record of the operations of the Temple sacrifices, evidently in anticipation of their eventual restoration. Armed revolt against Rome, both in the Diaspora and most especially in the homeland, continued.[9] The last major insurrection, during the reign of Hadrian in 132–35 C.E., was led by Simon bar Kochba, the Son of the Star (an allusive reference to the messianic image in Nm 24:17), who was recognized by no less an authority than Rabbi Akiva as the messiah. With his defeat, and the construction of a pagan city on the site of Jerusalem, militant messianism discredited itself as a viable expression of Jewish piety. Turning to Torah, recalling the days of the Babylonian devastation and the return of the exiles, Jews expressed their longing for independence through prayer—prayer for the restoration of Jerusalem and the rebuilding of the Temple, the consolation of Zion, the raising of the fallen tabernacle of David.[10] Rome was not Seleucid Syria, and the example of the Maccabees had to be put aside.

Apocalyptic Eschatology

This period of intense political turmoil, popular unrest, and occasional armed confrontation which stretches from Antiochus Epiphanes to the emperor Hadrian forms the tragic and highly charged political backdrop to

8. Roman historians were also aware of the popular belief in these messianic prophecies, Tacitus, *Hist.* V.13; Suetonius, *Vespasian* 4:5.

9. See esp. S. Applebaum, *Jews and Greeks in Ancient Cyrene,* and Smallwood, *Jews under Roman Rule,* pp. 389–427, on the Jewish revolt in the Diaspora in 115–17; on the Bar Kochba revolt, Smallwood, pp. 428–66, and Applebaum, *Prolegomena to the Study of the Second Jewish Revolt.* See also Schürer, *HJP* 1:514–57.

10. On the chief synagogue prayer, the *Amidah* or *Shemoneh-Esreh* (the Eighteen Benedictions), see Schürer, *HJP* 2:454–63. While the final form of the prayer postdates the destruction of the Second Temple in 70, the prayer itself is much older. On the blessings after meals (*Birkat hamazon*) and the Amidah, see also Moore, *Judaism in the First Centuries* 1:174–79. For a historical and exegetical analysis of all of these, J. Heinemann, *Prayer in the Talmud.*

the life and public career of Jesus of Nazareth. Hope in God's salvation, in the teeth of such misery, was periodically expressed by military endeavor. But this hope and the courage and conviction to act on it both created and were sustained by a particular orientation toward God and the world that scholars have named *apocalyptic eschatology*.[11]

Apocalypse means the "revelation of hidden things." *Eschaton* means "the end." Apocalyptic eschatology thus means the revelation of knowledge concerning the end of time, which will bring God's definitive, and ultimate, intervention in history. Certain key items associated with this event appear variously, and in various combinations, in Jewish apocalyptic literature. Chief among these are that God will establish his Kingdom; that Jerusalem, and thus the Temple, will be rebuilt or restored; that the exiles will be gathered in; the unrighteous punished; idolatry vanquished; and suffering and travail will be replaced by an everlasting peace.

The reader will recognize in this list major themes from the prophetic response to Israel's experience under Assyria and Babylon. Indeed, at the heart of apocalyptic is the same conviction that inspired the prophets: God's covenant with Israel is everlasting, the apparent counter-evidence of present events notwithstanding, and therefore God will surely redeem and restore his people. But something crucial has changed here. The "restored" Israel is an idealized Israel, one that the scriptures never claimed to have been: a people entirely dedicated to Torah, with a priesthood and a Temple universally recognized as pure, under a perfect monarch, living and left in peace. And its perfections are universalized: what for the earlier prophets was to be a historical event in the life of Israel becomes, in apocalyptic writings, what God will bring about at the end of time, changing the nature of historical reality itself. Apocalyptic eschatology thus projects onto the universe the experience of the Exile and Return from Babylon. The entire world will experience Israel's redemption, for it will signal the redemption of the entire world.

Happy people do not write apocalypses. The apocalyptic description of the joyful future that awaits—that is in fact imminent—is the mirror image of the perception of present times, which are seen as uniquely, indeed terminally, terrible. Small wonder then that apocalyptic literature flourished in this troubled period between the Maccabees and Bar Kochba, a literature whose esoteric symbolism could cloak a political critique. The final enemy was always the apocalyptic "Babylon," be it incarnated as the Seleucid Empire or Rome.

But apocalyptic symbolism provided more than just protective camouflage for potentially dangerous political statements. It also enhanced the prestige

---

11. Consensus definitions exist for neither word. I use the phrase in this book to convey the idea of expecting the End soon. Sanders avoids this terminological awkwardness by speaking of "Jewish restoration theology" (*JJ*, passim); see also chap. 3, n. 1.

and mystique of these writings and gave them almost unlimited interpretive elasticity. The more obscure the symbolism, the more privileged the reader who understood it and the more elevated the revelation. The hearer of the apocalyptic message could know what those outside could not: that the almost insulting arbitrariness of history actually concealed patterns of significance that converged and would shortly be manifest in the hearer's own day. Current events need not dishearten since, as those privy to such revelations knew, they really pointed to an impending salvation. Moreover, the denser or more esoteric the symbolism, the more flexible the text. For symbolism invites interpretation; and reinterpretation preserves the relevance of a text for future readers: its symbolic code can always be made to fit a new context. Thus, though apocalyptic predictions might be disconfirmed, they never need be discredited.[12] And if adversity and oppression continue, the vision of the End will only be reinforced.

Thus the crisis of foreign oppression, which had earlier called forth the prophetic writings of the seventh and sixth centuries B.C.E., produced a revival of the prophetic vision beginning in the second. Some of these later prophets—men such as John the Baptist, Jesus, Theudas, and the Egyptian—made direct pronouncements on their own authority and left no writings. Those who did write could "borrow" authority from earlier tradition, either interpreting classical writings in light of their own apocalyptic convictions or ascribing authorship of their own visionary writings to an authoritative figure from the past.

The Essenes of Qumran, a separatist community, exercised both these options. They produced extensive commentaries on classical sources (Torah and the prophets) while composing their own visionary literature. The author of the Book of Daniel, interpreting events during the Maccabees' revolt against Antiochus, chose to place his composition in the period of the Babylonian Captivity, when the historical Daniel lived. The astounding "accuracy" of Daniel's prophecy—actually veiled descriptions of current events—served to enhance this text's authority.

Other visionaries chose personae from the glorious days of Israel's past. A psalm of "Solomon," appearing shortly after Pompey's capture of Jerusalem in 63 B.C.E., predicted the ultimate triumph of God and his chosen, the anointed king. In another screed, probably from the first century C.E., "Moses" confided to Joshua a vision of the travails before the final triumph; while "Baruch," the companion of Jeremiah, depicted (sometime after 70 C.E.) the coming resurrection of the dead. "Enoch" (second century B.C.E. to first

12. See the literary study of Frank Kermode, *The Sense of an Ending*. Harvey, *Jesus and Constraints*, pp. 66–97, provides a good discussion of the logic of apocalyptic thought. For a sociological perspective, see the study of Leon Festinger, Henry W. Reicken, and S. Schachter, *When Prophecy Fails*.

century C.E.?), whom popular legend, on the basis of Gn 5:24, held to have been translated directly to heaven and who was therefore a particularly well-placed source of revelations, spoke of the renovation of Jerusalem and the coming judgment of the Son of Man. Another anonymous apocalypticist used an entirely different strategy: by appropriating the form of Greek hexameter verses that traditionally expressed the visions of pagan oracles, the Sibyls, he had a Gentile spiritual authority predict the ultimate turning of the Gentiles toward the God of Israel.[13]

All these writings voiced the belief that the End was fast approaching and the final restoration of Israel was at hand. But this conviction was expressed in a great variety of ways, for apocalyptic Judaism, like Judaism generally, tolerated a broad spectrum of interpretation. Thus in this literature we find no strict consistency or systematic body of doctrine, but rather a certain coherence of concepts, images, and expectations. We might distill from these the following general outline of events expected near or at the End:

The oppression of the righteous (Israel) by the unrighteous (Gentiles, Jewish apostates, etc.) is about to enter a final phase in which both social and natural order will be aggressively disrupted. Earthquakes, floods, and celestial disturbances will mirror human anarchy, where armies clash and even family members turn against one another. When things finally reach their worst, on the Day of the Lord, God will take active control of events. Either he himself will lead the battle against the forces of evil (Zec, Assumption of Moses), or else he will send his prophet Elijah to anoint his messiah, who will lead the Army of God. Or perhaps he will send his messiah himself (2 Bar), or delegate the military duties to a nonhuman hero figure, the Son of Man (2 Esd).

This turn of events will be sudden. The forces of good will utterly vanquish the hostile powers, demonic or human, and the Kingdom of God will finally, truly be established. And in this kingdom will dwell two peoples: restored Israel and the morally transformed Gentiles. Jerusalem, renewed and glorious, will gather to herself all her scattered children from the farthest reaches of the earth, both the living and the dead (Is 26:19; Ez 37:1–14; Dn 12:1–3—an extension of the idea both of the in-gathering of the Exiles and of the vindication of the righteous). And all the nations of the earth, abandoning idolatry, will likewise come to Jerusalem to worship God at the new Temple (Is 2:2ff.; Mi 4:1; 1 En 90:30–33; Sib Or 3.616,716). If a messiah rules over this kingdom, he knows that the true king is God (Ps Sol). A last judgment will precede a universal renewal in which nature itself will be transformed: the earth will yield up abundant riches, the lion will lie down with the lamb. And the peace of God, mediated through his Torah, will emanate from Jerusalem to the whole world.

13. These texts may be found in the anthology edited by J. H. Charlesworth, *Old Testament Pseudepigrapha*, 2 vols. For a systematic presentation of apocalyptic eschatology, Schürer, *HJP* 1:514–47.

Nothing in this scenario, except for the sequence travail/bliss, is fixed. There is no consensus, for example, on whether all the dead will be resurrected or only the saints; on who will lead the apocalyptic battle; on how many of the Gentiles will perish in their sins or turn in the end to God. Most important of all, for this study, is the breadth of speculation concerning the apocalyptic redeemer figures, the Son of Man and the messiah.

The expression Son of Man occurs in three explicitly apocalyptic works: in Daniel, chapter 7, and in two later writings which draw on Daniel, 2 Esdras and 1 Enoch. In his vision, "Daniel" relates briefly, "behold, with the clouds of heaven there came one like a Son of Man. He came before the Ancient of Days [God], and was presented before him, and to him was given dominion and glory and kingdom" (7:13–14). "One like a son of man" means "something or someone in human form" (cf. Ez 38–39, where God addresses the prophet: there the periphrasis simply means "you," i.e., a human). But Daniel seems to refer here to a corporate entity, the eschatological Israel of the saints. Thus "one like a Son of Man" was given "dominion and glory and kingdom" (7:14), while the saints, after much persecution and suffering, receive "dominion" and greatness and "everlasting kingdom" (7:27). In other words, when Daniel prophesies that Israel's suffering will lead to its vindication at the end of time (12:9), he seems to speak in terms of a "son of man" much as Isaiah, in similar circumstances, had spoken in terms of a "suffering servant."[14] Daniel does not equate such a figure with the messiah, whom he names later in his text as a human being who falls in battle. "After the sixty-two weeks, the messiah will be cut off and be no more" (9:26). Here the author most likely refers cryptically to a particular political figure slain in a struggle over Jerusalem, to whom historians have assigned various identifications.

On the other hand, 2 Esdras 13 sees the Son of Man as a supernatural redeemer, though resembling a human being, whose gaze and voice cause humanity to tremble. The author of Enoch identifies this figure with the heavenly Enoch, seated on God's throne of glory. The spirit of righteousness is poured out on him; the word of his mouth slays sinners; he is a staff to the righteous and a light to the Gentiles (1 En 46–48). Such description draws on messianic imagery, and indeed the author elsewhere calls Enoch the Lord's Elect One.

By contrast, the messiah of biblical and rabbinic tradition is definitely and truly human. In the Hebrew Bible, the term (which occurs only thirty-nine times) usually designates the current ruler of Judah or Israel: being anointed with oil was the way one assumed office in the ancient Near East. Accordingly, we also find *meshiach* (anointed one) in reference to the High Priest (e.g., Lv 4:3, 5, 16). But at one point the entire people are called "God's anointed" (Ps

105:15; 1 Chr 16:22), and elsewhere so is Cyrus the Persian, "whose right hand I have grasped, to subdue nations before him" (Is 45:1), no doubt because Cyrus was a mighty warrior who executed judgment on Babylon and freed the exiles to go home.

But the historical anchor for the messianic tradition is the warrior king David. Thus in intertestamental apocalyptic writings, we may find two messiahs at the final battle, one priestly and one military (1 QS 9:11), or only one messiah (e.g., 2 Bar), or no messiah at all (Assumption of Moses). But where we do find a messiah, he is a human being, albeit divinely endowed and empowered to lead God's forces in the eschatological battle.[15] Like the David esteemed by tradition, the messiah will be someone in whom are combined the traits of courage, piety, military prowess, justice, wisdom, and knowledge of Torah. The Prince of Peace must first be a man of war: his duty is to inflict final defeat on the forces of evil. But—and, in light of the symbol's resonance with the royal and military Davidic tradition, unsurprisingly—we find in the Judaism of this period no idea that the messiah is to die to make atonement for sin. The dying messiah falls in battle, a prelude to the coming messiah son of David; the one whose sufferings expiate the sins of others in the Servant Songs of Isaiah is the people of Israel.[16] These two concepts might be conjoined in a later, and significantly different, first-century apocalyptic movement; but within traditional Judaism they were distinct.

Thus, given their evocation of the independent monarchy, the Return from Babylon, and that fundamental myth of redemption, the Exodus, the term *messiah* and indeed the whole tenor of apocalyptic eschatology express a memory and a hope of liberation that no astute ruling foreign power could fail to perceive as threatening. Any such religious revivalism in a polity such as Israel, where religion and politics were scarcely distinguishable in principle, would have had a decidedly political aspect. Small wonder then that Jews in this period who proclaimed the nearness of the Kingdom of God, and perhaps of his messiah, would find themselves the objects of Rome's active displeasure.

PALESTINIAN JUDAISM IN THE TIME OF JESUS

In the political tinderbox of early first-century Palestine, despite (or perhaps, in part because of) the constraints imposed by Rome, Judaism flourished in vigorous variety. Josephus reviews four of the major groups within Judaism at

15. Some rabbis later held that the *name* of the messiah had existed before creation, i.e., that it had been created before the world, along with other realities of paramount importance: Torah, repentance, the Garden of Eden, Gehenna (Hell), the Throne of Glory, and the Temple (bPes 54a). Such statements indicate the religious significance of the given concept, not its metaphysical existence. Cf. 1 En 62:7 for the preexistence of the Son of Man.

16. Traditions concerning the dying messiah are conveniently collected in R. Patai, *Messiah Texts,* pp. 104–21. See also Schürer, *HJP* 1:547–49.

this time—the Sadducees, the Pharisees, the Essenes, and the Zealots—which, for the benefit of his pagan audience, he calls "philosophical schools." If we add to these the categories of charismatic healers and prophets and of peasants (*amme ha-aretz*) unaffiliated with any of these groups, we may orient ourselves in the religious topography of Palestinian Judaism at the time of Jesus.

Sadducees

The Sadducees were the "school" composed mainly of the sacerdotal aristocracy of Jerusalem. Their piety focused particularly on the Temple, since as priests they were responsible for the performance of the sacrifices. This fact accounts for two others: the political quietism of the Sadducees, and their disappearance after the war of 66–73.

The priestly aristocracy had functioned as a ruling elite for several centuries by this period. With the collapse of Hasmonean power in the mid-first century B.C.E., the priests became the mediators between the general populace and the foreign governing authorities (especially Roman colonial officials), with whom they could share a common culture, since they tended to be more Hellenized than other sections of the population. As a good working relationship with Rome helped guarantee the uninterrupted operation of the Temple, these aristocrats inclined toward the governing powers politically as well. Nonetheless, with the serious disintegration of the political situation in 66, it was Eleazar the son of the High Priest who triggered revolt by prohibiting sacrifices on behalf of the Empire (*BJ* 2.17,2).

The Sadducees' spiritual orientation is difficult to reconstruct, for they left no texts of their own. The evidence we have comes from hostile witnesses: the rabbis (the spiritual descendents of the Sadducees' rivals, the Pharisees); Josephus (a Pharisee himself, despite his priestly background); and the gospels (which on certain issues reflect the Pharisaic point of view, e.g., Mk 12:18–27 and parr.). Alone of all the groups in this period, the Sadducees apparently did not believe in resurrection, a position which indicates their overall attitude toward the correct interpretation of Torah. They were "strict constructionists," arguing that only what stood explicitly in the written text was religiously binding and authoritative: all else was interpretation.

Josephus states that the Sadducees' position on this and other issues alienated public opinion, so that "when they become magistrates, unwillingly and by force sometimes they addict themselves to the notions of the Pharisees, for otherwise the multitude would not bear them" (*AJ* 18.1,4). It is difficult to know whether this statement reveals anything other than Josephus' own position. Together with the Pharisees, the largely Sadducean priestly aristocracy comprised (and probably dominated) the Sanhedrin, the Jewish supreme court in Jerusalem that exercised judicial, civic, and religious authority.[17]

17. Sanders, *JJ*, pp. 309–17, discusses the nature of Jewish leadership during the Roman occupation; see also Schürer, *HJP* 2:199–226 (the Sanhedrin), 404–14 (the Sadducees).

Ultimately, however, Rome decided the outcome of the Sadducean/Pharisaic rivalry, for with the war came the destruction of the Temple and the end of any sort of Jewish political government. Thus deprived of their raison d'être, the Sadducees faded from Jewish history.

Pharisees

The Pharisees, who according to Josephus numbered approximately six thousand during the reign of Herod the Great (AJ 17.2,4), formed together with the scribes a "school" of lay interpreters of Torah. They held the Temple in highest esteem, as the material on the Temple preserved in the Mishnah, and so transmitted by them, indicates. But the institution most associated with them was the synagogue. Here worship took the form of community prayer and readings from scripture.

Josephus attributes to the Pharisees a recognized position of leadership during the early first century that neither their numbers nor other evidence seems to support. Since their spiritual heirs, the rabbis, came to define normative Judaism from the second century C.E. onward, it is easy to grant to the Pharisees a retrospective dominance that in their own period they did not in fact enjoy. If we can speak of a "normative Judaism" in a period of so much diversity, this would be what the majority of Jews felt their religion required of them: the sacrifices and practices mandated by biblical law. The Pharisees observed these but interpreted them according to the Oral Law, traditions for interpreting the written Torah that the Pharisees traced back through Ezra and Nehemiah in the early Second Temple period through the prophets to the judges and ultimately to Moses on Sinai, who received them from God.[18] (When Paul tells the Philippians that he was a Pharisee on the issue of the Law, he means that he accepted as sacred and authoritative both Oral and Written Torah; Phil 3:5). Oral Law makes the written text more flexible, so that the Pharisees could find scriptural support for post-biblical beliefs and, as we know from the disputes between the great teachers from the late Second Temple period preserved in the Talmud, a wide range of possible interpretations.[19]

The lineaments of Pharisaic political commitments are less easy to perceive, but indirect evidence suggests that they were as much touched by eschatological hopes as most other Jewish groups, the Sadducees excepted, in this period. It was a Pharisee named Zadok who led the tax revolt in 6 C.E. together with Judah the Galilean (AJ 18.1,1); and it was a rabbi (and hence heir to the Pharisaic traditions), Akiva, who more than a century later declared Bar Kochba the messiah. From the example of Paul and the attestations in Acts, it would seem that some Pharisees found the message of the early Jesus commu-

---

18. mAvot 1.1. See also Moore, *Judaism in 1st Centuries*, 1:251–62.
19. On Hillel and Shammai see ibid., 72–82.

nity, itself a variant messianic movement, congenial enough to join.[20] For the most part, however, the Pharisees seem to have been politically prudent, hoping and praying for God to commence the final days rather than attempting to inaugurate the End themselves.

Essenes

On the Essenes we have two very divergent sources of information. The first is descriptions by outsiders—Pliny the Elder, Philo, Josephus—who present the Essenes as a celibate philosophical community, somewhat on the model of the Neopythagoreans.[21] Most Essenes, these sources tell us, did not marry; they held property in common, living and eating together daily; they did not worship in Jerusalem but remained in their own communities, where they lived a strictly regulated life of prayer and study; and they exceeded all other men in the pursuit and practice of virtue.

The discovery of the Dead Sea Scrolls in 1948 demonstrated once again the value of first-hand evidence over against second-hand (however contemporary) description.[22] For while the Hellenized characterization of the Essenes as philosophers does not contradict what the scrolls reveal, neither does it adequately describe the community. The Essenes saw themselves as living on the edge of time, in the very last days; and they dedicated every moment and aspect of life to preparing, after their fashion, for the coming Kingdom of God.

The historical origins of this separatist group seem to lie in the period of the Maccabees. At that time, Jonathan, the brother of Simon, accepted the office of High Priest even though he was not a member of the correct sacerdotal family. Another priest, known in the scrolls as the Teacher of Righteousness, protested Jonathan's appointment and was forced into exile with his followers. So intense was this group's hatred of the Hasmoneans that they actually rejoiced when, in 63 B.C.E., Pompey conquered Jerusalem and defiled the Temple they considered already polluted by the ministrations of their priestly opponents (1 QpHab 9:4–7). This sullying of the sacred office by a political leader might be what lies behind the Essene expectation of *two* messiahs, one priestly and one military (1 QS 9:1; 1 QSa 2:11ff.).[23] In light of

20. On the Pharisaism of the early movement, see J. Klausner, *Jesus of Nazareth*, and Sanders' more recent discussion, *JJ*, pp. 51–53. According to Josephus, the Pharisees in Jerusalem were on good terms with James the brother of Jesus as late as c. 62, *AJ* 20.9,1.

21. Pliny the Elder, *Natural History* V.15,73; Philo, *quod omnis probus* 12.75–13.91; Josephus, *BJ* 2.8,2–13; *AJ* 13.5,9; 18.1,2. For discussion of this literature see Schürer *HJP*, 2:555–74.

22. It is now generally assumed that the community of the Dead Sea Scrolls was Essene. For a modern translation of this library, Geza Vermes, *The Dead Sea Scrolls in English*, 3d ed. (Harmondsworth 1968); for discussion, Vermes, *The Dead Sea Scrolls: Qumran in Perspective*, and Schürer, *HJP*, 2:575–90; 3:380–469.

23. On the Qumran tradition of two messiahs, Schürer, *HJP*, 2:550–54.

their experience, perhaps they felt that the two functions and offices should be kept distinct.

The members of this sect saw themselves as the privileged recipients of the true covenant, the message of Moses and the Prophets now interpreted correctly in light of the preaching of the Teacher of Righteousness. They kept aloof from their coreligionists, never entering the Temple and, since they followed a solar rather than a lunar calendar, observing the great festivals on different days from the rest of the nation. A solar calendar was particularly appropriate for a group which saw itself as the Sons of Light. They felt obliged while in this world to live in continuous worship and strict ritual purity—to the point where most forswore sexual relations—in anticipation of the approaching Final Battle.[24] Then they would join with the celestial Sons of Light against the forces of darkness and evil. These sectarians, to the outside a quiet scholarly community sequestered by the Dead Sea, lived their days studying and commenting on scripture in order to perceive therein, hidden to all but the True Israel (that is, themselves), the divine plan for the End.

The end that overtook them came in the form of the Roman legions whom they had long ago identified as the final foe. At the zealot fortress of Masada, archeologists have uncovered fragments of Essene literature: perhaps, during the course of the war that was for them the last, the Essenes had embraced the military activism of the zealots. The Essene community did not survive the war.

Insurrectionists

Josephus traces the genesis of the disastrous war in 66–73 back to Judah the Galilean and Zadok the Pharisee, who had led the revolt in 6 C.E. "All sorts of misfortunes sprang from these men, and the nation was infected with this doctrine [i.e., that God would assist armed Jewish rebellion] to an incredible degree; one violent war came upon us after another . . . [so that] the very Temple of God was burnt down by their enemy's fire" (*AJ* 18.1,1). Josephus speaks variously of different armed anti-Roman groups in this period as "brigands" (*lēstai*), "revolutionaries" (*stasiastai*), "dagger-men" (*sicarii*), and "zealots." Though these groups did not agree with one another, as their internecine struggles during the siege of Jerusalem testify, they held in common a sublime confidence in their cause. Their persistent willingness to confront Rome despite overwhelming odds points to the fact that they operated within an apocalyptic framework, inspired by the hope that, once they began the struggle, God would finish it.[25]

These men would look to the Maccabees for their inspiration: as God had

---

24. Philo, Pliny, and Josephus all say that the Essenes rejected marriage, but Josephus also reports a branch that did marry, *BJ* 2.8,12; see also Schürer, *HJP*, 2:578.

25. On sicarii and zealots, Schürer, *HJP*, 2:598–606.

aided his warriors against Antiochus Epiphanes, surely now he would do no less against Caesar. Their master plan was similar. Although their initial sphere of operations might be the highways of the Galilee or the Judean hills, ultimately they too focused on liberating Jerusalem and cleansing the Temple. Hardships endured before God's final intervention were simply to be expected; and even when the city itself lay in flames so fierce that those in Masada, some thirty miles away, could see it burning, the rebels "declared with beaming faces that they cheerfully awaited the end," having left nothing to the enemy (*BJ* 6.7,2).

Pharisaic in their religious orientation but activist in their politics, those of the "school" of Judah the Galilean looked forward to the day, which in their eyes they were helping to bring about, when God would be "their only ruler and Lord" (*AJ* 18.1,6). Ultimately their conviction, combined with the ineptitude and cruelty of the Roman provincial government, mobilized enough of the rest of the nation so that it held off imperial troops for almost three years. The rebel-held fortress of Masada withstood three years longer, its defenders—more than nine hundred men, women, and children—dying by their own hand rather than surrendering to the enemy (*BJ* 7.9,1).

Charismatics

Insurrectionists battled the forces of evil as they saw them manifested in foreign armies. Charismatics carried on their battle against enemies not human but demonic: possession, disease, and sin itself. Signs and wonders were the charismatics' stock in trade, and through them they signaled the intimacy of their relationship with God, who granted them their powers.[26]

Both Josephus and later rabbinical sources, as well as the New Testament, preserve the memory of these individuals. A certain Eleazar expelled demons from possessed persons; Hanina ben Dosa of Galilee worked cures from a distance and, out of piety, embraced poverty. Other charismatics commanded nature: both Honi the Circle-drawer (called Onias in Josephus) and his grandson Hanan enjoyed reputations as rainmakers. One irate Pharisee, affronted by the impertinence of Honi's successful petition for rain, complained, "What can I do with you, since even though you importune God, he does what you wish in the same way that a father does whatever his importuning son asks him?" These wonder-workers themselves were aware of their special relationship with God: Hanan the rainmaker even prayed that his audience would distinguish between himself and the one who truly granted rain, the *Abba* in heaven.[27]

26. My discussion of the charismatics is greatly indebted to Vermes, *Jesus the Jew*, esp. pp. 59–82.

27. Honi, mTaan 3:8; *AJ* 14.22,4; Gen Rabba 13:7; Hanan, bTaan 23b; discussion in Vermes, *Jesus the Jew*, pp. 69–72, 210–13; cf. J. Jeremias' earlier analysis of these passages in *Prayers of Jesus*, pp. 60–61.

Other charismatics were prophets of the End, spokesmen for God, calling the people to prepare for the approach of the Lord. Such were John the Baptist and Jesus. Miracles of course validated one's claim to speak for God. The gospels attribute many to Jesus; Josephus, as we have already noted, tells that Theudas promised to part the Jordan River; the Egyptian, to collapse the walls of Jerusalem; others, to perform marvels before those who followed them out into the desert (*AJ* 20.5,1;8,6; *BJ* 2.13,5). Josephus calls those in this latter group "deceivers," as ex post they must have seemed. But the promise of such mighty works would have been interpreted, in the atmosphere of intensifying hostility to Rome, as announcements of God's approaching Kingdom.[28]

Amme ha-aretz

The vast majority of first-century Palestinian Jews fit none of these categories; they were simply *amme ha-aretz*, "people of the land," peasants. And while ultimately the spirituality of the Pharisees exercised a lasting effect on later Judaism, it was the commitment of the amme ha-aretz to their ancestral religion that ensured its survival.

Common people, obviously, were neither priests nor scholars. They were accordingly relieved of most of the obligation to observe the laws of ritual purity that were incumbent upon the priests. If they wished to fulfill their religious obligations according to the Pharisaic interpretation, they had to study it and thus acquire some education—a fact which sometimes occasioned resentment on both sides.[29]

The main arenas of religious practice, however, were universally recognized and were as accessible to the amme ha-aretz as to his more learned neighbors: the home, the synagogue, and the Temple. In the home, Jews observed most especially the food laws (*kashrut*), the laws of family purity (rules governing permissible times for sexual intercourse between spouses), and the domestic rituals of the holidays. At the synagogue, the community gathered on the Sabbath, and often on the second and fifth days of the week, to hear the Torah and to pray. At the Temple, Jews congregated especially during the chief festivals (Passover, Shavuot, Sukkot). So many would come, Josephus reports, that the Romans always garrisoned extra troops in Jerusalem during the holidays (*BJ* 2.12,1). An individual at any other time could go to the Temple as a pilgrim or to make a personal sacrifice. We cannot ascertain the number of common people who came to the Temple for personal worship, but archeolog-

---

28. Sanders, *JJ*, pp. 170–73.

29. "Rabbi Akiva said, 'When I was an *am ha-aretz*, I used to say, "I wish I had one of these scholars, I would bite him like an ass."'" His disciples said, 'You mean like a dog.' He replied, 'An ass's bite breaks the bone; a dog's does not'" (bPes 49b). See Sanders, *PPJ*, pp. 152–57, and *JJ*, pp. 188–199, on modern scholarship's polemical conflation of the amme ha-aretz with "sinners."

ical evidence shows that the Temple was prepared, indeed designed, to accommodate great numbers of worshippers.

This, then, was the Palestinian Judaism of Jesus' day. The great external fact with which all these groups had to come to terms was Rome. This they did in ways that varied even within a particular group. Sadducees for the most part chose accommodation; but it was the High Priest's son who initiated the revolt in 66 (*BJ* 2.17,2). Pharisees looked forward to the establishment of the Kingdom of God and even, like Zadok, engaged in military insurgence to help bring it about; but other Pharisees, like Yohanan ben Zakkai, repudiated the entire effort and left besieged Jerusalem to the Romans.[30] The Essenes originally hailed Rome for humiliating their Hasmonean enemies and then came to view it as the apocalyptic force of darkness itself. Indeed, reminders of Rome's presence were everywhere, most especially the onerous taxes that weighed on the common people and, together with the encouragements of the insurrectionists, incited them to rebel time and again.

This political situation was of religious concern because, as I have repeatedly noted, Judaism did not draw a distinction between the two spheres: an idolatrous occupying force posed a religious problem. These different groups thus interpreted their religious obligations in light of it. Though ultimately they arrived at various conclusions, they all started within a broad consensus on what was religiously important: the people, the Land, Jerusalem, the Temple, and Torah. Jesus, as an early first-century Jew, would have participated in this consensus. It is now our task to see how this might have been so.

30. Yohanan escaped the city and established a scholarly community at Yavneh (Jamnia) from which, in the wake of the Second Temple's destruction, rabbinic Judaism developed. See esp. J. Neusner, *Life of Yohanan ben Zakkai*.

Chapter 6
Toward a Historical Image of Jesus

We have surveyed the various images of Jesus conveyed by Paul's letters and the gospels. From the diverse and independent Jewish sources that we have reviewed—Biblical scriptures, apocalyptic writings, Philo, Josephus, and later rabbinical works—yet another image of Jesus may be derived. This indirect derivation, based on our reconstruction of Jesus' early first-century Jewish environment, is the task of this chapter.

I shall proceed by distilling an outline of Jesus' story as given in the gospels and, necessarily to a lesser degree, in Paul, recalling *grosso modo* the evangelists' own interpretation of these events. Such an outline is extremely hypothetical, depending as it does ultimately on Mark, who freely constructed the narrative framework of his story for his own purposes. Restricting ourselves to those episodes that pertain to the public career of Jesus, we shall stop where it stops, with his death on the cross. We shall then review the individual items of this outline in light of what we know about Jesus' first-century context. In so doing, we can explore the divergence between what the New Testament presents and what is historically probable and try to account for this divergence. Finally, and briefly, I shall assemble the conclusions gathered from this rereading of the documents into a narrative sketch of the "historical Jesus."

THE FIRST READING

The four gospels unanimously assign to John the Baptist the premier place in inaugurating the public career of Jesus. Mark states the fact outright; Matthew, Luke and John offer various obfuscatory scenarios (Mk 1:9–11; Mt 3:13–17; Lk 3:21–22; Jn 1:29–34). Shortly after this event, Jesus begins his own ministry and gathers his first disciples, twelve of whom form a special inner group (Mk 3:14–19 and parr.).

Jesus' ministry almost immediately occasions crisis and conflict. The Pharisees protest his violation of the Sabbath and the laws of purity and criticize his consorting with sinners, whether Jewish or Gentile. They, however, hold themselves aloof from those most needing guidance and comfort, namely the sinful and the poor. The Pharisees thus reveal themselves to be pious hypocrites, scrupulous in small matters of ritual observance but negligent of more important ethical demands. Against them, Jesus repudiates the rules and announces the good news that God is loving and merciful and forgives repentant sinners. Thus antagonized, the Pharisees plot to destroy him. At this point Jesus predicts not only his own future suffering, but also that of his disciples.

Finally, at Passover, Jesus goes up to Jerusalem. His entry stirs messianic hopes, and he is hailed as the harbinger of the Davidic kingdom (Mk 11:10) or as royalty himself (Mt 21:9; Lk 19:38; Jn 12:12–15). He then enters the Temple area, driving out the money-changers and overturning their tables, earning the enmity of the Jewish leadership in Jerusalem (Mk 11:15–19 and parr.; cf. Jn 2:13–22).

After continuing to teach in the city, Jesus and his disciples prepare either to celebrate a Passover seder (Mk 14:12–16 and parr.), or to eat together the night before the beginning of the holiday (Jn 13:2ff.). During the meal, Jesus presents the bread and wine as his body and blood poured out for many (so the synoptics; Jn has no corresponding scene) and predicts his imminent betrayal.

From this point on, an incredible amount of activity is condensed into a single night. Following supper, Jesus and his disciples, save Judas, retire to a garden. Here Judas betrays Jesus into the hands of a crowd sent by the chief priests and elders (Mt 26:47), or by the chief priests, elders, and scribes (Mk 14:43), or by the chief priests and officers (Lk 22:47; cf. vv. 3–6), or to a band of Roman soldiers together with representatives of the chief priests and the Pharisees (Jn 18:3; cf. v. 12, where the Pharisees drop from view). He is then led before the High Priest and the entire Sanhedrin and sustains both a nocturnal trial during the first night of the festival (Mt 26:57–60//Mk 14:53–64), and, at dawn, a second convention either of the chief priests and elders (Mt 27:1–2) or of the chief priests, elders, scribes, and the whole Sanhedrin (Mk 15:1). Or, following his arrest, he is detained at the High Priest's house for a single morning trial (Lk 22:66–71). Or, on the day before Passover, he is led to the house of Caiaphas the High Priest and questioned by Annas (Jn 18:12–28). Following these episodes, according to all accounts, Jesus is then led before Pilate.

Before the Jewish authorities, whoever and however many they were, the interrogation turns upon issues we might label "religious": Had Jesus threatened to destroy the Temple? (Mt 26:60ff.//Mk 14:57ff.). Had he claimed to be the messiah, or the Son of God, or both? (Mt 26:62 and parr.: Jn records no statements by Annas; 18:19–24). Before Pilate, however, the issue is straight-forwardly political: "Are you the King of the Jews?" (Mt 27:11; Mk 15:2; Lk 23:3; Jn 18:33, one of the few instances of verbal agreement among all four gospels). Jesus answers evasively in the synoptics; in John, he implicitly accepts the title by responding, "My kingdom is not of this world" (18:36). Pilate, who clearly prefers not to be involved in this case (in Lk he even goes so far as to send Jesus to Herod the Tetrarch, 23:6–16), suspects the motives of Jesus' accusers and seeks various ways to save him (Mk 15:1–15 and parr.). Finally, Pilate offers a choice to the crowd suddenly assembled at his doorstep: Shall he release Jesus, or one Barabbas, a known murderer and insurrectionist?

The people demand Barabbas. Pilate, anxious lest he alienate public opinion, at this point renounces any further responsibility in the matter (Mk 15:14–15 and parr.; cf. Jn 19:6, 12–16). He orders Jesus scourged and led away to crucifixion, where he is hanged between two criminals (Mk 15:27 and parr.; Mt uses the term for political brigands, *lēstai*, 27:38). The titulus on the cross reads "King of the Jews" (Mt 27:37; Mk 15:26; Lk 23:38; Jn 19:18, another point of agreement among all four gospels).

While on the cross, Jesus endures further humiliations and insults. The Jews mock him, the criminals revile him from their own crosses, soldiers gamble for his clothes, he is offered bitter wine to drink (Mk 15:22–32 and parr.; cf. Lk 23:40–43; Jn 19:30). Finally, as the sky grows unnaturally dark, the earth shakes, and the curtain of the Temple tears in two, Jesus utters a loud cry and dies (Mk 15:33–37 and parr.).

THE SECOND READING

New Testament historians attempt to sort out fact from later tradition by applying the various critical methodologies reviewed in the first section of this study—dissimilarity, multiple attestation, and so on—to the evangelical accounts of Jesus' ministry. But dispute on the status of individual passages seems virtually endless: a saying or story that evinces a clear "ring of authenticity" for one scholar often displays to another, just as unambiguously, the earmarks of ecclesiastical origin.

Scholars of the first half of our century, stoically acknowledging the nonhistorical interests of the gospel writers and the distance in time, language, and outlook between them and Jesus, embraced a radical skepticism. Consoled by the rigor of their intellectual consistency, they abandoned all hope (at least consciously) of retrieving the Jesus of history. More recently, however, academic attention has refocused on the gospels, examined not for individually authentic or inauthentic statements but for such inferences as can be drawn from them in light of relevant historical knowledge—of Judaism, of first century Palestine, of Roman legal procedure and colonial policy, and so on.

This second approach, in many ways a reaction to the first, has produced something like a consensus on those "almost indisputable facts" that can be known about the public career of Jesus.

The two most secure such facts are those that mark his career's beginning and end: Jesus' baptism by John and his crucifixion by Pilate. These pass the first half of the test of dissimilarity: nothing in early first-century Judaism speaks of a baptized or executed messiah. And, *faute de mieux*, reports of these two events survive in early Christian tradition, despite their being obvious embarrassments. The church, as evidenced by all the various evangelical efforts to mitigate the awkwardness (e.g., John did not really want to baptize Jesus, but Jesus insisted; Pilate did not really want to execute Jesus, but the Jews and finally even Jesus insisted), was stuck with these two facts. They stood too firmly in the tradition to be dropped; the best the various communities could do was soften their effect.

The intuition of earlier scholars was sound: "what really happened" during Jesus' ministry is not recoverable from the evangelical descriptions of what happened. But by examining these descriptions in light of our knowledge of Jesus' historical context, we can establish with reasonable security what *possibly* happened, what *probably* happened, and what *could not possibly* have happened. With this goal in mind, let us review the preceding outline of Jesus' career, from his initiation by John to his encounter with Pilate.

John the Baptist and Jesus

We know of John from two sources: Josephus, *Antiquities* 18.5,2, and the gospels. Josephus reports that John was a pious man who baptized Jews "for the purification of the body when the soul had previously been cleansed by righteous conduct." Translated into traditional terms, John baptized those who had already done tshuvah, repented of their sins. Sins are not forgiven by baptism *ex opere operato:* John is not dispensing a sacrament. Rather, sins are forgiven because the sinner has already repented; he demonstrates his repentance by being baptized in the Jordan. In Josephus' account, in other words, baptism is an alternative or analogue to a sin offering at the Temple.

Josephus continues that so many were so stirred by what John said that Herod Antipas, fearing popular insurrection ("for the people seemed likely to do everything he might counsel") had him executed. But why should Herod have feared this, if all John preached was penitence, purification, and piety? Here the gospels fill in what Josephus leaves only implied. John called to the people to repent their sins in order to prepare for the judgment preceding God's Kingdom: "Repent, for the kingdom of heaven is at hand!" (Mt 3:2). John, in other words, like so many Jews of his day, believed that the hour of Israel's restoration had dawned, perhaps even that the messiah was about to arrive.[1] The potential political import of this message would not have been lost on Herod. Nonetheless, what sealed John's fate was not his message per se, but his message combined with his personal popularity. Such a preacher of such a message, with a committed following, could at any moment ignite revolt.

Jesus heard John's apocalyptic message and responded to it by receiving baptism. Later Christians clearly had difficulty with this fact. Matthew's John almost refuses to baptize Jesus—"John would have prevented him"—but Jesus persuades him by acknowledging the reasonableness of John's protest: Jesus *is* John's superior, but nonetheless he too should fulfill all righteousness (Mt 3:13–15). Luke subordinates John to Jesus from birth (Lk 1:5–80) and passes over the baptism scene in great haste with a subordinate clause (3:21). John the Evangelist emphasizes the relative inferiority of the Baptist to Jesus throughout his gospel (Jn 1:6–8, 19–37; 3:25–30; 4:1, etc.). Historians tend in the face of these evangelical efforts to suspect that the opposite was true: that in their lifetimes John was the more popular leader.[2]

Did the Holy Spirit then appear like a dove? Did a voice from heaven announce to bystanders, or to Jesus alone, or possibly only to John, that Jesus was the beloved divine Son? Of course we cannot know; and these stories as they now stand bear too clearly the stamp of later tradition. But they do point to the fact that it was after his contact with John and his reception of the apocalyptic message that Jesus began his own mission also preparing Israel for the Kingdom.

The Mission and Message of Jesus

How did Jesus take this apocalyptic message to Israel? According to the gospels, in several ways. He presented himself as the uniquely authoritative spokesman for God's Kingdom. He demonstrated his authority by working exorcisms and miracles. And whether by personal example or explicit instruction, he taught against the prevailing Jewish understanding of Torah, while exhorting his followers to live by a new, radical ethic. This question of Jesus and the Law we shall take up later;[3] here we focus instead on the probable content of his positive teachings.

Several strong themes appear in the didactic passages of the gospels. Jesus is

1. All four gospel accounts propose this, by way of foreshadowing Jesus' appearance, Mk 1:7–8 and parr. Cf. Harvey, *Jesus and Constraints,* pp. 75, 89, who seems to interpret the call to repentance as an effort to *avert* the End.

2. Josephus, who to reviews this period, apparently spoke more of John than of Jesus; but his text is difficult, having been much reworked by later Christian interpolators troubled by this discrepancy. See Schürer, *HJP* 1:428–41, with bibliography; also Brandon, *Jesus and the Zealots,* pp. 359–68. According to Acts 18:25 (Apollos), John's baptism had penetrated the Diaspora.

3. See "The Conflict with the Pharisees" and "Hostility to Jesus and the Passion Predictions" later in this chapter.

depicted as especially drawn to the poor, whose very poverty enriches them spiritually (Mt 5:3–12; cf. Lk 6:20–23). So binding is the obligation to care for them that Jesus enjoins an ethic of voluntary poverty on his wealthier followers: "Go, sell all you have, and give it to the poor" (Mk 10:21 and parr.; cf. Mt 5:42//Lk 6:29–30). He also urges breaking off normal ties to family and property, perhaps even to the point of advocating celibacy "for the sake of the kingdom of heaven" (Mt 19:10–12; though cf. the absolute prohibition of divorce, Mk 10:2–9). Evil is to be met with nonresistance; the enemy, with love rather than hatred (Mt 5:38–6:4//Lk 6:27–36). And sinners should not fear exclusion from the community of the redeemed: indeed, because they now follow Jesus, even the most notorious of them—tax collectors and prostitutes—may precede the priests themselves into God's Kingdom (Mt 21.31).

Much in this portrait probably recalls authentic aspects of Jesus' career and message. He probably did work miracles and exorcisms: for one thing, he had a popular following, which an ability to work cures would account for (Mk 1:23–28, 32, 39). Such abilities, in an age of so many healers and miracle-workers, would confer no unique distinction upon Jesus; but coupled with his moral message and his call to prepare for the Kingdom, they may have enhanced his reputation as an authoritative prophet.[4]

Certain of the moral teachings that the evangelists ascribe to Jesus appear in a stratum of Christian tradition earlier than and independent of the gospels, namely, the letters of Paul. Paul too absolutely prohibits divorce ("not I but the Lord"; 1 Cor 7:10–11), exhorts his communities to celibacy (7:29), and teaches that family relations, ideally, should be subordinated to preparations for approaching redemption (7:1–16, 25–40). Persecutors, Paul says, should be blessed; vengeance eschewed; injustice tolerated (Rom 12:9–13:14; cf. 1 Cor 6:7). And the poor back in Jerusalem are the special responsibility of his Gentile churches, who should therefore give cheerfully to their support (2 Cor 9; 1 Cor 16:1–3; Gal 2:10; Rom 15:25–29). The appearance of these teachings in both the gospels and Paul implies a common source: primitive Christian tradition. Might that tradition go back to Jesus himself?

Very likely. These teachings express traditional Jewish beliefs (for instance, that the support of the poor is a religious obligation)[5] or interpretations of such beliefs put forward by other first-century apocalyptically-minded Jews, and so fit Jesus' historical context. The Essenes too, for example, embraced an ethic of celibacy motivated by the desire to prepare for the coming Kingdom,

4. On the relation of healing to religious authority within Judaism, Vermes, *Jesus the Jew,* pp. 86–98; also Sanders, *JJ,* pp. 157–73. Harvey associates Jesus' miracles in particular with the eschatological prophecy in Is 35, *Jesus and Constraints,* pp. 98–119.

5. Support of the poor was a typical expression of Jewish piety; see, e.g., Harvey, *Jesus and Constraints,* p. 143; Moore, *Judaism in 1st Centuries,* 2:162–79. So important did Jews consider this obligation that it was one of the few *mitzvot* (divine injunctions) emphasized during the conversion ceremony of a proselyte; see L. H. Schiffman, "At the Crossroads," pp. 122–25.

and they too minimized status distinctions within their community by eschewing private property.[6] The evangelists, of course, see Jesus teaching such things in contradistinction to Judaism ("You have heard it said . . . but I say . . ."). But these precepts are better understood as the extension or intensification of the ethics encoded in the Torah. Murder brings condemnation (Ex 20:13; Dt 5:17)—but anger is the equivalent of murder (Mt 5:22); adultery is sin (Ex 20:14; Dt 5:18)—but lust itself is already adultery (Mt 5:28); swearing falsely is bad (Lv 19:12)—but swearing itself is wrong (Mt 5:34), and so on. This intensification of ethical norms in the interests of moral regeneration is a phenomenon typical within communities committed to the belief that time is rapidly drawing to a close.[7]

The apocalyptic context of such teachings accounts as well for much of their sheer impracticality. No normal human society could long run according to the principles enunciated in the Sermon on the Mount: total passive non-resistance to evil—indeed, compliance with injustice (Mt 5:38–48//Lk 6:27–36)—and an absolute refusal to judge (Mt 7:1–2//Lk 6:37–38) would simply lead to the exploitation of those abiding by such rules by those who did not. This impracticality in turn allows us to glimpse the intensity of expectation that motivated Jesus' mission and the community that formed around him: the Kingdom was *at hand*. Those who followed Jesus, therefore, really could attempt to conduct their lives according to these demands, since—as Paul, preaching the same ethics in a similar situation of intense expectation, said elsewhere—"the form of this world is passing away" (1 Cor 7:31).

The intensity of this expectation and the social impracticality of these ethics return us to the issue of Jesus' self-presentation as an authoritative spokesman for the coming Kingdom. Christian eschatology as such, in distinction to Jewish eschatology, expresses even at its oldest and most vibrantly apocalyptic level—again, Paul's letters—the paradox of "now/not yet." The Kingdom, and hence Jesus' second coming, loom in the near future; and yet within the *ekklēsia* the Spirit has already been given; the power of the evil *stoicheia* has already been broken; redemption, spiritually if not physically, has already been won (e.g., 1 Cor 2:14–16; 3:16; chaps. 12–14; Gal 4:3–9; Rom 8:10–17, etc.). This theme continues into the canonical gospels where, particularly in Luke and John, the "now"—realized eschatology—subsumes the "not yet" of apocalyptic (Lk 10:9; 11:20; 17:21; Jn 11:25; 14:18–23; etc.).

Jesus' resurrection compelled Paul to profess the presentness of redemp-

6. For a sociological appreciation of these egalitarian eschatological ethics, see John G. Gager, *Kingdom and Community*, pp. 32–37; and Gerd Theissen, *Sociology of Early Palestinian Christianity*, pp. 33–46.

7. "In most renewal movements within Judaism, a stricter interpretation of the Torah was bound up with the imminent expectation of the kingdom of God," Theissen, *Palestinian Christianity*, p. 77; see pp. 77–95. Jesus apparently exercised the timeless Jewish prerogative of choosing to emphasize some aspects of Torah more than others; see Sanders, *JJ*, pp. 245–69.

tion; creation's bondage to decay, its futurity (Rom 8). And the evolving evangelical emphasis on realized eschatology saved Christian tradition from the embarrassments of its apocalyptic past while enhancing the spiritual prestige and value of the church, whose establishment thereby became the object of Jesus' mission. A realized eschatology, in other words, so explains away the difficulty of the continuing delay of the End that it fails the criterion of dissimilarity: the provenance of such a teaching, according to this reasoning, must be the post-resurrection church. Those scholars who want to argue that Jesus really did announce a present rather than future Kingdom somewhat compromise their case by relying, necessarily, on the later strata of gospel tradition.[8] A Jesus preaching such a Kingdom would have been an excellent Christian theologian but a baffling early first-century Jew.

Yet the existence of this strong tradition of intensified Jewish ethics may indicate the preresurrection source of a realized eschatology in Jesus' own preaching. Why would Jesus make such demands of his followers? Why would they listen to him? *Because, as authoritative spokesman of the Kingdom, Jesus created around himself a community of those who would live, prolepticly, according to the "new" Torah written upon their hearts, the Torah according to which all Israel would live when the Kingdom came:*

> Behold, the days are coming, says the Lord, when I will make a new covenant with the house of Israel and the house of Judah. . . . I will put my Torah within them, and will write it upon their hearts; and I will be their God, and they shall be my people. And no longer shall each man teach his neighbor and each his brother, saying, "Know the Lord," for they shall all know me. . . . for I will forgive their iniquity, and I will remember their sin no more.   (Jer 31:31–34)

A radical ethic of love, passive nonresistance, egalitarianism, and propertylessness is impractical in the long run, given man's nature—"for the imagination of man's heart," as God comments after the Flood, "is evil from his youth" (Gen 8:21). But Jesus did not expect a long run; nor did he or his tradition expect life, particularly social and therefore ethical life, to be the same after the Kingdom came as before. Those who accepted him as the Kingdom's authoritative, final forerunner, and who therefore looked forward to the imminent restoration of Israel and redemption of the world, were in a privileged position: having received and accepted advance word, they could prepare for the event they knew was coming. And, accordingly, following the example of their master, they prepared themselves by already, in the last moments of the Old Aeon, living by the intensified, internalized precepts of the Torah that would order Jewish life in the New. And by virtue of this ethical preparation, they could be "first" in—or perhaps into—the kingdom of heaven.

8. The classic argument for Jesus' own "realized eschatology" is found in C. H. Dodd, *Parables of the Kingdom.*

The Twelve Disciples

There is good reason, on first consideration, to question the evangelical report that Jesus had an inner circle of twelve disciples.[9] For one thing, there is no agreement on who they were: the names vary between gospels (Mt 10:2–4; Mk 3:16–19; Lk 6:14–16; Acts 1:13). Further, the concept itself is too conveniently metaphorical: the twelve disciples represent the twelve "new" tribes of the New Israel, the church. This fails the second half of the criterion of dissimilarity.

But Paul, earlier than and largely independent of gospel tradition, also attests to such a group. When arguing with the Corinthians about the resurrection of the dead, he asserts:

> For I delivered to you . . . what I also received, that Christ died for our sins in accordance with the scriptures; that he was buried, that he was raised on the third day in accordance with the scriptures, and that he appeared to Cephas, and then to the twelve. Then he appeared to more than five hundred brethren . . . then to James, then to all the apostles. Last of all . . . he appeared also to me.   (1 Cor 15:3–7)

But why twelve? If the story of Judas' betrayal is historical, then only eleven disciples should have witnessed the Risen Christ. Several copyists, aware of this problem, "corrected" 1 Cor 15:5 to read "eleven." Matthew asserts both that "the twelve" have a future role to play in the church and the Kingdom (sitting on twelve thrones judging the twelve tribes; 19:28), and that only eleven witnessed the Risen Christ in Galilee (28:16). Luke relates a story about choosing a new twelfth disciple (Acts 1:21–22). That the number twelve is insisted upon despite the awkwardness of retaining it may be construed as the measure of the strength of the early tradition. In light of the betrayal, the number twelve would have to go back to before the crucifixion. If so, then perhaps to Jesus himself.

As noted above, twelve is a highly significant number in Judaism, for it calls to mind the twelve tribes of Israel. By Jesus' day, ten of these tribes had ceased to exist. That Jesus did indeed speak of twelve chief disciples, called twelve specific individuals to be such, and saw them as playing a major role in the dissemination of the good news that the arrival of the Kingdom was imminent, would reinforce the view that he looked to the restoration of Israel, a major theme of Jewish apocalyptic eschatology. An Israel including the ten tribes lost to Assyria in the eighth century B.C.E. would require an eschatological miracle. The twelve disciples may thus have symbolized the restored—and hence eschatological—Israel, the Israel Jesus believed to be at hand.

The Conflict with the Pharisees

The return to Palestine was regarded as a meritorious work, performed only by a small "religious elite." The realities of the "holy city" [i.e., Jerusalem] might,

9. See esp. Sanders, *JJ*, pp. 95–106.

however, bring as much disillusionment to someone returning there as Renaissance Rome did to Martin Luther as a pilgrim. In the temple, the Sadducaean priestly nobility were exploiting the pious visitors; as the predominant spiritual movement in Palestine, Pharisaism, with its subtle casuistry and its esoteric arrogance, was not especially attractive either. . . . ethical monotheism and the idea of universalist mission met with only limited understanding.[10]

This description, from a recent essay, immediately anchors one in a familiar world. Here we have early first-century Judaism, inherently elitist (few could make such an expensive voyage), focused on meritorious works. The priestly aristocrats abused their flock, which their legalistic opponents, the Pharisees, held in contempt. The religion had so lost its way that it no longer understood the very concepts that stood at the heart of its own scriptures, namely, ethical monotheism and the mission to the Gentiles. Small wonder that, with the arrival of a religious movement that was true to these principles, spiritually desiccated *Spätjudentum* ceased to be a viable religion.

The above quotation, and the analysis it conveys, have been with few exceptions definitive of the entire field of New Testament scholarship. The topic "Jesus and the Pharisees" has long functioned as a sort of shorthand for "Grace versus Legalism," "Christianity versus Judaism"—and even, as the above quotation reveals (Young Man Luther and Renaissance Rome), "Protestantism versus Catholicism."

The broader explanation for the origin and vigor of this attitude must be sought in the study of religions itself, particularly in the sociology of religion, which can help us to analyze the role of conflict and competition in the formation of group identities. I shall take up that discussion in the concluding chapters of this study. Here we must consider two immediate, and historical, explanations: the nature of the New Testament documents themselves, and the historical origins of modern New Testament scholarship.

All four gospels, despite the variety of their theological focus and presentation of Jesus, unite stylistically, or strategically, at this point: the Pharisees are the dramatic foils for Jesus. They provide a dark backdrop against which the truth of the Gospel can shine forth. Religiously, they are everything that Jesus is not. They scorn sinners; Jesus seeks them out. They focus on manmade rituals and rules (Sabbath observance, food laws, purity laws, Temple sacrifice); Jesus is concerned with weightier matters—forgiveness of sin, true repentance, love of God and neighbor, and so on. Such evangelical characterizations are clearly polemical, and polemic rarely provides reliable description.[11] Why, then, in a field generally so cautious and self-consciously critical, do New Testament scholars routinely confuse historical reality with theological polemic, and in the name of pursuing the former reproduce the latter?

10. Hengel, "The Origins of the Christian Mission," in *Jesus and Paul*, p. 57.

11. On the historiographical consequences of applying this observation consistently, see Sanders, *JJ*, p. 337–38.

The answer, in no small part, lies in the origin of the discipline in the new biblicism of the Protestant Reformation. The phrases "works righteousness," "dead legalism," "hypocrisy," "anxiety about merit" enter scholarship as historically analytical concepts with the Pauline commentaries of Martin Luther. But Luther's descriptions of the stultifying religiosity of Paul's opponents in Galatia, and by extension of Jesus' opponents in Palestine, had another, closer target: the practices of the Renaissance Catholic Church. In describing the Gospel's ancient enemy, Luther made clear the identity of its modern counterpart, and so turned ancient polemic to contemporary use.

This Protestant conflation of Catholic/Pharisee has of course long been noted, often by Protestant scholars themselves. In this more ecumenical age, they have by and large renounced it—though not entirely, as our lead quotation demonstrates. But the disparagement of the Pharisees continues largely unabated, despite the excellent work of those scholars who, availing themselves of diverse Jewish sources, have argued—one would have thought decisively—against this misrepresentation.[12]

This caricature of Pharisaism in particular, and Judaism in general, severely compromises our understanding both of the life and teaching of Jesus and of the images of him conveyed by the New Testament texts. The evangelists, reading the post-70 situation of Jewish/Christian debate back into the lifetime of Jesus, presented the Pharisees as his chief opponents; while Luther perceived and modeled the sixteenth-century intra-Christian debate in terms drawn from this late first-century conflict. Modern New Testament critics, unwittingly replicating the polemics of both Luther and the evangelists in their own scholarship, thus perpetuate a double anachronism.

Two significant facts intervene between the lifetime of Jesus and the composition of the gospels: first, Rome had destroyed Jerusalem; and, second, the majority of Jews had declined to perceive Jesus as a messiah. The war with Rome affected the new movement in numerous ways. It provided yet another incentive for the Gentile Christian disengagement from Judaism: Gentile Christianity, already evolving in ways different from Jewish Christianity—a fact evident in Paul's letters—now had a vital political reason to disassociate both itself and its messiah from a people in such bad odor. Hence these Christians not only underscored the nonpolitical character of Jesus' message and messiahship but also so segregated him from his historical context that often he appears as a leader without (Jewish) followers.

Rome's victory also affected the perception of Jesus' crucifixion. Crucifixion, as we have repeatedly noted, was a Roman form of punishment reserved particularly for political troublemakers. In the wake of the seven-year-long Jewish insurrection, a Gentile Christianity wishing to champion a *crucified*

12. See esp. the milestone study by George Foot Moore, "Christian Writers on Judaism" (1921!), pp. 197–254; and Sanders' bibliographical essays in *PPJ*, pp. 33–59, 434–42.

messiah would have to divest both terms of their opprobrium in a Gentile context. This is chiefly the task of the Passion narratives, as we shall see; but the evangelists laid the groundwork for the Passion in their presentation of the opposition to Jesus' ministry. That opposition, they argue, was Jewish, not Roman. The result: Rome and Christianity are both on the same side against the Jews.

The evangelists argue further that this opposition was specifically Pharisaic—yet another effect of the war with Rome, as well as the measure of Christian frustration with Jewish nonresponse. For the political insurrectionists in the front line of the struggle—zealots, sicarii, and so on—had been militarily crushed and (at least temporarily) discredited; the Essene community destroyed; and the Sadducees, with the loss of the Temple and any pretense of Jewish government, had virtually disappeared. The only organized group to have survived the war reasonably intact was the Pharisees. Contemporary post-70 Gentile Christianity accordingly faced an adversarial or indifferent *Pharisaic* Jewish audience; and this is the situation projected, through the gospel narratives, onto the ministry of Jesus as well.

These retrospective controversies are thus somewhat contrived. In the episode of the paralytic, for example (Mk 2:1–12 and parr.), Jesus says, "My son, your sins are forgiven" (2:5), to which the scribes respond, "It is blasphemy! Who can forgive sins but God alone?" Modern scholars, who seem to assume that something like this exchange actually occurred, read the first remark in light of the second and conclude that Jesus deeply shocked and offended his Jewish audience by daring to speak for God, or by putting himself in God's place by forgiving sins, and so on. But the connection between illness and sin, and hence healing and the forgiveness of sin, is attested in Judaism both contemporary with and after the lifetime of Jesus. In the context of a cure, such a comment would hardly seem remarkable, much less blasphemous.[13] So also with speaking on God's behalf: within Judaism, priests, prophets, or any inspired person could claim to speak for God. Those unpersuaded might deem the spokesman wrong or misguided, but they would have little reason to find the claim itself blasphemous.

Other scenes of controversy seem to stem from the evangelists' pedagogic and polemical concerns, as well as from their unfamiliarity with the Judaism of Jesus' day. The gospels' Pharisees, for example, are obsessively concerned to avoid ritual impurity. Judaism, however, was concerned less to prevent impurity (incurred, for example, by childbirth, marital intercourse, or contact with a corpse, all activities actually enjoined by Torah) than to establish the means to remove it after it had been contracted (so that the person could

---

13. Sanders remarks on this passage, *JJ*, p. 273–74; Vermes, *Jesus the Jew*, p. 66–67, adduces a passage from one of the Dead Sea Scrolls, the *Prayer of Nabonius:* "I was afflicted with an evil ulcer for seven years . . . and a *gazer* [exorcist? healer?] pardoned my sins. He was a Jew."

participate in family and community life).[14] The gospels' Pharisees are incited to murderous plots by Jesus' curing a man's withered hand on the Sabbath (Mk 3:1–6)—not knowing, evidently, that the Sabbath had not been transgressed.[15] The gospels' Pharisees object to Jesus' mission to tax collectors, sinners, and the poor—groups they are depicted as despising—apparently forgetting two central tenets of Judaism: that through repentance and atonement, forgiveness is available to all sinners; and that the community has explicit and divinely enjoined obligations toward the poor. In their anxiety to ensure universal conformity to their standards of observance, the Pharisees follow Jesus everywhere, watching his house to see whom he eats with and how (Mk 2:13–17 and parr.), checking to see whether his disciples first wash their hands (7:1–2).

As portraiture, this is caricature. Elsewhere, and inadvertently, the gospels and Acts reveal the opposite of what they wish to convey: namely, that much of Jesus' teaching, even as they present it, is Pharisaic; and that the early Jesus movement drew some of its first followers from the ranks of the Pharisees (Acts 15:5), Paul being the most conspicuous. But even if, despite the prima facie implausibility, these controversies between Jesus and the Pharisees had actually occurred, what then? In circa 30 C.E., the Pharisees were only one of a number of groups in Palestine, and a small minority at that. They neither represented nor controlled the Judaism of Jesus' day. If they had disagreed with Jesus (on what issues is now very difficult to say) they might have refused to eat with him or otherwise avoided his company; or they might have disputed with him. But there is little else they could have done. The Pharisees in fact all but disappear from the Passion narratives, where the Sadducean nobility and especially the High Priest emerge as the chief movers behind Jesus' execution. All these considerations indicate that, at the very least, the evangelists' image of a Jesus beleaguered by constant Pharisaic opposition draws more on the circumstances of their own day than on the Palestinian ministry of Jesus.

14. "Impurity," in other words, implies no moral censure: a menstruant is not thereby a sinner, nor is one who has just given birth, nor one who has just buried a corpse. "There is nothing wrong with such people; they are only forbidden by biblical law to enter the temple area. . . . Recourse to the immersion pool, and waiting for the sun to set, cleansed most impurities" (Sanders, *JJ*, pp. 182–83). Note too that these purity regulations are *biblical,* not rabbinic; as such, they would have been the concern of any observant Jew, and not, as the gospels portray, exclusively of the Pharisees.

15. Altering nature is to be avoided on the Sabbath; therefore, prohibited actions include making something or carrying something in the public domain. (All prohibitions are suspended when life is at risk.) Mark's Jesus is thus guilty of no infraction. Cf. Jn 5:2–10, where the Jews object not to the cure, but to the paraplegic's carrying his pallet; and 9:1–16, where the Pharisees protest Jesus' making a clay of spittle and earth to cure the blind man. On the Markan controversy scene, see Barrett's intelligent discussion, *Jesus and the Gospel Tradition,* p. 63.

Hostility to Jesus and the Passion Predictions

The gospels present Jesus as moving in an atmosphere of thickening danger. The longer he continues his ministry, the more sinister the situation becomes until, inexorably, and just as he had predicted, his mission ends in violence. He suffers death from Rome; but first, the evangelists are at pains to point out, he suffers hostility and rejection from the Jews, especially the Pharisees. The gospel narratives, smoothing over the disjuncture between Rome and Israel, argue that, although Jesus was executed by Rome as a political offender, his death had been arranged by Jews whom he had offended religiously. What was his religious offense?

Most New Testament scholars, taking their cue from the controversy stories, have tried to locate that offense in Jesus' supposed attitude toward the Law. Since Jesus both forgave sins and taught on his own authority, this explanation goes, he essentially announced in his person and ministry that the authority of the Law had come to an end. Henceforward salvation would be accorded to whoever responded in faith to him. In other words, by proclaiming the Gospel, Jesus at least implicitly proclaimed also the end of Judaism as a religion, and therefore of Israel as God's elect. Jews hearing such a message, Jesus knew, would naturally kill the messenger; and that, through the agency of Rome, is what they did.

There are two problems with this proposal, one methodological and the other historical, and they are linked. Methodologically, it is out of joint with the times. It imports Paul and a particular understanding of his mid-first century mission to the Gentiles of the Diaspora back into Palestinian intra-Jewish mission of Jesus. Paul argues against *fellow Christian missionaries,* not Jews per se, that Gentiles need not be circumcised in order to enter the community of the redeemed (Gal 1:6). Baptism suffices. Circumcision, which for Paul as for his tradition was the sign of the covenant par excellence, is not necessary *for the Gentile in Christ.*[16] But Jesus had never addressed this issue. He had never had to. His mission did not extend to Gentiles. Later ecclesiastical tradition, endeavoring to reveal a reason for Jewish hostility to Jesus, must focus on Paul, whose message *was* offensive both to other Christians (Galatians) and to Jews (2 Cor 11:24). But in Jesus' historical context, the situation precipitating this debate about whether to observe Torah—that is, the Gentile mission—simply did not exist.

Further, Paul never defends his Law-free mission to the Gentiles by an appeal to a teaching of Jesus, nor does he claim that such was even *implicit* in any of Jesus' teachings. Here we touch upon the historical problem with the

16. Circumcision was essential for male converts to Judaism (see Schiffman, "Crossroads," pp. 125–27). No Jewish source, however, seems ever to state that circumcision was *universally* required for salvation: the Gentiles' eschatological inclusion in the Kingdom of God was contingent only upon their abandoning idolatry.

proposition under review. *If Jesus during his ministry had abrogated the Torah, apparently neither his own disciples nor Paul himself knew.* Paul had to argue his case regarding the Gentiles and Torah some twenty years after Jesus' death before Christians in Jerusalem who had known Jesus "in the flesh," namely, James, Peter, John, and possibly the "false brethren" as well (Gal 2:1–10; cf. vv. 11–14). Neither they nor he evoked a teaching of Jesus to clarify the situation. Further, Paul says repeatedly that the source of his Law-free gospel was not human tradition but his vision of the Risen Christ. It is difficult, then, to sustain the position that Jesus during his lifetime publicly taught against the Torah, and thus that such teachings were a source of mortal conflict between him and his contemporaries.

What, then, can we say about that other scholarly conjecture—that Jesus, preaching that God was a loving and merciful Father who forgave repentant sinners and preferred mercy to sacrifice, would have astounded and offended his listeners? That it fails as credible explanation. Such a message simply would not have come as news to Jesus' Jewish audience, whose people had been preserving scriptures and creating liturgies stating as much for at least half a millennium. Nor does it seem credible that they would be so affronted by someone preaching such a message that they would feel impelled to kill him.

But suppose Jesus preached this message with a peculiar slant. Perhaps he assured sinners that they would have a place in the coming Kingdom whether or not they made the *traditional* public sign of repentance, an offering at the Temple. Acknowledging Jesus' authority as prophet of the Kingdom—the event that would have prompted their penitence—would suffice.[17] They would thus be welcomed into the community forming around Jesus, which through his revelation had privileged knowledge that the Kingdom was at hand, and which accordingly attempted to live before its arrival according to the intensified moral demands of Torah that Jesus preached and by which society in the Kingdom would abide. Once it came, these former sinners would enter the Kingdom before many of the more respected members of Jewish society (e.g., Mt 21:31).

On this hypothesis, accepting Jesus and repenting—as earlier hearing John's call, repenting, and receiving baptism—would function as an alternative or analogue to a Temple offering. The question here, then, is not, Does God desire mercy and not sacrifice? but: What constitutes an acceptable demonstration of tshuvah, of turning away from sin and back to Torah? Jesus' answer, as John's earlier, might have struck more traditional contemporaries as idiosyncratic and even egotistical (Mt 11:18–19//Lk 7:33–34).[18] Such a

---

17. For a different reconstruction, cf. Sanders, *JJ*, pp. 106–116, 207, 270–81.

18. "Here, and in the preaching of Jesus generally, there is an egoism that is inconsistent with good Jewish piety," Barrett, *Jesus and Gospel*, p. 63.

message may have particularly irritated the priests, who were responsible for performing these sacrifices. (They later figure prominently in the Passion narratives.) But did Jesus really pose a serious threat to the performance of biblically mandated Temple sacrifices? It is hard to think so.

The Gospel of John proposes a different reason for Jewish plots against Jesus: fear of Rome. Immediately following the raising of Lazarus, the chief priests and Pharisees, according to John, convened the Sanhedrin:

> Some of the Jews [who had witnessed this miracle] went to the Pharisees and told them what Jesus had done. So the chief priests and the Pharisees gathered the council, and said, "What are we to do? For this man performs many signs. If we let him go on thus, every one will believe in him, and *the Romans will come and destroy both our holy place and our nation.*" (Jn 11:46–48; emphasis mine)

Why should the Romans destroy the Temple and the nation if Jesus amassed a large following? Because they might perceive in such a crowd a threat to their government, just as they did in the crowds that followed Theudas and the Egyptian, other charismatic leaders who purportedly worked great signs in the period before the war. To preempt Rome's punishing all Israel for Jesus' following, the chief priests and Pharisees in John's gospel maneuver Rome into punishing Jesus alone. As Caiaphas, the High Priest, says here, "it is expedient for you that one man should die for the people, and that the whole nation should not perish" (11:50). We shall return to the Johannine scenario when we consider the Passion narratives. Here I simply note its superiority to the synoptic proposals in that it offers both a more credible "offense" on the part of Jesus and a more direct connection between his offense and his execution.

Did Jesus, perceiving the hostility that his ministry provoked, foresee his own death? According to the evangelists, he did, and he explicitly told his followers what to expect: that in Jerusalem he would be handed over to the chief priests and elders; he would suffer many things and be killed; and on the third day he would rise again (Mk 8:27–33; 9:30–32; 10:33–34 and parr.). The very detail of the predictions prompts the reader's suspicions that these are descriptions after the fact, worked back into Jesus' ministry by the evangelists, who nonetheless fail to integrate them into their story. For once in Jerusalem, the disciples are overwhelmed by precisely the events the Passion predictions should have prepared them for, and Jesus' resurrection seems to catch them every bit as much by surprise.

No Jew, and especially no Galilean, preaching the imminent end of the current order and gathering any kind of following, could have expected to endear himself to Rome. And no remarkable degree of perspicacity would be required for such a popular leader, in these circumstances, to anticipate that he might end his days on a cross, that is, killed by Rome. Perhaps Jesus really did think that his life was in danger; perhaps he even confided his suspicion to his disciples. This is possible, even plausible.

But the Passion predictions as they now stand, both in their detail and in their intent, precisely reverse this reconstruction. They focus on the danger posed not by Rome but by the chief priests, elders, and Jewish leaders in Jerusalem. They reinforce the gospels' overall theme that Jesus' message was offensive religiously (i.e., to Jews), not politically (i.e., to Romans). The predictions thus prepare the reader for the crucial role given the Sanhedrin in Jesus' death, as if a Roman colonial administrator—especially one of Pilate's reputation—would not otherwise have noticed a Galilean charismatic with an enthusiastic following coming into holiday-crowded Jerusalem. Jews, not Romans, the gospels argue, were hostile to Jesus; Jews, not Romans, were threatened by his message; Jews, through Romans, engineered his death; and all had been long ago predicted in scripture.

To conclude: it is difficult to find a source of religious conflict between Jesus and his Jewish contemporaries. Jesus might have suspected that his ministry, for political reasons, put his life at risk: he had the immediate example of John the Baptist before him. He might have confided his suspicions to his followers. His death, nonetheless, took them by surprise.

With the claim made soon after his death that Jesus was the messiah, his death had to be explained. Crucifixion confirmed Jesus' status within Christian tradition only in light of the faith in his resurrection. It is this faith that moved the early proclamation from "Jesus is messiah *despite* his death on the cross" to "Jesus is messiah *because of* his death on the cross"—the evolution and argument that stand behind the evangelical passion predictions.

The Days in Jerusalem

The gospels assert both that Jesus entered Jerusalem amid much public fanfare for the holiday of Passover and that the Sanhedrin figured prominently in events leading to his execution once he was there. Accepting the first assertion as historical calls the second into question.

The trip to Jerusalem at Passover is the crescendo of Jesus' ministry. Jesus enters the city like a Davidic king, that is, like a messiah (Mk 11:1–10 and parr.; Mt 21:5 and Jn 12:15 cite Zec 9:9), precisely during the chief festival of liberation. He is hailed as messiah by the crowds. And shortly thereafter he dies the way a messianic pretender would have died under Rome.

The direct and causal connection between these events—that Jesus' entry explains his execution—is the strongest argument in favor of its historicity. And in this depiction of his followers' exuberance, their confidence that they were about to witness the miraculous arrival of God's Kingdom, and their specifically messianic expectation, we may have a faithful reminiscence of this moment in Jesus' ministry. But if we take the gospel accounts of Jesus' entry at

Passover as essentially historical, then we have difficulty with what they further relate: that Rome did not immediately react to such sedition, as surely it would have during a holiday so notoriously inflammatory that troops were kept on special alert (*BJ* 2.12,1), that Jesus' immediate followers were not also arrested and killed, as surely they would have been had Rome perceived them as parties to such an incident; and that the Sanhedrin had to bring Jesus to Rome's attention, when a significant public demonstration such as the gospels describe should and would have sufficed.

Thus the messianic entry fits thematically the tradition that Jesus went up to Jerusalem at Passover and historically the fact of his crucifixion. But it makes all the more mysterious the traditions that the Sanhedrin or the chief priests, for religious reasons, instigated his arrest.

The Incident at the Temple

Shortly after entering Jerusalem at Passover, Jesus provoked some kind of incident at the Temple that earned him the mortal enmity of the chief priests. John places this event early in Jesus' ministry, where its significance is mostly symbolic: it sets the tone for Jesus' relations with official Judaism and fore-shadows the Passion (2:13–22). In the synoptics, however, this is one of the dramatic events at the end of Jesus' career that leads to his crucifixion. Luke's abbreviated account says only that Jesus drove out "those who sold" (19:45–46). Mark, and following him Matthew, also speak of his overturning the tables of those who changed money and sold pigeons (Mk 11:15//Mt 21:12; so too Jn 2:15). This would have taken place in the Courtyard of the Gentiles, where such activities were conducted. How should we interpret this report?

The gospels provide one interpretation. Jesus' action was a protest against such commerce within the Temple precincts: apparently he considered it inherently dishonest. "Is it not written, 'My house shall be called a house of prayer for all the nations?' But you have made it a den of robbers" (Mk 11:17 and parr.; cf. Jn 2:15–17, an elaboration on this theme). Modern commentators, following the evangelists' lead, have often concluded that such commercial enterprises did indeed compromise or pollute the Temple, and that by driving out those so engaged, Jesus was symbolically restoring or reforming Temple worship.

Unfortunately, while this reconstruction makes Jesus at home in modern Western religion, it alienates him from the Judaism of his own time. For the practices that, on this interpretation, he undermines were integral to the religious function of the Temple, whose principal role was to serve as the place for the sacrifices enjoined by God on Israel through Moses at Sinai. These sacrifices necessitated a system ensuring a supply of unblemished animals (e.g., the pigeons in Mk 11:15), which pilgrims purchased for sacrifice—as presumably Jesus' parents did when they "presented" their baby at the Temple (Lk

2:24). These pilgrims, coming from all parts, brought various currency; and moneychangers, doubtless for a charge, converted these to the Temple's standard coinage, which bore no offensive images.

Moneychanging and the sale of animals, in other words, were necessary to the normal functioning of the Temple, which was universally regarded as vitally important. Josephus reports that in 63 B.C.E. the priests continued the sacrifices even as Pompey laid siege to the city and stormed the Temple (*AJ* 14.4,3). Even the Essenes, long alienated because of their quarrel with the incumbent priesthood, nonetheless sent votive offerings for the sacrifices in the very Temple they would not step foot in (*AJ* 18.1,5). As for the people generally, says Josephus, "to think of leaving off those sacrifices is to every Jew plainly impossible, who are still more ready to lose their lives than to leave off that divine worship which they have been wont to pay to God" (*AJ* 15.7,8). Thus if Jesus were protesting not the sacrifices themselves but the support services necessary for the sacrifices, his gesture would lack practical significance. And if he were protesting the Temple sacrifices per se, he would be all but unique in his time and especially among his people.[19]

It is natural, of course, to impute religious uniqueness to Jesus. But one last historical consideration casts doubt in this instance: evidently his own disciples after his death continued to worship and offer sacrifices in the Temple (Acts 2:46; 3:1; 5:12, 42; 21:23–27; cf. Mt 5:23–24, where Jesus gives explicit teaching on how a Christian should sacrifice at the altar). True, the disciples do not appear as models of mental agility in the gospels. But had Jesus at such a dramatic moment and in such a dramatic way condemned so central an aspect of Jewish worship as perverse or impure, could the disciples have registered nothing?

The synoptic tradition at two other crucial points links Jesus with the Temple. Sometime shortly after this incident, Jesus predicts the Temple's destruction when teaching about the End of the Age (Mk 13 passim, esp. vv. 1–3, and parr.). And later, during his trial before Jewish authorities, he is accused by "false witnesses" of having threatened to destroy the Temple and to rebuild it—Mark adds "not with hands"—in three days (Mk 14:57–60, cf. Mt 26:60–62; Acts 6:14). This accusation recalls the similarly worded Passion predictions: "The Son of Man must . . . be killed, and after three days rise again" (Mk 8:31). John, who combines the Temple's "cleansing" with the saying about its destruction, makes the reference to the Passion explicit ("but he spoke of the temple of his body"; Jn 2:21).

Considered together, these traditions connecting Jesus' death with his prediction of the Temple's destruction suggest both the meaning of his action in the Temple and the reason why the chief priests, so prominent in the Passion narratives, enter the story here. Overturned tables symbolize not purification

19. Sanders, *JJ*, pp. 62–67.

but destruction.[20] Through this disruptive gesture, Jesus symbolically enacted the impending *apocalyptic* destruction of the Temple. This was another way of stating in the idiom of Jewish apocalyptic eschatology what he had preached throughout his ministry, namely, that God's kingdom was at hand. For just as Israel under Babylon had endured the Temple's destruction and the Exile before the redemption of the Return and the rebuilding of the Temple, so now the current Temple's destruction would point ahead to eschatological redemption, the Kingdom, when the glorious Temple of the New Age, "not made by hands" (Mk 14:58), would appear. As the author of Tobit had prophesied some two centuries earlier:

> They will rebuild the House of God, though it will not be like the former one until the times of the age are completed. After this they will return from the places of their captivity [i.e., the Ingathering of the Exiles at the End], and will rebuild Jerusalem in splendor, and the House of God will be rebuilt there with a glorious building for all generations forever. (14:5)

In sum: Jesus' gesture (overturning tables in the Temple court) near the archetypical holiday of national liberation (Passover) in the context of his mission ("The Kingdom of God is at hand!") would have been readily understood *by any Jew watching* as a statement that the Temple was about to be destroyed (by God, not human armies, and certainly not literally or personally by Jesus himself), and accordingly that the present order was about to cede to the Kingdom of God.[21]

This interpretation of the "cleansing" also explains the prominence in the Passion narratives of the chief priests. Mark and Luke foreshadow the priests' role in Jesus' death with this episode (Mk 11:17–18//Lk 19:46–47); Mark and Matthew, depicting Jesus before the Sanhedrin, suggest that the High Priest regarded his threat concerning the Temple's destruction as a religious offense (Mk 14:57–60//Mt 26:60–62). Prima facie this was not so. The classical prophets had uttered similar warnings about the First Temple,[22] and Tobit clearly had the Second Temple in view. Further, Josephus reports that one Jesus son of Ananias, just before and subsequently throughout the siege of

---

20. Ibid., pp. 68–90, carefully reviews the evidence and current academic discussion on this point. On Tobit 14:5, ibid., pp. 80–81.

21. Cf. Harvey, *Jesus and Constraints*, pp. 133–34, who argues that Jesus' gesture was (deliberately?) obscure or interpretively open-ended, "a new and creative prophetic gesture with which Jesus . . . challenged his contemporaries to draw their own conclusions." My sense is that an interpretive free-for-all ill conforms to the urgency of a public, apocalyptic ministry, especially at a moment of climax.

22. Notably Jeremiah, whose sermon concerning the Temple provoked the anger of Jerusalem's citizens and led to his arrest (Jer 26:1–19). But Jeremiah's circumstances were considerably different from Jesus' (an impending invasion vs. a long-standing occupation); and a prophecy of the Temple's destruction per se—as the case of Jeremiah illustrates too—did not constitute a violation of Torah; see Hare, *Jewish Persecution*, pp. 26–30.

Jerusalem in 66–70, continuously bewailed the Temple's coming destruction. Both Jewish and Roman authorities flogged him for his disruptive and disturbing behavior, but neither charged him with having broken the law, whether civil or religious. And during the siege itself, when the Jewish authorities were completely autonomous, no further steps against him were taken (*BJ* 6.5,3).

So why would the priests have acted against Jesus if he publicly predicted the Temple's destruction? Again, because of the readily recognizable meaning of his gesture in overturning tables in the courtyard. To so openly—perhaps flamboyantly—tell a crowd, during such a holiday, after such a ministry, when an official such as Pilate was in Jerusalem, that their liberation was at hand and that God's Kingdom approached, *no matter how apolitically and nonmilitarily that Kingdom was conceived*—was tantamount to shouting "Fire!" in a crowded theatre. The priests, ever the intermediaries between the populace and the Romans, were peculiarly responsible for maintaining civic order. And if, as the synoptic gospels claim, Jesus continued to preach in the Temple during the period before Passover (Mk 11:27–13:1 and parr.; cf. 14:49), and particularly about the signs of the End (Mk 13 passim), the priests' fears about his potential effect on the crowds—or, through imperial spies, on Pilate (cf. Lk 20:20)—would not have diminished as the holiday approached.

The Last Supper

The synoptic gospels state that Jesus' last meal with his disciples was the Passover seder, although they do not present it as such. John, who moves the action of the final days back twenty-four hours, simply calls this last gathering a supper. At this meal, seder or not, Jesus is said to have spoken of his own body and blood, symbolized in the bread and wine, as a new covenant, looking forward to the establishment of the Kingdom. Thus Mark:

> And as they were eating, he took bread, and blessed it and broke it, and gave it to them and said, "Take, *this is my body*." And he took a cup, and when he had given thanks he gave it to them, and they all drank of it. And he said to them, "This is *my blood of the covenant, which is poured out for many*. Truly, I say to you, I shall not drink again of the fruit of the vine *until that day when I drink it new in the kingdom of God*." (14:22–25)

And Paul:

> For I received from the Lord what I also delivered to you, that the Lord Jesus on the night when he was betrayed took bread, and when he had given thanks, he broke it and said, "*This is my body which is for you*. Do this in remembrance of me." In the same way also the cup, after supper, saying, "This cup is *the new covenant in my blood*. Do this, as often as you drink it, in remembrance of me." For as often as you eat this bread and drink this cup, you proclaim the Lord's death *until he comes*. (1 Cor 11:23–26)

The celebration of a common meal seems to have been an early and prominent feature of Christian worship. This meal was modeled on traditions about the Last Supper, which is indeed why Paul relates the passage cited above. The tradition united the motives of Jesus' death, vicarious suffering ("my blood . . . poured out for many" in Mark, "my body, which is for you" in Paul), and the coming of the Kingdom.

What historically might stand behind such a tradition? The idea of a communal banquet celebrating the arrival of the Kingdom of God existed in contemporary Judaism among the Essenes, who anticipated such a meal presided over by the Priest and the messiah (1 QSa 2:17–22), and who regularly observed a communal meal in anticipation of the "messianic banquet" at the End (1 QS 6:4–6). Later apocalyptic texts (Baruch, Enoch, Apocalypse of Elijah) speak both of an abundance of food at the End and of dining with the messiah. Other passages in the gospels depict the coming Kingdom in terms of a banquet (for example, Mt 8:11). If Jesus himself also anticipated the arrival of the Kingdom, perhaps that very night near or on the Passover before he was arrested, he might well have celebrated a special meal with twelve of his disciples, so numbered to symbolize the restored, eschatological Israel. We cannot of course be certain, but this much is not antecedently impossible.[23]

The eucharistic formula poses other problems, requiring as it does not only Jesus' foreknowledge of his impending death but also his own theological interpretation of it as expiatory sacrifice. That the righteous suffer before the coming of the Kingdom is, as we have seen, one of the motives of Jewish eschatological thinking; and Jesus, to the degree that he did foresee his own death, may have viewed it in this light. Did he then specifically associate the bread and wine of the meal with his own body and blood, and these with the eschatological (q.v. "new"; cf. Jer 31:31) covenant? Again, we cannot be certain; but the early Christian communities certainly did, as they too celebrated by eating together in anticipation of a messianic banquet that would signify not their messiah's arrival but his glorious return.

Arrest and "Trials"

As we noted above, at this point in the gospel narratives all four accounts condense a remarkable (not to say improbable) amount of activity into a single night. The closer we come to the Passion, the thicker the evangelists' theological overlay in their presentation of events. And as the activities proliferate, the details diverge.

All four gospels assert that Judas, one of the Twelve, betrayed Jesus to an arresting posse (the composition of which is variously described) that then brought Jesus before the High Priest and perhaps others. (Paul says only that Jesus "was betrayed," without saying by or to whom.) The evangelists imply

23. See Barrett's discussion, *Jesus and Gospel*, pp. 50–53.

that Judas—whether motivated by money (Mt 26:15) or Satan (Lk 22:3)—took the initiative; and they explain the authorities' preference for surreptitious betrayal over straightforward arrest as the measure of Jesus' popularity. Thus Judas "sought an opportunity to betray him to them in the absence of the multitude" (Lk 22:6; cf. Mk 14:1–2 and parr.). So too the Fourth Gospel, which states that Judas knew where Jesus would be (a garden across the Kidron Valley), and so led *Roman* troops there, thus circumventing the enthusiastic crowds in Jerusalem (Jn 18:1–12; cf. 12:19).

The gospels must postulate strong popular support for Jesus in order to accommodate the tradition about his betrayal (cf. I Cor 11:23, cited above). Thus Jesus was ambushed when away from the crowds, who otherwise would have created a disturbance. An enthusiastic following would also begin to account for Jesus' execution and for the community that formed so quickly, and with such commitment, after his death. This all makes good historical sense—although it highlights the improbability of what the gospels further relate, namely, the crowd's wholesale defection between nightfall and morning.

The legal or practical grounds for Jesus' arrest (e.g., disturbing the peace, sedition, etc.) are nowhere stated, which enhances the evangelical theme that Jesus died for religious reasons. Certain hints, however, point another way. At the moment of his arrest, Mark's Jesus exclaims, "Have you come out as against a robber (*lēstēs*, a political outlaw), with swords and clubs to capture me? Day after day I was with you in the Temple teaching, and you did not seize me" (14:48–49). Perhaps Jesus was arrested as a lēstēs: he was certainly executed as one, crucified between two others (*duo lēstai*, 15:27); and he was charged with making a seditious claim, that is, that he was "The King of the Jews" (15:26; more on this below). But if this were the reason for Jesus' arrest and subsequent execution, he would have been led directly to the Roman authorities. Instead, according to all four accounts, he was taken before the High Priest.

The High Priest

Here as elsewhere, our sources diverge. Mark and Matthew depict two separate trials before the full Sanhedrin in what remained of the first night of Passover and into the early morning. In Luke the Sanhedrin convenes only once, in the morning. In John there is no Sanhedrin trial, but Jesus is interrogated either by Annas or Caiaphas (the account is garbled)[24] and then led from the High Priest's house to the praetorium early in the morning of the day before Passover (18:28). The synoptics convey a lively trial scene—the court seeking incriminating testimony, many false witnesses perjuring themselves, and Jesus remaining silent. Finally (according to Mk and Mt) the High Priest takes matters into his own hands and demands: "Are you the Christ, the Son

24. See Paul Winter's comments, *On the Trial of Jesus*, pp. 44–45.

of the Blessed?" (Mk 14:61; "of God" Mt 26:63). Jesus responds straightforwardly ("I am"; Mk) or obliquely ("You have said so"; Mt and Lk; cf. Jn 18:33ff.) and then goes on to speak of the exalted Son of Man. The court deems this blasphemous (Mk and Mt; Lk reports no charge, 22:70-71), whereupon the guards mock Jesus and abuse him. Then, inexplicably, he is led off to Pilate.

The historical difficulties with this episode are legion and have been minutely discussed in many studies.[25] The trial as it is reported violates the traditions of Jewish legal procedure as set out in the late second-century text *mishnah Sanhedrin*. The court could not convene at night, nor on a major feast day. Contradictory evidence would have disqualified the charge. And what Jesus says, or what his examiners take him to imply, does not constitute blasphemy. Had some capital charge been sustained against Jesus, no trace of it remains in our documents.

The thickest fog surrounds the question of the Sanhedrin's competence in this period to execute capital cases for offenses to religious law.[26] The evidence, and the arguments, are fairly evenly divided, while the evangelical accounts themselves, tendentious and artificial, do not inspire confidence. Why, after purportedly finding Jesus guilty of blasphemy, would the Sanhedrin convey him to Roman authorities, like some medieval inquisition handing a heretic over to the secular arm? John alone offers an explanation: the Jews inform Pilate (who otherwise would not have known?) that they are not empowered to execute anyone (18:31). But even John suggests that the Romans were called in by prophetic, not legal, necessity: "This was to fulfill the word which Jesus had spoken to show by what death he was to die" (18:32). Jesus had to die by crucifixion, a Roman penalty. But, had Jesus been found guilty of a capital religious offense (again, no record of which remains) and executed by order of the Jewish court, there would have been no crucifixion. With prior Roman permission were it requisite, without if it were not, Jesus would have died by stoning.[27]

If we relinquish the effort to see the Sanhedrin trial as history, we can perceive more clearly the theological effect it achieves. This scene crowns the gospels' presentation of a Jesus who died for religious reasons (hence at Jewish instigation), not political ones (hence not at Roman initiative). The query the High Priest is made to utter—"Are you the Christ, the Son of the Blessed?"— is precisely the Christian confession. Jesus *is* the Christ, he *is* the Son of God; and so he is presented here, in effect dying for Christianity.

25. The arguments are reviewed ibid; see also D. R. Catchpole, *Trial of Jesus.*

26. Barrett, *Jesus and Gospel*, pp. 53–62; on the competence of the Sanhedrin, Schürer, *HJP* 2:218–26. Sanders comments, "it is also clear from Josephus that whoever was in power— whether a Hasmonean, a Herod, or a Roman procurator—could execute or free whom he wished without a formal trial" (*JJ*, p. 317).

27. Cf. bSanh 43a, where Jewish tradition assumes that if the Sanhedrin did condemn Jesus (i.e., for religious offenses), he died by stoning.

But even if such words had passed between the High Priest and Jesus in 30, they would have meant one thing to them and quite another to readers of the gospels forty or more years later. In the Jewish context, *messiah* would have denoted "leader," most particularly a royal and military leader (apocalyptic or otherwise) whose special dignity as the chosen instrument of the divine plan could be indicated by the title Son of God; but he would have been fully and normally human. A dissenting hearer might think that the person making such a claim for himself was wrong, but he would have no reason to consider the claim itself blasphemous. In later Hellenistic Christian circles, however, *messiah* had a special *theological* significance and Son of God a particular *metaphysical* content that were in fact offensive to most Jews. Such Christological development was the interpretive work of the churches reflecting back on Jesus' death and resurrection. Only through anachronism can it be seen as an issue between Jesus and his contemporaries.

The appeal of such a scenario, despite its inherent improbability, rests in its theological power, its clear enunciation at a moment of highest pathos and drama of the Christian confession. As such, its image of Jesus served later Christian communities as the example of Christian discipleship par excellence: Jesus had suffered as they themselves were suffering for confessing the Gospel of Christ as Son of God. Additionally, of course, the trial scene articulates a social fact: Jewish communities for the most part, and certainly by the end of the century, did not so confess Jesus as Christ. This later rejection of later claims becomes through the evangelists a retrojected paradigm, and nowhere more so than in the Sanhedrin trial where the High Priest, the symbolic representative of Judaism, repudiates the truth of the Gospel.

What can be said historically to underlie these progressively embellished accounts of priestly action against Jesus on the night of his arrest? If we accept the gospels' version, however broadly, then Jesus was guilty of some infraction of religious law and condemned for such by the Sanhedrin. Rome had to perform the execution, given the Jewish court's diminished powers in capital cases, but the initiative came from the priests. Against this reconstruction, however, stand three facts. First, no capital violation of Torah seems to stand in any of the gospels' accounts of Jesus' teaching. Second, even if Jesus did speak "against the Temple" (e.g., predicting or threatening its imminent destruction and the establishment of an eschatological Temple "not built by hands"), this would not in itself constitute a legal or religious offense and so would not suffice to bring him before the Sanhedrin, much less to a sentence of death. Third, the evidence that the court could not exercise authority in capital cases is extremely ambiguous.[28] The traditional scenario, however, absolutely requires it, for there is no other way to posit Jewish initiative but Roman fiat.

---

28. The suspension of the Sanhedrin's privilege to try capital cases for the period "forty years until the Temple's destruction" is also attested in various later Jewish sources (ySanh 1.18a;

On balance, John's account seems more credible: Jesus was interrogated by one or more priestly officials and then led to Pilate. But why? Here we return to Jesus' symbolic gesture in the Temple courtyard and his message of the impending Kingdom. The Passion narratives probably preserve the kernel of a reliable historical reminiscence here, since the priests were the middlemen between the populace and the Roman occupation government. If they feared that Jesus' activity before Passover might inspire popular agitation, and so provoke Roman hostility, they may have tried to forestall disaster by handing him over to Pilate, or by facilitating his arrest, lest Pilate indiscriminately "chasten" the city, as he on other occasions is known to have done (cf. Jn 11:47–53).[29]

But none of the gospels portrays the situation thus. The priests do not say, "Here is the chief troublemaker, but don't worry: the rest of his followers have fled." Rather, they say, "Here is the troublemaker" and then have to plead with Pilate to take steps. Such a course of events also makes impossible any sort of publicly acclaimed entry into Jerusalem. Had Jesus arrived in any way like the gospels show him arriving, the priests would not have had to bring him to Pilate's attention.

How then can we grant historical status both to the entry and to these reports of priestly initiative in Jesus' arrest, in light of the irrefutable fact that Jesus was executed by Rome? By positing that Pilate, or his spies, may have had an eye on Jesus ever since his tumultuous entry. Evidently Jesus' supporters at that time had not been sufficiently numerous to warrant immediate action, or else, we may assume, Pilate would have taken it. But Jesus' subsequent prophetic action at the Temple, and his continued preaching about the imminent Kingdom, were attracting and exciting crowds, perhaps in increasing numbers, as Passover approached. The priests, knowing what Pilate was capable of, may have intervened at this point. Engaging a disaffected disciple to arrange an ambush, they would have worked in concert with Roman troops to bring Jesus into custody.

Once Jesus had been apprehended, the High Priest could question him "about his disciples and his teaching" (Jn 18:19). Were they revolutionaries?

---

bShab 15a; bAvZar 8b). Nonetheless, sentences passed by Jewish courts under Roman rule were apparently carried out—the execution of James the brother of Jesus, and certain others, being one well-known example. (See "Jewish Persecutions of the Early Mission" in chap. 8.) "Those who were found guilty were put to death according to Jewish juridical practice and there is no mention in the legal proceedings or in the execution of the sentence that the judgment needed the confirmation of the Roman authorities; and the convicted were not remanded to them for the execution of the sentence," S. Safrai, "Jewish Self-Government," p. 399.

29. When Jews in Jerusalem gathered to protest his appropriation of Temple funds for a municipal project (building an aqueduct), Pilate interdispersed armed Roman soldiers in mufti throughout the crowd, who at his signal clubbed the protestors and occasioned a stampede, so that "large numbers perished"; *BJ* 2.9,4; cf. *AJ* 18.3,2.

No. Did they have any plans to riot, seize the Temple, or harass Roman troops during the holiday? No: divine force, not human, was bringing in the Kingdom, as the authorities would soon discover. Terminating the interrogation, the High Priest could then send Jesus on to Pilate with the assurance that Pilate need not expect an outbreak of violence if he gave Jesus the penalty he deserved. Pilate, satisfied, could then concentrate his attention on Jesus alone.

Pilate

The issue before Pilate is clear: Sedition. In all four accounts Pilate demands, "Are you the King of the Jews?" Jesus responds ambiguously (Mk 15:2 and parr.; Jn 18:33ff.) and shortly thereafter receives the usual Roman penalty for sedition.

We have already reviewed most of the hints that Jesus was somehow associated with contemporary movements of national liberation: one of his followers, Simon, was a "zealot" (Lk 6:15; Acts 1:13); his followers both hoped (Lk 24:21) and proclaimed (esp., e.g., the Triumphal Entry) that "he was the one to redeem Israel," that is, that he was the messiah as understood by Jews at that time. Jesus protests at his arrest that he is not an insurrectionist (Mk 14:48); but he is associated with one (Barabbas), dies as one together with two others, and the *titulus* over the cross declares this to have been his crime. Some scholars have seen in these data evidence that Jesus was himself involved in political messianism of the sort associated with Judah the Galilean or Bar Kochba; but unless we discount the irenic and politically nonconfrontational traditions in the gospels and Paul as protective camouflage vis-à-vis Rome, this seems unlikely. Also, it is hardly possible that Rome would have allowed the original disciples to form a community and reside in Jerusalem had they been part of an active movement of political opposition.

But Jesus need not have preached insurrection to have been perceived as politically disruptive by Rome or even by the chief priests, that Jewish group most concerned to keep things quiet in those unquiet times. A large following and the vocabulary of apocalyptic eschatology, with its hope of a new kingdom and a new order, would have sufficed. Josephus provides ample evidence of how Rome dealt with such, and both he and Philo note that Pilate was not one to waste time on legal niceties. Were Jesus in this category of perceived troublemakers, his execution could have followed very swiftly upon his arrest.

The Roman hearing as it now stands in the gospels serves as the narrative companion piece to Jesus' interrogation before the priests. Pilate's reported conduct as reluctant judge is scarcely credible as history, but it was very important theologically and politically to the communities that stood behind these gospels.

Theologically, this scene is the high-water mark of Jewish malice toward Jesus. They accuse him before Pilate of "many things" (Mk 15:3); specifically, and falsely, of fomenting revolution: "We found this man perverting our nation, and forbidding us to give tribute to Caesar, and saying that he himself is Christ a king" (Lk 23:2). "If you [Pilate] release this man, you are not Caesar's friend; every one who makes himself a king sets himself against Caesar" (Jn 19:12). The more the tradition evolves, the worse the Jews become. In Mark, the chief priests simply accuse Jesus (the charge is not specified) and persuade "the crowd" (which appears out of nowhere; 15:8) to demand his crucifixion. In Matthew, "the people" explicitly assume the responsibility for his death, which Pilate refuses to take ("His blood be upon us and on our children!"; 27:25). In their efforts to secure Jesus' condemnation, Luke's chief priests bear false witness to both Pilate and Herod (23:2, 5, 10), and Pilate delivers Jesus up "to their will." According to John, once the Jews secure Pilate's necessary authorization, they perform the execution themselves, though by Roman, not Jewish, means: "Then he [Pilate] handed him over to them to be crucified" (19:16).

As the Jews are inculpated, Pilate is progressively exculpated, emerging finally as a considerate and sympathetic figure. In Mark he asks, "Are you the King of the Jews?" and then urges Jesus to defend himself against the charges of the chief priests (15:2–4). Wondering at Jesus' silence and perceiving that the priests press their claims "out of envy," Pilate makes a last-ditch effort to save him by permitting "the crowd" to choose between Jesus or Barabbas, in accordance with his custom (otherwise unattested) of releasing a prisoner during the feast. The Jews demand Barabbas, a known murderer and insurrectionist, whom Pilate (incredibly and irresponsibly) proceeds to release. Still protesting Jesus' innocence ("What evil has he done?"; 15:14), he finally consents to the crucifixion.

Matthew's Pilate, even more conflicted, receives a message from his wife urging him to "have nothing to do with that righteous man" (27:19). Protesting Jesus' innocence, he publicly washes his hands of the whole affair (27:24). In Luke, he pronounces Jesus innocent of any crime, tries to avoid the issue by passing him over to Herod for judgment, and repeatedly insists that Jesus is blameless (23:4, 6, 13, 20, 22). And in John, where release of a prisoner changes from Pilate's custom to the people's (18:39), Pilate's reluctance is so great that he tells the importuning Jews to do the job themselves (19:6). Finally even Jesus must persuade him to continue with the crucifixion. Arguing that heaven has mandated Pilate's role, Jesus explicitly assures him that the High Priest has "the greater sin" (19:11).

To repeat: given Jesus' manner of death, we can only assume that Pilate, and not the High Priest or the Sanhedrin, was responsible. The task of the trial narratives is to reverse the burden of that responsibility in the face of the fact, too central to the tradition to be dropped or altered, that Jesus died on a cross. Pilate had indeed acted—but only, they urge, because he was compelled by the Jews.[30]

---

30. Succinctly summed up in Acts 3:13b–15.

The evangelical account of the story behind Jesus' death receives support from a passage in a much earlier document: 1 Thes 2:14–16. In the middle of Paul's warm and fond praise for the Thessalonian community, the following appears:

> For you, brethren, became imitators of the churches of God in Jesus Christ which are in Judea; for you suffered the same things from your own countrymen as they did from the Jews, *who killed both the Lord Jesus and the prophets, and drove us out, and displease God and oppose all men* by hindering us from speaking to the Gentiles that they may be saved—so as always to fill up the measure of their sins. But God's wrath has come upon them at last!

There are many impediments to accepting this as authentically Pauline. Its sweeping condemnation of "the Jews" contrasts strongly with the way Paul speaks of his own people elsewhere (e.g., Rom 9–11). Its invocation of the prophet-martyr tradition and its accusation of a Jewish spiritual stinginess toward the Gentiles implies an acquaintance with the later synoptic tradition. And finally the past completed action of the final phrase—"God's wrath has come upon them at last!"—most readily calls to mind the Temple's destruction in 70. But the strongest argument against Pauline authorship of this passage is Paul's undisputedly authentic statement in 1 Cor 2:8: "None of the rulers (*archontes*) of this age (*aiōn*) understood this [secret and hidden wisdom of God]; for if they had, they would not have crucified the Lord of glory." The archons of this aeon, I have argued, are to be understood as astral, nonhuman entities. But if Paul did refer here to the human agents in Jesus' death, the "rulers of this age" could only be the Romans.[31]

Both the gospel accounts and this Pauline interpolation were composed in the period immediately following the terrible war of 66–73. The church had every reason to want to assure prospective Gentile audiences that the Christian movement neither threatened nor challenged imperial sovereignty the way the Jewish people had, *despite* the fact that their founder had himself been crucified, that is, executed as a rebel. Thus the gospels draw the greatest possible contrast between Jesus and Barabbas, a man who, these accounts urge, actually was a revolutionary, and whom the Jewish people naturally preferred. And while this political context did not in and of itself determine all the elements of the trial scenes, it surely provided additional incentive to these Christian communities to dissociate themselves from the Jewish nation. In this, ironically, they may have shared an important concern with those Jewish priests who historically had dissociated themselves and the nation they represented from Jesus: the danger of even seeming to stand in political defiance of Rome was too great, the potential price too high.

---

31. The arguments against Pauline authorship of this passage, and its congruence with later strata of Christian tradition, are laid out in Birger A. Pearson, "1 Thessalonians 2:13–16."

The Crucifixion

Whether at any time in his ministry Jesus claimed for himself the title *messiah*—the evidence on this point is extremely ambiguous—he certainly died as if he had.[32] From Pilate, Jesus was led away to the cross. For his disciples, this was a crushing defeat, particularly bitter after their jubilant entry with Jesus into the city only a short time earlier, when they had expected to witness the arrival of the Kingdom of God (Mk 11:10 and parr.). Whether they at any time had regarded Jesus as a messiah—and the evidence on this point, too, is extremely ambiguous—his crucifixion would have disabused them of such an idea. Someone executed by Rome as an insurrectionist might be revered as a political martyr, but the brute fact of his death would invalidate any claim to messiahship.[33] The messiah, to function as messiah, had at least to be alive.

But later Christians, looking back to Jesus' crucifixion in light of their belief in his resurrection, radically reinterpreted the meaning of the cross. Since his resurrection had followed upon his crucifixion, the cross came to be seen as the necessary prelude to this great event. Condensing death and eternal life into one symbol, Christians esteemed the cross as the paradoxical expression of Jesus' ultimate vindication (hence John's repeated puns on exaltation/crucifixion). They thus reversed the terms of the problem originally posed by Jesus' death: only a crucified messiah is the true messiah. Scriptural support for this proposition extended the argument: only the crucified messiah fulfills the scriptures.[34]

We should keep this theological development in mind when we turn to the evangelists' accounts of Jesus' death, for it informs their strategy of presentation. The testimonia shaping the details they report enable the evangelists both to interpret and to validate the Passion: their narrative is an extended demonstration that Jesus died "according to the scriptures." Thus Jesus submits in silence to calumny (Is 53:7) and abuse (Is 50:6); he refuses wine and myrrh (Prv 31:6?) or wine and gall (Ps 69:21). His garments are divided (Ps 22:18); he cries from the cross (variously, Ps 22:1 or 31:5); once he has died, the soldiers do not break his bones (Ps 34:20), though one does pierce his side (Zec 12:10). But Jesus' death does more than conform to scriptural prophecy. It calls forth miraculous portents: the sun darkens and the earth shakes

32. See the review of scholarly opinion in Harvey, *Jesus and Constraints*, pp. 145–50. Consensus seems to hold that *messiah* was a post-resurrection title (see, e.g., Barrett, *Jesus and Gospel*, pp. 19–24, 65–66; G. Bornkamm, *Jesus of Nazareth*, pp. 169–78); Harvey argues that reconstruction of the events of Jesus' ministry and its conclusion are simpler if one assumes that he or his followers did claim this title for him during his lifetime (pp. 137–43).

33. But cf. N. A. Dahl's important essay, "The Crucified Messiah," which argues that Jesus' death as a messianic pretender would, in light of the resurrection, have served as the source of the messianic attribution. *Crucified Messiah*, esp. p. 26.

34. Hence the didactic and polemical function of the Passion predictions. See also Bornkamm's survey of the testimonia in the Passion narrative, *Jesus*, pp. 156–57.

(recalling Jesus' earlier description of events preceding the Parousia, Mk 13:5–8, 24–27 and parr.); the bodies of "saints who had fallen asleep" are raised (a miracle expected to precede the messianic age, Mt 27:52); and the curtain of the Temple is torn in two (a symbol of its impending destruction before the New Age, Mk 15:38 and parr.).[35] The gospels, in brief, present a crucifixion that conforms Jesus' death to the Christian definition of "messiah."

What historical conclusions can we draw from these theologically freighted accounts? First and foremost, that Jesus' crucifixion came as a terrible shock to his followers. The tremendous effort and ingenuity that the gospels expend to domesticate the crucifixion, to integrate it into the message of the Risen Christ (the Passion predictions, the scriptural citations, the post-resurrection explanations, etc.) is the measure of its resistance to reinterpretation. However Jesus may have felt that his life was in danger, whatever he may have said to his followers to that effect, when they all traveled to Jerusalem that Passover, Roman oppression was not what they expected to see triumph.

Second, while we may suspect the historicity of individual details in the Passion narrative, we have little reason to doubt the general impression of Jesus' behavior that they convey. Once arrested, he did not resist. True, the wholesale defection of his disciples may have closed off this option; or he may have submitted himself to what, inexplicably, now seemed the will of God; or, stunned by this totally unexpected turn of events, he may have been too dispirited to react.[36] All this is possible—as is the chance that he did resist and called his disciples to do so and that later tradition repressed this fact for apologetic or practical reasons. But the evangelical portrait of a pacific Jesus fits well with a theme prominent in the traditions both about his ethical teachings and about the coming Kingdom: violence was to be avoided, and the Kingdom would come without force of arms.[37] Beyond the simple practice of the ethics that he preached, then, Jesus' utter acquiescence to Rome might indicate his confidence in his own message. Rome's dominion, through his agency, was about to give way to the eschatological Israel and the dominion of God.

Third, Jesus' crucifixion, taken together with his proclamation of the Kingdom, indicates his status as a political figure. This is not to say that Jesus was an insurgent, like Judah the Galilean. Nor is it to say that Rome mistakenly thought he was: otherwise, Pilate would have arrested and crucified Jesus' followers too. But *Jesus was an apocalyptic preacher, and the nature of*

35. On this, see esp. Gaston, *No Stone*, pp. 480–81; Brandon, *Jesus and the Zealots*, p. 228; for the standard Christian theological interpretation of this episode, Bornkamm, *Jesus*, p. 167.

36. Cf. Barrett, *Jesus and Gospel*, pp. 47–49, on the disciples at Gethsemane.

37. On the nonmilitary aspect of these traditions, Sanders, *JJ*, pp. 74–75; 231–32.

apocalyptic is political. Its message of an impending new order at least implies a condemnation of the present one; it is in religious idiom the expression of a political critique.[38] The distinction between Jesus or John the Baptist, on the one hand, and Judah or his sons, on the other, is thus not that the former are religious while the latter are political. The one is pacifist (i.e., communicating his message, or expecting to see it realized, without recourse to arms), the other military; but both are religious, and both are political.

Both are also nationalist. Jewish restoration theology focuses on the redemption of a particular people, Israel; brought back from exile to a particular land, *ha-Aretz, the* Land. If other peoples participate in the Kingdom, then they leave their gods behind and worship in the renewed Jerusalem, specifically in "the house of the God of Jacob." Apocalyptic theology, in other words, partakes of the broad Jewish consensus on what was religiously important: the people, the Land, Jerusalem, the Temple, and Torah.[39]

The gospels, despite their distance from Jesus' own religious context and their antipathy to such an outlook, nevertheless preserve traces of his participation in this consensus: his calling twelve disciples to represent all the tribes of eschatological Israel; his intensification of the ethical norms embodied in Torah; his journey to Jerusalem to greet the coming Kingdom; his prophetic gesture at the Temple, in anticipation of a Temple not made by hands; his prophecy of the imminent fulfillment of God's promises to Israel revealed in Torah. Thus, though Jesus may have proclaimed that the Kingdom would be established not by armed rebellion but by an act of God, Jesus' Jewish audience would have known—as would Pilate—that such a kingdom exalted Israel and precluded imperial dominion. In the tinderbox of early first-century Palestine, crucifixion of such a prophet would be a prudent Roman response.

With the crucifixion, Jesus' public ministry ends. When the evangelists resume their story, they recount the miracle to which they trace their own religious origins: Jesus' resurrection from the dead. Various individuals and communities in various situations—the disciples in Palestine, Paul and his Diaspora communities, the Christian writers of the second and third generations of the movement—responded in various ways to their belief in Jesus' resurrection. By analyzing their responses, we can begin to account for the

38. On the political nature of apocalyptic activity, Gager, *Kingdom and Community,* pp. 27–28; Theissen, *Palestinian Christianity,* pp. 59–76.

39. On the religious nationalism of Jesus' message, Sanders, *JJ,* e.g., pp. 116–19; 222; 228–41; Brandon, *Jesus and the Zealots,* emphasized an activist, military nationalism, at least on the part of Jesus' immediate followers; cf. W. D. Davies, *Gospel and the Land,* p. 365, who sees such traditions as the work of the later church, which "increasingly draped [Jesus] in an apocalyptic mantle and specifically Jewish expectations."

development and diversity of the images of Jesus that we find in our New Testament texts. But an analysis of traditions originating in faith in the Risen Christ requires that we have in mind an image of their historical starting-point, Jesus of Nazareth. I shall therefore pause here to summarize the results of our review of the gospel story.

Chapter 7
Jesus of Nazareth

The following recapitulates the conclusions of the previous chapter. The qualifications appropriate to such historical reconstruction—"perhaps," "it may have been that," "possibly," and so on—I have used sparingly, in order not to numb the reader with excessive repetition. Much in the sketch that follows is speculative, though I have tried to indicate in the anterior discussion my reasons for what I propose synthetically below.

Jesus was born in Nazareth in one of the most turbulent periods of Jewish history. Roman imperial policies had collided with the traditional hopes of Jewish restoration theology to produce a highly charged atmosphere in which many different individuals and groups preached and sought to put into practice a liberation viewed as religious and political both. Judah the Galilean, his sons and grandson, the Pharisees and the Essenes, John the Baptist, Jesus, Theudas, the Egyptian—all brought to their people, in various ways and with various interpretations, the message that the current order was about to succumb to the kingdom of heaven. In such a situation, many Jews looked for signs of the coming redemption, and especially for God's Redeemer, the messiah. "The people at this time," reports Lk 3:15, "were in expectation, and all men questioned in their hearts concerning John [the Baptist], whether perhaps he was the messiah."

Jesus himself received John's message of repentance in preparation for the coming Kingdom, and was baptized in the Jordan. After John's arrest and execution, Jesus continued to preach the message of the Kingdom, attracting some of John's now leaderless disciples. But unlike John, whose hearers apparently had to go to him, Jesus took his message to his audience, wandering from town to town with his disciples. Again unlike John, whose baptism followed upon repentance, Jesus received, and indeed sought out, people who were yet sinners. Repentance need not precede, but could in fact proceed from, the reception of his good news that redemption approached.

The Kingdom Jesus proclaimed would bring radical changes and even reversals in the current social order. Whereas status and authority now rested in those wielding positional, political, or financial power, when the Kingdom came, "many that are first will be last": penitent tax collectors and harlots would enter before chief priests and elders; the poor would precede the rich; the lowly would inherit the Land.[1] He who understood and truly believed Jesus' proclamation should tolerate and even comply with the demands of the present unrighteous regime, for God had numbered its days and would soon act himself to destroy its dominion. If, as the gospels report, Jesus indeed called his followers to abandon property and normal family relations in order to follow him, we might take the exigency of his message to indicate how soon he expected to see it fulfilled. The Kingdom was *at hand.* He who had ears to hear and eyes to see should take radical steps to prepare for it.

In the brief interim between his preaching and the arrival of the Kingdom, Jesus' followers might feel the disapproval of family or peers; but soon marriage and traditional family structures would be no more as eschatological humanity became one family. Further, the dead as well as the living would participate in this new community, for God would vindicate all those who had suffered persecution and died for the sake of righteousness. The End would bring a universal judgment of both the quick and the dead; but following judgment would come redemption, when God the Father gathered all people to himself—former sinners, scattered Israel, and ultimately even the no longer idolatrous Gentiles.

While such news would naturally appeal more to those who felt themselves cut off from the benefits of power than to those who enjoyed them (the point made by the story of the wealthy man, Mk 10:17–23ff. and parr.), nonetheless, many Palestinian Jews from various walks of life—the poor and the well-off, tax collectors and zealots, prostitutes and Pharisees—were attracted to Jesus, whose authority as spokesman for the coming Kingdom was clearly demonstrated in the exorcisms and cures he performed. Some traveled with him on his missions; others remained in towns, providing for him when he passed through.[2] But all felt bonded together in a new community, called by their special knowledge of the approaching End to a new level of moral awareness; practicing the intensified ethics preached by Jesus according to which, when the Kingdom came, all eschatological humanity would live.

1. Mt 5:5, the meek shall inherit *tēn gēn,* the same word used in Dt 3:7 LXX for territorial Israel, but cf. Davies, *Gospel and Land,* p. 361f. *Gē* may have the same implication in Acts 1:8, where the Resurrected Christ charges his disciples to witness to him "in Jerusalem and in all Judea and Samaria and to the end of *tēs gēs.* See D. R. Schwartz, "The End of the GĒ."

2. On this form of social organization, see Theissen, *Palestinian Christianity,* pp. 8–23.

How these people interpreted his preaching and regarded Jesus himself is now difficult to say. Some probably saw Jesus as a divine prophet, like John alive once again; others, as a new Elijah, preparing the way for the Lord. From the authority of his proclamation, his representation of the twelve tribes of the restored Israel among his own disciples, and his role as leader, some inferred that Jesus himself was the messiah whose presence signaled the hour of Israel's redemption.

How and whether Jesus thought of, invited, or accepted any of these designations we cannot know. Nor can we know the size of his following or the ways that it publicly demonstrated its enthusiasm for him and his message. We must assume that it was large, loud, and potentially disruptive enough to occasion some concern on the part of the priestly aristocracy of Jerusalem, whose job it was to mediate between Roman power and the populace. Perhaps they were even sufficiently alarmed to discuss Jesus during a session of the Sanhedrin (Jn 11:47).

Finally, during the procuratorship of Pontius Pilate, Jesus went up to Jerusalem to celebrate Passover. The sources speak of this trip as the climax of his ministry. He went, perhaps, in the expectation that his ministry was about to end in the final Passover, when the Kingdom would arrive. He might have proclaimed his conviction to the enthusiastic crowds that followed or greeted him, speaking to them of the imminent End-time to be ushered in not by force of arms, but by the act of God. They in turn might have hailed him as the messiah. Proceeding to the Temple, Jesus then pronounced the nearness of the End through a prophetic gesture. Overturning tables in the outer court, he symbolically enacted the impending destruction of Herod's temple, soon to be replaced by the eschatological Temple of God.

How long Jesus preached in Jerusalem, and how much he agitated the crowds as the night of Passover approached, we cannot know; but at a certain point the Roman governor had had enough. Alarmed by the possibility of an indiscriminate use of Roman force, the city's priestly authorities, aided perhaps by a disenchanted former disciple of Jesus, arranged in collaboration with Pilate's troops to arrest Jesus by night, away from his excitable following. Aware of the growing danger of his situation, Jesus confided to his disciples that he might have to suffer at Rome's hand before he accomplished his mission. But redemption was close—so close that their celebration together near or on the night of Passover immediately anticipated the impending messianic banquet in the Kingdom. When he next drank wine, Jesus told them, he would be in the Kingdom of God. Later that same night, a posse of Roman soldiers, assisted by some officers of the Temple guard, surprised Jesus and arrested him. His disciples fled in such fear and confusion that the soldiers did not trouble to arrest them, too.

What Jesus had hoped would be the final Passover of the world turned out, instead, to be the last for him. Interrogated briefly by the High Priest, Jesus was condemned by Pilate, who executed him as a messianic pretender together with other enemies of the imperium. Thus Jesus' ministry, begun in such confidence, motivated by such a great hope—the restoration of Israel and the redemption of the world—ended in violence on a Roman cross.

III
THE CHRISTS OF THE CHURCHES

Chapter 8
Responses to the Resurrection

J esus' mission ended on the cross. The mission that was to spread in his name, however, in a sense begins at this point. Within days of his death, to certain of his close companions, Jesus appeared, risen from the dead.[1] This small company, which had followed Jesus in the Galilee and, in panic, deserted him in Jerusalem at the moment of his arrest, regrouped in radically new circumstances. For two of the prime promises of the messianic age, the resurrection of the dead and the vindication of the righteous, had been realized in the person of their executed leader.

What actually occurred during these post-crucifixion manifestations is now impossible to say. Our earliest report, Paul's, is itself late (c. 55?) and secondhand ("I delivered to you as of first importance what I also received"; 1 Cor 15:3). Mark "predicts" and Matthew reports post-resurrection appearances to the apostles in the Galilee; Luke and John set them in Jerusalem. The gospels unanimously name women, though variously identified, as the first witnesses to the empty tomb, and Matthew and John, to the risen Christ as well; Paul cites Peter ("Cephas") and then the Twelve. We can draw securely from this evidence only the baldest conclusion: that despite the absolute certainty of Jesus' death, his immediate followers with equal certainty perceived—and then proclaimed—that Jesus lived again.

The disciples' experience of Jesus' resurrection stands at the heart of the early Christian movement. This fact points indisputably to its origins in the

---

1. The Markan Passion predictions give "after three days" (8:32; 9:31; 10:34), but the narrative has Jesus die on Friday and rise on Sunday (15:42; 16:2). The later synoptics correct the Passion predictions to read "on the third day" (Mt 16:21; Lk 9:22), which confirms the earlier Pauline tradition (1 Cor 15:4). One possible scriptural source for this tradition is Hosea 6:2: "After two days he will revive us; and on the third day he will raise us up, that we may live before him." See Conzelmann's comments, *1 Corinthians*, pp. 255–56.

eschatological hopes of first-century Judaism, with its belief in the resurrection of the dead and vindication of the righteous when the Kingdom came. That Jesus' followers perceived Jesus to have been so raised and so vindicated tells us, further, the degree to which he had forged his followers into a committed community and prepared them for an eschatological event. The one they all expected when they went up to Jerusalem was the arrival of the Kingdom, the fulfillment of Jesus' message. Instead, abruptly and brutally, this message was disconfirmed, their leader killed by the enemy who incarnated the ungodly powers of the present order. But shortly thereafter Jesus' followers experienced an *unexpected* eschatological event: Jesus was raised. The community could continue; disconfirmation became confirmation.[2] For what else was Jesus' resurrection but a vindication of his message, a sign of just how close the Kingdom really was?

How long Jesus' followers continued to have such experiences we cannot say: the evidence of Paul (1 Cor 15:4–7) and Acts (1:3; 13:31) suggests that they extended over some period of time. This caesura between the apostles' perception of Jesus' resurrection and their proclamation of it is one of the most crucial and intriguing "prehistoric" moments of the primitive community, one for which we have no direct sources. Mark's gospel simply stops at this point; the others conflate the resurrection appearances with a charge from the Risen Christ to convert the nations. Only in the opening chapters of Acts do we glimpse, behind Luke's mannered presentation, the community's agitation and excitement in this interregnum between Easter and the mission. The disciples and brethren gather together, experiencing the Risen Christ who for weeks speaks to them of the Kingdom (1:3); they pray together daily (1:14; 2:1), communalize all property, share meals, and worship together in the Temple (2:44–46). They were expecting, not a world mission, but the Kingdom of God.

At some point, however, the community must have begun to reinterpret the eschatological significance of the resurrection. Clearly it could not in and of itself have signaled the approach of the Kingdom, because still the Kingdom did not come. What thus might have been a second, and equally fatal, disconfirmation of the faith of Jesus' followers instead became the occasion for a further reinterpretation that allowed the community to continue. If Jesus' resurrection were not his eschatological Parousia, then surely it could not be far away. And in this interim between Jesus' resurrection—a sort of Parousia *manquée*—and his definitive Second Coming, the disciples felt called to continue Jesus' mission, preparing Israel for the End they now knew, on the evidence of his resurrection, to be fast approaching.

2. For the dynamics of "cognitive dissonance"—the distress felt when a crucially important belief is apparently disconfirmed—and its transmutation into sustained missionary activity, see the study by Festinger, Reicken, and Schachter, *When Prophecy Fails.* Gager, *Kingdom and Community,* applies this study to the early Christian community, pp. 40–44.

This situation of intense and energetic missionary activity, propelled by a belief both fervently held and inevitably disappointed, unites the movement led by Jesus with the movement formed in his name. Paul and Mark share it; the later gospels are shaped by it. For the original message—that Jesus authoritatively announced the coming Kingdom of God—was continually threatened by the simple passage of time. Successive disappointments gave rise to new interpretations as the tradition reworked what was too central to relinquish.

This study of the images of Jesus began by surveying the variety of interpretations conveyed in the gospels and Paul. Examining these critically, I reconstructed a plausible image of their historical starting-point, Jesus of Nazareth. We are now in a position to consider these canonical images once again, this time aware of the dynamics of expectation and disappointment that stand behind them. For each represents a different moment in the reinterpretation of a figure and a message whose meaning had to change to accommodate new circumstances—the nonresponse of Israel, the reception of the Gentiles, the delay of the End. Reconceiving Jesus and the Kingdom, Christian tradition in various ways continually adjusted itself to success—that is, to its own vigorous existence—as its central prophecy failed. And as part of its adjustment to this unexpected future, the tradition grew away from its own past.

For the original community of Jesus' followers, like Jesus himself, had stood recognizably within the bounds of traditional Judaism and traditional apocalyptic expectation. After their experiences of the Risen Christ, they continued to worship in the Temple and to look forward to redemption—now linked to the glorious *second* coming of their vindicated leader—speedily and in their days. And with the delay of the End, they undertook to complete the preparation of Israel. Soon the message of Jesus and the coming Kingdom spread to the synagogue communities of the Diaspora. But at this point, the missionaries encountered active hostility—not from Rome, but from fellow Jews. And by the end of the century, the churches, now largely Gentile, that traced their origins back to this apostolic community repudiated the Torah, viewed the Roman destruction of Jerusalem with undisguised satisfaction, and claimed the biblical promises to Israel for themselves.

The New Testament texts reveal the late first-century Christological developments that underlie, accompany, or express this evolution. But what connects their images of Christ the Lord, the Davidic messiah and preexistent divine Son, to the primitive kerygma, the proclamation of the earliest community? How did those who had known Jesus in the flesh speak of him after his resurrection? And how would their interpretation of Jesus explain what we know from Paul: that within two years of the resurrection, their message had spread from the Jewish homeland to the synagogues of the Diaspora; that it so agitated these communities that a zealous Pharisee persecuted his synagogue's *ekklēsia;* and that by mid-century a Law-free mission in Christ's name existed among the Gentiles, but that Israel for the most part had remained aloof from the Gospel?

THE KERYGMA OF THE EARLY MISSION

So soon after his death, and so definitively, did the original apostles identify the crucified Jesus as the messiah that within two decades the equivalent Greek term, *Christ,* functioned as part of his name. Their message to the Jews of the Diaspora, echoed by Paul ("what I also received"; 1 Cor 15:3), proclaimed that Jesus the messiah, crucified and raised, was about to return in power with the Kingdom. But this double proposition had to be defended and explained. Why is Jesus the messiah? And (especially since the hope of a *second* coming so deviated from traditional messianic expectation) why had he died?

The messianic claim, as we have seen, grew out of the facts of Jesus' ministry, whether or not he himself ever made such a claim. One's place in the Kingdom was determined by one's response to Jesus—that is, he claimed eschatological authority;[3] he was the leader of a community anticipating the Kingdom, and most particularly of a group that represented redeemed Israel (i.e., the Twelve); his enemies as well as his followers thought of him as, or believed that he claimed to be, the messiah, because as such was he executed. Further, his followers construed his resurrection as a vindication of his message: the Kingdom was indeed at hand, and Jesus was indeed, in a unique sense, its messenger. True, this vindication was of a private nature, initially limited to those who already believed in him. But soon his Parousia, in the vanguard of the coming Kingdom, would publicly broadcast his vindication. Appearing after death for the second time, Jesus at his Parousia would perform precisely as a traditional messiah was supposed to perform. Exalted, glorious, leading the hosts of heaven against the forces of darkness, Jesus would execute judgment on the wicked and establish the Kingdom of God (1 Thes 4:16; 1 Cor 15:24ff.; Mk 13:24ff. and parr., etc.).

But why had he died? Here we come to the great creative contribution of Christian theology to first-century Jewish messianism. "Christ died for our sins, according to the scriptures" (1 Cor 15:3). Paul asserts this as part of the primitive kerygma; later, the synoptic Passion stories narratively echo one of the scriptures that Paul, and the apostles before him, may have had in mind:[4]

> He was despised and rejected by men;
> > a man of sorrows, and acquainted with grief . . .
>
> . . . .

3. See Martin Hengel's remarks in *The Charismatic Leader and His Followers,* pp. 15, 67–68.

4. The influence of Is 53 is contested; see F. F. Bruce, "Date and Character of Mark," p. 85–86 and literature cited; also Harvey, *Jesus and Constraints,* pp. 22–25.

Surely he has borne our griefs
  and carried our sorrows . . .
  . . . .
. . . he was wounded for our transgressions,
  he was bruised for our iniquities;
upon him was the chastisement that made us whole,
  and with his stripes we are healed.
  . . . .
The Lord has laid on him
  the iniquity of us all.
He was oppressed, he was afflicted,
  Yet he opened not his mouth;
like a lamb led to slaughter . . .
  . . . .
By oppression and judgment he was led away . . .
  . . . .
although he had done no violence,
  and there was no deceit in his mouth.
  . . . .
. . . he bore the sins of many,
  and made intercession for transgressors.   (Is 53:3–12)

Jesus the messiah, his disciples maintained, had died to atone for the sins of others. In fact, they said, his suffering, atoning death, and subsequent resurrection marked the dawn of redemption, the approach of the Kingdom of God. How did they come to such an interpretation?

According to the tradition about the Last Supper, preserved variously in Paul (1 Cor 11:23–26) and Mark (14:22–25), Jesus himself spoke of his own death as a sacrifice for others ("for you"; "for many"). This tradition may preserve a historical reminiscence: perhaps, as the atmosphere in Jerusalem grew increasingly threatening, Jesus suspected that he might die before the Kingdom arrived. At their last meal together in anticipation of the messianic banquet, he may have said as much to his disciples. Having believed that his mission would end with the Kingdom, Jesus may now have revised that expectation: his death, rather, would be one of the travails, like the present Temple's apocalyptic destruction or the prophesied astral disturbances, that would immediately precede its arrival. Jesus' logia in both Paul and Mark connect his coming death to the coming Kingdom. But still—in neither does Jesus say something like, "This is my blood which is poured out for *the expiation of the sins of* many." So whence the idea of an *atoning* sacrifice?

The roots of this idea may lie in Jesus' remembered relationship with sinners. If Jesus had held that their reception of his message, their subsequent repentance, and their "following" him—that is, living according to the intensified ethics of his communities in anticipation of eschatological society—suffered to ensure them a place in the Kingdom, then their commitment might substitute for the traditional public sign of repentance, a sin or guilt offering at the Temple. Faith in Jesus as the authoritative spokesman for the Kingdom, in other words, might replace a Temple offering. Later, those who believed in his resurrection and in his approaching Parousia may have interpreted his death in light of this teaching, ultimately condensing the two: Jesus himself thus becomes the sinners' atonement sacrifice.[5]

The various elements of this primitive Christology already existed in earlier Jewish thought, especially apocalyptic: the messiah would come, perhaps on the night of Passover; his coming would herald the arrival of God's Kingdom; with the Kingdom would come the resurrection of the dead; before it comes, the righteous will suffer; suffering atones for sin, and so on.[6] The early community interpretively recombined these originally distinct traditional elements as they gave meaning to the fact of Jesus' death in light of their faith in his resurrection. They themselves of course saw this process of interpretation differently. Events had made them realize, if belatedly, that scripture had long ago foretold that the messiah would die for the atonement of sin (cf. Lk 24:19–27, 44–47). Now, finally, they understood, for they themselves had seen scripture fulfilled in their own day.

But the New Testament texts claim that Jesus is more than messiah. They also identify him as Son of Man, Lord, and Son of God. What further can we learn about the earliest kerygma from these different designations?

The phrase *Son of Man* is notoriously obscure. As we have seen, it appears in several Jewish apocalyptic works, where it refers to the vindicated saints of Israel (Daniel) or to a heavenly redeemer figure with messianic connotations (Enoch).[7] Elsewhere in Jewish Aramaic writings, *son of man* can mean simply "man," "one," or, reflexively, the speaker himself.[8] In the New Testament, *Son of Man* appears frequently although almost exclusively in the gospels (otherwise only in Acts 7:56 and Rv 1:13 and 14:14), where the evangelists present Jesus as using the phrase to refer to himself. Thus whoever scorns Jesus, the Son of Man will scorn when he comes in judgment; the Son of Man will suffer and die in Jerusalem; the Son of Man will come again in glory, and so on.

Scholarly debate continues both on the titular use of this phrase, that is, *the* (heavenly? preexistent?) Son of Man, and on its range of meanings in the

---

5. For the same point made from a different perspective, see Martin Hengel, *Son of God*, p. 68 n. 123.

6. See discussion in "The Expectation of Redemption," in chap. 5.

7. See discussion *loc. cit.*

8. This is discussed in Vermes' seminal treatment, *Jesus the Jew*, pp. 160–91, and his follow-up essay, "The Present State of the Son of Man Debate," in *Jesus and Judaism*, pp. 89–99. See also Barnabas Lindars, *Jesus Son of Man*.

Palestinian Judaism of Jesus' day. But the phrase itself, awkward Greek but unremarkable Aramaic, obviously entered the tradition early and continued to be authoritative. If, because of its associations with the apocalyptic pattern of the suffering and vindication of the righteous (Dn 7, 12), Jesus himself had frequently used Son of Man to evoke the experience of the saints in the face of the coming Kingdom, or if, less metaphorically, he habitually referred to himself or those who followed him by this designation, the disciples may well have recalled it when later professing the suffering and subsequent exaltation of the messiah whose return they now expected.

The complete absence of the phrase from our earliest written source, Paul, might seem to argue against its role in the primitive apostolic kerygma. But the audiences of Paul's letters are exclusively Gentile, and his use of *Jesus Christ* replicates the functional definition of Son of Man (i.e., one who suffered, was vindicated, and will be vindicated when the Kingdom comes). Paul may simply have decided to spare himself and his Greek-speaking communities an unnecessary neologism. Mark, on the other hand, our earliest extant source for reconstructing the Palestinian "biographical" traditions, made Son of Man the Christological centerpiece of his gospel.[9] In sum, then: did the original disciples declare the message of Jesus Christ, the crucified and vindicated Son of Man (– "man"?), whose death atoned for the sins of Israel and whose imminent Second Coming would accompany the Kingdom? Very probably.

Lord and *Son of God*, despite their own Aramaic links to the tradition, are more problematic. Paul frequently designates Jesus as *kyrios* (Lord). His association of this title with the Parousia (e.g., in 1 Thes 4 and 5, where it occurs 15 times in 46 verses) apparently recalls an Aramaic formula: "*Marana tha!* Our Lord, come!" (1 Cor 16:22; cf. Rv 22:20). In non-Christian Jewish Aramaic literature, *mare*, a respectful form of address ("sir," "milord"), has a wide range of applications. It might designate fathers, husbands, authorities both secular and religious, miracle-workers, and even, albeit infrequently, God himself.[10]

Doubtless some of Jesus' Aramaic-speaking followers would have used *mari* when courteously addressing him. Christian tradition, however, turned this word's Greek equivalent, *kyrios*, into a term acclaiming Jesus' special status and unique nature as preexistent Lord. Thus we find in the gospels exegetical arguments for his superiority to David based on Ps 110.1 (LXX): "How can the scribes say that the Christ is the son of David? David himself, inspired by the Holy Spirit, declared, 'The Lord [*kyrios;* Heb. YHWH] said to my Lord [*kyrios;* Heb. *adonai*], Sit at my right hand, until I put your enemies at your feet.' David himself calls him Lord; so how is he his son?" (Mk 12:35–37).

---

9. See discussion on Mk in chap. 9.
10. Vermes, *Jesus the Jew*, pp. 103–128; Hengel, *Son of God*, pp. 77–83.

This use of *Lord,* with its suprahuman implications, begins to overlap with *Son of God,* another phrase with an Aramaic bridge to primitive tradition. Mark's Jesus in Gethsemane prays to God as *Abba,* "Father" (14:36). So too do Paul's congregations cry "Abba, Father!" since they through the Spirit are "sons by adoption" (Gal 4:6; Rom 8:15). Finally, the gospels portray Jesus as habitually referring to God as "Father" (Gk: *patēr*), "our Father," or (particularly in John) "my Father."

These New Testament passages reflect standard Jewish usage, in which God is addressed or described as Father in scripture, prayer, and commentary. Nonetheless, some scholars have wanted to see in Jesus' particular use of *abba*—less formal, more intimate and affectionate than the Hebrew *ab*—an indication of Jesus' personal consciousness of his uniquely close relationship with and to God.[11] This interpretation asks *abba* to bear the burden of later theological developments, which made particular claims about Jesus' unique metaphysical nature as divine Son. The Aramaic *abba* is indeed a term of intimate address. As such it was used by Jewish charismatics, such as Hanan the Rainmaker: the ability to work miracles implied intimacy with God.[12] Jesus, who also worked miracles, may indeed have prayed to God as *Abba,* and the word's multiple attestation in primitive tradition supports the view that he did. But clearly he was not the only Jewish miracle-worker in this period to do so.

If God is a Father, who is his son? In scripture, any number of entities and persons.[13] Angels, monarchs, prophets, just men, the entire nation of Israel—all could properly be called "son(s) of God." But in post-biblical Judaism, *son of God* came particularly to designate the Davidic—that is, royal—messiah (cf. 2 Sm 8:14; Ps 5:7, the so-called Coronation Psalm). *If* the apostles used this term of Jesus, it would have been by attraction to *messiah: Son of God,* in other words, would have been an alternative messianic designation. But even this is unlikely, for *son of God* is really the language of royalty, and Jesus had not been a royal messiah (hence the point of Mark's use of Ps 110:1, cited above).

Within thirty years of Jesus' death, however, these terms are no longer linked. *Messiah* does denote Davidic royalty, but *Son of God* denotes something far greater: a unique, preexistent, divine entity. Thus Paul: "Paul, a servant of Jesus Christ . . . [God's] Son, who was descended from David according to the flesh [= messiah], and designated Son of God in power

---

11. See J. Jeremias, *Prayers,* esp. 11–65; cf. Vermes' corrective, *Jesus the Jew,* pp. 210–13, and "The Gospel of Jesus the Jew II: The Father and his Kingdom," in *Jesus and Judaism,* pp. 30–43; see also Harvey, *Jesus and Constraints,* pp. 168–69.

12. See "Palestinian Judaism in the Time of Jesus," in chap. 5, for discussion of Jewish charismatics.

13. See Hengel, *Son of God,* pp. 41–56.

according to the Spirit of Holiness by his resurrection from the dead" (Rom 1:1–4).

The resurrection, Paul proclaims, reveals Jesus' status as Son of God. But this divine Son and Lord originates in heaven. He descended to earth, died on the cross, was exalted at his resurrection *back* to heaven, and is about to come down from heaven again (e.g., Phil 2:6ff.; 1 Cor 2:7; 2 Cor 8:9; Gal 4:4; Rom 8:3). Were those who had followed Jesus in the Galilee and who had known him "according to the flesh" the source of this teaching? This is possible. But it seems more likely to me that this is Paul's contribution, granted to him, perhaps together with his gospel and apostleship, "not from men nor through man, but through Jesus Christ and God the Father" (Gal 1:1). We shall consider it shortly.

Here, however, we should conclude our reconstruction of the primitive kerygma conveyed to Jews of the synagogue communities by those who were apostles before Paul. They proclaimed Jesus as the crucified messiah. His starting place was earth (a "son of man"); he was exalted to God's right hand at his resurrection; he would come again shortly in glory to defeat evil, judge, occasion the resurrection of the dead, redeem Israel, and establish the Kingdom. His death on the cross as a messianic pretender, a fact of history, the apostles invested with redemptive significance: he died to expiate the sins of others. His resurrection vindicated his message: the Kingdom *is* coming.

Why, finally, did these apostles see Jesus as the messiah? *Not* because of his resurrection. That event signaled, rather, the nearness of the End, since at the End the dead (or perhaps only the righteous dead) were to be raised. It thus confirmed Jesus' message, and consequently his status as messenger. But nowhere did Judaism anticipate a dying and rising messiah; and the apostles, like Paul after them (Rom 1:3–4), would have had no reason to infer from his resurrection that Jesus was the messiah.[14] What else do we know about Jesus, then, that would explain his apostles' messianic interpretation of him? Only that he was their *leader,* one who apparently claimed exceptional personal authority as the final forerunner of the Kingdom.[15]

Jesus, both before and especially after his execution, was not a credible messianic candidate, and his apostles knew it. If Mk 12:35–37 recalls any historical incident, Jesus knew it too. The messiah everyone expected was the Davidic messiah. Paul himself attests to the strength of the royal tradition: if Jesus is the Christ, then he must be "descended from David according to the flesh," and so, without troubling to argue the case, Paul states he was (Rom 1:3; cf. 15:12, quoting Is 11:10). Later, traditions evolved to support this view, and thus we find in the birth narratives of Matthew and Luke genealo-

14. Ibid., p. 62 and n. 115.
15. Cf. Sanders' reconstruction, *JJ,* pp. 234–37.

gies that ingeniously supply Jesus the Galilean with the correct messianic lineage.

The original apostles revered this Davidic tradition. But they also revered their resurrected leader whom—unlike Paul and the later evangelists—they had personally known. Thus inhibited from providing Jesus with a messianic past, they conformed him to Davidic tradition by giving him a messianic future. Destroying the enemies of God, judging the nations, perhaps even renewing or rebuilding the Temple, gathering all the tribes of Israel—when Jesus came again, he would come the way the royal messiah was supposed to come. And he was coming very soon.

JEWISH PERSECUTIONS OF THE EARLY MISSION

So far I have reconstructed a messianic movement whose message, despite one glaring oddity—its messiah had died and been raised—essentially recapitulated the traditional hopes and commitments of Jewish restoration theology. Its first apostles, themselves Jews, shortly after the resurrection took this message of the impending redemption of Israel to Israel. They traveled via the network of synagogue communities spreading throughout the Jewish homeland to the Diaspora, fervently preaching the coming of the Kingdom and their messiah's return. And, since these Diaspora synagogues naturally included greater numbers of affiliated Gentiles than did their Palestinian counterparts, more and more Gentiles, too, had the opportunity to hear and embrace the Gospel.

Scholars have attempted, in light of these two facts about the early mission—that the apostles preached the gospel of a crucified messiah, and Gentiles received it—to explain a third: the Jewish persecution of Jewish followers of Jesus. For this last we have unimpeachable evidence: the first-hand report of the former persecutor, Paul himself. For, sometime before his call to be an apostle (c. 33?), Paul had "persecuted the *ekklēsia* of God" that had formed within his community in Damascus (Gal 1:13; cf. v. 23; 1 Cor 15:9; Phil 3:6).

But we must first ascertain *what* Paul did before we can ask why he did it. What, in this context of a mission by Jews to Jews, would "persecution" have meant?

Acts, which purports to describe this period of the church's development, depicts Jews both in Jerusalem and in the Diaspora as violently hostile to Jewish Christians. In Jerusalem, Luke claims, shortly after the Ascension, the priests and Sadducees twice arrest without charges some apostles, whom the Sanhedrin subsequently releases (4:1–23; cf. 5:17–42, where the apostles are first "beaten," i.e., lashed; 5:40). Shortly thereafter, the Sanhedrin convenes to hear Stephen, who had been arrested at the instigation of other Greek-speaking Jews. These Jews accuse him of speaking against the Temple and the Law, teaching that "Jesus of Nazareth will destroy this place [i.e., the Temple], and will change the customs which Moses delivered to us" (6:8–14). Either by order of the court or by a mob, Stephen is then stoned (7:54–60; note Paul's presence, 8:1). That same day, "a great persecution" arises against the church in Jerusalem, so that everyone "except the apostles" flees the city (8:1–2).

Luke reports no other anti-Christian activity in Jerusalem until circa 44, when Herod Agrippa orders James the son of Zebedee beheaded during the intermediate days of Passover (12:1ff.; Luke gives no motive). Seeing that this pleases the Jews, Herod then arrests Peter, who miraculously escapes and leaves Jerusalem "for another place" (12:3–17). Some fifteen years later (c. 58?), Jews from Asia accuse Paul of "teaching men everywhere against the people and the Law and this place" and of defiling the Temple with Gentiles. They incite a mob to seize him in the Temple (21:27ff.). When other Jews pressure the Sanhedrin to have Paul killed, Roman troops put him into protective custody (23:12–24). Despite the importuning of the high priest Ananias, Luke concludes, Paul passes from Felix the governor to Festus, and ultimately on to Rome (24:1–28:30).

So in the Diaspora: religious contention invariably leads, in Luke's account, to violent persecution—imprisonments, executions, mob fury, and attempted assassinations. Luke makes this case especially in his presentation of Paul. Paul himself, in his own letters, says only that he persecuted the ekklesia "*kath' hyperbolēn,*" (to the utmost; Gal 1:13).[16] But Luke supplies a description of this activity: Paul witnesses and approves the murder/execution of Stephen in Jerusalem (8:1); he has Christians imprisoned (8:3, cf. 9:2; 22:4; 26:10); he votes the death penalty whenever the Sanhedrin tries them (implying both that he was a member and that it happened frequently, 26:10); in "raging fury" he plans to extend his activities to Damascus (26:12; also 9:2; 22:5). And once the shoe is on the other foot, the Jews of the Diaspora plot continuously to murder Paul (9:19–24, 26–30; contrast with the relatively benign Roman involvement, 13:12, 50; 14:2, 19; 17:5; 18:1–13, etc.).

How reliable is Acts' picture of these Jewish persecutions? Where we have independent evidence—Paul for the Diaspora, Josephus for Jerusalem—Luke does not fare well. Paul himself, for example, nowhere seems to understand "persecution" as "execution." When he complains of Jews "persecuting" him in the Diaspora, he specifies receiving "thirty-nine lashes," the maximum number allowed by synagogue courts (2 Cor 11:24).[17] Further, and again against Luke, Paul asserts that his activity began in Damascus, not Judea (cf. Gal 1:22–23). And in any case, local synagogue courts in the Diaspora during

---

16. For this translation of *kath' hyperbolēn,* see discussion in A. J. Hultgren, "Paul's Pre-Christian Persecutions of the Church," pp. 107–09.

17. See Hare's discussion of disciplinary flogging, *Jewish Persecution,* pp. 44–46.

this period do not seem to have had authority to execute capital cases (cf. Acts 26:10, which in turn complicates the Sanhedrin's prior relationship with Pilate in the matter of Jesus' execution, Lk 22:70–23:5).

Of the situation in Jerusalem, then, the historical Paul tells us nothing. Josephus, however, relates briefly in the *Antiquities* that "James the brother of Jesus the so-called Christ, and some others" (unidentified), were seized sometime around 62 by one Ananus, the newly appointed High Priest (*AJ* 20.9,1). This Ananus, "a bold man and very insolent," and like all Sadducees very rigid in judging offenders, then convened a Sanhedrin, accused the prisoners of breaking the Law, and had them executed (i.e., stoned). Other Jerusalemites— most likely Pharisees—fair-minded and strict in their observance of the Law, objected to Ananus' action.[18] Some complained to Agrippa II of its injustice; others, to the Roman governor Albinus of its illegality (apparently the Sanhedrin could not be convened without the governor's consent). Ananus was subsequently deposed.

Looking at Acts with Josephus in mind, and bracketing the theological concerns of late first-century Gentile Christianity that shape Luke's presentation, what can we say about the pattern of Jewish persecutions of Jewish Christians in Jerusalem? First, that the very earliest incidents all seem to involve the Sanhedrin. Stephen's death by stoning implies that he had committed a grave religious offense, but no trace of that remains in Luke's report, and the offense Luke adduces—sharp disagreement over the religious status of the Law, the Temple, the Jewish people, or Jesus (6:11–15)—clearly derives from the evangelist's own day. Also, if the Sanhedrin had authority in such capital cases, Pilate's role in Jesus' death would have been superfluous. Luke's historically incoherent citywide persecution that targets only Greek-speaking Jewish Christians suggests that controversy, if there were such, would not have been over religious issues, for then the original apostles would have been affected too (Acts 8:1ff.).

The Sanhedrin all but drops from view in later incidents. James' execution and Peter's arrest seem politically motivated—Herod beheads James and executes Peter's guards when Peter escapes.[19] It may be significant too that, once again, these things take place during Passover, when the city habitually hovered on the edge of popular insurgence. Luke's last incident, Paul's arrest, follows these events by almost fifteen years; and its instigators are not the high court, but a mob. Finally, while the High Priest clearly had a hand in the death of Jesus' brother James, Josephus reveals as well that, as late as 62, relations between the Jerusalem church and the Pharisees were so good that the latter,

18. Hare, *Jewish Persecution*, p. 33, discusses the identification of the objectors.

19. Had James' offense been religious, execution should have been by stoning (Brandon, *Jesus and the Zealots,* p. 97); the guards pay the penalty that should have been visited upon their escaped charge, Peter (Hare, *Jewish Persecution,* pp. 30–32).

offended by Ananus' action, secured his dismissal. Josephus further suggests that the charges against James were trumped up: something other than concern for the Law, which this precipitous trial violated, must have motivated Ananus.

In sum: while early anti-Christian activity in Jerusalem seems to have been connected to the Sanhedrin, Luke's description is too heavily overlaid with later developments for us to know now what precisely this activity was. His portrait, indeed, gives an impression he surely did not intend: that Jerusalem was a fairly quiet place for the church. Except in the period immediately following Jesus' execution, the Jewish authorities hardly troubled Christians there at all—indeed, we might infer from Josephus that, on the whole, good relations prevailed. And while Paul himself attests to Jewish anti-Christian activity in the Diaspora, Luke's lurid depiction of a stylized violence motivated by murderous envy and anachronistic theological concerns, again on the evidence of Paul, cannot be relied on. What then did Paul, as one of these hostile Diaspora Jews, actually *do* when he "persecuted"?

Probably what he later received as an apostle and named persecution: lashing (2 Cor 11:24). Jewish law specifies two sorts: *makkot arbaim*, the thirty-nine lashes, traditionally a punishment administered for specific violations of negative commandments; and *makkot mardut*, a disciplinary lashing administered at the discretion of the local court. The number of lashes given in this latter instance would also be up to the court's discretion; but if the defendant were to be punished *kath' hyperbolēn* (to the utmost), he could receive up to the customary legal maximum, thirty-nine.[20]

Paul's situation both as persecutor and persecuted suggests that he gave and received makkot mardut, discretionary lashing. But why? The polemic in Galatians, where Paul briefly alludes to this period, coupled with the equally polemical remarks he makes elsewhere about his former zeal for the Law and the hardships he currently endures because he does not "preach circumcision" (Phil 3:6; cf. 1 Cor 15:9; Gal 5:11), have led to an almost universal consensus. Paul as a Jew persecuted Jewish Christians, in this view, because they challenged religious principles fundamental to Judaism. Whether because they preached a crucified messiah or because they received Gentiles without requiring circumcision, these Christians violated Torah in the name of salvation in Christ.

The Scandal of the Crucified Messiah

How would a belief that a crucified messiah was about to return to establish the Kingdom of God so disturb a community that synagogue authorities would subject to public lashing those Jews who so believed? Scholars have

---

20. Hultgren, "Paul's Persecutions," p. 103; cf. Paula Fredriksen, "Paul and Augustine," pp. 13–14. mMakkot 3 details Jewish legal procedure for administration of this penalty.

offered two explanations: first, that proclaiming the arrival of *any* messiah would occasion legal offense; or, second, that proclaiming specifically a messiah who had been crucified would occasion religious offense.

According to the first explanation, Jews believing that Jesus was the messiah would have ceased to observe the Law and would actually have preached against it, since the Law was cancelled with the coming of the messiah. Paul the zealous Pharisee would thus have been roused to anger by a message that encouraged forsaking the Law in the name of Christ; later, after his revelation, he would champion the same.

This scenario requires a Christian movement that, within a few years of Jesus' death, preached a Law-free Gospel, a sort of pre-Pauline Pauline Christianity, directed not to Gentiles, but to Diaspora Jews. However, everything we know about Jesus' original disciples indicates that they kept the Law.[21] Scholars, following Luke, finesse this difficulty by an appeal to the mysterious Hellenists of Acts (Stephen et al., Acts 6:1–8:2; cf. 11:19–21). Only the more parochial Palestinian apostles, despite a message at least implicit in the Gospel, nonetheless kept the Law; the cosmopolitan Hellenists, according to this argument, rejected it.[22]

But then why would the Torah-observant Jerusalem apostles not themselves have taken offense? And why some sixteen years later would the Law-free community in Antioch be a source of contention and distress if James, Peter, and John had already known and cooperated with this earlier nonobservant Hellenist community right in Jerusalem? (Cf. Acts 6:5ff. and chaps. 10, 15; Gal 2:1–15.) Further, nothing in the Judaism of this period indicates that Jews who thought the messiah had arrived would feel called upon to cease observing Torah: again, the Jerusalem community, though proclaiming Jesus as messiah, kept the Law, as apparently did those Jews who joined other first-century messianic movements. Finally, when Paul preached against full Torah-observance to his Gentile communities, he nowhere argued that Christ's coming had overthrown the Torah as such, that is, even for Jews.[23] A tradition that the arrival of the messiah would end the Law, in other words, seems securely attested only in modern New Testament scholarship and not in ancient sources, be they Jewish or Christian.[24]

21. See "The Gospels: The Second Reading," in chap. 6.

22. E.g., Hengel, *Jesus and Paul.*

23. "As to the main outlines of Paul's teaching concerning the Law there is little doubt—they are set forth at length in his own letters, especially Romans and Galatians. . . . The Mosaic Law, he insists, is holy and spiritual (Rom 7:12,16); it not only was, but still is, valid; even [Gentile] Christians who accept its yoke are bound to follow it in all details (Gal 5:3)" (Morton Smith, "The Reason for the Persecution of Paul and the Obscurity of Acts," p. 262). See most recently the work of Lloyd Gaston, who uses this fact as his interpretive point of departure for understanding the epistles.

24. See esp. B. J. Levy, "Torah in the Messianic Age." Paul "*never appeals to the fact that the Messiah has come as a reason for holding the law invalid*" (Sanders, *PPJ*, pp. 479–80).

Other scholars, acknowledging that the arrival of the messiah would occasion no legal offense, suggest rather that proclaiming as messiah someone who had died specifically by crucifixion would be a religious offense. Why? Because of the malediction pronounced in Dt 21:23, repeated by Paul in Gal 3.13: "Cursed of God is every man hanged from a tree." Jesus nailed to a cross—that is, "hanged from a tree"—would thus in Jewish eyes have died under the divine curse pronounced by the Law. He therefore could not be accepted as messiah without, at the same time, defying the Law.[25]

But an utter lack of evidence compromises this proposal, too. In no Jewish writing of this period, Paul's included, do we find crucifixion itself taken to indicate a death cursed by God or by the Law. The reasoning in Gal 3:10–14, the premier support for this view, is extremely difficult precisely because it recapitulates the letter's entire argument. The cross of Christ, Paul says here, removed the curse of the Law since Christ became a curse by dying a death cursed by the Law. Therefore, he concludes, resuming his main theme, the blessing of Abraham has passed to the Gentiles so that they can receive the Spirit through faith—unless, of course, they listen to Paul's opponents and receive circumcision.

Even by Pauline standards, this is a snarled passage. Wending his way from "curse" to "blessing," Paul cites any number of scriptural verses, Dt 21:23 among them; and he must conflate "hanging on a tree" with "crucifixion" to do so.[26] But the Deuteronomic verse itself refers not to a mode of execution, as Paul must have known, but to the display of an already and otherwise executed criminal's body. The deceased's crime, further, would have been religious, not civil. The "curse" obtains because the deceased, on the finding of the Jewish religious court, was (presumably) guilty of blasphemy or idolatry; not because hanging itself, regardless of the agent in the execution (Rome, for instance) says something about the deceased's spiritual status.[27] Dt 21:23, in other words, is a loose fit with the facts of Jesus' death, but rhetorically it gets Paul where he needs to go.[28]

25. This is a prominent interpretive position, often held by those scholars who recognize that proclaiming an arrived messiah would not lead to legal offense. See Fredriksen, "Paul and Augustine," pp. 11–13 and literature cited.

26. The same conflation appears in another first-century Jewish text, 4 QpNahum ii.12 (Vermes, *Dead Sea Scrolls*, p. 232): note that no "curse" is mentioned. Cf. F. F. Bruce, "Curse of the Law," p. 31 and n.; T. C. G. Thornton, "Trees, Gibbets and Crosses," *JTS* n.s. 23 (1972), pp. 130–31.

27. "None is hanged [after execution] save the blasphemer and the idolator" (mSanh 6.4), though the sectarians at Qumran would apparently allow for execution by hanging (i.e., crucifixion) as a punishment for treason or maligning the Jewish people (11 Q Temple 64.6–13). See also Winter, *Trial of Jesus,* chaps. 7–8.

28. "The answer [of Gal 3:13] is introduced because of the *Stichworte* which lead the argument from 'Gentiles' to 'blessing' to its opposite, 'curse.' Thus Gal. 3:13 is not the keystone of the argument, but has a subsidiary place in explaining how the curse (3:10) is removed" (Sanders, *PLJP*, p. 25).

We may grant the rhetorical force of Paul's argument without generalizing from it to a common Jewish view of crucifixion as ipso facto religiously offensive to Jews, especially in light of other evidence. Nowhere, for example, do the eight hundred Pharisees crucified under Alexander Janneus (*AJ* 13.14, 2) or any of the thousands of Jews crucified in the rebellions against Rome seem to be held as having died "cursed of God." On the contrary, the rabbis apparently associate this Roman mode of execution with an event of great positive significance for their religion: the binding of Isaac, who carried the wood for his sacrifice "as a man carries his cross on his shoulders" (Gen Rabba 56:3). And finally, the experience of the original apostolic community actually presents counter-evidence: It resided in Jerusalem unmolested for decades at a time; it too proclaimed a crucified messiah.

What then should we conclude about the scandal of the cross? First, that in light of their experience of Jesus' resurrection, early Christians turned necessity into virtue by seeing in Jesus' cross a premier theological justification for its violation of traditional expectation: the messiah died for the sins of many. But we should not try to construct from this religious reinterpretation of Jesus' death a theological reason for the ultimate Jewish reaction, or lack of reaction, to it.[29] Christ crucified is a scandal to Jews "who demand signs" (1 Cor 1:22)—evidence, that is, that this messiah had brought with him the messianic age.[30] But nothing in Judaism *required* seeing a crucified man as cursed of God, nor do we have an instance of Jews actually having done so.

Finally, the argument that a criminal's death—that is, crucifixion—is scandalous and that, accordingly, the message that the messiah had been crucified would scandalize, reflects a Gentile, not Jewish, perspective. Romans indeed saw in Christ *hominem noxium et crucem eius*, "a criminal and his cross."[31] But why would a Jew? (Would Lollards see Hus as a heretic because the church had burned him at the stake?) Why would a nation that had seen generations of its own so executed agree with the hated imperial force responsible that such a death was a scandal? Why, in brief, would Jews reject a Jew for a Roman reason? The Jewish perception of crucifixion, particularly in this period of political unrest, would most naturally tend toward the opposite view: Rome's "criminals" were her subject peoples' heroes.[32]

---

29. "This verse has been made the hair on which to hang mountains of nonsense about Jewish resistance to the substitution of a spiritual Saviour for a military Messiah" (Smith, "Persecution of Paul," p. 263).

30. A problem, by the end of the 1st c. C.E., in Gentile Christian circles as well: "Scoffers will come in the last days with their scoffing . . . saying, 'Where is the promise of his coming? For ever since the fathers fell asleep, all things have continued as they were from the beginning of creation'" (2 Peter 3:3–4).

31. M. Felix, *Octavius* 29,2; see Martin Hengel's survey of Roman views in *Crucifixion*, pp. 22–83.

32. "The cross was the symbol of Zealot sacrifice before it was transformed into the Christian sign of salvation" (Brandon, *Jesus and the Zealots*, p. 145). Cf. Hengel's treatment of Jewish attitudes toward crucifixion, *Crucifixion*, pp. 84–90 and passim.

The Inclusion of the Gentiles

What then is left, in what we know about the early Christian mission, that can explain its "persecution" by Diaspora Jews? Only its apparent reception of and by "the uncircumcised," that is, Gentiles. How shall we interpret this fact?

Given the open relations between synagogues and sympathetic Gentiles in the Diaspora, it is difficult to say. As we have already seen, Diaspora synagogues routinely permitted interested Gentiles to attend services and hear the scriptures without making any "legal," that is, halakic, demands on them. The curious and occasional outside observer concerned simply to acquaint himself with a powerful God; the crowds who participated with Alexandrian Jews in the annual celebration of the Torah's translation into Greek; God-fearers who moved freely between the pagan and Jewish worlds; committed men and women studying for full conversion—all these Gentiles could and did enter the synagogue community as they would, just as those journeying to Jerusalem could and did offer sacrifices at the Temple.[33] Under normal circumstances, the boundary between the synagogue as a religious community and the larger outside world was a fluid one.

Turning from Judaism's quotidian practices regarding sympathetic Gentiles to speculations concerning their fate at the End, we find, not surprisingly, a broad range of opinion. Both scripture and intertestamental Jewish writings speak variously of a coming apocalyptic destruction (though of the unrighteous Gentiles, not Gentiles per se), or of the Gentiles' ultimate subjugation to a redeemed Israel, or of their cooperative participation and full inclusion in the Kingdom (e.g., Is 2:2–4; 49:23; 54:3; Zec 8:23; 1 En 90:3; Bar 4:25–35; Ps Sol 17:25ff.). In the rabbinical literature, however, and thus in that Judaism that survives and flourishes in the post-Second Temple period, this last view predominates. The community of the redeemed, said the rabbis, would have a mixed population; Gentiles too would have a place in the world to come.[34]

Are these "saved" Gentiles only those who had already *converted* to Judaism before the Kingdom came? Apparently not. Once a Gentile converted fully

---

33. The God-fearers are especially intriguing. These Gentiles "attend synagogue and pray and give alms. . . . Some . . . join study-groups to read and discuss the Law and take part in directing the community's charitable activities"; and, if members of the city council, they also perform the public sacrifices required of their office (Reynolds and Tannenbaum, *Aphrodisias*, pp. 56–58). Commodian, a late Latin churchman, complains that Jews permit Gentiles both to attend synagogue and to worship idols (ibid., pp. 62–63). Finally, the rabbis hold that such Gentiles are free to offer sacrifices to God anywhere, unlike Jews, who in principle could do so only at the Temple in Jerusalem (ibid., p. 64 and literature cited nn. 277–79).

34. See esp. Sanders, *JJ*, pp. 212–21, cf. 92–95; and his earlier treatment, *PPJ*, pp. 206–12; Schürer, *HJP* 2:530. The *Alenu*, an important synagogue prayer that perhaps predates the destruction of the Temple (since it makes no mention of rebuilding it), looks forward to the day when all the nations of the world recognize the nullity of idols and acknowledge the God of the universe.

to Judaism, he was held to be a Jew, fully responsible to and for the obser-
vances mandated in the Torah.[35] The "righteous proselyte" becomes part of
Israel and as such is blessed along with the nation in the chief synagogue
prayer, the Amidah.[36] To say that converted Gentiles are not in the category of
"Gentiles redeemed at the End" is thus a tautology, since a convert is already a
Jew.

Does this then imply that those Gentiles who remained pagan up to the End
would be "eschatologically" converted, receiving Judaism and thus, in the
case of males, circumcision as well when the Kingdom came? Nothing in the
literature expressing or interpreted as expressing apocalyptic hope speaks of
such conversion.[37] Their redemption, rather, depended upon their spiritual,
and hence moral, "conversion": Gentiles were expected, when the Kingdom
came, to *turn from* idolatry (and the sins associated with it, e.g., Rom 1:18–
32) and *turn to* the worship of the True God. *But moral conversion is not
halakic conversion.* These Gentiles would not, by abandoning their idols, have
the legal and religious status of "converts," that is, Jews. They would remain
Gentiles and *as Gentiles* would they be saved.[38]

Judaism's general openness toward sympathetic Gentiles, coupled with
traditions about their inclusion at the End, in turn sheds light upon the earliest
Christian mission. Once in the Diaspora, the Gospel spread so quickly to
Gentiles because Gentiles were present in the Diaspora synagogues to hear it.
And the original apostles so readily accepted these Gentiles because they saw
in their response, as with their leader's resurrection, yet one more sign that the
Kingdom approached—indeed, its effects were already manifest. "In those
days ten men from the nations of every tongue shall take hold of the robe of a

35. See Justin's remarks on Gentile converts to Judaism, chap. 2, n. 11. Philo comments that
the proselyte, in the final days, will be marveled at and held blessed by all, having joined
eschatological Israel, since not race but "virtue" matters to God, "who takes no account of the
roots [Gentile pagan origin] but accepts the full-grown stem" (*de praem. et poen.* 26.152).

36. "Over the righteous and over the pious; and over the elders of thy people of the house of
Israel; and over the remnant of their Torah scholars; and over the righteous proselytes; and over
us [i.e., the praying community] may thy mercy shower down, Lord our God" (13th Benediction;
text from Schürer, *HJP* 2:457).

37. The Talmud cites R. Eliezar as saying, in fact, that Israel in the messianic age will not
receive proselytes (bYeb 24b). The discussion clearly presupposes the existence of "eschatological
Gentiles": who else but a non-Jew could convert to Judaism? I do not see, then, how Sanders can
maintain that "very likely the general expectation of Gentile *conversion* at the end was common"
(*JJ*, p. 217, emphasis mine).

38. Hence "the nations" of Is 2:2; the "many" who will turn to God, worship him, and share
in Israel's salvation (Sib Or 3.616); the "entire humankind" (*kol benai basar*) who will turn from
their idols to God, in the *Alenu.* This long-standing theme within Jewish restoration theology, the
gratuitous redemption of Gentiles in the Final Days, accounts for Paul's remark in Gal 3:21, as
translated by Gaston: "I do not set at nought the grace of God; for since through the Law is (the)
righteousness (of God), Christ consequently has died as a free gift." See "Paul and the Law in
Galatians 2–3," esp. pp. 39–52.

Jew, saying, 'Let us go with you, for we have heard that God is with you'" (Zec 8:23).

What *religious* grounds, then, would Paul and his community have for persecuting such a group? I have already discounted as improbable the conjecture that the apostles to Damascus, even if they were among the group Luke labels "Hellenists" (i.e., Greek-speaking Jews; Acts 6:1), had abandoned the Law and in Christ's name urged other Jews to do so. But what if these apostles were permitting Gentiles into their ekklesia without requiring them to keep the Law or, more specifically, to be circumcised? Paul is persecuted sometime around 55 (by Jews? more likely by Jewish Christians, cf. Gal 1:6, 5:11) for not circumcising Gentile Christians; perhaps circa 33 this is why he persecuted.

But the same factors that explain the early apostles' ready inclusion of Gentiles—namely standard Jewish practice and a strong and articulated apocalyptic tradition—render this inclusion, and hence the question of circumcision, impossible as an issue between Paul and the ekklesia in 33. *Gentiles in Paul's own synagogue could attend services without receiving circumcision:* why should Paul and his community then persecute a subgroup in their midsts that followed just this practice? Was it because these apostles maintained that Gentiles, too, had a place in the world to come? But so did Isaiah, Micah, Zechariah, and Tobit; so did the Alenu; so, drawing on this tradition, did Philo and, later, the rabbis; and in this period, accordingly, so probably did the Pharisees. If Paul protested this opinion, then he and the leaders of the Damascus synagogue, not the members of its ekklesia, violated "the traditions of [the] fathers" (Gal 1:14).

Perhaps it was the intimate social intercourse between Jewish and Gentile members within the ekklesia that offended the larger community. Beside seeing each other in the synagogue, these people would gather in a member's house, perhaps as frequently as once a week, to celebrate a common meal in anticipation of the Second Coming and the messianic banquet (1 Cor 11:26). We know from Paul's later correspondence that this situation of "mixed eating" in Antioch caused concern to James and the "circumcision party" (Gal 2:11–14); and we know that the ritual status of wine and meat—whether they had been dedicated to idols and were thus not kosher, that is, ritually fit to eat—troubled even some Gentiles in Paul's congregations (1 Cor 8:1–13; 10:23–29a; Rom 14:13–20). Do these facts shed light on the situation in Damascus in 33?

Mixed table-fellowship itself could not have been the issue: Jews could and did eat with Gentiles. The discussions preserved in the Mishnah that detail the correct procedure on such occasions attest to the frequency with which they occurred.[39] But in the mixed situation of the ekklesia, a Gentile member might

39. See Hare, *Jewish Persecution,* pp. 8–9, for a discussion of the rules for mixed eating presented in mAvZar 5:5, which is concerned about the ritual purity of wine at such a meal.

celebrate the eucharistic meal for the community in his house and therefore serve nonkosher food and wine. Jews might eat nonkosher food only when life was at stake. If Jewish members of the ekklesia ate nonkosher food in Gentile Christian households, they would indeed violate the Law.

Could this be why the pre-Christian Paul "persecuted" the Jewish members of the Damascus Christian community? Possibly. But here we should recall that Jews belonged to their religious communities voluntarily. They were always free to withdraw or even (as Philo's own nephew did) apostasize.[40] If they were publicly flogged by the religious authorities every time they privately violated the laws of kashrut, they could vote with their feet. In such a situation—especially in the Diaspora, and especially in a period before halaka was standardized and codified—zealous officials would soon have depleted the Jewish population within their synagogues.

But what if these Damascene Christians, Jew and Gentile alike, energetically proclaimed that those "in Christ" need not be concerned with food dedicated to idols, since idols were naught? (cf. 1 Cor 8:1–6). That the biblically mandated food laws did not matter? Were these the elusive pre-Pauline Pauline Christians through contact with whom Paul himself came to embrace the "Law-free" Gospel? But if the mission had been run along these lines since before Paul's change of heart around 33, his conference with the pillars of the Jerusalem community some sixteen years later is all but inexplicable. And again, had things been so clear for so long, the confusion and bad feeling at Antioch, where Peter initially ate with the Gentiles and later withdrew (Gal 2:1–14), and the scruples of some Gentiles in Paul's own later communities (1 Cor 8:1–13; 10:23–31; cf. Rom 14:13–23), are hard to account for.

Could circumcision then have been the fundamental issue after all? Clearly some people mid-century objected strongly to the church's admission of uncircumcised Gentiles, Jewish tradition notwithstanding. Paul complains bitterly against their intrusion into his communities. Perhaps, in the 30s, he had been on the other side of this same issue and so had persecuted the church.

Again, possible but not likely. For the people hounding Paul and his congregations about circumcision appear to be Christians themselves (Gal. 1:6ff.; Phil 2:3ff.?), perhaps Gentile converts to Judaism who then joined the Christian mission (Gal 6:13).[41] The church's inclusion of Gentiles with or without the requirement of circumcision, in other words, appears to have occasioned

---

40. On Tiberius Alexander, Philo's nephew and an important figure in the Roman war against the Jews in 66, see Josephus, *AJ* 20.5,2.

41. Or perhaps Gentile *Judaizers*, Gentiles who observed elements of Judaism without becoming converts. See esp. Johannes Munck, *Paul and the Salvation of Mankind*, pp. 87–134; Lloyd Gaston's reconstruction, "Paul and Torah," and his "Israel's Enemies in Pauline Theology." See also Gager, *Origins of Anti-Semitism*, p. 236f.

an *intra*mural controversy, a question of concern and interest only to those already within these groups.

A question, further, that most probably did not arise in the context of the very earliest mission, when the Parousia was expected at any time. If male Gentiles received the kerygma, why burden them with a requirement, never demanded of them by the synagogue, to convert fully to Judaism and be circumcised? Clearly at some point in the years intervening between Jesus' death and Paul's trip to Jerusalem at mid-century, circumcision had become an issue (Gal 2:1–7, 12). I shall account for it when we consider Paul's mission. But to conclude here: noncircumcision cannot adequately account for Paul's pre-Christian persecution of Jewish Christians.

What, finally, do we know about the ekklesia in Damascus around 33? That, on whatever conditions, it probably included Gentiles who were exposed to the Christian message through the synagogue. The content of this message was: Jesus the messiah, crucified for the atonement of sin and raised to the right hand of God, is about to return to execute judgment on the wicked and establish the Kingdom. We have failed to derive from these two facts any religious reason for Paul's persecution of this group. What other reason might he have had?

The Gospel in the Diaspora

But for one necessary adjustment in their preaching—explaining why the messiah had been crucified—nothing that the early apostles claimed about Jesus would have been foreign to other Jews. In particular, neither their belief in a crucified messiah nor their ready inclusion of Gentiles within their groups would have offended Jews religiously. So why would Paul and others "persecute"?

Here we must consider the mood of the movement in the years immediately following Jesus' death. An intense expectation that the Kingdom was about to arrive had motivated the ministry of Jesus. His disciples shared this belief, and when Jesus called them to Jerusalem to witness the final redemption, they followed. The crushing events of that Passover radically challenged their faith in Jesus' message; just as radically, the resurrection appearances reconfirmed it. These Christophanies multiplied: first only Peter and then the twelve, later more than five hundred "brethren," and finally "all the apostles" saw the Risen Christ (1 Cor 15:4–7). Once again the community gathered in the expectation of the End. And waited.

At some point not long thereafter, this group burst into sustained and energetic missionary activity. Some apostles went to the Jews in Palestine. Others, presumably the bilingual among them, went to the Diaspora. Had the apostles concluded that the Kingdom tarried because they first had to carry Jesus' message to "all the towns of Israel"? (Mt 10:23). Did they then construe their call to extend to "all the towns where Israel dwells," that is, the Diaspora? Or was this solution to the delay of the End granted to them by the Risen Christ? (Mt 28:19; Acts 1:8).[42] The sources suggest a combination of all these factors. The salient point, however, is that the early mission was an extension of the ministry of Jesus in three ways: (1) it saw itself as continuing his work to prepare Israel for the Kingdom; (2) it was motivated by the same excited conviction that the Kingdom was at hand; and (3) the message of Jesus, subjective genitive ("the Kingdom is at hand") necessarily became the message of Jesus, objective genitive ("the Son of man [i.e., Jesus himself] is coming in power to establish the Kingdom").

Into Paul's synagogue in Damascus, then, sometime shortly after the year 30, came apostles energetically proclaiming the imminent subjection of the present order to the coming Kingdom of God. The glorious messiah who would lead the hosts of heaven had been known to them personally: Jesus of Nazareth. He had been crucified by Pontius Pilate only a short time ago, but they had experienced the power of his resurrection. Did this surprise their listeners? But the scriptures themselves clearly spoke of these things. . . .

If we can generalize from the picture later presented in Paul and in Acts, these missionaries would have found opportunities at the regular Sabbath service to speak, debate, and perhaps demonstrate the authority of their message with charismatic healings and exorcisms. Normally present as well on such occasions would be Gentiles voluntarily attached to the synagogue. They too would hear this message of the crucified and coming messiah; and if they responded in faith, the missionaries would see this as one more proof of the nearness of the End. The ekklesia subsequently formed in Christ's name, a mixed group of Jews and Gentiles, would continue to worship in the synagogue while also congregating separately (in the evening following the Sabbath?) to celebrate a common meal that both recalled Jesus' last supper with his disciples and anticipated the approaching messianic banquet in the Kingdom. Prayer and prophecy, interpretation of scripture, perhaps even ecstatic speech—all these activities would confirm the ekklesia's faith in the power and the nearness of the Spirit of God.

How would other Jews have regarded this excited and vocal subgroup in their midsts? The belief in a messiah known to have died might strike them prima facie as odd or incredible. But the enthusiastic proclamation of a messiah executed very recently as a political insurrectionist—a *crucified messiah*—combined with a vision of the approaching End *preached also to Gentiles*—this was dangerous. If it got abroad, it could endanger the whole Jewish community. The ekklesia might protest that the Kingdom would be brought about by a miracle, not armed uprising. But the traditional language for expressing such a belief—hosts of heaven, battles against the wicked, judg-

---

42. Whose instruction, initially, may have been only to go to the ends of *ha-Aretz*, the land of Israel. See Schwartz, "End of *GE*."

ment and condemnation of evil—was invariably martial. Besides, if the wicked are punished in the End, and the Romans had just killed this messiah, what were these people claiming was about to happen to Rome? Bad enough if Jews spoke of such things among themselves. But the *ekklesia* was full of Gentiles, rushing perhaps to their unaffiliated Gentile neighbors with this "good news" of impending redemption. This latter group, whether out of malice or fear (justifiable, in light of the later attacks on Gentile populations by insurgent Jews when war broke out in Palestine in 66),[43] might then inform the government that the Jewish community harbored messianists from Palestine who spoke of coming battles.

The synagogue court had no jurisdiction over its Gentile sympathizers. But it could discipline those Jews who, seemingly oblivious to the politically sensitive nature of declaring a coming *christos,* endangered the well-being of the entire community. The form that discipline would take was makkot mardut—lashing. Were Paul an officer of the court, he would be responsible for the administration of its decisions, perhaps executing its orders *kath' hyperbolēn* (Gal 1:13), to the maximum thirty-nine lashes allowed by the Law.

This reconstruction is of course speculative. But it has two significant advantages over the traditional explanations for Paul's persecutions reviewed above. It requires neither anachronism (the retrojection of issues arising from Paul's mid-century mission to the Gentiles into the early 30s, when as a Jew he persecuted Jews) nor the invention of a Jewish exegetical tradition unattested in any of our data (crucifixion ipso facto as curse, by appeal to Dt 21:23).

It also recognizes the politically precarious situation of urban Jewish communities in the Diaspora. Particularly in this troubled period, these could be subject to the violent hostility of the Gentile majority and depended on Rome for protection. With that protection removed, such communities could be attacked and even slaughtered with impunity—as was Alexandria's in 38 C.E., and Paul's home community in Damascus, when war broke out in 66 (10,000 slain, *BJ* 2.20,2; 18,000 slain, *BJ* 7.8,7).[44] Diaspora synagogues might well

43. The experience, for example, of Hippus, Gadara, Scythopolis, and Pella (*BJ* 2.18,1), Greek cities in territorial Palestine. Almost 50 years later, the Gentile population of Cyrene in North Africa was slaughtered at the beginning of an initially successful anti-Roman revolt in the Diaspora: the rebels, en route to Jerusalem, got as far as Alexandria, where hastily dispatched imperial troops finally defeated them. Schürer, *HJP,* 2:85–183, reviews the effects of the war in 66–73 on the Hellenistic cities; see 1:529–34 on the rebellion of 115–17. On this rebellion see also Applebaum, *Jews and Greeks;* Smallwood, *Jews under Roman Rule,* pp. 389–427.

44. For the anti-Jewish riots in Alexandria, see Philo, *in Flaccum* and *ad Gaium;* Josephus, *AJ* 18.8,1. Josephus' list of Jewish urban populations slaughtered at the outbreak of the war in 66—20,000 dead, for example, in Caesarea (*BJ* 2.18,1; 7.8,7); 2,000 (the entire community) in Ptolemais (*BJ* 2.18,5); 13,000 in Scythopolis (*BJ* 2.18,3–4; 7.8,7)—attests to the reasonableness of the anxiety these Jews might have felt as messianic rumors spread to the general public. For a fuller list, with discussion, see Schürer, *HJP,* 2:85–183.

fear alienating or antagonizing Rome. News from Palestine spreading via the synagogue of a coming messiah might do just that.

Diaspora Jews, anxious about the Roman perception of and reaction to an enthusiastic messianic group in their midst, would thus share a concern with the High Priest, or the chief priests, who had taken a part in Jesus' arrest. But, as Acts and Josephus attest, anti-Christian activity soon quieted down in Jerusalem, whereas in the Diaspora it continued. Why then, if communities both at home and abroad found this messianic preaching politically dangerous, would the Sanhedrin have been so much less active against the church than the synagogue courts were?

The answer may lie with the fact that Jerusalem, unlike Damascus or the cities in Paul's eventual itinerary, had a Jewish majority. The starting situation was both less threatening and socially less volatile. Also, in the course of the four decades until the destruction of the Second Temple, the Sanhedrin had other noisily apocalyptic popular movements and *living* messianic preachers to worry about.[45] As long as normal conditions obtained—that is, in any situation short of outright war—the Jewish community in Jerusalem was fairly secure. But in the Diaspora, and especially in a situation of messianic agitation, things could, and ultimately did, worsen abruptly.

Jewish Christians themselves in this early period just a few years after Jesus' execution would have seen matters differently. They felt themselves on the verge of witnessing the fulfillment of the biblical promises to Israel, and from the synagogue they proclaimed this conviction to others. One sign of the nearness of the End had already been granted to them: the resurrection of their crucified leader. As the mission continued, signs multiplied. Apostles worked miracles; communities "filled with the Spirit" prophesied; the Gentiles hearkened to the word of the Lord. And they recalled and repeated, from the teaching of Jesus himself, what was to be the final sign of the imminent End: the destruction of the Temple in Jerusalem, to be renewed or superseded by the eschatological Temple of God.

THE APOSTLE TO THE GENTILES

> Christ . . . appeared to Cephas, then to the twelve. Then he appeared to more than five hundred brethren at one time . . . then to James, then to all the apostles. Last of all, as to one untimely born, he appeared to me. For I am the least of the apostles, unfit to be called an apostle, because I persecuted the church of God. But by the grace of God I am what I am, and his grace toward me was not in vain. On the contrary, I worked harder than any of them, though it was not I, but the grace of God which is with me.   (1 Cor 15:3–10)

Paul included himself in the original circle of apostles who witnessed the Risen Christ. His personal circumstances, however, differed considerably

45. See "Insurrectionists," discussed in chap. 5.

from theirs. He lived in the Diaspora; he had never known Jesus "according to the flesh"; and he had once "persecuted" the ekklesia. After receiving this vision of the Christ, Paul left Damascus for Arabia, then returned, and only "after three years" did he go up to Jerusalem, "to those who were apostles before me," namely Peter (Cephas) and James (Gal 1:16ff.). We do not know what he did in this interim,[46] nor do we know whether he contacted other Christian missionaries while in Arabia (he implies in this passage that he did not: "I did not confer with flesh and blood"; 1:16). In this time between his call and his first trip to Jerusalem, then, Paul's sole exposure to the kerygma seems to have been through the Christians whom he had persecuted in Damascus.

These Christians, both those native to the Damascus community and those who had come to them from the original group in Palestine, were Jews. They continued to worship in the synagogue and to observe the Torah as they awaited the glorious return of the messiah whose crucifixion had atoned for sin and whose resurrection announced the impending close of the age. But Paul, writing of these days some twenty to twenty-five years later, had taken his gospel explicitly, if not exclusively,[47] to Gentiles. To them he spoke of the preexistent divine Lord and Son through whose death even the Torah had been superseded in the economy of salvation. And he dated the origin of these views to his days as a persecutor in Damascus (Gal 1:13–15).

How had Paul come to such a Gospel?

Cosmic Evil, Cosmic Christ

Jesus' *point de depart* in Palestinian tradition was earth. After his resurrection, he had ascended to the right hand of the Father; soon he would descend, returning to establish the Kingdom. But Paul prefaced this Christological pattern with another half cycle: descent (in obedience to the Father)/ascent (at the resurrection)/descent again (at the Parousia). Before his life in the body, the Son had played a crucial role as God's agent in Creation (1 Cor 8:6); with his resurrection, he signaled its imminent transformation (Rom 8:19ff.).

Scholars have long sought some explanation in Paul's background that could account for his view of Christ. Is his in fact the gospel of the "Hellenists," Greek-speaking Christian Jews who, according to Acts, left Jerusalem

46. See discussion of this period in H. D. Betz, *Galatians*, pp. 66–73.

47. 1 Thes 1:9, "you turned to God from idols to serve a living and true God"; 1 Cor 12:2, "you know that when you were Gentiles you were led astray to dumb idols"; Gal 4:8, "formerly when you did not know God, you were in bondage to beings that by nature are no gods"; Rom 1:5, "among all the gentiles, including yourselves." See too Sanders, *PLJP*, p. 181.

To repeat: the fact that these Gentiles went from idolatry to being "in Christ" does *not* mean that they had not been God-fearers. Rather, it suggests the opposite: what other population in the Empire (1) would have moved from idolatry to Jewish monotheism and (2) would have been able to follow (better, perhaps, than many modern historians) the logic of Paul's arguments from scripture, than this population who would have been exposed to the LXX through the synagogue?

to carry the good news back to the synagogues of the Diaspora (11:19ff.)? Or is this view the measure of pagan influences on Paul, who thus speaks to his Gentile congregations in the language of the mystery cults with their dying and rising divine redeemers? Or is its matrix the Jewish speculations on God's divine preexistent Wisdom through whom God had formed the universe and who was rejected by men?[48]

As the literature itself demonstrates, all things are possible, but not all things are helpful. Postulating Hellenistic Christian influence just pushes the problem back a step: why and how would the Hellenists have come to this view of Christ, and so shortly after the execution of Jesus? And the conjecture that Paul drew on esoteric concepts of divine mediation, whether Jewish or pagan, still leaves the chief question unanswered: what would have prompted him to associate personal divine preexistence and unique eternal sonship with a human being? And what would the original apostles who had followed Jesus in the Galilee, or, in James' case, grown up with him, make of such a claim?

While debate continues over the environmental influences on Paul's Christology, scholars agree on its immediate cause: his experience of the Risen Christ. But we cannot say how he perceived this event when it occurred. His allusions to it, in letters written after a lifetime of missionary work, function strategically to support arguments he makes at mid-century. Lacking any comparative evidence from around 33, we cannot gauge the degree to which this later polemical context shaped his report.

The passage quoted above, for example, prefaces Paul's protest against what he considers an inadequate understanding of the resurrection. Some Corinthians had failed to understand the implications of Christ's resurrection for those "in Christ." Paul thus begins by saying that, while he had once persecuted the ekklesia, his vision of the Risen Christ had so turned him around that he was now one of God's most conscientious apostles (1 Cor 15:8–11). Then comes Paul's real point: "Now if Christ is preached [in particular by Paul] as raised from the dead, how can some of you say that there is no resurrection of the dead? But if there is no resurrection of the dead, then Christ has not been raised. . . . For if the dead are not raised, then Christ has not been raised" (15:12–13, 16).

But since Christ has been raised (15:20), all "in" him, both the living and the dead, will be transformed when he returns (15:23, 35, 42–54). It is to support *this* point that Paul brings in his "call." Not only has Paul seen Christ: he has been given such a large measure of grace that he went from least fit (v. 9) to most fit (v. 10). Would not the authority of his interpretation of this event correspond to this great measure of grace?

---

48. Hengel combines both the Hellenist and the Wisdom explanations, *Jesus and Paul,* esp. pp. 48–64; and *Son of God,* pp. 66–83; Rudolph Bultmann anchored this Christology—esp. through its use of the term *kyrios* (lord)—to Greek mystery cults. See, e.g., *Theology of the New Testament,* pp. 51–52, 133–52, 164–83.

The situation in Galatia and Philippi is more highly charged. "Other apos tles" preaching "another gospel" had invaded Paul's territory. Do they urge circumcision on Paul's Gentile community, and speak of the Law, and call Paul's Jewish credentials into question? Ah, says Paul, he had once been like them: a Hebrew of Hebrews, zealous for the Law—"blameless," in fact, as to his righteousness under the Law. But such zeal was and is misguided, indeed antithetical to salvation in Christ, these other Christians' claims notwithstanding. Paul knows this from his own experience: such zeal had even driven him to persecute the church (Gal 1:13–14; Phil 3:6). But then God himself and Jesus Christ had revealed to Paul the truth of the (i.e., Paul's) Gospel. Could these rival apostles who preached circumcision claim so much?

This revelation of Christ had been the occasion of Paul's turning from persecutor to apostle. But what was its content? Again, given the retrospective and polemical nature of Paul's allusions to it, we cannot say.[49] But we may infer at least that it convinced Paul that the End really was at hand (Rom 13:11), and that it really would be ushered in by the crucified and risen messiah. His response, whether immediately thereafter or "after three years," was to preach the Gospel to the Gentiles.

By *Gospel* Paul meant neither "sayings of the Lord"[50] nor episodes drawn from Jesus' earthly mission—precisely the content of the later gospels. The political and historical metaphors of more traditional Jewish apocalyptic eschatology retained even by these later works could not adequately express Paul's vision of the enormous evil overcome and about to be overcome by the Risen Christ. He thus transposed the apocalyptic struggle between good and evil into a different key, from the historical to the cosmic. Paul proclaims that the powers of the evil cosmic rulers of this aeon, who in their ignorance had crucified the "Lord of glory" (1 Cor 2:8), had been broken by power of Christ's resurrection. The believer, once baptized into the death of the Son, himself becomes part of Christ's risen body, so that these forces have no more power over him (Gal 4:3–7). Thus receiving the spirit of sonship as a consolation, the Christian could look forward to the redemption of his own body, indeed of all creation, with the imminent return of the Lord (Rom 8).

Moral Evil and the End of the Law

Thus far, despite his radical divinization of the Risen Christ, Paul seems to stand within the same religious universe as the early apostles. Those features peculiar to his "high Christology" (preexistence, unique sonship) extend the kerygma of the suffering and glorified messiah. Paul painted the apocalyptic vision on the broader canvas of the Hellenistic universe, and he needed a

49. See my arguments, Fredriksen, "Paul and Augustine," pp. 3–5, 28–34.

50. He reports very few, e.g., 1 Thes 4:15ff. (events at the End), 1 Cor 7:10–11 (marriage and divorce), 11:23–26 (the eucharistic tradition).

cosmic Christ to defeat cosmic evil. There is logic to this argument, and even some consonant Jewish traditions.[51] But in discussing moral evil, Paul goes well beyond—indeed, goes against—any sort of Jewish thinking. For when God sent his Son to die on the cross, Paul maintains, he did more than break the powers of the archons. God also revealed that righteousness lay not with the Law—which in fact led only to sin and death—but uniquely with life in Christ.

With this issue of Paul's views on Christ and the Law, we enter into the deepest exegetical quagmire of New Testament scholarship. Scholars, their confusion facilitated by Paul's own apparent inconsistency (cf., for instance, 2 Cor 3:4–9 and Rom 3:1–2), do not agree even on *what* Paul said, much less why he said it. Interpretations currently fall into one of three categories, one traditional and the other two revisionist. As part of our effort to understand what stands behind Paul's image of Christ, I shall briefly review these here.

Paul Rejects Judaism

From the later New Testament writings through Augustine and Luther to modern historical criticism, this interpretation predominates. Briefly stated, it holds that through Christ, Paul realized that Judaism as a religion was both deadening and dead. The Torah only tangled man in self-righteousness, inducing him to think that he could earn salvation through the accumulation of good works ("legalism"). The spiritual result was hypocrisy (doing good works for the wrong reason, that is, for one's own benefit), complacency ("Since I did these works, I am righteous"), or anxiety ("How can I ever do enough?"). Indeed, zeal for the Law, motivated by this desire to earn salvation, led (and leads) to sin, since righteousness comes only as the unmerited gift of God's grace. In the language of existential theology, Paul announced that Judaism as a religion of works-righteousness leads to anxiety and alienation. Jewish self-righteousness (a type of religiosity not limited to Jews) thus inhibits the reception of grace.[52]

Various problems attend this interpretation. First, it cannot account for all Paul's positive statements about the Law—that it is one of Israel's great privileges (Rom 9:4), the key to decent community life (Gal 5:14) and the standard for community behavior *even for Gentile Christians* (1 Cor 14:34). One *can*—and Paul did—attain righteousness under the Law (Phil 3:6); and the Christian too, though "in the Spirit" and "under grace," must nevertheless follow it (e.g., Rom 13:8ff.). Second, this reading makes Paul's moral reasoning incoherent, since—despite his characteristically Jewish insistence on God's

---

51. See Hengel's valuable discussion, *Son of God,* pp. 21–23, 41–56, 57–84.

52. This describes a mainstream, and extremely influential, school of NT scholarship that has particularly characterized German approaches to Jesus as well as Paul. See Sanders' incisive critique of this interpretive tradition, *PPJ,* pp. 33–59, 426ff.

justice, mercy, and righteousness— it holds that Paul believed in a God who gave a Law that he knew no one could possibly fulfill, or who condemned men for their zeal in fulfilling his own commandments.

Third, these exegetical and ethical difficulties are compounded by a major historical one: outside traditional Christian polemic and exegesis, there is no evidence for the existence of the Judaism that Paul, according to this theory, describes. In the literature where Judaism speaks for itself, Israel's election, embodied in the giving of the Torah, is viewed as God's gracious gift. Obedience to Torah is the proper response to the gift of Torah, but it does not *earn* salvation as such. "Election and ultimately salvation cannot be earned, but depend on God's grace" and mercy.[53] And in the inevitable event of moral failure, the tradition specifies various ways, spiritual and material, to atone for sin. What in historical Judaism, then, corresponds to Paul's putative "description"?

Historians, uneasy at finding themselves more familiar with Paul's native religion than apparently he was himself, search for plausible targets for his invective. Rabbinic ("Palestinian") religion was not legalistic, but perhaps Hellenistic Judaism was. Or the opposite: Hellenistic Judaism was universalistic and humane; rabbinic Judaism self-righteous and judgmental. Or perhaps Paul really protests the absolutism of apocalyptic Judaism, which urged those who would be saved to earn their way through meritorious works.[54]

Others, unsatisfied with all these attempts, urge that the traditional interpretation be abandoned altogether. Paul did not really reject Judaism when he criticized the Law. Against what, then, does he speak?

Paul Rejects Judaizing

More recently, some historians and theologians have argued that Paul's target is not Juda*ism*, but Juda*izers,* Gentile Christians (perhaps proselytes to Judaism) who held that circumcision was necessary for salvation in Christ.[55] We know that such people had created a pastoral problem for Pauline churches in Asia Minor by the end of the first century. Perhaps they are the object of Paul's own critique.

On this interpretation, Paul nowhere denigrates Torah, circumcision, or the promises to Israel, but simply holds them to be *irrelevant for the Gentiles,* on behalf of whose eschatological salvation he has been called to work. The Gentile need not become a Jew to enter the Kingdom; rather, through Christ

53. See ibid., pp. 85–87.
54. Hellenistic Judaism as oppressive, e.g., Samuel Sandmel, *Genius of Paul,* pp. 15ff., H. J. Schoeps, *Paul,* pp. 25–37; rabbinic Judaism—the usual choice in such "reconstructions"—see n. 52 above; Hellenism and apocalypticism, C. J. G. Montefiore, *Judaism and Saint Paul,* p. 95; J. Zeisler, *Pauline Christianity,* p. 100.
55. See n. 41 above.

he receives the revelation of God's righteousness apart from the Law, a righteousness that depends on faith that in Christ he has indeed been justified. Through baptism into Christ (as opposed to circumcision, which is for Jews), Gentiles receive the Spirit, which in turn enables them to conduct the social and spiritual life of the ekklesia according to the principles of Torah (1 Thes 3:13; 5:23; Phil 1:10, Gal 5:14; 1 Cor 14:34–36; Rom 13:8–10). Accordingly, the Gentile who elects full conversion to Judaism spurns God's gracious offer of justification through faith in Christ and, by assuming the Law, seeks his own righteousness based on "the works of the Law."

Paul thus speaks "not to the exclusion of Judaism, but rather to the inclusion of Gentiles."[56] Christ does not abrogate Torah. Rather, God has a double covenant with humanity, to the Jew first and also the Greek: through the Torah with Israel; and, now that the end of the ages is upon humankind, through Christ with the Gentiles.

The double covenant model is attractive for many reasons. First, it takes seriously both the fervor of Paul's eschatological expectation and the missionary context of his work: he preaches to the Gentiles. Circumcision, the Sabbath, and the food laws would seem burdensome obligations to Gentiles, and so God revealed to Paul that, in view of the approaching End, "another righteousness," without the Law, was available to Gentiles in Christ.[57] Second, it places Paul coherently within his religious context, first-century Judaism. Scholars need neither endorse a caricature of Judaism nor invent reasons rooted in Paul's psyche to make sense of his hostile statements: he directs them against Judaizers, not Judaism per se. Also, it accounts for his seeming contradictions. Circumcision (and by extension, the entire Law) is not required of Gentiles for salvation (as any of Paul's Jewish contemporaries, Christian or not, would have agreed); but nevertheless the Law is holy and the commandment is holy, just, and good (Rom 7:12). Finally, this interpretation explains the striking and baffling absence from Paul's letters of the Jewish concept central to keeping the covenant: tshuvah, return to the Torah, repentance. Paul addressed Gentiles. They were not *re*turning to God, but turning for the first time.

This interpretation allows Paul to be a first-century Jew rather than a misplaced fifth-century Augustinian, sixteenth-century Lutheran, or twentieth-century existentialist theologian. That is its great strength. Additionally—an advantage in this age of increased ecumenicalism—it clears Paul of the charge of antisemitism and so makes him an attractive figure theologically. But can we responsibly "reinvent" an ecumenical Paul? What about his attack on Peter at Antioch? He did not endorse Peter's decision as a Jew to observe Torah (i.e., the food laws) while allowing the Gentiles, justified by faith in

56. Gager, *Anti-Semitism*, p. 215.
57. Gaston's argument, summarized and expanded ibid., pp. 197–264.

Christ, to drink whatever they pleased. Rather, Peter "stood condemned" for *not* disregarding the Law (Gal 2:11ff.). In his metaphor of Israel as the true olive tree, the wild branches, the Gentiles, have been grafted on. But the native branches have been broken off: they must be *re*-grafted by God (Rom 11.17 24). This does not seem to be the language of "two covenants."

Paul speaks both positively and negatively about the Law. Emphasizing his negative comments and construing them as actually descriptive leads to a historically false image of his native religious environment. Apportioning the positive statements to Judaism and the negative ones to Gentile Judaizing creates an even-handed theology that cannot account for Paul's insistence that both Jew and Gentile will be redeemed by Christ (Rom 11:26). How else, then, can we read Paul?

Paul Rejects Everything but Christ

A third interpretation holds that Paul's negative statements about the Law are indeed directed against Judaism, not because he misunderstood his own religious tradition, but because after his experience of the Risen Christ, Paul condemned as useless for salvation anything other than being in Christ. The attempt to find antecedents to explain Paul's position are thus doomed to frustration, because there are none. Paul never held that the Law was inherently bad or inherently impossible to fulfill; but after the revelation of Christ, it is simply irrelevant for salvation, and therefore it should be condemned when proposed as salvation's prerequisite. "This is what Paul finds wrong in Judaism: it is not Christianity."[58]

Paul's extreme position, on this construction, results from his encounter with the Risen Christ as universal redeemer. Up until his call, Paul had not seen salvation as a problem; afterward, he had to construct a problem grave enough to have required a solution as radical as God's sending his own Son as redeemer.

From what, then, does Christ redeem man? From the antithesis of God, namely, Evil. Paul's thought here is uncompromisingly "ancient," not "modern"; for this evil is not simply moral (and thus human), but cosmic. Christ's blood indeed atoned for man's transgressions—that much Paul would have inherited from the early kerygma. But how does it affect cosmic evil—Sin, Death, the Flesh, the astral *stoicheia* (elements), and all the powers by which man is dominated while in the "present evil aeon"?

It is to this point that Paul introduces his critique of the Law. Righteousness under the Law *is* possible: Paul felt that he himself had achieved it (Phil 3:6). But that righteousness cannot effect the transfer necessary to move one from the lordship of Death to the lordship of Life, that is, Christ. Only the righteousness available through faith in Christ, whose death and resurrection

---

58. Sanders, *PPJ*, p. 552.

broke the enslaving power of Death, can do that. The Law indeed has many advantages (Rom 3:9), but not with respect to salvation. The Law cannot save, because only Christ saves.

This interpretation, too, has many advantages. It moves to the foreground Paul's call, which, given its radical effects, may properly be deemed a "conversion." It emphasizes the first-century quality of Paul's eschatology: the mythic concept of Lordships, the corporate nature of salvation (baptism into Christ's body), the enslavement to astral powers outside of Christ, the emergency situation brought about by the impending End. It also explains why Paul does not mention repentance or forgiveness: "repentance, no matter how fervent, will not result in a change of lordships."[59] Finally, it ties Paul's "most profound conviction about himself" as apostle to the Gentiles immediately to his commitment to his Law-free, exclusive Gospel: *"It is the Gentile question and the exclusivism of Paul's soteriology which dethrone the law, not a misunderstanding of it or a view predetermined by his background."*[60]

But to the degree that it recapitulates some of the major points of the first, or "classic," interpretation of Paul, this view also recapitulates some of its weaknesses. To hold that Paul's conversion resulted in an unprecedented and otherwise unexplainable position vis-à-vis Judaism is to render his historical and cultural context essentially irrelevant to his theology.[61] And to stipulate as the theological center of his message Paul's conviction that "God shows no partiality" (Rom 2:11), so that both Gentiles and Jews are saved on the same basis—faith in Christ—is to make God, again, into some version of Descartes' Evil Genius: why would God have presented his Law as his will and the path of righteousness and life, in order only to reveal, at the eleventh hour, that its real purpose was to condemn? This theory, reasoning backward from the extreme effect of Paul's call, explains why Paul says that the Law condemns (so that all need to be saved, to preserve divine impartiality, etc.). But it hardly explains how Paul could see the perpetrator of such a deception as a just God ("Is there injustice with God? God forbid!"; Rom 9:14).

Review of these interpretations only confirms what our earlier reading had already revealed: Paul is extremely difficult to understand. Our efforts suffer for standing at so many removes from him, both temporal and cultural. We cannot, for example, believe (at least not in the way that Paul did) that the world is about to end; nor can we as either Christians or Jews appreciate the "anguish and dilemma" of someone who at a unique moment in time was both.[62] Furthermore, Paul's long respectability at the heart of the New Testament canon makes him harder to see: almost two thousand years of exegesis

---

59. Ibid., p. 500.
60. Ibid., p. 496–97.
61. So too Gager, *Anti-Semitism,* p. 203.
62. Sanders, *PLJP,* p. 197.

tying him to later periods of Christian culture frustrate our efforts as historians to see him in his own. And, finally, from the evidence of his own letters, Paul was more successful at communicating excitement and conviction than clarity. He confused his own congregations. We come by our own confusions honestly, and by now we lack too many pieces of the puzzle to assemble a completely coherent picture of either the man or his message.

Perhaps, however, we can succeed at reconstructing his situation. By the time he wrote the letters now in the Christian canon, Paul had been a missionary in a movement which had been expecting and preaching the imminent return of the Risen Lord for nearly a quarter of a century. Time, inexplicably, had stretched on since the first Easter; on, indeed, with the mission to the synagogues in the Diaspora; and it showed signs of continuing even once the Gospel spread from Israel to the nations. Let us—resigning ourselves at once to the incompleteness of any reconstruction—try to understand Paul's image of Jesus and his Law-free Gospel against this background of the original community's continuing expectation and the Kingdom's continuing delay. Unable to know from this distance exactly what Paul said, we may nonetheless be in a position to understand why he said it.

The Gentiles, the Law, and the Close of the Age

The first missionaries preached the imminent return of their crucified messiah as part of the eschatological scenario about to unfold with the arrival of the Kingdom. Paul encountered them at a time when their conviction and urgency were very great—within a very few years of Jesus' execution and resurrection. Some twenty-five years later, the Apostle to the Gentiles exhorted the community at Rome with no less urgency: "Now salvation is nearer than when we first believed; the night is far gone, the day is at hand" (Rom 13:11). How had Paul sustained for a quarter century his conviction that he was living on the edge of the aeon? How did he see in this passage of time a confirmation of his message that the End was at hand? And how did those who were apostles before Paul continue in this expectation?

We see in the closing chapters of Romans how Paul had integrated his own self-image as uniquely appointed apostle with his Law-free mission to the Gentiles and with the approach of the End. The interim before the Kingdom came would last as long as Paul's mission itself. *He* was bringing in the "full number of the Gentiles" (11:25). He had preached from "Jerusalem as far round as Illyricum" and now there was no longer "any room for work in these regions" (15:23). After his trip back to Jerusalem "in the priestly service of the Gospel of God" to bring the offering of the Gentiles (that is, the collection made in his churches, and in a sense these Gentiles themselves) to the original community there, Paul would press on to Rome and ultimately Spain (15:23–29). And once he had brought in the "full number of Gentiles," the final events could unwind.

The ultimate source of Paul's sense of vocation and his assessment of his uniquely important role in bringing God's plans to completion lies beyond historical examination, in his personality and in his own view of his call. But we do know how he exercised this vocation and vindicated this assessment: by tirelessly preaching the Law-free Gospel of salvation in Christ to the Gentiles. Was this, too, Paul's singular contribution to the movement?

In light of traditional Jewish hopes for the eschatological salvation of the Gentiles and the early movement's ready embrace of them, I have argued, this seems unlikely. True, the attitudes toward Gentiles expressed in scripture itself are mixed. At the End, Israel's role as a light to the nations is to result in the Gentiles also turning and worshiping the only true God (e.g., Is 2:2–3; 49:6). Or, at the End the wealth of the nations will pour (as tribute?) to Jerusalem (45:14); or the Gentiles will serve Israel (49:23).[63] Early Christianity's ready inclusion of Gentiles, however, proves that it, like the Hellenistic Judaism represented by Philo and the pseudepigrapha, and like the rabbinic inheritors of Pharisaism in the following century, stood within the "liberal" stream of Deutero-Isaiah. The Kingdom of God would include two peoples: Gentiles, redeemed from idolatry, and Israel, redeemed finally from exile.

Inclusion is not conversion. Conversion, as we have seen, is a "normal" function of Judaism, complete with scriptural precedents (Ruth) and various halakic requirements, among which is circumcision for males. But inclusion, in the context of the early mission, points again to the movement's origins in the traditional hopes of Jewish restoration theology. *For the Christian mission as a Jewish apocalyptic movement admitted Gentiles from the beginning without the requirement that they convert to Judaism, and thus as Jews be responsible to and for the Law.*

Put differently, the Law-free Gospel to the Gentiles was not Paul's original contribution to early Christianity. James, Peter, and John endorsed Paul's Gospel, despite the importuning of the "false brethren," because that had always been the basis on which Gentiles had been admitted (Gal 2:1–10). And this was so not because Jesus himself had preached or implied the abrogation of the Torah, nor because in the crucifixion and resurrection of their messiah this group realized that the Law had come to an end, but because such was consonant with that stream of Jewish apocalyptic tradition with which the earliest movement—also Jewish, also apocalyptic—identified itself.

Clearly, by the late 40s, consensus on this issue was breaking down. Paul had been able to preach his Gospel to the Gentiles for some sixteen years before needing to defend it to the pillars in Jerusalem (Gal 2:1; cf. 1:18). "False brethren" questioned whether the mixed Antiochene community should continue on the same basis as before; also, they urged that Titus, Paul's

---

63. See discussion of Gentiles in "Hellenistic Judaism," chap. 2, and "The Expectation of Redemption," chap. 5.

Gentile co-worker, be circumcised. Later, Peter and all the Jews withdrew from mixed table-fellowship at Antioch, "fearing the circumcision party" (2:11ff.). What had changed between 30 and 49, and why?[64]

We must consider this period of time within a larger context: the development of Christianity in the first century and its origins in the proclamation of Jesus of Nazareth. Jesus had announced that the Kingdom was at hand. After his resurrection, the apostles took that message, now altered slightly to accommodate the eschatological miracle they had just witnessed, to the synagogues of Judea and, shortly thereafter, the Diaspora. Those receiving their message—Jews, together with some Gentile God-fearers—formed or joined an ekklesia within the synagogue. But within 50 years, the movement was predominantly Gentile; and within 150, the church regarded Jewish Christians as heretics.[65]

This shift in populations occurred in part because earliest Christianity, as a variant type of apocalyptic Judaism, operated within an entirely unique and unprecedented situation. After Easter, the world could no longer be the same place, nor was it—yet it was. And though the ekklesia had already received the eschatological gift of God's spirit (Jl 2:28; cf. 1 Cor 12–14; Acts 2:1–36), clearly the resurrection of the dead, the Parousia of the Lord, and the transformation of creation were yet to be (e.g., 1 Thes 4:16; 1 Cor 15:23; 2 Cor 4:14; cf. 2 Thes 2:2). Jesus' resurrection, in other words, coupled with the delay of the End, plunged the early Christian movement into a kind of eschatological twilight zone. And as time and this anomalous situation continued, the movement's effectiveness within its native religious community declined (e.g., Rom 11:5, 7).

The failure of the Gospel within Israel, together with the continued delay of the Kingdom, was a major trauma for the Christian movement, perhaps second only to the initial shock of the crucifixion itself. Paul sees it as nothing less than an act of God, a mystery ultimately of good consequence (Rom 11:25); the evangelists, and later ecclesiastical tradition, as both the proof and the measure of Israel's iniquity.

Historians have often sought in the Christian message itself a theological explanation for Israel's rejection of the gospel. Frequently attention has focused, as we have seen, on the image of the crucified messiah. Such a messiah was inherently unacceptable to Israel, this argument runs, whether because Israel expected only a military messiah and could accept no other, or because a messiah who had died "under the curse of the Law" was religiously offensive, or because the idea itself was so unprecedented, and so on. These "explanations" fail to consider the fact that a crucified messiah was evidently *not*

---

64. Gaston speaks of the 40s as a decade of crisis for the early movement, *No Stone*, p. 429–30.

65. See chap. 10, on the ultimate fate of the Jewish church.

inconceivable: Jews could and did conceive it. The message failed, rather, because its central and motivating claim—that crucifixion actually confirmed Jesus' status as messiah—could not be accommodated to mainstream Jewish messianism, which linked the coming of the messiah to the coming of the messianic age (see 1 Cor 1:22). Early Christian descriptions of the Parousia, both in Paul's letters and in the later gospels, are the measure of the strength of this Jewish tradition. Jesus' classically messianic performance at his Second Coming was to offset his untraditional earthly ministry.[66]

A messiah, crucified or otherwise, was not a messiah in the eyes of Jewish tradition if after his coming the world continued as before. The charismatic atmosphere of the early ekklesia compensated for those already inside the new movement. They had been given the Spirit and soon would see Christ come in glory. But to those outside, empirical reality would weigh heavily against any claim of the messiah's having already arrived: righteousness was not flowing down like waters; men continued to beat plowshares into swords; the dead had not been raised; the Land was still captive. And as the period between the resurrection and the Parousia stretched on, Christian claims would have seemed progressively less credible to those Jews who adhered to traditional messianic expectation.

Further, in the Jewish homeland itself, politics and popular spirituality combined repeatedly in the period before the war in 66 to provide a number of more acceptable messianic candidates. Increasing anti-Roman sentiment and millenarian activity would have distracted attention from the claims of a pacific group anticipating the return of a messiah already known to have died by Rome's hand. And, finally, the movement's very success among the Gentiles would have combined with these other factors to undermine its persuasiveness to Jews. When the church was still predominantly Jewish, Gentile participation was a welcome affirmation of the Gospel; as it became more and more Gentile, it compromised its identity as a renewal movement *within* Judaism, and hence its chances for success among Jews.[67]

We see in Paul's brief description of the "Jerusalem Council" in Galatians 2 the outlines of one set of Jewish Christian responses to the double disconfirmation of the Kingdom's delay and Israel's increasing nonresponse. With the delay of the End, this group of "false brethren," as Paul calls them, "the circumcision party," may have begun to press for Gentile *conversions* to the Christian movement rather than simple inclusion. They may have begun to revise considerably the movement's timetable and so have decided to consolidate the community within Judaism (where it placed itself in any case) by

66. See the further development of this idea in Rv 19:11–21.

67. Theissen, while construing the issue of Gentile inclusion differently from the way I present it here, nonetheless also sees the eventual disproportion of Gentiles to Jews in the movement as a reason in itself for Christianity's failure within its community of origin (*Palestinian Christianity*, pp. 113–14).

normalizing their Gentile membership.[68] Or, more likely, they may have seen a causal relationship between the Kingdom's delay and the already apparent failure of their mission to Israel. If they could speed the preparation of Israel, then the messiah would return, and with the salvation of Israel would come the redemption of the whole world. Clearly the considerable number of Gentile adherents could not commend to Jews the message of Christ as the fulfillment of God's promises to Israel. And Paul's Gentile co-worker, Titus, almost literally embodied the problem. What headway could the Gospel of the Crucified make among Jews if it countenanced Gentiles expounding Jewish scriptures—especially since these Gentiles, as Gentiles, could not teach in the synagogues and therefore preached to audiences elsewhere?

Too many Gentiles, too few Jews, and no End in sight. But could anything disconfirm the truth of the Gospel? Of course not, argued the circumcision party; and they fell back on the traditional view of the final redemption, within which the new movement—and Jesus himself—had always operated: *only once the Kingdom came would Gentiles as such be redeemed.*[69] Its delay was due to the nonresponse of Israel, for which these apostles took responsibility. In their haste, they had misconstrued their obligations both to Gentiles within the church and to unconvinced Jews outside. For now, in view of the pressing need to complete the mission, let Gentile Christians join Israel fully through halakic conversion, lest they unnecessarily impede Jews from receiving the truth of the Gospel.

Could anything disconfirm the truth of the Gospel? Of course not, argued Paul; and drawing on the revelation of Christ granted him by God to be an apostle to the Gentiles, he saw these same discouraging facts in a different light.[70] Jews did not heed the Gospel? This was part of God's plan: he in fact was deliberately hardening their hearts until Paul (and others, though Paul does not keep them in mind in Rom 11) brought in the full number of Gentiles. Too many Gentiles? Again, God had so planned it, forming Paul in his mother's womb to be his special emissary to the Gentiles in these final days (Gal 1:15). The Kingdom tarried? No; rather, it waited until Paul could complete his mission. At that moment, these unnerving facts would be turned around. When the full number of Gentiles had been brought in, the remnant of

68. Paul's rivals in Corinth, the "superlative apostles" who were also Jewish (2 Cor 11:5, 22), apparently were *not* flogged by synagogue authorities, as Paul had been, or else Paul could not have used that experience to build his case that he had suffered more for Christ than they (so too Hare, *Jewish Persecution*, p. 46). Had these apostles, who preached another Jesus from the one Paul preached (11:4), abandoned hope of an imminent Parousia and thus ceased preaching a *coming* messiah? This would account for their preaching Jesus yet not being flogged: their nonapocalyptic message would not have threatened the well-being of their host Jewish Diaspora community.

69. Hence the traditions preserved in the later gospels that Jesus explicitly limited his mission to Israel, e.g. Mt 10:6; 15:24.

70. See too Sanders, *PLJP*, pp. 185–96, *JJ*, pp. 93–95.

Jews currently chosen by grace for the Gospel would be joined by "all Israel" (Rom 11:5, 12, 26, 32). Israel's rejection of the Gospel had brought reconciliation to the nations of the world; their ultimate reception of the Gospel would mean "life from the dead" (11:15) and the redemption of all creation (8:21). Paul knew he was right by virtue of divine revelation. Anybody preaching a gospel different from his was an enemy of the Gospel of God. "Let them be anathema!" (Gal 1:8).

Paul carried the day in Jerusalem, when the "pillars" agreed, in conformance with the practice of the earliest mission, not to require proselytism of Gentile members. Paul, they suggested, would be particularly responsible for preaching the Gospel to the Gentiles; they would continue their work within Israel (2:6ff.). This is how Peter later ran afoul of both sides at Antioch. Together with the other Jewish members of that community, he ate with Gentile members; later, when men from James came, he withdrew, "fearing the circumcision party"—perhaps, that is, believing that he hampered the mission to Israel by appearing to violate the laws of kashrut.[71] Paul alone found this objectionable; and since we have only his view of things, we know neither how Peter and the others responded nor how the Antiochene church itself regarded his outburst (2:14–15). Apparently, however, his tenure in Antioch ended on a sour note, for Paul left the community there and does not refer to it again outside of Galatians.

But Paul's solution to the twin problem of Jewish nonresponse and the delay of the Kingdom represents a triumph of lateral thinking. For Paul broke out of the box into which traditional Jewish apocalyptic, from the prophets through Jesus to the original post-resurrection community, had placed the Gospel. Israel is not the linchpin of the Kingdom, he argued. No use imposing circumcision on Gentile believers for the sake of uninterested, if not hostile, Jews. The Spirit of God clearly rested on Paul's Gentile communities. Once Paul had brought the full number of Gentiles into Christ, then the Kingdom could come. Of course there could be no Kingdom without Israel—God had long ago given his promise, and it could not be broken (Rom 9–11; 15:8). But Israel's reception of the Gospel would take an eschatological miracle, for which Paul was uniquely responsible. He worked to redeem the Gentiles; Israel, God's beloved, would be redeemed by God himself.

Christ according to the Spirit

Jesus of Nazareth preached the coming Kingdom to Jews in the Galilee and Judea; after his resurrection, his apostles took his message to the Israel of the Dispersion as well. Paul radically expanded the scope of both the early mission

---

71. "It was probably Peter's responsibility to the circumcised, which might be hindered if he himself were not Torah-observant, not disagreement with Paul's mission as such, which led him to withdraw from the Gentiles in Antioch" (Sanders, *PLJP*, p. 19).

and its view of Jesus as he reinterpreted the story of salvation embodied in the biblical promises to Israel in light of his personal experience of Christ's resurrection and his own apocalyptic hope. The unique answers he offered to questions concerning the delay of the Kingdom, the meaning and significance of Torah, and the sequence of events at the Eschaton served, in the long centuries that neither he nor his fellow apostles imagined would follow, as the foundation of a Gentile Christian polity.

Paul's gospel should not have proved so adaptable. It was too much motivated by his belief that his was the final generation and that he himself would live to participate in the events at the End. This confidence in the nearness of the Kingdom, which Paul shared with the first apostles and with Jesus himself, lends itself badly to institutionalization. Subsequent Christian tradition rescued Paul from later embarrassment by framing him, in the canon, with the deeschatologized Paul of Acts, the bureaucratic Paul of the Pastoral Epistles, and the philosophical Paul of Ephesians and Colossians.[72] But the germ of transcultural and transtemporal relevance already lay in Paul's own letters. His expansion of the mission and of Christ's role in the economy of salvation revolutionized the conceptual framework in which the first apostles and, mutatis mutandis, Jesus of Nazareth had operated.

For apocalyptic eschatology had been born of the historical experience of the Jewish people. It expressed Israel's faith in God's justice and mercy, most especially as these were manifest in his covenant with Israel. Present miseries were seen to confirm God's commitment to his people; he intended adversity to turn them back to Torah. Thus exile ultimately could only mean return; destruction, rebuilding; depletion, renewal; oppression, liberation. The more dire the enemy who oppressed Israel—Assyria, Babylon, Seleucid Syria, Rome—the more glorious the compensatory image of Israel's imminent restoration, until finally the redemption of Israel became the redemption of the entire world.

The redemption, further, of *this* world. Apocalyptic redemption affirms creation. When the Kingdom came, it would come on earth, which God had made. Hence the Pharisees, and later the rabbis, insisted that the dead who participated in the Kingdom would be raised with physical bodies. The quality of physical existence would change—the earth would bring forth fruits in abundance; the lion would lie down with the lamb; men would live in peace and justice—but not the fundamental fact of physical existence itself. God's Kingdom on earth could gloriously recapitulate the idealized features of the Davidic monarchies: the nation would be reconstituted, the lost tribes restored, and the "word of the Lord" would go forth from Jerusalem to all the peoples of the earth, who would gather to worship at the Temple.

Paul's vision, too, is Jewish. He sees God intervening definitively in history

---

72. On this process, the work of John Knox, *Marcion and the New Testament*.

to redeem his creation, and he describes this vision in terms drawn directly from scripture. But we search in vain to find Paul praising the future Jerusalem or the eschatological Temple. Images of earthly fecundity or social harmony do not figure in his presentation. The coming Kingdom will be "in the air" (1 Thes 4:16), in the heavens (Phil 3:20) where no flesh can dwell (1 Cor 15:50). The resurrection is *spiritual,* not physical (1 Cor 15). The powers oppressing "the saints" are cosmic, not merely political: Sin, Death, the Flesh itself, which pervert the Law[73] and cause all creation to groan in its bondage to decay (Rom 8:21). These demonic powers killed God's own Son (1 Cor 2:8). They threaten Paul's communities and hamper his mission (2 Cor 2:10; 1 Thes 2:18), though they have already been defeated by the power of Christ's resurrection and will soon be utterly destroyed.

Jewish history and the Jewish commitment to God's nature as revealed in Torah created the dynamics of apocalyptic eschatology. Paul retains these dynamics but renounces their particularity. His vision of the End is no drama of national liberation writ large. On the contrary, in Christ and therefore in the coming Kingdom, such earthly distinctions between peoples and persons dissolve: "There is neither Jew nor Greek; there is neither slave nor free; there is neither male nor female; for you are all one in Christ Jesus" (Gal 4:28). What place has the land of Israel, the city of Jerusalem, the walls of the Temple—in brief, the *realia* of Judaism—in such an expansive and inclusive vision?[74] What place has a prediction of the Temple's destruction, which would recall the redemption from Babylon and speak of salvation in its territorial idiom as return to the Land? What place has Torah, which distinguishes Israel from the nations and even (as at Antioch) divides the body of Christ? God's promise to Abraham stands: it is irrevocable. "In you shall all the nations be blessed" (Gen 12:3; Gal 3:8; Rom 9:4ff.; 11:2, 29). But the heir to this blessing is Christ (Gal 3:16), and Abraham is the father of all who believe, whether Gentile or Jew (Rom 4:12). In brief, *Paul denationalizes Jewish restoration theology.*

Accordingly, Paul also denationalizes Christ. Only in Romans, where he briefly introduces Jesus as "descended from David according to the flesh" (1:3; cf. 15:12), does Paul present the messiah of Jewish tradition. Otherwise, Christ's significant point of origin is not the flesh (his putative Davidic descent) but the Spirit, which reveals him at his resurrection as the divine preexistent Son (1:4). At the Parousia, Christ will execute his military duties in the final battle against evil, exactly as the Davidic messiah would. But he destroys cosmic foes, "every rule and every authority and power," not the apocalyptic Babylon (1 Cor 15:24; cf., for example, Rv 18:2). Since the traditional vocabulary of Jewish apocalypticism drew so directly on particular events in Jewish

73. See Meeks' discussion, *Urban Christians,* pp. 184–85.
74. The phrase is Davies', *Gospel and Land,* p. 366.

history, Paul, where he can, avoids that vocabulary. Where he cannot—as with the term *Christ*—his radical definitions dissolve such constraints.

Finally, even though Paul orients his gospel toward the coming final redemption at the Parousia, he argues that the turning of the aeon, through Christ's resurrection, has *already* occurred. Thus neither Christ's coming in the flesh, nor his death on the cross, nor his imminent return, but rather the fact of his resurrection, to which Paul himself is witness, redeems believers from sin (1 Cor 15:17) and ensures the ultimate transformation of their bodies (1 Cor 15:42–48; Phil 3:10). No need, then, for the Temple's destruction to signal the dawn of redemption: that signal had already been granted in the resurrection of Christ.

Thus Paul radically redefines the concept of redemption as he does the concepts of Kingdom and Christ: through the originally political vocabulary of liberation, he praises a reality that is utterly spiritual. And his vision so shrinks the significance of contemporary politics that Paul, fully aware of the human agents of Jesus' execution, nevertheless can tell Christians at Rome to honor all governing authorities since they, appointed by God, "are not a terror to good conduct, but to bad" (13:1ff.). Pilate, Felix, Festus, Caligula, Nero . . . the rapid approach of the Kingdom paradoxically allows Paul to take a long view (13:11).

How did Paul come to conceive such a Kingdom and such a Christ? The sources reveal a constellation of factors, though not the causal connections between them. Paul was a Jew of the Greek Diaspora, concerned to preach the Gospel to the Gentiles; his Gospel excised the nationalist context and content from Jewish restoration theology and presented a scheme of salvation in the cosmopolitan idiom of Hellenism.[75] He thus minimized the political aspects of this messianic movement while presenting his message in terms already meaningful to his Gentile audience. Further, Paul saw the period between the resurrection and the Parousia as coincident with his own mission to the Gentiles. Unsurprisingly, then, he upheld the standard synagogue practice of including Gentiles without requiring full conversion (i.e., circumcision), despite mounting pressure from both Gentile and Jewish Christians. To require circumcision would have retarded the Gentile mission considerably.[76]

But against the synagogue's practice of admitting Gentile God-fearers who

---

75. "One of the startling aspects of early Christianity is that, at a very early date, Gentiles, for whom the question of the land could not possess the interest that it had for Jewish Christians, soon became the majority. By the time the New Testament documents came to be written, even by the time of Paul, the Gentile flood had already overtaken the Church. . . . [This fact] carried with it the demolition of the question of the land" (ibid., pp. 369–70).

76. The Graeco-Roman world generally regarded circumcision as a peculiar barbarity of Judaism, and the emperor Hadrian (117–38 C.E.) banned circumcision by broadening the application of an earlier law against castration. See the material collected in Molly Whittaker, *Jews and Christians*, pp. 80–85.

continued in their own religions, Paul rigorously insisted that his Gentiles "in Christ" absolutely abandon idolatry. Here again we see the measure of his conviction that, through Jesus' resurrection, the New Age had *already* spiritually dawned. His Gentiles had to conduct themselves as if they were already in the Kingdom. And this, according to the expectation of Jewish restoration theology, meant that they realize that their former gods were no gods, and that they worship no other god but God (e.g., 1 Thes 1:9ff.; 1 Cor 10:7–22; cf. 2 Cor 6:15–7:1; Gal 4:1–11).[77]

About Jesus of Nazareth Paul evinces little interest. He reports few of his sayings and admits freely that he had not known Jesus "according to the flesh." Paul sees Jesus' significance and status as eschatological redeemer granted not in his biography (where he was born, what he preached, whom he called) but in his resurrection. Christ's resurrection redeems the believer in the "present evil age" when, baptized into Christ's death, he spiritually joins Christ's resurrected body while awaiting the transformation of his own at the End. Paul's gospel, accordingly, relates not Jesus' teachings, but Paul's teachings about the meaning of Christ's resurrection, from which Paul reasons backward to Christ's divine sonship and forward to his imminent Parousia. Paul in his letters thus does not preach *about* Jesus; rather, he preaches *that* Jesus has descended, ascended, and is about to descend again in power. Finally, Paul derives his authority as apostle not from any contact with the historical Jesus but from his experience of the Risen Christ (Gal 1:12–16; 1 Cor 9:1).

Paul's emphasis on Christ's resurrection and his experience of the Risen Christ at his call to be an apostle to the Gentiles returns us, from another direction, to the question of Paul's denationalized, apolitical, pneumatic messianic eschatology. Put simply: the Christ whom Paul encountered was not in a physical body. This fact may account for Paul the Pharisee's striking departure from that most characteristic of Pharisaic teachings: the resurrection of the flesh (cf. Phil 3:5, 20–21). Physical revivification of the righteous at the End of Days (Dn 12:2), especially as a vindication of those who suffered religious persecution (2 Mc 7), was a central tenet of the Pharisaic interpretation of Torah and one of the major points of dispute between them and the Sadducees. Jesus' own position on this issue, on the evidence of the later gospels, was Pharisaic. Paul, however, asserts strenuously that Christ's resurrection was *not* physical, but spiritual. And as Christ's raised body is, so shall the Christian's be. Paul proves this by arguing that the bodies even of the living will be transformed at the Parousia: those who "sleep" and those left alive will both be changed when Christ returns. And, against later evangelical tradition,

---

77. This means it would be less socially disruptive for a pagan to be a God-fearer within the synagogue than a God-fearer within the ekklesia.

Paul defends this teaching by an appeal to dominical authority: "For this we declare to you by the word of the Lord" (1 Thes 4:15).

Christ could not have been raised physically, else where would his body have gone? Flesh and blood cannot ascend to the right hand of God. And inasmuch as Paul infers from Christ's body the nature of the believer's body at the End (1 Cor 15:47ff.), he sees the abode of these spiritual bodies in a spiritual Kingdom, "in the air" (1 Thes 4:17). Hence also Paul's choice of an apolitical apocalyptic enemy: not Rome, nor indeed any earthly power, but the astral archons of the Hellenistic cosmos (cf. "the prince of the upper air"; Eph 2:2).

Those who were apostles before Paul, who had followed the earthly Jesus and witnessed the Risen Christ, presumably (again against evangelical tradition) did not see a physical body either. Was their vision of the approaching Kingdom likewise transformed? In light of the material ultimately derived from this circle of followers and preserved in the later gospels, this seems unlikely. Sayings and stories about marriage and divorce, drinking and eating in the Kingdom, the position and authority within the Kingdom of both Jesus and his disciples, the twelve tribes, and the new or renewed Temple—all point toward the traditional Jewish concept of a structured human society (albeit a morally transformed society) in a Kingdom on earth (albeit a transformed earth). The Temple, Jerusalem, and the reconstituted people of Israel would stand at its center.[78] Explicitly nonmilitary, brought about by the act of God, this Kingdom was nonetheless explicitly nationalist—the redemption of *Israel*—and therefore implicitly political.[79]

Not so Paul's. For him, whether because he had imbibed the Diaspora's cosmopolitanism or because of his particular experience of the Risen Christ, the Kingdom transcended these categories. Paul too envisioned an objectively real, historical fact, the absolute transformation of present reality (cf. Lk 17:20–21). All Israel and the full number of the Gentiles would participate. But the Kingdom would not be a glorified Israel, nor would a temple figure in the eschatological service of God. As with Paul's present earthly communities, so with the approaching Kingdom: all would be equally "sons of God" through God's Son, united through the Spirit, clothed in immortality, a genuinely new creation.

We glimpse Paul for the last time in Romans. He writes from Achaea, preparing to depart for Jerusalem with the Gentile collection; he intends to

---

78. On the nationalism, existing together with universalism, of Jewish restoration theology in general and that of Jesus and the earliest apostles in particular, see Sanders, *JJ*, pp. 61–119.

79. See Gaston's remarks on the probable political content of Jesus' preaching in *No Stone*, pp. 423–24.

visit Rome on his way from Jerusalem to Spain (Rom 15:24–26). According to Acts, Paul's presence in Jerusalem precipitated a crisis, and he was brought to Rome under arrest (21:17–28:31). Still later tradition holds that he was martyred there.

The next Christian text we have, the Gospel of Mark, follows the letters by less than fifteen years. In that brief interval, however, much had changed. Jerusalem lay in ruins; a major prophecy of Jesus had been realized; and the first generation had passed away.

Chapter 9
Between the Resurrection and the Parousia

Had Paul's apparent indifference to traditions from and about the earthly Jesus been universal, the Gospel of Mark never could have been written. It is by drawing precisely on such traditions that Mark, through the device of a life story about Jesus, presented the message of the crucified messiah. But a crucial distance intervened between Mark and the early first-century Jewish Palestine in which Jesus of Nazareth had preached, from which the traditions of Mark's church—however much altered in the course of their transmission—ultimately derived, and within which Mark chose to set his story. For Mark was a Gentile, of the second Christian generation. He thus virtually embodied the unsettling situation that had fissured the apostolic generation in the 40s: the Gospel's failure among Jews, its success among Gentiles, and the delay of the End.

Simply by existing, then, Mark's church challenged the authority of the very historical tradition that it preserved. But Mark did not see things this way. On the contrary, he embraced as affirmations what he might otherwise have avoided or repressed as embarrassments. Dramatically, insistently, Mark emphasized that Israel had always rejected the Gospel, from the earliest days of Jesus' mission (2:6–7, 16–17, 24–25) to the last (Jerusalem and the Passion narrative, 11:18–15:38). The Gentiles had always been receptive. Jesus had preached to them too (e.g., multitudes from the Gentile cities of Tyre and Sidon, 3:8; 5:1–20; 7:25ff.) and had foretold that they would hear the Gospel before the Son of Man came in glory (13:10, 24–27). Mark repeated forthrightly and with great conviction Jesus' teaching that his own hearers would live to see God's kingdom (9:1; 13:30; cf. 14:62). And he also related, albeit more obliquely, the prophecy that Jesus' mission would end in the destruction of the Temple (14:58; 15:29; cf. 11:15; 13:2, 14).

The unfavorable response of the Jews, the enthusiasm of the Gentiles, and these ostensibly unfulfilled prophecies thus did not undermine Mark's community's tradition. On the contrary, he argued: these seemingly troublesome facts, correctly interpreted within the context of that tradition, actually confirmed the tradition's authority. Accordingly, Mark created from this tradition its own interpretive context: a narrative about its origins in Jesus' mission between his baptism and his resurrection.

The Son of Man and the Church

The term *historical biography* cannot be used without qualification to categorize Mark's gospel. He is not a historian in either the ancient or the modern sense; nor does his spare sketch of Jesus' career pretend to be a full picture of his life. Yet the term is not wholly inappropriate, for Mark does offer a story, set in the past, whose ostensible subject is the earthly Jesus.

However, Mark wrote to convey not historical information, but religious instruction. The innovative literary product which resulted, the gospel genre, enhanced the authority of this instruction. For the gospel had a distinct rhetorical advantage over the more traditional forms of religious declaration, whether Christian or Jewish—the letter, the sermon, the commentary, or the apocalypse. Because Mark presented the kerygma as historical biography, he did not need to appeal to another authority, be it tradition (written[1] or oral; cf. 1 Cor 15:3) or revelation (cf. Gal 1:12). Instead, he could communicate his instruction more directly, by presenting it through the words, actions, and experiences of the foundational authority, Jesus himself.

A key item in this instruction is Jesus' identity. Mark places the Christological question—"Who do you say I am?"—at the structural and dramatic midpoint of his gospel, the confession at Caesarea Philippi (8:29). But his Jesus seems at pains to avoid answering it. When Peter in this passage responds, "You are the Christ," Jesus does not acknowledge his answer but charges him to remain silent, as he earlier commanded demons who recognized him as Son of God (8:30; cf. 1:34). The evangelist himself is scarcely more helpful. While he and his community clearly held Jesus to be the Christ and the Son of God, Mark neither defines nor develops either concept. Is Jesus the Christ because, either in life or death, his deeds conformed to certain messianic prophecies (cf. Mk 11:1ff.//Mt 21:1ff.)? Is he the Son of God because before his earthly life he existed together with God (2 Cor 8:9), or assisted in creation (Jn 1:3), or reconciled God and man through his death (Rom 5:10)? Mark never says.

---

1. Commentaries, for example, ground their innovations in the prestige of the traditional text they interpret, as we see in the Qumran library.

Mark, and Mark's Jesus, give only one unambiguous answer to this crucial Christological question: Jesus is the Son of Man. Even here, Mark does little to clarify the obscurity of this term, which originated in the old, Aramaic tradition. Beyond identifying the Son of Man with Jesus, Mark defines it not in terms of its content so much as its function: not what the Son of Man *is,* but what he *does.* Thus the Son of Man exercised authority in defiance of the norms of Jewish piety (2:2–23). Jewish officials consequently rejected his teachings and successfully plotted his death (chaps. 11–15, specifically predicted in 8:31; 9:31; 10:33). But the Son of Man fulfilled his own predictions, rising from the dead on the third day (16:1–8), and he will come again in glory to gather his elect (13:26–27). In brief, Jesus' experiences as Son of Man define both the narrative structure of Mark's gospel and the content of its message.

They also establish the pattern to which Jesus' "future" followers, Mark knew, would conform. The Son of Man will be delivered up (9:31); so will they (13:9,11). He will be brought before authorities and scourged (8:31; 10:33–34); so will they (13:9). Hatred and contempt is his lot (9:12) and theirs (13:13). He will be put to death (8:31; 9:31; 10:34), and whoever would follow him must be prepared likewise to take up his cross (8:35). Mark's gospel thus identifies the life of his church, through the replication of this experience of suffering, with the life of Jesus as Son of Man.[2]

Not only the suffering but also the glory; for Mark interprets the life of the Son of Man and of his church in terms of the traditional apocalyptic pattern, the suffering and vindication of the righteous. The Jesus who endured rejection, hostility, and persecution—that is, the earthly Jesus—was triumphantly vindicated (as he had predicted) at his resurrection. As with the Son of Man, so with his followers: they too will be vindicated—provided they hold fast to their faith (8:38; 13:13)—when the Son of Man returns, an event that will mark the end of the age and the establishment of God's Kingdom (9:1).

The hour of this final vindication, Mark and his Jesus assert—clearly in three places; more subtly, as we shall see, in the treatment of the resurrection—has dawned. Mark places the first such statement exactly between Jesus' first prediction of his own and his later disciples' passion (8:31–38) and the Transfiguration, when Jesus' glorious post-resurrection status as Son of God is manifest to Peter, James, and John (9:2–9). "Truly, I say to you, there are some standing here who will not taste death before they see that the Kingdom of God has come with power" (9:1). Later, in Jerusalem, Jesus similarly concludes the "Markan apocalypse": "So also, when you see these things take place [i.e., the woes listed in 13:2–25, and the mission to the Gentiles, v. 10], you will know that he [the Son of Man, 13:26] is near, at the very gates. Truly, I say to you, this generation will not pass away before all

2. See esp. Gaston, *No Stone,* pp. 370–409.

these things take place" (13:29–30). And at the climax of his trial before the Sanhedrin (the consequence of which is proleptically mourned and connected with another reference to the Gentile mission, 14:6–9), Jesus tells the High Priest, "You will see the Son of Man seated at the right hand of Power, and coming with the clouds of heaven" (14:62).

Thus the End will follow upon certain events, specifically the resurrection, wars fought by messianic pretenders, the mission to the Gentiles, and the Parousia. All these things, asserts Mark, will come to pass within the lifetime of those who first followed—or rejected—Jesus. Why, given the late date at which he writes, would Mark say this? And what makes him so certain? To answer these questions, we must first consider the ways that other social fact, the unfavorable Jewish response to the Gospel, and the other traditional prophecy, that Jesus' mission would terminate in the destruction of the Temple, shaped Mark's view and presentation of the past, and hence of the future.

The Son of Man and the Temple

The early kerygma, the product of the apostles' response to the resurrection, had proclaimed Jesus as the crucified and risen messiah whose imminent *second* coming would immediately precede the Kingdom. Already by mid-century, few Jews accepted this message;[3] as time went on, ever fewer. But the early missionaries met with worse than skepticism or indifference. As Jews going to Jews, they also encountered the active opposition of Diaspora communities and the synagogue courts (e.g., Paul's own experience on both sides of this opposition, Gal 1:13 and 2 Cor 11:24). Well before Mark wrote, the mission to Israel had foundered.

Mark's Gentile community, a generation later, lay outside the jurisdiction, and very possibly the concern, of these courts. But the traditions Mark preserved retained the memory of this earlier experience, when (Jewish) Christians had been "delivered up to councils and beaten in synagogues" for preaching the Gospel (13:9a, 10).[4] And the continued existence of contemporary synagogue communities further evinced the Jews' persistent refusal to receive the Christian kerygma, now proclaimed to them for the most part by Gentiles.

When Mark undertook to portray the public career of Jesus, he projected these divergent responses to post-resurrection Christian claims back onto Jesus' own lifetime. The centurion's instantaneous confession at the moment of Jesus' death—"Truly this man was the Son of God!" (15:39)—climaxes an extended series of episodes whereby Mark, despite preserving a tradition that

---

3. Only a remnant so far, Rom 9:27; only the elect have obtained the Gospel, but the rest God has hardened, Rom 11:7.

4. On the anachronistic quality of such passages, which recall an era already past by the time the gospels are composed, see Hare, *Jewish Persecution,* pp. 104–05.

Jesus had restricted himself to Israel (7:26–29), nonetheless integrated sympathetic Gentile responses to the Gospel into Jesus' public ministry. His Jesus reaches out to Gentiles, usually after some confrontation with Jews, be they his enemies or his own disciples. Thus, though the Pharisees plot to murder Jesus, multitudes stream from pagan cities to hear him (3:1–8). His disciples' faith falters as they bear him to Gentile territory, but once there, Jesus preaches with great success (4:35–40; cf. in the county of the Gerasenes, 5:1–20). Jesus disputes with the Pharisees over the essentials of Jewish observance and then quits their company for Gentile audiences (7:1–31). Most strikingly, it is to a Gentile that Jesus reverses his usual policy of demanding silence after a cure. "Go home to your friends, and tell them how much the Lord has done for you, and how he has had mercy on you" (5:19). In such ways Mark argued through his gospel that the Gospel had presupposed the Gentile church—Mark's church—from the beginning.

So also with Jewish unbelief, which Mark situates as well in Jesus' lifetime. Christian frustration with Jewish hostility or indifference to post-resurrection claims about Jesus, Mark thereby explained, only recapitulated Jesus' own experience during his mission. Things had always been as they were now; the Jews had always resisted the Gospel.

But in proclaiming the Gospel through a construction of Jesus' past, Mark created an awkward problem. Was the Gospel rejected by Jesus' Jewish contemporaries the same as the Gospel rejected by Mark's? Did Jesus before his death and resurrection, in other words, proclaim as Mark's community did the post-resurrection Christ?

Mark's treatment of the post-resurrection titles *messiah* and *Son of God* bespeaks both the historical tenor of the tradition that he had inherited and his own sensitivity to it. He seems implicitly aware that Jesus was not so designated during his lifetime, but after. Hence he associates Peter's confession of Jesus' messiahship immediately with the Passion (8:29–31) and thence the Parousia (8:38–9:1). And he follows Bartimaeus' proclamation, "Son of David!", with Jesus' departure for Jerusalem, the long-foreshadowed site of his sufferings (10:46–11:1). So also with the Transfiguration (9:2–8). Jesus "charged them to tell no one what they had seen [i.e., his glorious revelation as divine Son] until the Son of Man should have arisen from the dead" (9:9; cf. Rom 1:4). Only supernatural entities—God (1:11 and here, 9:7) or demons (e.g., 5:7)—had so identified Jesus during the course of his ministry. The two humans to call him "Son of God," the High Priest (14:61) and the centurion (15:39), do so only in the context of his Passion.

Mark's Jews, then—at least up to Jesus' confrontation with the High Priest (14:60–64)—do not reject Jesus on account of his Christology. On the contrary, so reticent is Mark's Jesus on this topic, usually demanding silence when someone or something divines his true identity (true, that is, in light of post-resurrection faith) as Christ or Son, that Jesus scarcely seems to pronounce a

Christology at all. Then why did Jesus' contemporaries reject him? Having serendipitously avoided Christological anachronism, Mark here introduces a social one. For Mark imputes to the pre-resurrection Jesus, the earthly, "historical" Jesus, a critique of Jewish institutions and practices that undermines the Jewish understanding of Torah.

The true origins of this critique, certainly evident in Paul as well as in Mark, must be sought in the post-resurrection context of the mission to Gentiles initially within the Diaspora synagogues and the debate thereby engendered among the first generation of apostles.[5] But through Mark's narrative, Jesus *in his lifetime* becomes the authoritative source of the Gentile rejection of Torah. He criticizes Sabbath observance, fasts, and Temple sacrifice; he dismisses mainstream Jewish practice as the "tradition of men" (e.g., 7:1–23; 11:27–33). Why did the Jews reject Jesus? Because, Mark answers, Jesus had already rejected them together with their religion, preaching with deliberate obscurity "lest they should turn again and be forgiven" (4:12).

This theme of mutual hostility and rejection builds to a climax during Jesus' final days in Jerusalem. Mark begins the story of Jesus' stay in the capital by intercalating two episodes that together symbolically repudiate Judaism and foretell its coming demise: Jesus curses the fruitless fig tree ("May no one ever eat from you again"; 11:14; cf. v. 20–21) and disrupts the operation of the Temple (11:15–17). Shortly thereafter, he confounds in debate all the representatives of Jewish learning—the chief priests, scribes, elders, and Pharisees (11:27–33; 12:13–17, 18–27). Worse than mere opponents, these men (as Mark has hinted or asserted practically from the beginning of his gospel) will bring about Jesus' death (3:6; 8:31, cf. 9:31; 10:33; 11:18; 14:1, 10–11, 43, 55; 15:1–15, 31). Thus, while the simple fact of crucifixion might implicate Rome, Mark's Passion narrative makes clear that true responsibility for Jesus' death lay with these men, in particular the High Priest (14:60–64), and finally with the general population of Jerusalem as well (15:8, 11–15, 29).

But for Mark, Jesus' crucifixion represents more than Judaism's rejection of the Gospel. It also points ahead to the destruction of the Temple. Where Jesus speaks directly of the Temple's destruction ("There will not be one stone upon another that will not be thrown down"; 13:2), Mark only indirectly establishes its connection with Jesus' death. In this passage, Jesus states that the destruction will mark the approach of the End and thus the glorious *return* of the Son of Man (13:2–4, 14, 26–29). By implication, Jesus must have died and been raised at some earlier point.

However, when Jesus stands before the Sanhedrin, Mark links this prophecy about the Temple directly to Jesus' death. He reports it in the more belligerent form of a threat, and attributes it not to Jesus but to "false witnesses": "We heard him say, 'I will destroy this temple that is made with

<hr>

5. For example, the situation in Antioch, Gal 2:11–21.

hands, and in three days I will build another, not made with hands'" (14:58, mockingly repeated at the crucifixion, 15:29). The formula "destroy/in three days build" immediately recalls Mark's earlier predictions about Jesus: "The Son of Man must be killed . . . and after three days rise again" (8:31; 9:31; 10:34). Perhaps Mark's Christological interpretation of the prophecy explains his distancing Jesus from this form of it by assigning it to a third party. Since Jesus' death corresponds to the Temple's destruction, and since Jesus cannot be the agent of his own death, neither can he be the agent of the Temple's downfall—an implication that Mark likewise repressed when interpreting Jesus' action in the Temple courtyard as protest rather than prophetic sign.[6] Mark thereby enriches the irony of the Sanhedrin's role in Jesus' execution. Thinking that they can destroy Jesus, they only bring about the symbolic fulfillment of his prophecy, his own death and resurrection (cf. Jn 2:18–22).

This association of Jesus' death as Son of Man with the Temple's downfall broadened the theological implications of the crucifixion. By laying the blame for Jesus' death on the leaders of Judaism—indeed, by so shaping the dialogue between the High Priest and Jesus that the trial turns on *the* Christian confession of Jesus as messiah and Son of God (14:61)—Mark argued that the Jewish rejection of the Gospel foretold and indeed led to God's definitive and historical rejection of the Jews: the destruction of their nation, their city, and their Temple, all come about in Mark's own day. Thus, into his description of Jesus' final breath (15:37) and the centurion's response (15:39), Mark intrudes a curious report: "The curtain of the Temple was torn in two" (15:38). Perhaps originally the story attested to a positive relation between Jesus and the Temple, which rent its own garments to mourn his death. But in Mark, this primitive tradition becomes another prophecy of the coming destruction. The Temple's curtains tear "as though mourning the impending destruction of that place."[7] Thus Mark can conclude that the Jews, by destroying Jesus, ironically became the agents of their own destruction, and by that same action effected a transfer of the Gospel to the Gentiles (15:39).

But suffering is only one half of this cycle. Vindication follows. Jesus' suffering and death—his role as Son of Man—had led to his resurrection. Accordingly, Mark argued, the suffering of his true followers during a period marked by wars, false messiahs, persecutions, and the mission to the Gentiles—a period whose close would be signaled by the destruction of the Temple—would lead to their own vindication (13:2–27). Thus the downfall of the Temple meant more than the end of Judaism, more even than the

---

6. Similarly, Jn 2:19 has to transpose this tradition into the second person: "Jesus answered them, 'Destroy this temple, and in three days I will raise it up.'" "The change is necessary for the evangelist's explanation that the temple is Jesus' body. Jesus could not have said that he would destroy his own body" (Sanders, *JJ*, p. 73).

7. From the early 3d-century Christian apocryphal text *Clementine Recognitions*, 1.41.

vindication of the Gospel. Mark's story does make these polemical points, but its main message is both broader and more urgent. Mark, writing in the aftermath of the Jewish war, uses his inherited historical tradition to assert, through his story about Jesus, the same message originally announced by Jesus and preserved in that tradition: "The time is fulfilled, and the Kingdom of God is at hand."

Behind this message stand expectation and prophecy unfulfilled. Jesus of Nazareth had expected to see the Temple destroyed, the Kingdom come, and the new Temple established in 30, at or as the climax of his own mission, and Mark's community preserved the memory of Jesus' proclamation of this belief. But Mark also knew that Jesus' mission had ended with his death, albeit followed by his resurrection. And Mark knew that neither Jesus nor his generation had lived to see the Temple destroyed. Worse: Mark's had, and still the Kingdom had not come.

Mark through his gospel thus exhorts his church to remain strong in the faith, despite this seeming disconfirmation of the Gospel. Hence he emphasizes the authority of Jesus' teaching, the importance of faith, the need to endure until the End. By ingeniously creating a prophetic synonymity between events circa 30 and events circa 70, between the fate of the Son of Man and the fate of the Temple, Mark preserved the authority of the threatened tradition by deploying it. He demonstrated through his Passion narrative that this prophecy had already been fulfilled exactly when Jesus had said it would be: at the end of his ministry, with his death and resurrection. And pointing to recent events, Mark also preserved the original, apocalyptic content of the prophecy. For if "destruction/rebuilding" symbolically corresponded to the crucifixion and resurrection of the suffering Son of Man, then clearly the Temple's actual, historical destruction signaled the imminent historical fulfillment of Jesus' prophecy, the advent of the Kingdom—now to be ushered in, according to Christian faith, by the glorious Son of Man. The Temple's destruction indicated how close he was, indeed, already at the very gates (13:2–8, 14, 29).

This linkage of Jesus' death, resurrection, and Parousia with both the experience of the church and Titus' victory over Jerusalem also accounts for the gravitational pull that the Passion exerts over Mark's entire story. Throughout his gospel, Mark trains his audience's attention on Jesus' inexorably approaching death. By so affirming the authority of his tradition by integrating, through the Passion, the fate of the Temple with the kerygma of Jesus the Son of Man, Mark also bequeathed to the future generations he never envisioned an enduring image of the past; an image, conveyed particularly through the Passion narrative, that fixed his depiction of Jewish perfidy and malice—and thus his hostility toward Jews and Judaism—at the heart of his gospel. For Jewish perfidy "explained" both the death of Jesus and the destruction of the Temple. It reinforced Mark's historicizing Christology, whereby Jesus became the founder of Mark's Gentile church. And this reinforced in turn his Christologizing of Jerusalem's defeat, which thereby became a major assurance that the church's eschatological vindication was, after all, at hand.

The history-likeness of Mark's narrative thus arises from the stereoscopic quality of his image of Jesus the Son of Man, whom Mark views simultaneously from these two perspectives: that of the historical tradition, ostensibly around 30; and that of his own day, circa 70. And this stereoscopy allows Mark unobtrusively to present his own church as the final community of the elect heralded by Jesus during his ministry. For those who had followed Jesus then—even his own disciples—had by and large failed to grasp his meaning, embrace its message of suffering, and endure with constancy. They were a "faithless generation" (9:19; cf. 4:13–14, 39–40; 6:49–52; 7:18; 8:17–21; 9:6–10, 32; 14:4–7, 10, 50; esp. Peter's dull performance, 8:31–33; 9:6; 14:37, 66–72). And to such a generation Jesus would grant no sign (cf. 8:12).

Rather, the sign of the impending apocalypse foretold by Jesus to his contemporaries had been granted only to those of Mark's generation. Only they had endured persecution for Christ's sake and brought the Gospel to all nations (13:9–13). Only they had witnessed the false messiahs (Theudas? The Egyptian? The leaders of the revolt in 66?), the wars, and the abomination of desolation set up where it ought not be (Titus' military standard on the ruined Temple mount? 13:6–8, 14).[8] Accordingly, only they had seen the fulfillment of Jesus' great prophecy, the destruction of the Temple (13:2, 14). Therefore it was they who would live to see the Kingdom of God come with power (9:1; 13:26–37; cf. 15:32).

Mark nowhere makes this point with greater economy and eloquence than when concluding his gospel. Placing post-resurrection traditions like the Transfiguration and the charge to preach to the Gentiles within the body of his narrative, Mark relinquished any portrayal of Jesus after Easter. His gospel closes, instead, with the empty tomb. Here Mark's twin perspectives merge completely: the resurrection becomes the Parousia. And where those who had followed Jesus in his lifetime had failed and fled, those of the first and final Christian generation—Mark's generation—stood faithfully: enduring till the End, awaiting salvation, keeping watch for the return in glory of the Son of Man.

THE LATER SYNOPTIC GOSPELS: ESTABLISHING THE PRESENT

Time continued. Judaism continued. And the traditions from and about Jesus of Nazareth also continued, shaping and being shaped by a third generation of communities that gathered in his name.

8. These passages are more usually taken to refer to Caligula's attempt c. 40 to put his own statue in the Temple, e.g., see Denis Nineham, *Gospel of Saint Mark*, p. 353. For the "abomination of desolation" as a reference to Titus' standards, see Brandon, *Fall of Jerusalem*, pp. 174, 231–32.

In the gospels of Matthew and Luke we have two third-generation interpretations of the Christian message. Each expresses traditions unique to itself,
be they the creative contribution of the individual evangelists or the independent traditions of their respective communities. And each, as we have seen,
presents a distinctive image of Jesus. The distinctiveness of their images,
however, is offset by their common dependence on three written Greek
sources that both evangelists clearly esteemed: Q, a collection of sayings
attributed to Jesus; the Gospel of Mark; and the Greek translation of the
Jewish scriptures, the Septuagint (LXX).

The use that each evangelist made of these sources attests to a decisive and
monumentally important change in the consciousness of the Christian movement. These later writers, unlike Paul and Mark, no longer expected the
fulfillment of the promise of salvation in their own lifetimes. They affirm the
coming End of the Age and the Parousia of the Risen Christ, but not as
immediate possibilities. These great events loom on the edge of a receding
horizon: time interposes between the present and the End.

Matthew and Luke thus consciously address communities that they expected would continue into an indefinitely extended future. The greater role
they give to the teachings of both Jesus (Q) and scripture (LXX) attests to their
greater concern to provide their churches with authoritative instruction for
establishing and maintaining community life. And they make room for Q and
the LXX within Mark's basic story by constructing, from their unprecedented
perspective in the third Christian generation, a new view of the past—both the
"immediate" past of Jesus' ministry, and the scriptural, contextual past of the
nation of Israel.

Accordingly, as the chief narrative source for their view of the Christian
past, the Gospel of Mark had to be revised. Mark had not written for posterity. The Temple's then recent destruction had convinced him that the
fulfillment of Jesus' prophecy of the Kingdom was at hand. For Mark, the
future already impinged upon the present; and the "past"—Jesus' experience
as Son of Man—revealed not the movement's origins so much as its End.

This oscillation between two temporal poles, the (recent) past and the
(near) future, allowed Mark to structure his story around binary opposites:
suffering/vindication; that faithless generation/his faithful generation; the
"traditions of men" (Judaism)/the true worship of God (faith in Jesus as God's
unique messenger). These stark antitheses, the precipitate of Mark's apocalyptic convictions, simplified the potentially complicated relationship of his sec-
ond-generation Gentile community to the earlier, Jewish apocalyptic tradition
that it preserved. Thus to the question: Why, if Jesus had preached to Israel,
did Israel not believe as Mark's community did? Mark could answer: Because
it had never been meant to. Already during his ministry, Jesus had rejected
Israel. But he had generously reached out to Gentiles, and they in turn had
received his message with joy. Further, Mark could assert, the Kingdom had

never really been delayed. It was coming exactly when Jesus had said it would: following the destruction of the Temple.

Such a foreshortened perspective on first and final events could not endure indefinitely as the period of time following the fall of Jerusalem lengthened. Nor could it serve those communities that looked to the ministry of Jesus as a foundational past, an event that explained and gave meaning to their own continuing existence. Thus, while Matthew and Luke adopted Mark's overall narrative chronology, they altered his emphases and expanded his temporal framework to accommodate the larger historical stage now occupied by the third generation. And though they both utilized the same texts and adapted similar strategies in revising Mark, each evangelist evolved his own answers to the questions of Jewish nonresponse, the existence of the Gentile church, and the delay of the Kingdom. Accordingly, inevitably, each presented as well his own interpretation of the figure whose life and death stood at the heart of these questions.

The Gospel of Matthew

Matthew extended Mark's story about Jesus both forward and backward. Going forward, he picked up where Mark left off, with the empty tomb. Adding several post-resurrection Christophanies, Matthew concluded with the Risen Christ's charge to his remaining disciples: "Go and make disciples of all nations . . . teaching them to observe all that I have commanded you" (28:19–20). These "commandments," much of them instruction drawn from Q, help to swell Matthew's gospel to almost twice the length of Mark's. Matthew thus presents his own church's beliefs about Jesus as Jesus' own teaching, a sort of doctrine held by the apostolic generation both before and after the resurrection. Now Matthew's church followed those teachings first delivered by Jesus to his disciples, and indeed to all Israel.

Further, Matthew held, Israel had been the sole focus of Jesus' mission. Mark, confined by his narrow time frame, had integrated a mission to the Gentiles into the earthly Jesus' mission to the Jews. But Matthew could stretch out and, by placing the Gentile mission in the period after the resurrection, distinguish between the two. Accordingly, he revised those Markan episodes that depicted a Gentile mission already underway—dropping, for example, the Gerasene demoniac's faithful response to Jesus, Jesus' exceptional command that he proclaim his cure to his (Gentile) friends, the man's mission in the pagan Decapolis, and the universal amazement which resulted (Mk 5:19–20//Mt 8:34). Matthew's Jesus concentrates his efforts solely on his own nation ("I was sent only to the lost sheep of the house of Israel"; 15:24), and during his lifetime he orders the twelve disciples to do likewise (10:5, 23).

But Israel had failed. Heedless, hostile, the Jews of Matthew's gospel reject Jesus violently. They plot his murder, demand his execution, and voluntarily embrace responsibility for his death. Nor was their hatred of the Gospel thus exhausted: Matthew's Jesus warns his disciples to expect similar treatment at the hands of the Jews (5:10ff., 25; cf. 23:34).

But how could those people to whom the scriptural promise of redemption had been given fail to recognize the one who, in Matthew's presentation, so conspicuously fulfilled the scriptures? Mark's terse answer had implied that Jesus deliberately caused their failure, preaching to them in parables "*so that* they may indeed see but not perceive, and hear but not understand" (Mk 4:12). Matthew offers a more palatable explanation. The Jews really were the "sons of the Kingdom"; but because of their behavior—not toward Jesus alone but toward all God's prophets—the Kingdom had been taken away from them (21:43; 23:31ff.; cf. 3:12; 5:20; 8:12). Thus Jesus taught them in parables "*because* seeing, they do not see, and hearing they do not hear, nor do they understand" (Mt 13:13, but cf. vv. 12, 14–15). Jesus was not the unique occasion of Israel's failure. Rather, Israel had always failed.

By thus extending Mark's story backward into the history of Israel—narratively from the baptism, theologically from the ministry—Matthew could appeal to a popular *Jewish* tradition that Israel had always rejected and persecuted God's prophets. Complaints frequently appear in scripture, and particularly in the classical prophets, that Israel obdurately resists the divine call issued through these prophets to do tshuvah—to turn from sin and return to Torah. Jews of the late Second Temple period inferred from such passages that their unrepentant people had resisted to the point of actually murdering God's messengers. Eventually, they assigned to each prophet a martyr's death.[9]

Within Judaism, this self-critical tradition offered a theodicy. For Jews in the post-Exilic period, it affirmed God's justice in the face of the nation's sufferings by evoking the historical context—and consequence—of these earlier prophets' deaths: Israel's captivity in Babylon. Because Israel had not heeded God's call, God had exiled Israel from the Land. But in recalling this traumatic period, the prophet-martyr tradition also expressed Jewish faith and hope. For the Exile had led to redemption; punishment succeeded where exhortation had failed. Chastised, enslaved, uprooted, the nation had repented. And God had once again displayed his mercy and affirmed his covenant: he had forgiven penitent Israel and returned them to the Land. Jews under Rome could thus be consoled, for if God had forgiven an earlier generation even the murders of his prophets, then surely he would forgive those sins for which he punished Israel now. Through tshuvah Israel would again be redeemed.

But Matthew placed himself, as his church placed Jesus, outside of Judaism.

---

9. These legends are collected in the pseudepigraphic text *Lives of the Prophets*, extant in Christian manuscripts only. See Hare, *Jewish Persecution*, pp. 137–41, on the Christian appropriation of this Jewish tradition.

He therefore drew on this martyrological tradition polemically, breaking the dialectic of exile/*return*, sin/*repentance*, chastisement/*forgiveness* that stood at the heart of biblical prophecy. For the prophets, Matthew argued, had also stood outside of Judaism. His gospel's genealogy, birth narrative, and extensive prooftexting all showed how they had actually witnessed to Christ. Thus the Jews, by rejecting and indeed murdering Jesus and by continuing to reject the Christian prophets, only realized to the fullest their ancient and well-established pattern of shedding the blood of the righteous (23:32–37; cf. 21:11, 46). With the death of Christ, then, the mission to Israel, begun by the biblical prophets, was over. Henceforth the Gospel would go to the nations.

By so interpreting Jesus' suffering and death against this "historical" pattern of martyred prophets, Matthew dissolved the bond of prophetic and symbolic synonymity created by Mark between the Son of Man, the fate of the Temple, and the End of the Age. The "sign" toward which the Son of Man's death pointed became, in Matthew, not the Temple's destruction, but the "sign of Jonah," Christ's resurrection after "three days and three nights in the heart of the earth" (12:38–41). The Temple's destruction remained, as in Mark, the divine punishment visited upon Israel for having repudiated Jesus (23:38; cf. 37:51–54, where the tearing of the Temple's curtain is somewhat lost among other, more spectacular signs). But—as Matthew, writing a generation after Mark, surely knew—it did not signal the imminent Parousia (cf. Mk 13:4//Mt 24:3; also 23:37ff., where Matthew specifically distinguishes between the destruction and the Parousia). Finally, as Matthew diminished the apocalyptic import of the suffering Son of Man, so too did he reinterpret the later suffering of his church. Such suffering was simply to be expected (cf. Mk 13:9–11//Mt 10:17–21). It indicated, not the approach of the End, but rather the authenticity of the church's claim to be the true heir of the martyred prophets (5:11–12).

Matthew's expansion of the Markan narrative thus dispelled much of the apocalyptic tension of Mark's story. It thereby demolished as well Mark's rationale for drawing a sharp, almost absolute contrast between the two generations delimiting his original time frame. For example, Mark had merged Jesus' own family with his Jewish opposition. Fearing that Jesus has gone mad, his mother and brothers attempt to seize him; finding him, they summon him to come to them (Mk 3:21–32). But Matthew, through the birth stories, brings Jesus' family into the penumbra of the church. They are the first to know that Jesus is God's Son and messiah (Mt 1:20–25; 2:10, cf. vv. 2, 4), and they accordingly treat him with respect (cf. Mt 12:46//Mk 3:31; Mt drops Mk 3:21 entirely). Having extended the witness to Christ back to the biblical prophets, Matthew easily includes Jesus' own family in that witness, too.

Even more dramatically rehabilitated are the disciples, and especially Peter. In Mark they are ineffective, inconstant, almost inexplicably dimwitted. When the gospel closes, they have been off-stage for two chapters, last seen deserting

Jesus in Gethsemane or, in Peter's case, denying him in the High Priest's courtyard (Mk 14:50, 66–72). They stand closer to the "faithless generation" that Jesus condemned than to the final, heroically persevering generation who would witness the Son of Man coming in glory (9:19; cf. 8:31–9:1).

But with the shift from the second to the third Christian generation likewise came a shift in the perception of the disciples. They assumed a new stature and dignity, which Matthew protected by reworking offending passages in Mark. Thus where Mark's Jesus had rebuked the disciples for lack of understanding, Matthew's simply explicates the parable (Mk 4:13; Mt 13:18). In Mark, James and John ask Jesus for a high place in the Kingdom; Matthew attributes the offensive request to their mother (Mk 10:35–45; Mt 20:20–28). And where Peter's confession at Caesarea Philippi had elicited obscure reactions and ultimately a harsh rebuke, in Matthew it calls forth Jesus' lavish praise, whereby he establishes Peter as the rock of the (future) church (Mk 8:27–33; Mt 16:13–23). For Matthew's third-generation community, the disciples were no longer failures, but founders. Witnesses to and partners in the original mission to Israel (10:1–11:1), they linked the Gentile church to its Redeemer (28:16–20).

But just as he closes his gospel, Matthew surprisingly and strongly qualifies this image. Not all the disciples are worthy; some, indeed, doubt even as they receive their commission from the Risen Christ (28:17). Judas Iscariot had been only the most egregious offender: others within the apostolic circle betray Jesus later, and differently. For if in such circumstances they could fail in their faith, how could they not have failed when communicating Jesus' teaching to future churches?

These false insiders thus stand behind the "false churches" of Matthew's own day, those other Christian communities whose existence provokes him greatly. These communities also worship Christ; their members also prophesy, heal, and work miracles in his name (7:21–22). But evidently their interpretation of Christian tradition differed from Matthew's in ways that he found intolerable. Hence his Jesus condemns them as false prophets, wolves in sheep's clothing, trees bearing bad fruit (7:15–20). At the End of the Age, Christ will disown them (7:21–23). They will gnash their teeth; they will be burned with unquenchable fire (13:30, 41–43, 50).

The interpretive diversity of late first-century Christianity was the price of its success. As it vigorously survived the setbacks and disappointments of its earliest years, the movement outgrew the limits set by its original message of an imminent end. Spontaneously, instinctively, the church brought its past up to date as believers preserved the meaningfulness of the traditions about Jesus for their own day.

But the diversity that resulted—a diversity that his free reworking of Mark and Q both contributed to and exemplifies—angered and agitated Matthew. He responded by constructing a Jesus who would end this maddening situation when he returned to judge not only the nations but also his own church. For Matthew's Jesus is first of all the eschatological judge: it is as such that John the Baptist introduces him (3:10–12); and as such is he to be joined on the Day of Judgment by both penitent Gentiles and his twelve apostles (12:36–42; 19:28). Warning his hearers of the judgment that precedes the Kingdom of Heaven (13:24–50) and of the eternal punishment that awaits the damned (25:31–46), Matthew's Jesus lays down his own commandments. He will return to condemn those who had failed to do them, be they Jews, Gentiles, or (non-Matthean) Christians.

The diversity that accompanied the tradition's growth inevitably clashed with the church's increasing sense of itself as a singular community founded on certain beliefs established at a particular moment in time—by Jesus, through his teachings, during his earthly ministry. Hence the proliferation of various gospels that could conform that unique moment and their own particular communities to each other; and hence as well (as Matthew shows us) the addition of other Christians to the list of enemies of the Gospel. Thus Matthew looks with a certain satisfaction upon the day of the Parousia, though its dawn be yet far off. For then, finally, Jesus will establish what these perfidious false insiders had denied to his—and thus to Matthew's—church: a univocal Christian tradition.

The Gospel of Luke and the Book of Acts

Luke, like Matthew, essentially reproduced the chronology of Mark for his presentation of Jesus' earthly ministry. And, again like Matthew, he extended his narrative beyond Mark's temporal limits, adducing sayings by which to instruct his own church (Q) and integrating the story of Jesus and the church into the biblical history of Israel (LXX). But where Matthew traces Jesus' ancestry to Abraham, Luke goes back to Adam, and thence to God (Mt 1:1–2; Lk 3:38). Where Matthew closes his gospel with the Risen Christ commanding the eleven disciples to evangelize the Gentiles, Luke opens his second volume, the Acts of the Apostles, with the Risen Christ commissioning his apostles to witness "in Jerusalem, and in all Judea and Samaria and to the end of the earth": the mission to Israel is to continue (Mt 28:16–20; Acts 1:8). And while Luke foreshadows the conversion of the Gentiles early in his gospel, when Simeon praises the infant Jesus in the Temple (Lk 2:31–32; cf. 3:5–6), he depicts no such movement until well along in Acts (11:19–20). Up to that point, observant Jews compose and direct the church (e.g., Acts 3:1; 10:14). Thus, though he and Matthew draw on the same major sources, Luke's more commodious time frame allows him to present a quite different view of the Christian past.

Luke differs most strikingly from Matthew in his presentation of the "Jewish" Christian past, both biblical and near-contemporary. Matthew, as we have seen, designated the prophets as the prime scriptural witnesses to Christ;

and this, together with his evocation of the prophet-martyr tradition, provided him with a ready explanation for and interpretation of the Jewish nonresponse to the Gospel. Within the context of biblical history, the Jewish prophets had been resident aliens, strangers in the strange land of the "traditions of men." Prophetic Judaism, leading to and fully realized only in Jesus, thus represented for Matthew a perpetual counter-religion: although *in* Judaism, it had never really been *of* it. Thus his Jews violently reject Jesus virtually from the moment of his birth (Mt 2:3ff.); his Pharisees in particular grow murderously enraged by Jesus' philanthropic violations of the Sabbath (12:14); and ultimately the people themselves cry out for Jesus' blood and demand his destruction (27:20,25). Matthew's Jesus, in turn, condemns these Jews as unjust persecutors and hypocrites even before any confrontation has occurred (cf. 5:11–12; 6:2, 5, 16; 9:3–4, 32). The Jews' treatment of Christianity is the ultimate expression of the "law of history" whereby the Jews have always murdered God's prophets.

Against this picture of intractable and inevitable hostility, we find in Luke the portrait of a people eagerly expecting the Christ (Lk 3:15; cf. 2:11–20, 26). His coming, promised to Abraham, was spoken of not only by the prophets, but also by Moses—that is, by the Torah itself (e.g., 1:55, 73; 16:19–31; 24:27, 44; Acts 3:22; 26:22; 28:23, etc.). Luke thus understands biblical history "historically": the object of God's redemptive acts and the partner in his covenant really is the Jewish nation, Israel (e.g., Acts 3:25–26). An unrelieved and mutual hostility between Jesus and his Jewish contemporaries, such as Matthew and Mark portray, would compromise Luke's vision of the continuity and historicity of the salvation revealed in scripture. For Jesus as Lord and Son of God fulfilled the promise of salvation given to Abraham and the patriarchs: he is the Son of David and thus King of Israel (the point of the nativity canticles, Lk 1:32–34, 54–55, 68–79). For Luke, this means that Jesus was a Jewish leader with Jewish followers, and so he portrays them in his gospel and Acts.

Thus Luke's Jesus is a traditionally pious Jew (e.g., 4:16), who even as a child engaged Jewish teachers in dialogue and awed them with his understanding (2:46). During his ministry, Jesus provokes—with one conspicuous exception, to which we shall return—little anger or active opposition. On the contrary: even with the Pharisees he maintains good relations. And the Pharisees, though annoyed and embarrassed by Jesus' Sabbath violations (Lk 6:11, cf. Mk 3:6//Mt 12:14; Lk 13:10–17; 14:1–6), at one point even urge him to flee when Herod Antipas endangers his life (Lk 13:31–33; cf. 19:38–39). The people, too, are generally benign or supportive. "Multitudes" follow Jesus throughout his ministry and remain loyal even during the final days in Jerusalem, where they bewail his suffering, witness his execution, lament and repent for his death (23:27, 48–49).

Who, then, is Jesus' Jewish opposition? The scribes, chief priests, and

Sadducees of the religious hierarchy, often together with Jerusalem's excitable populace. These harass both Jesus and, later, the apostolic church (Lk 19:47ff.; 20:19–26; cf. Mk 12:13–17//Mt 22:15–22, who name Pharisees; Acts 4:1–3; 5:17–18; 9:1–2). But even they did not act out of malice, Luke argues. Ignorance, rather, and lack of understanding, had led them inadvertently to fulfill the prophets by condemning Christ (Acts 2:17; 13:27).

By presenting a Jesus who harmoniously realized God's most fundamental promises to Israel, Luke can also present an early Christian community religiously continuous with its Jewish environment. Like Jesus, the apostles and early followers are pious Jews, observing the Sabbath (Lk 23:56), worshiping in the Temple (24:53; Acts 3:1; 21:26), keeping the laws of kashrut (Acts 10:14; Lk does not reproduce Mk 7:17–23; cf. Acts 24:14). Through them, the Palestinian mission to Israel, already a success in Jesus' lifetime, wins many thousands of Jews after his death (Acts 2:41; 4:4; 6:1). And even those few Gentiles who encounter the Gospel during this Palestinian period are "Jewish" in their piety: the centurion at Capernaum loves Israel and builds a synagogue (Lk 7:5; cf. Mk 8:5–13); the Ethiopian eunuch ponders the prophets and does pilgrimage to Jerusalem (Acts 8:27–39); and Cornelius, together with his entire household, "fears God" (that is, worships in the synagogue), prays constantly, and supports the poor (Acts 10:1–4, 22, 31; cf. v. 36).

How then does the Gospel move from this Palestinian Jewish church to the church Luke knows, the Gentile communities of the Diaspora? At what point does the rupture between Judaism and Christianity, a fact of history by the time Luke writes, come into his story? His theological vision of their essential continuity, presented narratively with such care in both his volumes, makes portraying such a disengagement difficult. Nevertheless, in part because his larger time frame allows him to depict this disengagement as a development, in part perhaps because he is guided by the historical sources he claims to have consulted (Lk 1:1–4, equally introductory of Acts), Luke names this breaking point precisely: the conversions *en masse* of Gentiles attached to the synagogues of the Diaspora.

The scene recurs repeatedly from Pisidian Antioch (Acts 13:14–51) to Thessalonica (17:1–15) to Corinth (18:4–8). Paul enters a town and preaches in the synagogue, where he is heard by both Gentiles and Jews. Initially, the Jews are often interested and even receptive (13:42–44; 17:4; 18:4). But when they see the numbers of Gentiles embracing the Gospel, the majority of Jews reject it violently. In a sudden eruption of murderous rage and jealousy, they rise up against Paul, repudiate his arguments, and instigate persecution both locally and abroad (13:45, 50–14:5,19; 17:5–9, 13; 18:12–17; 20:3). But their efforts to prevent the spread of the Gospel, particularly to the Gentiles, achieve exactly the opposite result: spurred by their persecutions, the apostles travel ever more widely in the Diaspora, preaching the "Kingdom of God."

The Jews of the Diaspora are thus the true villains of Luke's piece. The

Sanhedrin and the people of Jerusalem had acted against Jesus in ignorance (3:17; 13:27; cf. Lk 23:34); but the Jews of the Diaspora act from malice and jealousy against his church. "I declared . . . also to the Gentiles, that they should repent and turn to God," Paul explains at his hearing before Agrippa II. "For this reason the Jews seized me in the Temple and tried to kill me" (Acts 26:20–21; cf. 22:21–22). By nearly accomplishing their goal, these Diaspora Jews (21:27) complete the role assigned to them in Acts: to move the Gospel from Jewish Palestine to the Gentile Diaspora. Their instigation of Stephen's death and thus the persecution of the church in Jerusalem scattered the disciples abroad, so that Gentiles, too, heard and received the Gospel (6:9–8:1; 11:19–21). Their murderous plots against Paul, newly designated by the Risen Lord "to carry my name before the Gentiles and kings and the sons of Israel," sent him from Jerusalem on to Tarsus and thence out to the Greek Diaspora (9:15, 29–30). Their final action against him ensures that the Gospel is brought from Jerusalem to Rome (25:12; 28:14–31).

Luke had foreshadowed this unhappy Jewish reaction to the Gentiles' reception of Christ in the earliest chapters of his gospel. There, the devout Simeon, the very first to praise the infant Jesus as a *universal* redeemer (Lk 2:29–32), is likewise the first to suggest that his advent would also bring division and ruin to many of his own people. "Behold, this child is set for the fall and rising of many in Israel/and for a sign that is spoken against" (2:34). Luke develops this idea in his description of an episode early in Jesus' ministry, when Jesus preaches in the synagogue of his native Nazareth (4:16–30). Hearing him obliquely declare his messiahship (4:18–21), his listeners are well-disposed but ignorant (4:22; cf. v. 15), not comprehending his status as Son of God ("Is this not Joseph's son?"; 4:22; cf. vv. 3 and 9, from the Temptation). Jesus then chides them for not accepting him and proceeds to relate two incidents in which God's prophets benefited Gentiles rather than Jews (4:24–27). Then, Luke reports, "When they heard this, all in the synagogue were filled with wrath. And they rose up and put him out of the city, and led him to the brow of the hill on which their city was built, that they might throw him down headlong. But passing through the midsts of them he went away" (4:28–30).

This abrupt and inexplicable reaction of murderous rage scarcely suits the immediate context of the pericope (cf. 4:14, 22), much less the generally irenic tone of this gospel. But it establishes the paradigm repeated continuously in Acts, once the church's mission goes to the Diaspora: initial openness, despite Christological ignorance; mild contention; Gentile response; jealousy, wrath, attempted murder; moving on to the next town. As Jesus was rejected by his own people in his home town, so too is his message of salvation ultimately rejected abroad by his own people, Israel.

True to his vision of the continuity of salvation, Luke is slow to depict the discontinuity and discord of the Diaspora mission. The threat of Judaism's disengagement from the Gospel is in fact never fully realized in Acts. Paul in anger and frustration often vows to preach henceforth only to Gentiles; but when he moves on, he invariably goes to the synagogue first (e.g., 14:1; 16.13; 17:2; 18:4, 19; 19:8). And it is from the synagogue congregation that his Gentile converts come.

What then of a mission to Gentiles independent of the synagogue? Mark had inconspicuously introduced such a mission into Jesus' earthly ministry (Mk 13:10; cf. 3:8; 5:1–20; 7:25ff.); Matthew has it commence from the Galilee at the command of the Risen Christ (Mt 28:19). For both these evangelists, the success of the Gentile mission stood in high contrast to the Gospel's foreordained failure in Israel. For Matthew in particular, it is the consequence of that failure.

But Luke, as we have seen, emphasized the Gospel's success in Israel. And though Jesus is to be a light to the nations (Lk 2:32), though the Risen Christ tells his apostles that they will take his name to all the nations (Lk 24:47; Acts 1:8), Gentiles hear the Gospel only eventually, and only after persecution, not inspiration, had driven Jewish disciples into the Diaspora (Acts 8:1; 11:19–21).

A Gentile mission properly so-called occurs only off-stage in Acts. Luke hints at it in the closing lines of his second volume, once Paul has arrived in Rome. Because Paul is under house arrest, the Jewish community must come to him: for the first time when expounding the Gospel to Jews, Paul does not speak from the synagogue (28:23). Once again, he argues from the Law and the prophets; once again, some Jews are convinced but most disagree; once again, Paul vows to go to the more receptive Gentiles (28:23, 24, 28). But in the midst of this now formulaic exchange, Luke adduces those lines from the prophet Isaiah alluded to at a much earlier point in his source, Mark, to pronounce God's rejection of Israel (Mk 4:10–12; cf. Mt 13:10–15):

You shall indeed hear but never understand,
and you shall indeed see but never perceive.
For this people's heart has grown dull,
    and their ears are heavy of hearing,
    and their eyes they have closed;
lest they should perceive with their eyes,
    and hear with their ears,
and understand with their hearts,
    and turn for me to heal them. (Acts 28:26–27; cf. Is 6:9–10)

Luke leaves Paul in Rome on this dual note of pessimism and confidence: pessimism about the Jews' ability to receive the Gospel, confidence in the Gentiles' positive response. Jews are not excluded by their very nature or the nature of their relationship to prophecy, as Matthew had argued. For Luke, the Gospel had already succeeded in Israel. These Roman Jews simply recall and confirm in the closing verses of Acts what Simeon had prophesied concerning Jesus in the opening chapters of Luke's gospel: that within Israel, perhaps precisely because its revelation goes also to Gentiles, Christianity would be "spoken against" (Acts 28:22; cf. Lk 2:32, 34).

Further, Luke throughout both works continually stresses that the repentant sinner will always receive the salvation of forgiveness in Christ. But he also insists that the Jews are to blame for the death of Christ (Acts 2:23, 36, cf. vv. 5–11; 3:13–18; 4:10; 5:30; 10:39); and this, coupled with his own evocation of the prophet-martyr tradition and its implication of racial guilt (Acts 7:51–53, cf. Lk 6:23) complicates his picture. A Gentile joining the church must repent his personal sins; but the Jew who would join, this implies, must repent as well the sin of killing Christ. And the contrary also holds true: the Jew who disbelieves the Gospel does not repent his "killing" Christ.

Thus as the church receives the salvation promised to Israel, she leaves the Jews behind. The future, as Luke knew, belonged to the Gentiles. And that future would be a long one.

On this issue—the de-eschatologizing of the kerygma—Luke goes well beyond Matthew in radically revising Mark. Not only does Luke drop or rephrase those passages where Mark suggests the timing of the Parousia (e.g., Mk 13:2//Lk 21:7; Mk 14:62//Lk 22:69), he also divests the terms *Kingdom* and *Son of Man* almost entirely of apocalyptic significance. Thus *Kingdom* functions virtually as a synonym for *Gospel*. Its arena is the historical mission of the church; it can be said to be in the "midsts" of assembled believers (Lk 8:1; 9:2; 10:9; 16:20–21). Luke's Son of Man, like Mark's, has authority on earth to forgive sins (5:17–26); he will suffer in Jerusalem (9:22, 44–45); he will reside in heaven (12:8–9; 22:69). The term clearly holds a place in the canon of Christological titles. But while Luke uses it comfortably to refer to the earthly Jesus, or the exalted Jesus, he does not have much to say about the *coming* Jesus. And when entering Jerusalem for Passover, Luke's Jesus actively discourages belief in the imminent appearance of the Kingdom (Lk 19:11; 21:8; cf. Acts 1:6–7).

The Temple is radically reclaimed from Mark's apocalyptic scheme. Luke quickly passes over the "cleansing" (19:45–46) and drops the cursing of the fig tree (cf. Mk 11:12–21). He represses the prophecy or threat of the Temple's destruction at Jesus' trial and crucifixion (Lk 22:66–71). And by displacing that prophecy to Stephen's trial in Acts, where he likewise imputes it to false witnesses, Luke puts the Temple's destruction at several removes from Jesus' Passion (cf. Acts 6:14; Lk 23:35–37//Mk 15:29–31). The destruction of Jerusalem, which Luke's Jesus mourns (Lk 19:41–44), "will be" purely punitive, the price paid by the Jews of that city for not having recognized Jesus (19:44; cf. 23:28–31). It implies neither God's blanket censure of Judaism nor the approach of the End (21:20–24).

So thoroughly does Luke claim the Temple for the church that he can end his gospel with the image—for Mark unthinkable—of the apostles "continually" in the Temple, rejoicing over the resurrection and blessing God (24:53). As the premier symbol of Judaism and the nation of Israel, the Temple repelled Mark for the same reason that it attracted Luke. Mark saw it as an enemy bastion, recently and rightly destroyed as the prelude to the Son of Man's return. But to Luke, the Temple represented a tangible link between the redemptive revelation of scripture and the revelation of Christ. To be sure, the Jewish authorities had failed to see this connection. They consequently misunderstood the Temple's true purpose and thought that God's worship demanded blood sacrifices. Luke, through Stephen, criticizes them on this account. Like any other idol—to which Israel in its past had also been known to sacrifice, and because of which God had previously destroyed the Temple and exiled his people (Acts 7:41–43; cf. Am 5:25–27)—the Temple was only "made with hands" (7:48; cf. vv. 41, 43). The work of God's "hand" far transcended it (7:49–50; Is 66:1–2). When "cleansing" the Temple, Jesus had stated its true purpose: it was to be a place of prayer, not sacrifice, for Israel (Lk 19:46, dropping "for all the nations"; cf. Mk 11:17; Is 56:7). Despite its misuse, however, the Temple is and was holy; Jesus himself called it "my Father's house" (Lk 2:49).

Finally, even more than Matthew, Luke is conscious of standing in an extended and extending tradition. His characters are concerned to guard its uniformity. Priscilla and Aquila instruct Apollos "more accurately" about the "way of God": he had spoken "accurately" about Jesus but was unfamiliar with the baptismal practices of the community in Jerusalem (Acts 18:24–28). Paul corrects the same problem with some disciples at Ephesus (19:1–7; cf. 8:14–17). The apostles likewise safeguard the Gospel from deviation. Peter severely reprimands those who break community discipline (5:1–11, on Ananias and Sapphira) or who embrace the Gospel for base reasons (8:18–24, on Simon Magus). Finally, everyone assembles in Jerusalem to coordinate missionary policy, so that from the Holy City throughout the Diaspora, the church will speak with one voice (15:1–34, the Apostolic Conference).

Thus Luke presents the first generation as a golden age of cooperation and unanimity within the church, suppressing instances of contention or diversity even as he reports them. He does admit, through Paul, that doctrinal diversity will increase with the passage of time, so that even disciples will be seduced. But this will happen only with the departure of the first generation (20:29–30).

Matthew, likewise aware of diversity within Christian tradition, both condemned it through the voice of the earthly Jesus and invoked its eventual eschatological condemnation by Christ the Judge at the Parousia. But Luke's historical perspective is longer than Matthew's, his theological temperament milder, his disinclination to invoke the Parousia much stronger. And what help to the church in the meantime is an eschatological selection indefinitely far away? Luke resolves the problem of diversity by introducing a character into his story who binds together both volumes of his "history of Christian origins," and indeed who unites the divine revelation in scripture with that of the church of Luke's day and beyond: the Holy Spirit.

All three synoptic evangelists assigned the same or similar functions to the Spirit in the early stages of Jesus' ministry,[10] but Luke both expands and more precisely defines its role in developing the church after Jesus' death (Lk 24:49, cf. 11:13//Mt 7:11; Acts 1:5). It empowers and protects the mission (Acts 1:8; 2:1–33; 4:31, etc.), inspiring Christian prophets as it had their biblical predecessors (7:55; 19:6). Most important, since it comes almost exclusively through those witnesses who stand in the "accurately" transmitted tradition going back through the apostolic community to Christ himself (e.g., 3:38; 9:17; 10:44–48; 19:2–6; cf. 18:24–26), it safeguards and distinguishes from perverse counterfeits Christ's *true* church.

Thus through the conduit of true apostolic succession, the Spirit transmits both Jesus' teachings and true charismatic power from the inspired generation of the first apostles to the community of Luke's own day. More: it joins the true church to the continuum of salvation as expressed and established through the scriptures. Thus no significant distinctions divide Luke's late first-century Gentile community from the Jewish church of the apostles, the preaching of Jesus Christ the Son of God, and the prophets and patriarchs who had witnessed to him beforehand. In and through the Spirit, all are one.

JOHN: THE ETERNAL WORD

The Christs of Matthew and Luke, for all their distinctiveness and originality, are nonetheless variations on the Markan theme. All three evangelists present a Jesus who preaches to fellow Jews about the Kingdom of God, whose miracles demonstrate his authority as God's messenger, and whose mission proceeds from the Galilee to its finale in Jerusalem. They see the Gospel message itself, Israel's ultimate response to it notwithstanding, as the complement or completion of the biblical promises of redemption. And while the past that each individual evangelist constructs as a setting for his Jesus coheres most closely, as we have seen, with the circumstances of the author's own day, certain themes and elements nevertheless emerge as historically possible, plausible, and sound.

The same is true of John. Indeed, on certain issues—the probable duration of Jesus' ministry, the Sanhedrin's concern for the political consequences of his preaching, the pitch of popular messianic excitement around Passover, the

10. The Holy Spirit, for example, comes to Jesus at the moment of his baptism (Mt 3:16//Mk 1:10//Lk 3:21–22); and it drives Jesus out to the desert to be tempted (Mt 4:1–11//Mk 1:13–14//Lk 4:1–13).

extent of the Jewish authorities' involvement on the night of Jesus' arrest, the date of his arrest relative to Passover—John's information seems historically more sound.[11] But such information is as incidental to John's chief concerns as his gospel's choppy narrative structure is to the highly crafted monologues and extended discourses that mark its true literary and theological center of gravity. For unlike the synoptists, who present their theologies in part through their constructions of Jesus' "historical" setting, John gives his straightforwardly as the teaching of the earthly Jesus himself, a Jesus who accordingly proclaims to his putative audience of early first-century Jews John's post-resurrection Christ.

John's Jesus is not the wandering charismatic Galilean who appears in the synoptics, but an enigmatic visitor from the cosmos above this cosmos, the preexistent, supremely divine Son (e.g., 1:1–4; 8:23, 42, 58; 17:5; 20:28). As he travels repeatedly between Jerusalem and the Galilee, this Jesus encounters, not fellow Jews, but sons of darkness, denizens of the lower cosmos who can never receive the word of God (8:23, 43–47; 10:25; 12:34; cf. 15:19–22). To those divinely chosen to receive it, Jesus brings the message of eternal life, of the glory of the Son and the Father, pronounced in the elliptical idiom of this gospel as much by Jesus' wondrous signs as by his own mysterious speech (e.g., 3:15, 36; 4:14; 5:24; 6:35–53; 11:1–4). The topic of his address is, most frequently, himself. An image of Jesus thus does not emerge from John's gospel: it dominates his entire presentation.

What sources and traditions stand behind John's Jesus? Lacking the sort of comparative data that the synoptic gospels provide for each other, it is difficult to say. Internal evidence—some verbal resemblances, certain clusters of episodes appearing in the same order—suggests that John knew at least some version of Mark, and possibly Luke.[12] However, such key synoptic terms as *righteousness, power,* and *good news* all fail to appear in John; *Kingdom* (as in Kingdom of God), used more than 120 times in the first three gospels, occurs in John twice (3:3, 5; cf. 18:36). Conversely, the synoptics use *truth* 10 times to John's 46; *world (kosmos)* 13 times to 78; and *Jews* 16 times to John's 67.[13] His familiarity with some strands of the synoptic tradition, then, did not inhibit his independence. Most scholars hold that John drew such unique traditions as the wedding feast at Cana (2:1–11) and the raising of Lazarus (11:1–44) from an (otherwise unattested) "signs" source; others, that he used a "discourse" source as well for Jesus' speeches; still others, that he reworked

---

11. John's gospel, by alluding to various Jewish holidays (2:13; 5:1; 6:4; 7:2; 11:55, etc.) implies that Jesus' ministry lasted about three years; on the Sanhedrin's concerns, 11:47–53; on the crowd's efforts to make Jesus king during Passover, 6:4, 15; on Jesus' interrogation before the High Priest, 18:19–24; on the timing of the Last Supper relative to Passover, 13:1–2.

12. See the review of this issue in C. K. Barrett's commentary, *Gospel according to John,* pp. 14–16, 34–35; Brown, *John,* pp. xliv–xlvi.

13. Barrett includes a comprehensive linguistic table, *Gospel according to John,* pp. 5–6.

some earlier, non-Christian myth of redemption to conform it to the Christian gospel genre. This scholarly uncertainty is the measure of John's literary and theological autonomy. His gospel, like his Jesus, is a mysterious stranger.

Nevertheless, those unsettling and interrelated facts that had so shaped the early Christian kerygma also confronted John. He too had to make sense of the Gospel's failure among Jews and success among Gentiles; of the Kingdom's delay and the church's growing diversity. His work, like that of the other evangelists and Paul, is in part a response to the dilemma posed by these facts. But in resolving this dilemma, John presents a Jesus whose saving revelation radically transposes the elements of the primitive tradition.

What does John's Jesus reveal? That he is the unique divine Redeemer who has come down and who will go back up. John articulates this revelation in part by unfettering the now traditional Christological titles—Messiah/Christ, King of Israel, Son of God, Son of Man—from the definitions given or implied in scripture (cf. Mt. 2:6//Mi 5:2; Mt 2:15//Hos 11:1). In John, these serve instead as synonyms for Jesus in his role as the divine descending/ascending mediator (e.g., 1:29–51; 3:13).

Other images, also culled from the LXX, express Jesus' redemptive identity even more innovatively. He is the Lamb of God who takes away sin (1:29, 35), the Good Shepherd who lays down his life for his flock (10:11–18). He is the "bread of life," "from heaven," giving his flesh as bread for the life of the world (6:35ff., 48–58); the "light of the world," who opens the eyes of the blind and guides his followers in the darkness (8:12; 9:1–41). The metaphors accumulate: Jesus is the source of Living Water (4:7–15), the Sheepgate (10:7–10), the Resurrection and the Life (11:25), the Way and the Truth (14:6), the True Vine (15:1). Thus, through his Christology, John rotates the axis of Christian tradition ninety degrees, away from the historical, horizontal poles of Past/Future to the spiritualizing, vertical poles of Below/Above. Collapsing the distinctions between the traditional Christological titles, eschewing their originally apocalyptic connotations by using them solely to denote Jesus as intercosmic mediator, John suggests through these latter, allusively sacramental images the many ways that Jesus continuously nourishes, supports, protects, and redeems the community of his chosen ones who must dwell in the lower realm.

The acts by which John's Jesus reveals himself are thus preeminently *signs*, indicators that point away from their own immediate context to one beyond. Not his exorcisms and healing miracles, not his fulfillment of prophecies, not his authoritative teaching, but his signs communicate Jesus' true identity as the Christ, the Son of God (20:31), the unique Redeemer from Above. He who apprehends this has been called by Jesus "out of the cosmos" to the realm of the Father to which the signs point (15:19).

But signs are by their nature ambiguous, a fact John invokes to account for the diversity of Christian tradition. Not all who believe as a result of seeing signs understand their true meaning (e.g., 2:23–25). If they think, with how-ever much piety, that Jesus is only a prophet (4:19; 6:14,36; 9:17); or if they think that Jesus is the Christ but have an inadequate understanding of what *christ* means (6:4, 15; the old messianic notion of earthly sovereignty; cf. the ironic Passion narrative, 18:33–19:21), then they are not "of God." Those who are "of God," on the other hand, do not need to see signs to know the Truth. Like those Gentiles that fateful Passover who, without prior contact, wished to see Jesus (12:20), so too "those who have not seen and yet be-lieve"—such as the faithful of John's own community and generation—"are blessed" (20:29). They alone are the divinely chosen whom Jesus knows; consequently, only they know Jesus, and thus only they know the Father (6:44ff.; 7:28; 8:19; 10:14; 13:18, etc.).

But why did so many of those who did witness Jesus' signs—that is, his Jewish contemporaries—fail to understand them (12:37)? In part, John ex-plains, because their own false priorities had turned them from the truth. When Jesus works two mighty signs—healing ("raising") a long-paralyzed cripple (5:2–17) and curing a man born blind (9:1–16)—all they can see is his technical violation of the Sabbath (in the first instance, he had the pallet carried; in the second he made clay). Jesus compounds this offense by arguing that God himself does not keep the Sabbath (5:17): by implication, it is not all that holy. Further, those Jews who objected to Jesus' activities on the Sabbath were either hypocritical or ignorant, for they broke the Law themselves. "Did not Moses give you the Law? Yet none of you keeps the Law" (7:19–23). If they did, it would have led them to Jesus; since they do not follow Jesus, they could not have been following the Law (5:45–47). Those few Jews who might have been sympathetic succumb to intimidation (9:22; 12:42; 16:2; Christian Jews are to be "expelled" from the synagogue).[14] And those committed to Jesus' destruction ultimately, in denying Jesus, deny Judaism. To Pilate's query, "Shall I crucify your king?", they respond, "We have no king but Caesar" (19:15; cf. Jgs 8:23; 1 Sm 8:6ff., etc.).

But such spitefulness and perversity are symptoms, not causes. The root reason why Jews do not accept Jesus, John explains, is that they *cannot*. They are not "of God," they do not "know God," and therefore they cannot recognize his Son (8:19, 47)—or, for that matter, even read Moses correctly (5:44–47). Jesus never called them, since he knew that they were not his sheep (10:26–27). In this sense, then, Israel did not reject the Gospel: the Gospel was never really offered to them (e.g., 6:63; 7:28; 8:14–20, 23–38, 42–47). And though the Jews' "failure" was divinely predestined (12:37–40, quoting Is 6:9–10), they are accountable nevertheless (15:22–24).

14. A reference to the *Birkat ha-minim*. As a point of historical fact, Hare says, "it must be noted that the *Birkath ha-Minim* involves self-exclusion only and does not constitute excom-munication from the synagogue" (*Jewish Persecution*, p. 55). See too R. Kimelman, "*Birkat ha-minim* and the Lack of Evidence for an Anti-Christian Prayer in Late Antiquity."

Once the Jews hand Jesus over to Pilate, their opportunity, such as it was, is over. From that point on, Jesus has no further direct communication with them (Pilate must shuttle back and forth, 18:33, 38; 19:4, 9). Jesus is on his way back "up" to the divine realm, of which they have no knowledge (8:14, 23). And even when he "comes again," after death, the Jews still will not know, because he will not make himself manifest to the cosmos (14:22). Rather, coming with the Father, Jesus will dwell "in" the believer, and the believer "in" them (14:18–23).

Thus John's Jesus, his presentation of the ministry, and his interpretation of the Parousia all stand in high contrast to the figure and message set out in the synoptic tradition. Yet it is to Mark, the most classically apocalyptic of those three gospels, that John not only contrasts most sharply but also corresponds most profoundly. Indeed, what is most characteristic of each is what is common to both.

Both evangelists articulate and reinforce their respective messages—and thus, their presentations of Jesus' message—by structuring their stories within a double context. For Mark, this is provided by history, by the events circa 30 and circa 70, the recent past and the impending future; for John, by the abiding juxtaposition of Above and Below, the realm of the Father and the realm of this cosmos. Both evangelists see as the chief purpose of Jesus' ministry his revelation of his identity as the authoritative Son of Man whose coming calls the world to judgment—Mark's Jesus when he comes again at the End (e.g., 8:38); John's, during his earthly ministry, when his appearance occasions a *krisis* in which one either believes that Jesus is the Son of Man (i.e., the one who has come down and will go up; 3:13) or else fails to attain eternal life (e.g., 3:14ff.; 5:27; 9:35–39). And both, finally, trace the Jewish rejection and Gentile reception of the Gospel back to the days of the earthly ministry itself. Both maintain that Jesus had never really tried to win Israel (Mk 4:10–12; Jn 15:16); and both portray Gentiles as seeking Jesus, and Jesus them (Mk 3:8; 5:1–20; Jn 10:16; 12:20).

But what of the nonarrival of the Kingdom, the delay of the End? How do these two evangelists reinterpret both moments of disappointment—the final Passover when Jesus went up to Jerusalem and the subsequent expectation of the later church?

Here Mark and John offer virtually contrapuntal responses. Mark's, as we have seen, is historical in several ways. His Jesus really does predict the coming End; that prediction really is tied to and in a sense realized in Jerusalem; and it is about to be fully realized, Mark believes, in the near future. His historical solution in turn affects his narrative. Tense, linear, highly structured, it sweeps the reader from the Galilee to Judea to the confrontation in the Temple court. Further, Jesus' death is a real death. He fears it (14:36); he suffers (15:34–37); it foreshadows a devastation as real and as total as the Roman destruction of the Temple (15:38). And his Parousia—Jesus' return after the destruction of the Temple, which will recapitulate his Easter appearance after the destruction of his body— will mark the real, historical finale of this age.

The verticality of John's double context changes all this. References to a traditional understanding of the End do appear in his gospel ("I will raise [the believer] up on the last day"; 6:40), but the believer, by believing, has already escaped condemnation and passed from death to life eternal (e.g., 3:16-18; 5:24). John's narrative, too, is dehistoricized to the degree that its sequence and structure is subordinate to revelatory discourse: the story is primarily a frame from which to hang Jesus' speeches. And finally, Jesus' death itself is not humanly real. No agony spoils his walk in the garden, no cry his dignity on the cross (18:1-6; 19:28-30). So completely has John identified Jesus' crucifixion with his glorification (e.g., 12:23, 32-33; 13:31) that the resurrection comes, not as a dramatic reversal, but as a continuation of the ascent begun with the cross.

Nowhere is the contrast between these two evangelists stronger and more telling than in the use each makes of traditions concerning Jesus' prophecy about the Temple. By initiating the final stage of Jesus' ministry with the incident in the Temple courtyard (Mk 11:1-18), and by echoing the language of the Passion predictions in the accusations during the Sanhedrin trial (14:58), Mark had created a correspondence between Jesus' death as the suffering Son of Man and the destruction of the Temple; between his resurrection, his Parousia as the glorious Son of Man, and the appearance of the eschatological Temple "not made by hands." Mark thus saw this prophecy, and the event it foretold, both historically and Christologically. He thereby encouraged his community to take heart, to believe that the terrible wars in Judea and the Temple's physical destruction indeed signaled the nearness of the End, the realization of Jesus' promise that the Son of Man would return in glory to redeem those of the generation that had witnessed these things (Mk 13:1-8, 14-27, 30).

But John's thought is post-apocalyptic, his universe stretched between Below and Above; his earthly Son of Man is enigmatic but does not suffer. Consequently, he has little use for a historical understanding of the Temple prophecy. Where Mark could use its antithesis of destruction/rebuilding to express both the Christological sequence death/resurrection and the historical sequence destruction/Parousia, John cannot: for him, crucifixion itself is a glorious lifting up, too immediately transformative and positive to correspond to destruction. Thus, though he preserves the original connection between the "cleansing" of the Temple and the prophecy of its destruction, John displaces this tradition from the final stage of Jesus' career to the earliest and emphasizes rebuilding. When Jesus says, "If you [Jews] destroy this Temple, in three days I will raise it up," John's Jews respond, "it has taken forty-six years to build this temple, and you will raise it up in three days?" (2:19, 22). So *exclusively* Christological is John's understanding of the Temple prophecy ("but he spoke of the temple of his body"; 2:23), so nonapocalyptic his eschatology, that the actual fate of the historical Temple is irrelevant both to John's Christianity and to the characters in his story—even Jews!

What then prompted the fatal animosity of the Jerusalem authorities toward Jesus? Mark had presented a two-stage process: Jesus' action in the Temple ("And the chief priests and scribes . . . sought a way to destroy him"; 11:18) and his Christology, revealed finally before the Sanhedrin by the High Priest's acute question ("Are you the Christ, the Son of the Blessed?" "I am"; 14:61–62). But John's Temple incident occurs much too soon to be part of his gospel's denouement, and his Jesus openly preaches a very high Christology ("I and the Father are one"; 10:30) throughout his career. Consequently, John did not need traditions about the Jewish authorities' involvement in Jesus' death to bear the weight of articulating Christian doctrine—his Jesus had already assumed that task. Less reworked than in the synoptics because less important to John's story, these traditions as he presents them retain a historical authenticity. The Sanhedrin took note of Jesus because the council feared Rome's potential response to his ministry (11:48); the night of Jesus' arrest, the High Priest questioned him "about his disciples and his teaching" (18:19).

Did John "know" Mark and accordingly construct a gospel against the Markan picture? Or was his acquaintance and concern with the synoptic tradition very slight and his own gospel based on other, independent traditions? Or are we dealing with the largely original composition of a creative theologian? We cannot be certain. But where John diverges from the synoptics most acutely, there, through the rifts in the traditions, we can glimpse the shape of the forces that led to the execution of Jesus of Nazareth.

Chapter 10
Jesus of Nazareth
in Christian Tradition

Paul of course was not indifferent to traditions from and about the earthly Jesus. He invoked their authority when instructing his communities on matters of crucial importance: the End (1 Thes 4:15ff.); marriage (1 Cor 7:10–11); the eucharist (11:23–26); the witnesses to Christ's resurrection (15:1–7). But the Gospel, for Paul, the message of salvation communicated by Jesus, lay not with any particular thing that Jesus may have said or done; nor did the believer's salvation depend upon familiarity with such teachings or deeds. Salvation, rather, came in and through the great eschatological fact of Christ's resurrection. By the grace granted through the Spirit in baptism, the believer could have a foretaste of this salvation, which would be realized finally and fully only at the Parousia.

Further, as the resurrection itself indicated, Christ's return in power was very near. Soon—certainly within Paul's lifetime—"the Deliverer [would] come from Zion" (Rom 11:26). At that point, God would cease hardening his own people, Israel, his sons whom he had chosen long ago to witness to his name and to bring his blessing to the nations (Gen 12:1–3; 15; 17:1–27; Rom 4). Since their divinely wrought resistance to the Gospel had brought redemption to the Gentiles, their historic role in God's plan of salvation was nearly complete (Rom 11:11–15). Soon, they too would receive God's Son (Rom 11:25–36; 15:8–13); soon, the final events would unwind; soon, God would reign supreme. "Rejoice in the Lord always; again I will say, Rejoice. . . . The Lord is at hand" (Phil 4:4). This is Paul's Gospel.

Mark's gospel is both profoundly similar and profoundly different. He too sees in the death and resurrection of Jesus Christ the Son of God the initiation of history's climax, the sign that God's redemption is at hand. He too expects to witness this redemption, which for him as for Paul will occur when the one who suffered and was raised returns in glory. And he, like Paul, writes mainly to communicate this expectation, to prepare his community for the fast-approaching End.

But when Paul expressed these convictions, he spoke as a Jew. Their interpretive context was his native religion, Judaism; their historical significance, the consummation of the promise of salvation given by God to Abraham and the patriarchs, recorded by Moses and the prophets, realized by the Davidic redeemer Jesus Christ. True, Paul viewed this context—that is, Judaism—from his singular perspective as one called to be an apostle, perhaps *the* apostle, to the Gentiles. And the traditions about the earthly Jesus known to Paul through those who were apostles before him naturally informed his perspective. But his Gospel articulates and affirms a vision that is characteristically, indeed quintessentially, Jewish.

Mark also believed that God had revealed himself in the man Jesus, had actively intervened in history, and would shortly bring history to a dramatic, definitive close. He thereby assumed some of the most peculiarly Jewish ideas of first-century Mediterranean religion. But he did so as one who stood outside their native culture. Consequently, Mark related to these ideas at one remove: not through Jewish history, religion, or scripture (which Mark rarely invokes), but through the traditions about Jesus himself. Mark thus situates the redemptive facts of Jesus' crucifixion and resurrection within the story of the career related by these traditions, a career that he views as an eschatological event in itself. Accordingly, he begins his gospel where he sees the Gospel beginning: with the Son of God's earthly ministry, inaugurated by John's baptism of Jesus (1:1–11).

By looking to Jesus' ministry, rather than to Judaism, as the interpretive context for the Christian message of salvation, Mark linked his understanding of this message to a particular view of recent and current events. Recollections of Jesus' prophecy concerning the Temple and of the role played by the Jewish authorities in his arrest, together with the more recent experiences of frustration and hostility engendered by the early missions to Diaspora Jews, had already affected the "historical-biographical" traditions about Jesus by the time they reached Mark. Mark's perspective as a Gentile on the war between Rome and the Jews shaped them further. Ultimately, as conveyed by Mark's narrative portrait of the past, these traditions served as both bridge and barrier. They let pass to Mark's Gentile Christian community the fundamentally Jewish expectation of God's approaching Kingdom; they blocked any sympathetic view of Jesus' Jewish context.

Again, the comparison with Paul is instructive. Both Paul and Mark held that the salvation wrought through Jesus had ended the redemptive function of the Law. But Paul's attitude is intricate, inconsistent, anguished. While he maintains that observance cannot be required of Gentiles, he nonetheless ultimately upholds the Law's sanctity and great moral value (e.g., Gal 5:14; Rom 3:21–31; 13:8–10). The Law had witnessed to Christ; indeed, Christ was its *telos,* the end toward which it had been directed (Rom 3:21–22; 10:4). If redemption in Christ now superseded the requirements of the Law, especially for Gentiles (Gal 5:2), this was so because of the eschatological miracle of his resurrection.

Further, nothing in Paul's Christian commitment drove him to condemn that great Jewish institution established to serve as the place for the sacrifices mandated by Torah: the Temple in Jerusalem. True, in his extant correspondence, Paul hardly speaks of the Temple at all. Nor does he evince any knowledge of or interest in Jesus' prophecy concerning its impending apocalyptic destruction—perhaps because in his view Christ's resurrection had superseded the Temple's destruction as the eschatological sign of the approach of the Kingdom. Where he does refer to the Temple, however, Paul speaks with unreserved esteem and classic Jewish piety. God's spirit dwells therein; it is holy; God will destroy its destroyers (1 Cor 3:16–18).[1] Its rites (*latreia*) are one of the glories and privileges of Israel (Rom 9:4).[2] So holy and Spirit-filled is the Temple that Paul invokes it as an appropriate metaphor for his Gentile converts, whose bodies through baptism have become "members" of the body of Christ (1 Cor 6:13–20). And Paul conceives his own work as a "priestly service," bearing the "acceptable" offering of the Gentiles to Jerusalem (Rom 15:15–16, 26–27, 31).

But Mark, who came by his apocalyptic expectation through the "historical-biographical" tradition, saw the earthly Jesus, not the Risen Christ, as the one who had "ended" the Law. He does not make this point didactically so much as dramatically. His Jesus repudiates the Law by continuously confronting and challenging the authority of those who represent it: the scribes, Pharisees, elders, Sadducees, and priests. And Jesus' arch enemy, the one who condemns him unjustly to death, is the particular representative of the Temple: the High Priest.

Within this dramatic presentation of uncomplicated antagonism, Jesus' original prophecy concerning the Temple takes on new meaning. Mark still held, as Jesus of Nazareth had, that the Temple's destruction pointed forward to impending redemption. But for Mark, it also pointed back one generation, to the crucifixion of Jesus brought about, in his view, by the Sanhedrin. Thus, while the Temple's destruction did indicate that salvation was at hand, that salvation was for Christians only (e.g., 13:2–4, 14, 20, 24–31). For Jews, it simply finalized the divine repudiation of their religion and their nation pro-

---

1. In this passage Paul refers to the believer's body, but the point is that he imputes this degree of importance and holiness both to the Temple and to the person "in Christ."

2. This means that Paul, mid-century, praises the traditional animal sacrifices mandated by Torah and observed in Jerusalem.

nounced by Mark's Jesus during his lifetime, signaled at the moment of his death by the miraculous tearing of the Temple's curtain, and consummated through Titus' legions.

Mark's simplicity in repudiating Judaism and reaffirming the approach of the End could not withstand the Kingdom's delay and the kerygma's transmission to the third Christian generation. The unexpected necessities of legitimating the church's continued existence and envisioning a Christian future led later communities to develop more complicated accommodations to their tradition's apocalyptic, Jewish past. For those standing within the synoptic tradition, this meant, as well, revising Mark.

In so doing, the later synoptists dissolved the tension that Mark had created and sustained between concealment and revelation, between Jesus as the suffering Son of Man and Jesus as the Risen Christ and Son of God. Matthew, for example, no longer reserves *Christ* and *Son of God* as post-resurrection titles. His Jesus is known as Christ in his own lifetime, for reasons both (ostensibly) traditional (birthplace and patrilineal descent, Mt 1:1–17; 2:5ff.) and untraditional (e.g., his healing miracles, 12:23). And, thanks to a miraculous conception, he is, quite literally, God's son (1:1–2:7, 15). As such, or as the Christ, he is even worshiped during his own lifetime (e.g., 2:2,11; 8:2; 9:18; 14:33; 15:25; cf. 28:9,17).

As Matthew places his church's claims about the post-resurrection Christ into the mouth of the earthly Jesus, he creates reasons both to repudiate Judaism and, seemingly, to embrace it. Thus, where Mark's Jews did not follow Jesus because he had not really revealed himself or his message to them (e.g., 4:10–12,25), Matthew's Jews *do* know and yet still do not follow: in essence, they explicitly reject Christianity. But too much of Matthew's image of Jesus depends on prooftexts from Jewish scriptures for Matthew to condemn Judaism as sweepingly as did Mark, who had scarcely used them. Matthew's repudiation is accordingly more nuanced. By creating in prophetic Judaism a perpetually victimized historical witness to Christ, he distinguishes between "good" Judaism (that which led to Jesus) and "bad" Judaism ("the traditions of men"). Likewise, there are two kinds of Law: what Matthew's community observes and what the Jews do. Whether Matthew and his community were themselves Jewish is a matter of scholarly debate; but Matthew unquestionably approaches Judaism through Christianity, interpreting its traditions and scriptures within the context of Christian revelation.

Luke, like Matthew, also collapses Mark's distinction between the pre-resurrection Son of Man and the post-resurrection Son of God and Christ. His Jesus is also literally God's son, born of a virgin and the "power of the Most High" and acknowledged as the (Davidic) Christ at birth (Lk 1:26–34; 2:11). Luke carefully develops these last two designations in relation to each other throughout his depiction of Jesus' earthly career, imputing to his Jewish characters knowledge not only of their traditional, biblical definitions (e.g.,

1:71; 2:25, 38), but also of his Christian ones (e.g., 3:15, cf. v. 3—their reason for thinking that John the Baptist might be the Christ; 5:8; 22:67–70; 23:35; cf. his substitution of *Christ* for *Son of Man* in the Passion formula, 24:26, 46). And while, again like Matthew, Luke gains a certain polemical clarity by extending Christianity's claims about Jesus back into the days of his earthly ministry, he also thereby gains an explanation of how and why some Jews during and after the ministry would have recognized Jesus as the Christ of the church.

Perhaps more important, both Luke and Matthew also gain an excellent way to distance their respective gospels from the energetic expectation of the Parousia that had so shaped the narrative of their mutual source. For Mark's story dramatically oscillates between Jesus' concealment and revelation: concealment during his ministry, revelation both circa 30 and shortly after 70. By so emphasizing the clarity of this final revelation, Mark imputes to the brief period between the resurrection and the Parousia—a period he believed, in light of the Temple's destruction, to be rapidly drawing to a close—a continuing obscurity. His parallel presentations of the Transfiguration and the scene at the tomb make this point. Both scenes ambiguously evoke the Parousia as well as the resurrection,[3] and both (despite the angel's injunction to speak in the latter case; Mk 16:7) present three witnesses who respond with fear, silence, and lack of understanding (9:6, 9//16:8). How, then, and when would Jesus' identity as Christ and Son of God be broadly proclaimed? Only when he returned as the glorious Son of Man (Mk 8:29–9:1; 14:61–62).

But the later evangelists, and John most extremely of all, depict a Jesus who makes known his Christological identity during his own lifetime, and who founds a church, again during his own lifetime, to continue his work of proclaiming the Christian Christ. They thereby break the eschatological identification of resurrection and Parousia that Mark had so carefully constructed. Resurrection now serves chiefly to confirm Jesus' prior and public claims; the Parousia recedes into the future. The period of intermediate obscurity between private and public revelations shifts back from the time between the resurrection and the Parousia to the time between imputed biblical witnesses and Jesus' appearance on earth. The revelatory event thus becomes, not Jesus' resurrection/Parousia, but his ministry. The Jesus of the later gospels, in other words, obviates the Christological function of the Markan Second Coming. That function now passed to the church, whose duty it was, in the ever-lengthening interim between the resurrection and the Parousia, to bring the good news—not so much that the Kingdom *would* come, but that the Christ the Son of God already *had* come—to the nations.

3. "Mk 8:31 speaks of the resurrection after the death of Jesus, and Mk 9:1 speaks of the parousia after the persecution of the church. There follows the story of the transfiguration, which some have held to be an anticipation of the resurrection and some . . . of the parousia. The whole point is that it is both, and one should not distinguish between them" (Gaston, *No Stone*, p. 469).

To forgo an imminent Parousia, however, was to relinquish as well the hope of a speedy end to ambiguity—in particular, to the infuriating social ambiguity presented by the existence of other, competing groups. Hence we find in these later gospels not only a developed and retrojected Christology but also an equally developed and retrojected polemic against the competition: other groups who baptize but are not Christian;[4] or who are Christian, but whose interpretation of tradition, practice, or Christ deviates from that of the evangelist's own community.[5] Such polemic was both the measure and the means of the development of a given community's religious identity: to know who one is not clarifies who one is.

It also explains why these different churches, very early on and continuing throughout the first several centuries of their existence, expended such great effort arguing not against pagans so much as against each other. Pagans, as outsiders, posed little threat to a Christian group's identity. But an alternative interpretation of the revelation of Christ or of the meaning of salvation in his name did pose such a threat: simply by existing, it relativized the claim of revelation. Hence each community, with anger and anxiety, would view others as "heretics," deviants from the revelation that it alone preserved or correctly interpreted.[6] The tone set by Paul's condemnation of diversity—"if any one preaches to you a gospel contrary to that which you received, let him be anathema!" (Gal 1:9)—would only grow harsher as time continued and diversity increased.

If Christian diversity challenged the young churches' developing sense of self, by that much more did that community whose religious mandate they claimed to supersede: the Jews. Judaism's wide-flung, stable societies organized around the synagogue, its sacred scriptures of universally recognized antiquity, its remarkable consensus on what was religiously important—the people, the Land, Jerusalem, the Temple and Torah—and its ability to accommodate diversity of interpretation within that consensus: all attested to a strong social and religious identity. By the period during which our documents were composed, Jews could trace their own tradition back nearly two millennia, to the calling of Abraham. They could well afford to disregard those claims, advanced increasingly by Gentiles, that the church alone understood the true meaning of God's revelation to Israel—especially when that interpretation energetically denied any legitimacy to the Jewish religious consensus.

4. E.g., the group that formed around John the Baptist and evidently continued after his death, toward which John the evangelist evinces hostility.

5. A polemic visible particularly in Matthew.

6. The burden of most of the later letters in the NT canon, for example, 1 Jn 2:18ff., where another Christian group is called antichrist; 2 Pt 3:15–16 warning against alternative interpretations of Paul's letters; 1 Tim 1:6–7, against deviant teachers; Titus 1:9ff. warning the faithful to keep to sound doctrine, against the teachings of "insubordinate men, empty talkers and deceivers."

Christian communities did not have that option. The continuing existence of the "Old" Israel, and the publicly apparent viability of an interpretation of scripture different from those revealed to and taught by the churches, too pointedly challenged the legitimacy and identity of the New. When the destruction of the Second Temple brought neither the Parousia nor the end of Judaism, these groups had to develop a polemic against a perceived opponent who would not go away—whose presence, indeed, confronted them from within the very scriptures to which they now laid claim. They had to explain to themselves, to potential converts, and, should they be so challenged, to skeptical Jews, how it was that the Jewish understanding of Jewish history and religion was false, and why those who had heard this Christian revelation most directly—Jesus' Jewish audience in Palestine—should have so completely failed to receive it.

The evangelists responded to this contemporary challenge by presenting the various images of Jesus that we have surveyed. By framing their image within a "historical" setting actually drawn from their own day, they had Jesus confront not early first-century Jews but a caricature of the evangelists' own opposition, the Pharisees of the late first-century synagogue. Thus, Jesus himself announced that Judaism ran counter to the will of God. But the Jews did not receive this message, tendered by God's own Son, because Jesus did not want them to (Mark). Or, since they had never understood prophecy, the Jews likewise could not accept Jesus (Matthew). Or, some Jews did accept Jesus, but ultimately most did not, resenting the inclusion of the Gentiles (Luke). Or, the Jews were never meant to receive this revelation, because they are not of God (John). Do these people, then, reject the Gospel? What could more clearly confirm the Gospel's claims?

Judaism was more than a standing challenge to Christian identity; it was also a competitor for Gentile adherents. During this period and long after, Gentiles continued to attach themselves to the synagogue for the same reasons that had always drawn them before: Judaism's monotheism, its antiquity, its articulated ethics and strong community, its claims to revelation, and its prestigious sacred text. The rise of Gentile Christianity is itself the best evidence of Judaism's appeal: the church, though it repudiated the synagogue, also used it socially and religiously as a model. Christianity thereby offered to Gentiles fewer of Judaism's disadvantages (circumcision for adult males; association with a nationality implicated, after the bloody revolts of 66, 117, and 132, in anti-Roman activity) but many of the same attractions (strong community, revealed ethical guidelines, and the scriptures themselves—already available, thanks to the Hellenistic synagogue, in Greek).[7]

But the churches competed for these Gentiles against a religious community

---

7. See Gager's remarks in *Kingdom and Community*, pp. 135–40, and his more recent discussion in *Anti-Semitism*, pp. 33–112.

both better established and more broadly recognized. Here Christianity again offers the best evidence of Judaism's abiding appeal. Christian invective, from the gospels through the writings of the second-century fathers and beyond, most often and most energetically targeted Judaism.[8] Why? If its goal were to wrest Gentiles from the errors of paganism, one would expect more attention to polemics against idolatry; if its goal were to condemn the unethical exercise of power, one would expect stronger criticism of the empire, which after all had executed the Savior and continued, sporadically, to persecute his followers. Why expend so much effort disparaging a community ostensibly engaged in compatible activity, turning Gentiles from idolatry to the worship of the God revealed in scripture? Because, to those Gentiles drawn to such religions and such communities, Judaism represented an attractive alternative to the church.

Only centuries later did Christianity finally contain the threat posed by the Jewish reception of Gentiles, when Constantine made conversion to Judaism a criminal offense. But the repeated enactment of such legislation testifies to Judaism's continuing attractiveness to outsiders.[9] In this early period, then, before there was a Christian state to impose sanctions, Judaism not only challenged the younger community's identity but also offered competition in the mission field. Thus we find among the various churches—those represented by the evangelists and those that evolved in the following century—near unanimity on this one issue alone. Whether Jews had always been evil or whether, up to the coming of Christ, they had indeed been God's people, Jews after Christ, if they remained Jews, stood condemned.

What then of the "Jewish Christians," such as those who had gathered around James in Jerusalem? Certainly they saw their faith in Jesus as continuous with their ancestral religion. But the fate of this earliest Christian community is a mystery. In the closing chapters of his book on the war of 66–73, the historian Josephus mentions a group of some six thousand who, prompted by a "false prophet," gathered on the last remaining colonnade of the ruined Temple as Titus' troops rushed in, "to receive the signs of their deliverance" (*BJ* 6.5,2). Were these James' people?[10] Or did they flee before the siege, resettling further east, as a much later, Gentile ecclesiastical tradition held?[11] Whatever the case, Jewish Christianity itself did not survive as a viable branch

---

8. Simon's *Verus Israel* is the comprehensive study of this *contra iudeaos* literary tradition.

9. Ibid., pp. 338–41, on imperial legislation directed against Jewish proselytism; also note citations to specific statutes in the *Codex Theodosianus*. More recently, T. D. Barnes writes, "Constantine translated Christian prejudice against Jews into legal disabilities. He forbade Jews to own Christian slaves and to seek or accept converts to Judaism" (*Constantine and Eusebius,* p. 252 and literature cited nn. 74–76).

10. Brandon speculates similarly, *Jesus and the Zealots,* p. 220.

11. Gerd Luedemann has argued convincingly against the historicity of this tradition in "Successors of Pre-70 Jerusalem Christianity;" see too Brandon, *Fall of Jerusalem,* pp. 167–84.

of the church. In the mid-second century, Justin Martyr disapprovingly mentions a Jewish group who believe in Christ, keep the Law, and induce Gentile Christians to do so (*Dial.* 47). By the end of that century, these Christians—named Ebionites by Irenaeus—are condemned as heretics. Not only do they circumcise and keep Torah; they also insist that Jesus, though indeed the crucified and risen Messiah, was solely and normally human (*adv. Haer.* 1.26, 2; III.21, 1; V.1, 3).

The Word sown on more Hellenistic soil produced a different Christology. These other Christians proclaimed that Christ had never been human at all.[12] Whether at the moment of the man Jesus' baptism or at the moment of his conception, the divine preexistent Christ had entered the world of flesh—but had not really assumed a body. Rather, as Paul said, Christ only appeared "in the *form* of a servant" and in "the *likeness* of men" (Phil 2·7–8). In Christ, the divine came as close as it ever possibly could to the human; but these two principles remained fundamentally separate.

Such Christology, called *Docetism* (from the Greek *dokein*, "to appear"), was a coherent expression of Hellenism's deep-seated ambivalence toward material reality. This ambivalence in turn expressed and was an expression of the pious desire to protect the perfect High God from any compromising proximity to imperfect existence. Pagan Hellenists, as we have seen, insulated their all-good, all-knowing, all-powerful deity from any implication in the evils of the lower cosmos by removing him from direct involvement in the organization of matter. He was purely spiritual and unchanging, and physical existence, inasmuch as it articulated divine principles, did so only by virtue of intermediaries. Christian Hellenists, through their belief in Jesus Christ, reduced this gulf between God and matter, spirit and flesh, as much as their system of thought would allow. Indeed, by proclaiming that the divine had intruded into history at a specific moment, they strained that system to the utmost. But like the Jewish Christians, though for very different reasons, the Docetists, too, insisted on an absolute separation between the human and the divine.

Between these two extremes, the theological expression of Christianity's double heritage, stood a diverse group of Christians who rejected both. Against the Ebionites, they insisted on Christ's divinity and the dissolution of the Law; against the Docetists, they proclaimed Christ's humanity and the relevance of the Creator God of the scriptures to the Christian dispensation. But to these scriptures they began to add a new collection of specifically Christian writings, ones that expressed their own views on the origins of the church. Thus, by the end of the second century, in this situation of inter-

12. This Christology is the object of some of the earliest inter-Christian protests in the NT canon, e.g., 2 Jn 7–8: "For many deceivers have gone out into the world, men who will not acknowledge the coming of Jesus Christ in the flesh. Such a one is the deceiver and the antichrist."

Christian and Christian–Jewish competition and controversy, the collection of writings destined to become the New Testament was first brought together. By the middle of the fourth century, the work of retrospectively creating the past was complete. The Christian canon included the Septuagint, but the New Testament superseded it; Christian imperial law made Judaism and various Christian groups pariah; and Orthodoxy could trace its genealogy directly from God's cursing the snake in Genesis to the courts of Constantinople.

Orthodox Christology affirmed a paradox: Christ was both fully God and fully man. But such a theological proposition violated the principles of the only intellectual language available to articulate it: the language of Hellenistic metaphysics. The church rose to the challenge, and in the Christological writings of the Greek Fathers and the debates of the great councils produced some of the most creative and brilliant philosophical reasoning of the late empire. Not since Philo of Alexandria had biblical thought and Greek come together so intimately.

Platonism was the intellectual underpinning of these Christological formulations. But Hellenistic metaphysics—like any other system of thought—could not endure forever as the touchstone of meaning. After the introduction of Galileo's map of the universe, the technological advances of the Scientific Revolution, and the social and cultural revolutions that followed in its wake, modern culture no longer looks to Plato. More current systems of thought—anthropology, psychology, psychoanalysis, phenomenology, existentialism, evolutionary science, medicine—now provide the meaningful constructs that in turn affect theological ideas of personhood. Modern Christianity, in consequence, must search for new ways to express its ancient faith in Jesus Christ as true God and true man.

For centuries, the church concentrated on "high" Christology, the theological investigation of Christ's divine nature. But since the Protestant and Catholic Reformations of the sixteenth century, and especially since the rise of scientific biblical criticism in the eighteenth, modern Christian thinkers have increasingly focused their efforts on the human dimension of the Incarnation. Attempting to see through the various expressions of the Christian message to its first messenger; seeking, through the careful reconstruction of his historical context, to compensate for the silence of the once-spoken word by more critically examining the written texts descended from it, scholars have forsaken metaphysics for history. Modern Christianity's continuing commitment to a theology of the Incarnation is thus expressed in its quest for the Jesus of history.

The church, by claiming faith in Jesus as the unique occasion of divine revelation, thus lays upon itself the obligation to do history. And to "do history" means to undertake, with as much information, sympathy, and realistic imagination as possible, the reconstruction of the religious, social, political, and cultural context in which Jesus of Nazareth lived and died. It entails, further, the renunciation of a simplistic reading of identity-confirming narratives, even if these are the ones offered by the gospels. Such a reading can only result in bad history. But bad history, for the church, results in bad theology, the subtle Docetism of anachronism. It marks the retreat from a fully and truly human Jesus, one who acted meaningfully and coherently at a particular moment of human time.

If history, for the church, is important, then undistorted history is very important. Only by meeting this obligation with intellectual integrity can the church, with integrity, continue to witness to that message proclaimed by the first apostles, expounded by Paul, and reflected in the gospels: that the horizontal plane of the human and the vertical plane of the divine met at the cross of Jesus of Nazareth.

Abbreviations

ANCIENT WORKS

Bible

Gn	Genesis
Ex	Exodus
Lv	Leviticus
Nm	Numbers
Dt	Deuteronomy
Jos	Joshua
Jgs	Judges
Kgs	Kings
Sm	Samuel
Chr	Chronicles
Ps	Psalms
Prv	Proverbs
Is	Isaiah
Jer	Jeremiah
Lam	Lamentations
Dn	Daniel
Hos	Hosea
Jl	Joel
Am	Amos
Mi	Micah
Zep	Zephaniah
Zec	Zechariah

Apocrypha

| Mc | Maccabees |

New Testament

| Mt | Matthew |
| Mk | Mark |

Lk	Luke
Jn	John
Rom	Romans
1 Cor	1 Corinthians
2 Cor	2 Corinthians
Gal	Galatians
Phil	Philippians
1 Thes	1 Thessalonians
Eph	Ephesians
Rv	Revelations

Pseudepigrapha

2 Bar	2 Baruch
1 En	1 Enoch
Sib Or	Sibylline Oracle
Ps Sol	Psalm of Solomon

Dead Sea Scrolls

1 QS	The Community Rule or Manual of Discipline
1 QSa	The Rule of the Congregation or the Messianic Rule
QpHab	Commentary on Habakkuk
4 QpNahum	Commentary on Nahum
1 QM	The War of the Sons of Light against the Sons of Darkness or the War Scroll
11 Q Temple	Temple Scroll

Philo

Quis rerum divinarum heres	Who Is the Heir?
de confusione linguarum	On the Confusion of Tongues
de vita Mosis	Life of Moses
de migr. Ab.	*de migratione Abraham;* Migration of Abraham
de spec. leg.	*de specialibus legibus;* On the Special Laws
de virt.	*de virtutibus;* On the Virtues
quod omnis probus	That Every Good Man Is Free
de praem. et poen.	*de praemiis et poenis;* On Rewards and Punishments
in Flaccum	Flaccus
ad Gaium	On the Legation to Gaius

Josephus

AJ	*Antiquitates Judaicae;* Antiquities of the Jews
BJ	*de Bello Judaico;* Jewish War
c. Apionem	Against Apion

Talmud (*m* suffix indicates that the text appears in the Mishnah; *b*, in the Babylonian Talmud; *y*, in the Jerusalem Talmud)

Pes	*Pesachim;* On Passover
Avot	Sayings of the Fathers
Taan	*Taanit;* On Fasting
Gen Rabba	*Genesis Rabba;* Commentary on Genesis
Sanh	*Sanhedrin*
Yeb	*Yebamoth;* On Levirite Marriages
Shab	*Sabbath*
AvZar	*Avodah Zarah;* The Worship of Idols

Christian Writers

EH	Eusebius, *Ecclesiastical History*
Dial.	Justin Martyr, *Dialogue with Trypho the Jew*
adv. Haer.	Irenaeus, *adversus Haereses;* Against Heresies
Strom.	Clement of Alexandria, *Stomateis;* Miscellanies

Pagan Writers

Hist.	Tacitus, *Historia;* History

MODERN WORKS

HJP	Schürer, *History of the Jewish People in the Age of Jesus Christ*
HTR	*Harvard Theological Review*
IDB	*Interpreter's Dictionary of the Bible*
IDBS	*Interpreter's Dictionary of the Bible, Supplement*
JBL	*Journal of Biblical Literature*
JJ	E. P. Sanders, *Jesus and Judaism*
JR	*Journal of Religion*
JSJ	*Journal for the Study of Judaism*
JTS	*Journal of Theological Studies*
NovT	*Novum Testamentum*
NTS	*New Testament Studies*
PLJP	E. P. Sanders, *Paul, the Law, and the Jewish People*
PPJ	E. P. Sanders, *Paul and Palestinian Judaism*
STh	*Studia Theologica*
ZTK	*Zeitschrift für Theologie und Kirche*

Glossary

aeon (Gk. *aiōn, aiōnes*): When referring to time, an age; in late Hellenistic religious thought, it can also mean a divine entity or, in the plural, evil supernatural beings or the power that such beings possess.

Alenu (Heb. "to us"): A prayer, now part of the synagogue service, that praises God for his revelation to the Jewish people. It proclaims his kingship and expresses the hope for his coming Kingdom, when all humankind will be liberated from idolatry and will worship the Creator. Its original provenance may be the worship service of the Second Temple period, since the prayer makes no mention of restoring the Temple and it alludes to the Temple practice of prostration during worship.

Amidah (Heb. "standing"): The core prayer of the synagogue service, also known as *ha-tefillah* ("the Prayer") and the *Shemoneh-Esreh* ("the Eighteen," the number of benedictions in the weekday Amidah). These blessings praise God, among other things, for reviving the dead (#2), delighting in repentance (#5), redeeming Israel (#7), and gathering in the exiles (#10); petition him to have mercy on the righteous, on converts, and on all who trust him (#13), to rebuild Jerusalem, reestablish David's kingdom, and renew the Temple service (#14–17). It concludes with a prayer for peace. The prayer is stratigraphic, some parts predating and others clearly postdating the destruction of the Second Temple.

Antiochus Epiphanes (d. 163 B.C.E.): Seleucid ruler of Syria, descendent of one of Alexander the Great's generals. He pursued a policy of Hellenization which ultimately led, in Judea, to the successful Maccabean revolt.

apocalyptic eschatology: Knowledge, often esoteric, concerning last things before the End of the Age. Certain themes in apocalyptic eschatology—such as the struggle between good and evil, the coming of a messiah, travails before the Kingdom comes or the subsequent glorification of Jerusalem and/or the Temple—are typical of Jewish restoration theology and thus of Judaism: the distinction between restoration theology and apocalyptic lies in the latter's conviction that the End is near.

archē, archai (Gk. "ruler" or "authority"): Earthly powers, but also—in Paul's letters and other first- and second-century Christian texts—angelic or demonic ones, or their domain or sphere of influence.

220

archon (Gk. *archōn, archontes*; "ruler" or "authority"). In later Hellenistic religious thought, the word can refer to evil powers, esp. hostile planetary or astral forces.

Birkat ha-mazon: Jewish blessings after a meal. These include a prayer that the fallen tabernacle (*sukkah*) of David might be raised.

Birkat ha-minim: An exclusionary benediction, the twelfth of the Amidah, that denounces Jewish *minim*—religious deviants within the community—and prays for their extirpation. The Talmud relates that it was composed toward the end of the first century C.E.; this, plus its content and the allusions in the Gospel of John to those who "confess Christ" being excluded from the synagogue (Jn 9:22; 12:42; 16:2), have led some scholars to conclude that the object of this prayer was the early Christians.

demiurge (Gk. "craftsman"): According to Plato, the divine agent who fashioned the visible universe to accord, as closely as matter would allow, with the intelligible world of the Forms.

Diaspora (Gk. "dispersion"): All lands outside Israel; in a spiritual as well as physical sense, a Jew living outside the Land (voluntarily or otherwise) would see himself in exile in the Diaspora.

Docetism (Gk. *dokein;* "to appear")· An early view of Christ's theological status that emphasized his divinity and correspondingly attenuated his involvement in flesh and matter: Christ appeared "in the *likeness* of flesh," this position held, without actually assuming a human body.

dunameis (Gk. "powers"): In late Hellenistic religious texts, particularly heavenly or astral powers (*dunameis tōn ouranon,* "the powers of heaven").

Ebionites (Heb. *ebioni'im;* "the poor"): Jewish Christians, who held that Jesus was fully and normally human and who continued to observe Torah. By the end of the second century, they were condemned by Gentile Christians as heretics.

ekklēsia (Gk. "assembly" or "gathering"): In Jewish biblical or intertestamental texts, particularly a gathering for religious purposes; hence Paul's use of the term. In later Christian circles, the word comes to designate specifically the Christian community, i.e., the church (e.g., Fr. *église*).

halakah (Heb. *halakh;* "to go"): The body of law in Judaism concerned with the observance of religious, personal, and social obligations. It includes both the written law (those found in Torah, the first five books of the Bible), traditionally regarded as delivered by God to Moses on Sinai; and the oral law, the interpretation of the written, also part of the Sinai revelation according to Pharisaic and later rabbinic tradition. Debates on and interpretations of oral halakah are found in the *Mishnah,* which comprises the earlier parts of the *Talmud.*

Hasmoneans: The family name of the ruling dynasty established by the Maccabees after their successful insurrection against Antiochus Epiphanes. The dynasty came to an end during the Roman period, when power passed to the family of Herod the Great.

Herod Family: Herod the Great was appointed king by the Romans in 40 B.C.E. He ruled from 37 to 4 B.C.E., and it was during his reign, according to Matthew and Luke, that Jesus of Nazareth was born. His son *Herod Antipas* (the ruler who beheaded John the Baptist) ruled the Galilee and Peraea until 39 C.E. Between 37 and 41 C.E. the territories that had been divided between Herod the Great's three sons were temporarily reunited under his grandson *Herod Agrippa I* (see Acts 12): this Herod's son, *Agrippa II,* ruled Northern Palestine until c. 93 (see Acts 25:13ff.).

Josephus, Flavius (c. 37–c. 100 C.E.): Jewish historian. In 66 C.E. he first fought against the Romans, but assisted them after his capture. His two great works are *de Bello Judaico,* a history of the war of 66–73, and *Antiquities of the Jews,* a history of his people from Genesis to the beginning of the war against Rome.

kerygma (Gk. "preaching"): With reference to earliest Christianity, the oral proclamation of traditions from and about Jesus.

koinē (Gk. "common"): A dialect of Greek that became the international language of the Hellenistic world.

logos (Gk. "word; reason; rational principal"): In Stoic philosophy, the universal rational principle permeating and organizing the material world. Philo of Alexandria, the Hellenistic Jewish philosopher, calls logos a sort of divine intermediary between God and physical creation and between God and man; later, the Gospel of John identifies logos with the preexistent Christ.

Maccabees: The Jewish family who led the successful revolt against Antiochus in 167 B.C.E.

messiah (Heb. "anointed"): Originally denoting anyone who had been set apart for a special function through anointing, such as a priest, the term became associated particularly with David and the kings descended from him. In later prophetic and apocalyptic thought, the messiah was to be a deliverer descended from David's house whose coming would mark the restoration of Israel, the in-gathering of the exiles, the redemption of Gentiles from idolatry, and an age of universal peace.

Mishnah (Heb. "repetition; instruction"): The body of orally transmitted Jewish law compiled c. 200 C.E.

paideia (Gk. "education"): Higher education, particularly in (pagan) philosophy.

Parousia (Gk. "presence" or "arrival"): The return of Christ in glory, his Second Coming, to inaugurate the final days and establish the Kingdom of God.

Philo of Alexandria (c. 20 B.C.E.–c. 50 C.E.): Hellenistic Jewish writer whose commentaries on scripture were informed by his training in Greek philosophy.

Passover (Heb. *pesach*): The Jewish festival commemorating the liberation from Egypt as described in Exodus. While the Temple stood, Jerusalem was a center for pilgrims during this holiday, one of the three great annual pilgrimage festivals. According to Jewish tradition, the prophet Elijah will appear on Passover night to announce the imminent coming of the messiah.

Ptolemy: The name of a dynasty of Hellenistic kings who ruled Egypt following the dissolution of Alexander's empire. During the reign of Ptolemy II Philadelphus (283–247 B.C.E.), according to the Talmud and Hellenistic Jewish legend, the Torah was translated into Greek.

Seleucids: A Hellenistic dynasty, descended from one of Alexander's generals, that ruled Syria after the breakup of Alexander's empire.

Septuagint (Gk. "seventy"): The Greek translation of the Torah, abbreviated LXX. Eventually the term came to designate the Greek translation of the entire Hebrew Bible.

Shavuot (Heb. "weeks"; Gk. "Pentecost"): One of the three great pilgrimage festivals, Shavuot is celebrated on the fiftieth day after the first day of Passover. According to rabbinic tradition, it commemorates the giving of the Torah on Sinai, fifty days after the Exodus (cf. Ex 19:1).

stoicheia (Gk. "sound" or "element"): In the sense used by Paul and later Hellenistic writers, the astral or cosmic elements of the universe, often assumed to be hostile.

Sukkot (Heb. "tabernacles" or "booths"): The fall pilgrimage festival, commemorating the time when the children of Israel lived in sukkot in the wilderness, after the exodus from Egypt.

synoptic gospels (Gk. *syn-*, "together," and *opsis,* "view"): The term applied to the first three gospels (Matthew, Mark, and Luke), because they share a common narrative chronology and many verbal details.

Talmud (Heb. "to learn"): The compendium of Jewish law that includes the *Mishnah* (collected c. 200 C.E.) and the discussions of the Mishnah, the Gemara (collected in the fifth and sixth centuries C.E.). Rabbis in Israel and Babylon produced Talmuds which are similar but not identical. A stratigraphic record of Jewish tradition, the Talmud encompasses teachings stretching in principle from the period of Ezra the Scribe, who returned to Jerusalem from Babylon in the fourth century B.C.E., well into the Imperial Christian era.

Torah (Heb. "teaching"): The first five books of the Bible, authorship of which is traditionally ascribed to Moses. More particularly, Torah also refers to the teachings and religious principles enunciated in the revelation at Sinai.

tshuvah (Heb. "to turn"): The rabbinic term for repentance, which implies turning from (sin) and turning toward (good).

Suggested Reading

Hellenism. On the creation of the Hellenistic world, and its effect on religious thought, Hans Jonas, *The Gnostic Religion,* 2d ed. (Boston 1963), pp. 5–27, provides a good overview. Both he and E. R. Dodds, *Pagan and Christian in an Age of Anxiety,* pp. 5–30, discuss the interplay of the Hellenistic construct of the universe, the human being, and Graeco-Roman religions. See also M. P. Nilsson, "The New Conception of the Universe in Late Greek Paganism," pp. 20ff. On pagan religion as such, see Ramsay MacMullen, *Paganism in the Roman Empire,* which includes a generous bibliography of secondary sources, pp. 207–34; the most recent discussion is found in Robin Lane Fox, *Pagan and Christian.* John Ferguson has written two extremely useful introductions, *The Heritage of Hellenism: The Greek World from 323 to 31 B.C.,* and *The Religions of the Roman Empire.* Also valuable is Peter Brown's discussion, *The World of Late Antiquity.* The Greek magical papyri are now available in English thanks to H. D. Betz, *The Greek Magical Papyri in Translation.*

Hellenistic Judaism. Two indispensable works for understanding Judaism in this period generally, and Hellenistic Judaism in particular, are M. Hengel, *Judaism and Hellenism,* and Emil Schürer, *The History of the Jewish People in the Age of Jesus Christ.* Victor Tcherikover, *Hellenistic Civilization and the Jews,* considers especially social and political history. Arnaldo Momigliano, *Alien Wisdom: The Limits of Hellenization,* esp. pp. 74–122, brilliantly traces the interaction of these two cultures. See also Marcel Simon's classic study, *Verus Israel,* esp. pp. 52–86, on Judaism in the Diaspora, and pp. 316–55, on Jewish proselytism; and George Foot Moore, *Judaism in the First Centuries of the Christian Era* (Cambridge 1966, orig. pub. 1927). Both of these books draw extensively on Hebrew and Aramaic as well as Greek sources. This period is surveyed most recently by Shaye Cohen, *From the Maccabees to the Mishnah,* which includes a generous discussion of secondary literature, pp. 237–44.

Also valuable are Marcel Simon's more introductory studies, *Jewish Sects at the Time of Jesus,* and, more recently, in collaboration with A. Benoit, the relevant chapters in *Le Judaïsme et le Christianisme Antique;* John J. Collins, *Between Athens and Jerusalem;* and John G. Gager, *The Origins of Anti-Semitism,* esp.

pp. 35–112. The festschrift for W. D. Davies, *Jews, Greeks, and Christians: Religious Cultures in Late Antiquity*, edited by R. Hamerton-Kelly and R. Scroggs, contains several excellent essays on particular aspects of Hellenistic Judaism: see esp. those by E. P. Sanders ("The Covenant as a Sociological Category and the Nature of Salvation in Palestinian and Hellenistic Judaism," pp. 11–44) and R. Hamerton-Kelly ("Some Techniques of Composition in Philo's Allegorical Commentary, with Special Reference to the *de agricultura*: A Study in Hellenistic Midrash," pp. 45–56). See also the essays in *Jewish and Christian Self-Definition*, vol. 2: *Aspects of Judaism in the Greco-Roman Period*, ed. E. P. Sanders, A. I. Baumgarten, and Alan Mendelson.

For the Jewish literature produced in the Hellenistic period: Philo's works, in Greek with facing English, may be found in the Loeb series, translated by F. H. Colson, G. H. Whitaker, and R. Marcus, 10 vols., 2 suppl. vols. (Cambridge 1929–62). E. R. Goodenough, *An Introduction to Philo Judaeus;* J. Daniélou, *Philon d'Alexandrie;* and Samuel Sandmel, *Philo's Place in Judaism*, introduce the reader to Philo's cultural and religious milieu as well as to his exegetical and intellectual program.

Anthologies, summaries, and/or discussions of those more folkloric—or at least less formally philosophical—Hellenistic works, many of which were later adopted and adapted by Christian communities, can be found in George W. E. Nickelsburg, *Jewish Literature Between the Bible and the Mishnah;* N. deLange, *Apocrypha: Jewish Literature of the Hellenistic Age;* Samuel Sandmel, *Judaism and Christian Beginnings* (New York 1978), esp. pp. 255–301; R. H. Charles, *The Apocrypha and Pseudepigrapha of the Old Testament*, 2 vols. (Oxford 1913); more recently, *The Old Testament Pseudepigrapha*, ed. J. H. Charlesworth, 2 vols. (New York 1985).

New Testament. New Testament introductions provide the best means into the complex (and overwritten) field of NT criticism. Two that I have found most useful are W. G. Kümmel, *Introduction to the New Testament;* and W. Marxsen, *Introduction to the New Testament*. These studies survey the standard problems of NT criticism—probable dates for composition of various texts; their literary interrelation, if any; probable community and place of origin; key theological concepts, etc.—and offer select bibliographies. Still valuable as well is M. S. Enslin's lucid study, *Christian Beginnings*.

Academic consensus dates the Pauline letters to the decade 50–60; for a revised chronology, see G. Luedemann, *Paul, Apostle to the Gentiles*. Consensus dates for the evangelists, the arguments for which appear in Kümmel, *Introduction to the NT*, are: Mark, c. 65 to some time shortly after 70; Matthew, Luke/Acts, and John, the final third of the first century. J. A. T. Robinson has energetically argued for a much earlier dating of these texts, which he would push back into the first Christian generation: see his *Redating the New Testament*. For the position that Mark is an abridgement of Matthew, see W. R. Farmer, *Synoptic Problem*.

For the Gospel of John, see the commentaries and studies of C. K. Barrett, *The Gospel according to St. John;* Raymond Brown, *The Gospel according to John;* R. Bultmann, *The Gospel of John* and *Theology of the New Testament*, 2:3–92; C. H. Dodd, *The Interpretation of the Fourth Gospel* and *Historical Tradition in the Fourth Gospel;* R. Schnackenburg, *The Gospel of John;* J. Louis Martyn, *History and Theology in the Fourth Gospel.* For a consideration of the social functions of Johannine theology, the seminal article by Wayne Meeks, "The Stranger from Heaven in Johannine Sectarianism."

Two perennially important issues in Johannine exegesis are, on the theological level, the extent to which John predicates divinity to Jesus and, on the sociological level, the ethnic/religious identity of the Johannine community, i.e., whether it was Jewish. The two issues are not unrelated. The Christological issue turns in part upon interpretation of the gospel's prologue, in part upon interpretation of the evangelist's use of *ego eimi* (I am) as perhaps a reminiscence of the Hebrew, biblical YHWH (e.g., Ex 6:7). See Brown's commentary, *John,* 1:533–38. Academic consensus now holds, on the strength of the gospel's anti-Jewish statements and the clear references in the text to an expulsion from the synagogue, that John's community was originally Jewish: Martyn, *History and Theology,* in particular should be consulted here; see also Raymond Brown, *The Community of the Beloved Disciple.* Some of these arguments in turn draw on the *Birkat ha-minim,* a Jewish invocation against religious deviance (and "deviants"): was this related to the Johannine community's expulsion from the synagogue? Cf., on this point, R. Kimelman, "Birkat ha-minim and the Lack of Evidence for an Anti-Christian Jewish Prayer in Late Antiquity."

For Matthew, see W. D. Davies, *The Setting of the Sermon on the Mount;* the articles by F. C. Grant in *IDB* 3:302–13, and by R. G. Hamerton-Kelly in *IDBS,* 580–83. Esp. useful for a sense of the social realities underlying the evangelist's presentation is the study by Douglas R. A. Hare, *The Theme of Jewish Persecution of Christians in the Gospel according to St. Matthew.*

For Luke, see H. Conzelmann, *The Theology of St. Luke; Studies in Luke-Acts,* ed. L. Keck and J. Louis Martyn; E. Haenchen, *The Acts of the Apostles;* and the articles by Vincent Taylor in *IDB,* 3:180–88, and by W. C. Robinson, Jr., in *IDBS,* pp. 558–60.

For Mark, see esp. the commentary by Denis Nineham, *Gospel of Saint Mark;* T. A. Burkill's study, *Mysterious Revelation;* M. D. Hooker, *Son of Man in Mark;* and the article by C. E. B. Cranfield in *IDB,* 3:267–77, and by Norman Perrin in *IDBS,* pp. 571–73. S. G. F. Brandon's two controversial studies, *The Fall of Jerusalem and the Christian Church,* 2d ed., and *Jesus and the Zealots,* set this and the other gospels in their political and cultural context; *Jesus and the Politics of His Day,* ed. E. Bammel and C. F. D. Moule, is a critical response to Brandon and the measure of the strength of his suggestions. On Mark, see esp. the essays by F. F. Bruce, "The Date and Character of Mark," pp. 69–90, and D. R. Catchpole, "The Triumphal Entry," pp. 319–34.

Works on Paul to which I am particularly indebted include E. P. Sanders, *PPJ* and *PLJP;* Krister Stendahl, *Paul among the Jews and Gentiles;* Johannes Munck, *Paul and the Salvation of Mankind;* H. J. Schoeps, *Paul: The Theology of the Apostle;* John Knox, *Chapters in a Life of Paul;* Wayne A. Meeks, *The First Urban Christians,* a study of Paul's communities; W. D. Davies, *Paul and Rabbinic Judaism,* and his essays in *Jewish and Pauline Studies;* and the articles by Lloyd Gaston. On Galatians in particular, see the commentary by H. D. Betz, *Galatians;* on Romans, those of A. Nygren (Philadelphia 1949), C. K. Barrett, *Commentary on the Epistle to the Romans;* and E. Käsemann, *Romans;* see also the study by Johannes Munck, *Christ and Israel: An Interpretation of Romans 9–11.*

Ancient Israel. The various articles in the Encyclopedia Judaica, 16 vols. + suppls. (Jerusalem 1971), and in *IDB* provide very good introductions to topics and issues in Jewish history. Good general histories of the biblical period include J. Bright, *History of Israel;* R. de Vaux, *Early History of Israel;* Salo Baron, *Social and Religious History of the Jews,* vol. 1. For religious history, see H. Kaufmann, *The Religion of Israel.* On the history of and behind the Hebrew Bible, see O. Eissfeldt, *The Old Testament;* and the more recent essays by P. R. Ackroyd, G. W. Anderson, S. Talmon, and G. Vermes in *The Cambridge History of the Bible,* ed. P. R. Ackroyd and C. F. Evans (Cambridge 1975), vol. 1.

Judaism in Palestine. For the period roughly from Alexander the Great (d. 323 B.C.E.) to the Bar Kochba revolt (132–35 C.E.), esp. for Palestine, see Schürer, *HJP;* Salo Baron, *The Jewish Community;* S. Zeitlin, *The Rise and Fall of the Judean State.* On Rome, see E. Mary Smallwood, *The Jews under Roman Rule;* on the war in 66–73 and its effects on Christian tradition, see Brandon, *Fall of Jerusalem* and *Jesus and the Zealots.* On Palestinian Judaism, consult Sanders, *PPJ* and *JJ;* Geza Vermes, *Jesus the Jew;* A. Büchler, *Types of Jewish-Palestinian Piety;* and Morton Smith, "Palestinian Judaism in the First Century," which warns against forgetting how deeply Hellenistic culture had penetrated Jewish Palestine. The indispensable primary sources are Josephus, *AJ* and *BJ,* available in facing Greek/English in the Loeb series, 10 vols. (Cambridge 1926–65).

John G. Gager, *Kingdom and Community,* esp. pp. 2–65, puts Jewish millenarian movements of this period in sociological and anthropological perspective, emphasizing the degree to which continuing Roman occupation provided their political preconditions. See also Gerd Theissen, *Sociology of Early Palestinian Christianity;* and the more recent book by R. Horsley and J. S. Hanson, *Bandits, Prophets, and Messiahs.* Michael Stone, *Scriptures, Sects, and Visions,* nicely combines social history with a focus on this literature; see also Abba Hillel Silver, *History of Messianic Speculation in Israel,* pp. 3–35. Apparently chronological speculations added to these expectations: the end of the world could be estimated by calculating its age. On this tradition, A. Harvey, *Jesus and the Constraints of History,* pp. 69–70; Lloyd Gaston, *No Stone on Another,* pp. 463–68, which includes copious references to the rabbinic material.

Other studies of and texts from the particular groups within Palestine: For the Pharisees, L. Finkelstein, *The Pharisees;* Moore, *Judaism,* 1.56–92 (the rise of the Pharisees; Shammai and Hillel; and the consolidation after 70 C.E. at Jamnia); J. Neusner, *From Politics to Piety;* Ellis Rivkin, *A Hidden Revolution,* and his article on the Pharisees in *IDBS,* pp. 657–63. The earliest written form of traditions from and about the Pharisees passed on to the rabbis was collected in the six tractates of the Mishnah, available in English translation as *Mishnayoth,* 3d ed., 6 vols. (Gateshead 1973). For mAvot I have also used the edition by R. T. Herford, *Pirke Aboth: The Ethics of the Talmud.* For the Dead Sea Scrolls, see the translation by Geza Vermes, *The Dead Sea Scrolls in English,* 3d ed. (Harmondsworth 1968), and his study *The Dead Sea Scrolls: Qumran in Perspective;* see also Sanders, *PPJ,* pp. 239–320. On the Qumran community, E.-M. Laperrousaz, *L'Attente du Messie en Palestine.* On political insurrectionists, besides the works already cited, see M. Hengel, *Die Zeloten;* and Y. Yadin, *Masada: Herod's Fortress and the Zealots' Last Stand.* The most intelligent consideration of the *amme ha-aretz*—who they were, what they believed and practiced, and how they were regarded by their more literate co-religionists—is in Sanders' *JJ*, pp. 174–211; see too his earlier treatment, *PPJ*, pp. 147–82.

On Jesus himself, the bibliography is enormous. I cite in the notes only works to which I am especially indebted, whether positively or negatively. Besides Sanders, Vermes, Brandon, Barrett, Davies, Harvey, and Hengel, the older studies of G. Bornkamm, *Jesus of Nazareth;* M. Goguel, *The Life of Jesus;* Charles Guignebert, *Jesus;* and Rudolph Bultmann, *Jesus and the Word* (New York 1958) and *Primitive Christianity in Its Contemporary Setting,* are valuable. On traditions about the Temple, consult Gaston's massive *No Stone on Another* and D. Juel's *Messiah and Temple.* All scholarship on Jesus in this century looks back to the classic study that first placed Jesus of Nazareth within his historical setting in first-century apocalyptic Judaism, Albert Schweitzer's *The Quest of the Historical Jesus.*

Sociological and Anthropological Studies. Classic studies of millenarian or apocalyptic movements include A. F. C. Wallace, "Revitalization Movements"; K. Burridge, *New Heaven, New Earth;* P. Worsley, *The Trumpet Shall Sound;* and Yonina Talmon, "Pursuit of the Millennium." Literary critic Frank Kermode's rich essay *The Sense of an Ending* investigates the logic of apocalyptic thinking, how it makes present events uniquely meaningful by imposing a plot on time, and how its calculations can be disconfirmed without being discredited. On the final point, from a sociological perspective, consult the study by Leon Festinger, Henry W. Reicken, and S. Schachter, *When Prophecy Fails.*

Bibliography

ANCIENT TEXTS

Jewish.
I cite biblical texts from the Revised Standard Version, except where I wanted to follow
the Hebrew more closely. In those few places, I translated myself. The intertesta-
mental Jewish writings are available in English; the most recent publication is *The
Old Testament Apocrypha and Pseudepigrapha*, 2 vols., ed. J. H. Charlesworth
(New York 1985). For the texts of the Essene community at Qumran, see Geza
Vermes, *The Dead Sea Scrolls in English*, 3d ed. (Harmondsworth 1968). Philo is
available, with facing Greek, in the Loeb series, 12 vols. (Cambridge 1929–62);
Josephus, in the same series, 10 vols. (Cambridge 1926–65).

    For the later rabbinical works: *Mishnayoth*, 3d ed., 6 vols. (Gateshead 1973);
Jerusalem Talmud, in modern French translation by Moïse Schwab (Paris 1871–
89); the *Babylonian Talmud*, with facing Hebrew/English in the Soncino edition
(New York 1965).

Christian.
I use the Revised Standard Version for New Testament citations except where I wanted
to follow the Greek more closely. In these instances, I translated myself. In addition:
Justin Martyr, "Dialogue with Trypho," *Ante-Nicene Fathers*, vol. 1, Grand Rapids
1973.
Ireneaus, "Adversus Haereses," *Ancient Christian Writers*, ed. C. A. Richardson, New
York, 1970.
Minucius Felix, "The Octavius," *Ante-Nicene Fathers*, vol. 4, Grand Rapids 1975.
Clement of Alexandria, "Stromateis," *Ante-Nicene Fathers*, vol. 2, Grand Rapids,
1975.
"Clementine Recognitions," *Ante-Nicene Fathers*, vol. 8 (1975).
Eusebius, "Oration on the Life of Constantine," *Nicene and Post-Nicene Fathers*, vol.
1, Grand Rapids 1976.
———, *Ecclesiastical History*, Loeb ed., 2 vols., Cambridge 1953.
———, *Praeparatio Evangelia*, 2 vols., Oxford 1903.
Roman.
Tacitus, *Annals and History*, Loeb ed., 2 vols., Cambridge 1932.

Suetonius, *Lives of the Caesars,* Loeb ed., 2 vols., Cambridge 1924.
Pliny the Elder, *Natural History,* Loeb ed., 10 vols., Cambridge 1938.

MODERN WORKS

Allport, G. W. and L. Postman, *The Psychology of Rumor,* New York 1965.
Alter, Robert, *The Art of Biblical Narrative,* New York 1981.
Applebaum, S., *Jews and Greeks in Ancient Cyrene,* Leiden 1979.
———, *Prolegomena to the Study of the Second Jewish Revolt,* A.D. *132–135,* British Archeological Reports, Oxford 1976.
Birdsall, J. N., "The New Testament Text," *The Cambridge History of the Bible,* ed. P. R. Ackroyd and C. F. Evans, Cambridge 1975, 1:308–76.
Bammel, E. and C. F. D. Moule, eds., *Jesus and the Politics of His Day,* Cambridge 1984.
Barnes, T. D., *Constantine and Eusebius,* Cambridge 1981.
Baron, Salo, *A Social and Religious History of the Jews,* 2d ed., vols. 1–2, New York, 1952.
———, *The Jewish Community,* Westport 1977; orig. pub. 1942.
Barrett, C. K., *Jesus and the Gospel Tradition,* London 1967.
———, *The Gospel according to St. John,* London 1958.
———, *The Gospel of John and Judaism,* Philadelphia 1975.
———, *A Commentary on the Epistle to the Romans,* New York 1957.
———, *The New Testament Background: Selected Documents,* New York 1961.
———, "The Interpretation of the Old Testament in the New," *Cambridge History of the Bible,* ed. P. R. Ackroyd and C. F. Evans, Cambridge 1975, 1:377–411.
Bauer, W., *A Greek-English Lexicon of the New Testament and Other Early Christian Literature,* 2d ed., rev. F. W. Gringrinch and F. Danner, Chicago 1979.
Beker, J. Christiaan, *Paul the Apostle: The Triumph of God in Life and Thought,* Philadelphia 1980.
Best, E., "The Revelation to Evangelize the Gentiles," *JTS* n.s. 35 (1984), pp. 1–30.
Betz, H. D., *Galatians,* Philadelphia 1979.
———, *The Greek Magical Papyri in Translation,* vol. 1, Chicago 1986.
Bickerman, E., *From Ezra to the Last of the Maccabees,* New York 1962.
Borgen, Peder, "Observations on the Theme 'Paul and Philo': Paul's Preaching of Circumcision in Galatia (Gal 5:11) and Debates on Circumcision in Philo," *Die paulinische Literatur und Theologie,* ed. S. Pederson, Aarhus 1980, pp. 85–102.
Bornkamm, G., *Paul,* New York 1971.
———, *Jesus of Nazareth,* New York 1960.
Brandon, S. G. F., *Jesus and the Zealots,* Manchester 1967.
———, *The Fall of Jerusalem and the Christian Church,* 2d ed., London 1957; orig. pub. 1951.
Bright, J., *History of Israel,* 3d ed., Philadelphia 1981.
Brown, Peter, *The World of Late Antiquity: From Marcus Aurelius to Mohammed,* New York 1971.
Brown, Raymond E., *The Gospel according to John,* 2 vols., New York 1966 /1.
———, *The Birth of the Messiah: A Commentary on the Infancy Narratives in Matthew and Luke,* New York 1977.
———, *The Community of the Beloved Disciple,* New York 1979.

Brown, Raymond E. and J. P. Meier, *Antioch and Rome*, New York 1983.

Bruce, F. F., "The Date and Character of Mark," *Jesus and the Politics of his Day*, ed. E. Bammel and C. F. D. Moule, Cambridge 1984, pp. 69–90.

——, "The Curse of the Law," *Paul and Paulinism: Essays in Honour of C. K. Barrett*, ed. M. Hooker and S. G. Wilson, London 1982, pp. 27–36.

Büchler, A., *Types of Jewish-Palestinian Piety from 70 B.C.E. to 70 C.E.*, New York 1968; orig. pub. 1922.

Bultmann, Rudolph, *Theology of the New Testament*, 2 vols., New York 1951–55.

——, *The History of the Synoptic Tradition*, New York 1963.

——, *Primitive Christianity in Its Contemporary Setting*, New York 1956.

——, *The Gospel of John*, Oxford 1971.

Burkill, T. A., *Mysterious Revelation*, Ithaca 1963.

Burridge, K., *New Heaven, New Earth: A Study of Millenarian Activities*, New York 1969.

Catchpole, D. R., *The Trial of Jesus*, Leiden 1971.

——, "The 'Triumphal' Entry," *Jesus and the Politics of His Day*, ed. E. Bammel and C. F. D. Moule, Cambridge 1984, pp. 319–34.

Cohen, Shaye J. D., *From the Maccabees to the Mishnah*, Philadelphia 1987.

Collins, John J., *Between Athens and Jerusalem: Jewish Identity in the Hellenistic Diaspora*, New York 1983.

Conzelmann, H., *The Theology of St. Luke*, New York 1961.

——, *1 Corinthians: A Commentary on the First Epistle to the Corinthians*, Philadelphia 1975.

Coser, L., *The Functions of Social Conflict*, New York 1956.

Dahl, N. A., *The Crucified Messiah and Other Essays*, Minneapolis 1974.

Daniélou, J., *Philon d'Alexandrie*, Paris 1958.

Daube, David, *The New Testament and Rabbinic Judaism*, London 1973 (orig. pub. 1956).

——, "Conversion to Judaism and Early Christianity," *Ancient Jewish Law*, Leiden 1981, pp. 1–32.

Davies, W. D., *Jewish and Pauline Studies*, Philadelphia 1984.

——, *The Gospel and the Land: Early Christianity and Jewish Territorial Doctrine*, Berkeley 1974.

——, *Paul and Rabbinic Judaism*, 4th ed., Philadelphia 1980.

——, *The Setting of the Sermon on the Mount*, Cambridge 1964.

deLange, N., *Apocrypha: Jewish Literature of the Hellenistic Age*, New York 1978.

Dodd, C. H., *The Parables of the Kingdom*, rev. ed., London 1961.

——, *The Interpretation of the Fourth Gospel*, Cambridge 1953.

——, *Historical Tradition in the Fourth Gospel*, Cambridge 1963.

Dodds, E. R., *Pagan and Christian in an Age of Anxiety*, New York 1970.

Donfried, K. P., ed., *The Romans Debate*, Minneapolis 1977.

Dupont, J., "The Conversion of Paul and Its Influence on His Understanding of Salvation by Faith," *Apostolic History and the Gospel*, ed. W. W. Gasque and R. P. Martin, Grand Rapids 1970.

Eissfeldt, O., *The Old Testament: An Introduction*, New York 1976.

Enslin, M. S., *Christian Beginnings*, New York 1938.

Evans, C. F., "The New Testament in the Making," *Cambridge History of the Bible*, ed. P. R. Ackroyd and C. F. Evans, Cambridge 1975, 1:232–83.

Falk, Z. W., *Introduction to Jewish Law of the Second Commonwealth*, 2 vols., Leiden 1972–78.

Farmer, W. R., *The Synoptic Problem: A Critical Analysis*, Dillsboro 1976.

Finkelstein, L., *The Pharisees*, 3d ed., 2 vols., Philadelphia 1962.

Ferguson, John, *The Religions of the Roman Empire*, Old Woking 1970.

———, *The Heritage of Hellenism: The Greek World from 323 to 31 B.C.*, London 1973.

Festinger, Leon, Henry W. Reicken, and S. Schachter, *When Prophecy Fails: A Social and Psychological Study of a Modern Group that Predicted the Destruction of the World*, New York 1964; orig. pub. 1956.

Fredriksen, Paula, "Paul and Augustine: Conversion Narratives, Orthodox Traditions, and the Retrospective Self," *JTS* n.s. 37 (1986), 3–34.

Fox, Robin Lane, *Pagan and Christian*, New York 1987.

Gager, John G., *The Origins of Anti-Semitism: Attitudes toward Judaism in Pagan and Christian Antiquity*, New York 1985.

———, *Kingdom and Community: The Social World of Early Christianity*, Englewood Cliffs 1975.

———, "The Gospels and Jesus: Some Doubts about Method," *JR* 54 (1974), 244–72.

———, "Some Notes on Paul's Conversion," *NTS* 27 (1981), 697–704.

———, *Moses in Graeco-Roman Paganism*, Nashville 1972.

Gaston, Lloyd, *No Stone on Another: Studies in the Significance of the Fall of Jerusalem in the Synoptic Gospels*, Leiden 1970.

———, "Paul and Torah," *Anti-Semitism and the Foundations of Christianity*, ed. A. Davies, New York 1979, pp. 48–71.

———, "Israel's Enemies in Pauline Theology," *NTS* 28 (1982), 400–423.

———, "Paul and the Law in Galatians 2–3," *Anti-Judaism in Early Christianity*, ed. P. Richardson, Waterloo, Ontario, 1986.

Geertz, Clifford, *Islam Observed: Religious Development in Morocco and Indonesia*, Chicago 1968.

Goodenough, E. R., "The Perspective of Acts," *Studies in Luke-Acts*, ed. L. E. Keck and J. L. Martyn, Philadelphia 1980.

———, *The Jurisprudence of the Jewish Courts in Egypt: Legal Administration by the Jews under the Early Roman Empire as described by Philo Judaeus*, New Haven 1929.

———, *Jewish Symbols in the Graeco-Roman Period*, 13 vols, Princeton 1953–68.

———, *An Introduction to Philo Judaeus*, 2d ed., 2 vols., Oxford 1962.

Goguel, M., *The Life of Jesus*, New York 1960; orig. pub. 1933.

———, "Remarques sur un aspect de la conversion de Paul," *JBL* 53 (1934), 257–67.

Goppelt, Leonhard, *Jesus, Paul, and Judaism*, New York 1964.

Grant, R. M., "The New Testament Canon," *Cambridge History of the Bible*, ed. P. R. Ackroyd and C. F. Evans, 1:284–307.

Grelot, P., *L'Espérance Juive à l'heure de Jésus*, Paris 1978.

Guignebert, Charles, *Jesus*, New York 1935.

———, *Le Monde Juif vers le temps de Jésus*, Paris 1969; orig. pub. 1935.

Haenchen, E., *The Acts of the Apostles*, Philadelphia 1971.

———, "The Book of Acts as Source Material for the History of Early Christianity," *Studies in Luke-Acts*, ed. L. E. Keck and J. L. Martyn, Philadelphia 1980.

Hamerton-Kelly, R. G., *Pre-existence, Wisdom, and the Son of Man: A Study of the Idea of Pre-existence in the New Testament,* Cambridge 1973.

Hamerton-Kelly, R. and R. Scroggs, eds., *Jews, Greeks, and Christians: Religious Cultures in Late Antiquity,* Leiden 1976.

Hare, Douglas R. A., *The Theme of Jewish Persecution of Christians in the Gospel according to St. Matthew,* Cambridge 1967.

Harnack, Adolf von, *The Mission and Expansion of Christianity in the First Three Centuries,* 2 vols., New York 1962.

Harvey, A., *Jesus and the Constraints of History,* Philadelphia 1982.

Heinemann, J., *Prayer in the Talmud,* Berlin 1977.

Hengel, Martin, *Judaism and Hellenism,* 2 vols., Philadelphia 1974.

———, *Crucifixion,* Philadelphia 1977.

———, *Between Jesus and Paul,* Philadelphia 1983.

———, *Acts and the History of Earliest Christianity,* Philadelphia 1979.

———, *The Son of God,* Philadelphia 1976.

———, *The Charismatic Leader and His Followers,* New York 1981.

———, *Die Zeloten,* 2d ed., Leiden 1976.

Herford, R. Travers, *Christianity in Talmud and Midrash,* New York 1975; orig. pub. 1903.

———, ed., *Pirke Avoth: The Ethics of the Talmud: Sayings of the Fathers,* New York 1962.

Homberg, B., *Paul and Power,* Lund 1978.

Hooker, M. D., *The Son of Man in Mark,* London 1967.

———, "Christology and Methodology," *NTS* 17 (1970–71), 480–87.

Horsley, Richard, "'How can some of you say that there is no resurrection of the dead?' Spiritual Elitism in Corinth," *NovT* 20 (1978), 203–231.

Horsley, R. and J. S. Hanson, *Bandits, Prophets, and Messiahs: Popular Movements in the Time of Jesus,* Minneapolis 1985.

Hultgren, A. J., "Paul's Pre-Christian Persecutions of the Church: Their Purpose, Locale, and Nature," *JBL* 95 (1976), 97–111.

Jeremias, J., *The Parables of Jesus,* New York 1963.

———, *The Prayers of Jesus,* Philadelphia 1967.

Jewett, R., *A Chronology of Paul's Life,* Philadelphia 1979.

Jonas, Hans, *The Gnostic Religion,* Boston 1963.

———, "The Soul in Gnosticism and Plotinus," *Colloque international sur le néoplatonisme,* Paris 1971, pp. 45–53.

Judge, E. A., "The Social Identity of the First Christians: A Question of Method in Religious History," *Journal of Religious History* 11 (1980), 201–17.

Juel, D., *Messiah and Temple: The Trial of Jesus in the Gospel of Mark,* Missoula 1977.

Käsemann, E., *New Testament Questions of Today,* Philadelphia 1969.

———, *Romans,* Grand Rapids 1980.

———, *Perspectives on Paul,* Philadelphia 1971.

Kaufmann, H., *The Religion of Israel,* Chicago 1960.

Keck, L. and J. Louis Martyn, eds., *Studies in Luke-Acts,* Philadelphia 1980, orig. pub. 1966.

Kee, H. C., *Miracle in the Early Christian World,* New Haven 1983.

Kermode, Frank, *The Sense of an Ending: Studies in the Theory of Fiction*, New York 1966; repr. 1981.
——, *The Genesis of Secrecy: On the Interpretation of Narrative*, Cambridge 1979.
Kim, S., *The Origins of Paul's Gospel*, Grand Rapids 1982.
Kimelman, R., "Birkat ha-minim and the Lack of Evidence for an Anti-Christian Jewish Prayer in Late Antiquity," *Jewish and Christian Self-Definition*, ed. E. P. Sanders, A. I. Baumgarten, and A. Mendelson, Philadelphia 1981, 2:226–44.
Klausner, J., *From Jesus to Paul*, New York 1943.
——, *Jesus of Nazareth*, New York 1925.
Knox, John, *Marcion and the New Testament*, Chicago 1942.
——, *Chapters in a Life of Paul*, New York 1950.
Koester, Helmut, *History, Culture, and Religion of the Hellenistic Age*, vol. I, Philadelphia 1982.
Kraabel, A. T., "Paganism and Judaism: The Sardis Evidence," *Paganisme, Judaisme, Christianisme: Mélanges offerts à Marcel Simon*, ed. A. Benoit, M. Philonenko, and C. Vogel, Paris 1978, pp. 13–33.
Kümmel, W. G., *Introduction to the New Testament*, rev. Engl. ed., Nashville 1975.
——, *Römer 7 und das Bild des Menschen im Neuen Testament*, Munich 1974; orig. pub. 1929.
Lampe, G. W. H., "A.D. 70 in Christian Reflection," *Jesus and the Politics of his Day*, ed. E. Bammel and C. F. D. Moule, Cambridge 1984, pp. 153–171.
Laperrousaz, E.-M., *L'Attente du Messie en Palestine à la vieille et au début de l'ère chrétienne*, Paris 1982.
Levy, B. J., "Torah in the Messianic Age," *Gesher* 7 (1979), 167–81.
Lindars, Barnabas, *Jesus Son of Man: A Fresh Examination of the Son of Man Sayings in the Gospels*, Grand Rapids 1983.
Linton, O. "The Third Aspect: A Neglected Point of View," *STh* 3 (1949), 79–95.
Lohfink, G., *The Conversion of St. Paul: Narrative and History in Acts*, Chicago 1976.
Luedemann, Gerd, "The Successors of Pre-70 Jerusalem Christianity: A Critical Evaluation of the Pella-Tradition," *Jewish and Christian Self-Definition: The Shaping of Christianity in the Second and Third Centuries*, vol. 1, ed. E. P. Sanders, Philadelphia 1980, pp. 161–73.
——, *Paul, Apostle to the Gentiles: Studies in Chronology*, Philadelphia 1984.
MacMullen, Ramsey, *Paganism in the Roman Empire*, New Haven 1981.
Malherbe, A. J., *Social Aspects of Early Christianity*, Philadelphia 1983.
Martyn, J. Louis, *History and Theology in the Fourth Gospel*, New York 1968.
——, *The Gospel of John in Christian History*, New York 1978.
Marxsen, W., *Introduction to the New Testament*, Philadelphia 1974.
McEleney, Neil J., "Conversion, Circumcision, and the Law," *NTS* 20 (1974), 319–41.
Meeks, Wayne A., "The Stranger from Heaven in Johannine Sectarianism," *JBL* 91 (1972), 44–72.
——, "Social Functions of Apocalyptic Language in Pauline Christianity," *Apocalypticism in the Mediterranean World and the Near East: Proceedings of the International Colloquium on Apocalypticism, Uppsala, August 12–17, 1979*, Tübingen 1983.

————, "'Am I a Jew?'—Johannine Christianity and Judaism," *Christianity, Judaism, and other Graeco-Roman Cults: Studies for Morton Smith at 60*, ed. J. Neusner, Leiden 1975, pp. 163–86.

————, *The First Urban Christians*, New Haven, 1983.

Meeks, Wayne A. and Robert L. Wilken, *Jews and Christians in Antioch in the First Four Centuries of the Common Era*, Missoula 1978.

Menoud, Philippe, "Revelation and Tradition: The Influence of Paul's Conversion on His Theology," *Interpretation* 7 (1952), 131–41.

Meyer, P., "Romans 10:4 and the End of the Law," *The Divine Helmsman: Studies in God's Control of Human Events*, ed. J. L. Crenshaw and S. Sandmel, New York 1980, pp. 59–78.

Momigliano, Arnaldo, *Alien Wisdom: The Limits of Hellenization*, Cambridge 1975.

Moore, George Foot, "Christian Writers on Judaism," *HTR* 14 (1921), 197–254.

————, *Judaism in the First Centuries of the Christian Era: The Age of the Tannaim*, 3 vols., Cambridge, Mass. 1927–30.

Montefiore, C. J. G., *Judaism and Saint Paul*, London 1914.

Munck, Johannes, *Paul and the Salvation of Mankind*, Atlanta 1977.

————, *Christ and Israel: An Interpretation of Romans 9–11*. Philadelphia 1967.

————, "La Vocation de l'apôtre Paul," *StT* 1 (1948), 131–45.

Neusner, J., *First Century Judaism in Crisis*, New York 1982.

————, *The Rabbinic Traditions about the Pharisees before 70*, 3 vols., Leiden 1971.

————, "The Use of the Mishnah for the History of Judaism prior to the Time of the Mishnah," *JSJ* 11 (1980), 1–9.

————, *A Life of Yohanan ben Zakkai, Ca. 1–80 C.E.*, 2d ed., Leiden 1970.

————, *From Politics to Piety: The Emergence of Pharisaic Judaism*, 2d ed., New York 1979.

Nickelsburg, George W. E., *Jewish Literature between the Bible and the Mishnah*, Philadelphia 1981.

Nilsson, M. P., "The New Conception of the Universe in Late Greek Paganism," *Eranos* 44 (1946), 20–27.

Nineham, Denis, *The Gospel of Saint Mark*, London 1963.

Nock, A. D., *Conversion. The Old and the New in Religion from Alexander the Great to Augustine of Hippo*, New York 1961, orig. pub. 1933.

Pagels, E. *The Gnostic Paul: Gnostic Exegesis of the Pauline Letters*, Philadelphia 1975.

Parkes, James, *The Foundations of Judaism and Christianity*, Chicago 1969.

Parvis, M. M., "Text, NT," *Interpreter's Dictionary of the Bible*, Nashville 1962, 4:594–95.

Patai, R., *The Messiah Texts*, New York 1979.

Pearson, Birger A., "1 Thessalonians 2:13–16: A Deutero-Pauline Interpolation," *HTR* 64 (1971), 79–94.

Perrot, Charles, *Jésus et l'histoire*, Paris 1979.

Raïsänen, Heikki, *Paul and the Law*, Philadelphia 1986.

Reicke, Bo, "The Law and This World according to Paul," *JBL* 70 (1951), 259–76.

————, "Judaeo-Christianity and the Jewish Establishment, A.D. 33–66," *Jesus and the Politics of His Day*, ed. E. Bammel and C. F. D. Moule, Cambridge 1984, pp. 145–52.

Reynolds, J. and R. Tannenbaum, *Jews and God-fearers at Aphrodisias: Greek Inscriptions with Commentary*, Cambridge 1987.

Rivkin, Ellis, *A Hidden Revolution: The Pharisees Search for the Kingdom Within*, Nashville 1978.

Robinson, J. A. T., *Redating the New Testament*, London 1976.

———, " 'His Witness Is True': A Test of the Johannine Claim," *Jesus and the Politics of His Day*, ed. E. Bammel and C. F. D. Moule, Cambridge 1984, pp. 453–76.

Robinson, J. M., "The Johannine Trajectory," *Trajectories through Early Christianity*, ed. J. M. Robinson and H. Koester, Philadelphia 1971, pp. 232–68.

S. Safrai, "Jewish Self-Government," *The Jewish People in the First Century*, vol. 1, ed. S. Safrai and M. Stern, Philadelphia 1974.

Sanders, E. P., *Jesus and Judaism*, Philadelphia 1985.

———, *Paul, the Law, and the Jewish People*, Philadelphia 1983.

———, *Paul and Palestinian Judaism: A Comparison of Patterns of Religion*, Philadelphia 1977.

———, ed., *Jewish and Christian Self-Definition*, vol 1: *The Shaping of Christianity in the Second and Third Centuries;* vol. 2, with A. I. Baumgarten and Alan Mendelson, *Aspects of Judaism in the Greco-Roman Period;* vol. 3, with Ben F. Meyer, *Self-Definition in the Greco-Roman World*, Philadelphia 1980–82.

Sandmel, Samuel, *Judaism and Christian Beginnings*, New York 1978.

———, *The Genius of Paul*, Philadelphia 1979.

———, *Philo's Place in Judaism*, Cincinnati 1956.

Schnackenburg, R., *The Gospel of John*, 3 vols., New York 1968–82.

Schiffman, L. H., "At the Crossroads: Tannaitic Perspectives on the Jewish–Christian Schism," *Jewish and Christian Self-Definition*, vol. 2: *Aspects of Judaism in the Greco-Roman Period*, ed. E. P. Sanders, A. I. Baumgarten and Alan Mendelson, Philadelphia 1981, pp. 115–56.

Schoeps, H. J., *Paul: The Theology of the Apostle in Light of Jewish Religious History*, Philadelphia 1961.

Schubert, K., "Biblical Criticism Criticised: With Reference to the Markan Report of Jesus' Examination before the Sanhedrin," *Jesus and the Politics of His Day*, ed. E. Bammel and C. F. D. Moule, Cambridge 1984, pp. 385–402.

Schürer, Emil, *The History of the Jewish People in the Age of Jesus Christ*, vols. 1–2, ed. and trans. Geza Vermes, Fergus Millar, and Matthew Black; vol. 3, ed. and trans. Geza Vermes, Fergus Millar, and Martin Goodman, Edinburgh 1973–86.

Schwartz, D. R., "The End of the GĒ (Acts 1:8): Beginning or End of the Christian Vision?" *JBL* 105 (1986), pp. 669–76.

Schweitzer, Albert, *The Quest of the Historical Jesus*, New York 1968; orig. pub. 1906.

Segal, Alan, *Rebecca's Children*, Cambridge 1987.

———, "Paul the Convert" (unpublished MS).

Silver, Abba Hillel, *A History of Messianic Speculation in Israel*, Boston 1959; orig. pub. 1927.

Simon, Marcel, *Verus Israel: Etude sur les relations entre Chrétiens et Juifs dans l'Empire Romain, (135–425)*, rev. ed., Paris 1964.

———, *Jewish Sects at the Time of Jesus*, Philadelphia 1967.

Simon, M. and A. Benoit, *Le Judaïsme et le Christianisme Antique*, 2d ed., Paris 1985.

Smallwood, E. Mary, *The Jews under Roman Rule: From Pompey to Diocletian*, Leiden 1976.

Smith, Morton, *Jesus the Magician*, New York, 1978.

———, "Palestinian Judaism in the First Century," *Israel, Its Role in Civilization*, ed. M. Davis, New York 1956, pp. 67–81.

———, "The Reason for the Persecution of Paul and the Obscurity of Acts," *Studies in Mysticism and Religion Presented to Gershom G. Scholem*, ed. E. E. Urbach, R. J. Zvi Werblowsky, and Ch. Wirszubski, Jerusalem 1967, pp. 261–68.

Stendahl, Krister, *Paul among the Jews and Gentiles and Other Essays*, Philadelphia 1976.

Stern, Menachem, *Greek and Latin Authors on Jews and Judaism*, 3 vols., Leiden 1974.

Stone, Michael, *Scripture, Sects, and Visions: A Profile of Judaism from Ezra to the Jewish Revolts*, Philadelphia 1980.

Talmon, Yonina, "The Pursuit of the Millennium: The Relation between Religious and Social Change," *Archives Européennes de Sociologie* 3 (1962), pp. 125–48.

Tcherikover, Victor, *Hellenistic Civilization and the Jews*, New York, 1977; orig. pub. 1959.

Theissen, Gerd, *Sociology of Early Palestinian Christianity*, Philadelphia 1978.

———, *The Social Setting of Pauline Christianity*, Philadelphia 1982.

Vansina, J., *Oral Tradition: A Study in Historical Methodology*, Chicago 1965.

Vaux, R. de, *The Early History of Israel*, Philadelphia 1978.

Vermes, Geza, *Jesus the Jew: A Historian's Reading of the Gospels*, Philadelphia 1981.

———, *Jesus and the World of Judaism*, Philadelphia 1984.

———, *The Dead Sea Scrolls: Qumran in Perspective*, rev. ed., Philadelphia 1981.

Vielhauer, P., "On the Paulinism of Acts," *Studies in Luke-Acts*, ed. L. Keck and J. L. Martyn, Philadelphia 1980 (orig. pub. 1966), pp. 33–50.

Wallace, A. F. C., "Revitalization Movements," *American Anthropologist* 58 (1956), pp. 264–81.

Whittaker, Molly, ed., *Jews and Christians: Graeco-Roman Views*, Cambridge 1984.

Wilckens, U., "Die Bekehrung des Paulus als religionsgeschichtliches Problem," *ZTK* 56 (1959), 273–93.

Winter, Paul, *On the Trial of Jesus*, rev. ed., ed. T. A. Burkill and G. Vermes, Berlin 1974.

Worsley, P., *The Trumpet Shall Sound: A Study of "Cargo" Cults in Melanesia*, 2d ed., New York 1968.

Yadin, Y., *Masada: Herod's Fortress and the Zealots' Last Stand*, New York 1966.

Zeisler, John, *Pauline Christianity*, New York 1983

Zeitlin, S., *The Rise and Fall of the Judean State*, 2 vols., Philadelphia 1962.

Index of Passages

Name Index

Subject Index

Abraham: prototypical convert, 16; divine promise to, 17, 71, 75, 76; in gospels, 21, 32, 36, 192; prototypical exile, 71, 76; in Paul, 147, 172, 206

Acts: and Paul, 27, 54–55, 171; and Holy Spirit, 27, 198; and Jerusalem church, 134, 142–45; Hellenists, 146, 157; and Diaspora synagogues, 193–96

Amme ha-aretz, 92–93

Aphrodisias inscription, 16n10, 149n33

Apocalyptic eschatology, 81–86, 88–93, 221, 229; and delay of End, x, xii, 62–64, 134, 135; and Jewish restoration theology, xi, 18n1, 82, 125, 130, 142, 175; and problem of evil, xi, 82; and charismatic prophets, 80, 83, 92; and Babylonian exile, 82, 113, 171; and Essenes, 83, 89–90; and political oppression, 83, 120, 124–25, 127; and insurrectionists, 90–91; and realized eschatology, 100–01, 173–74, 200, 203–04; and Jesus' resurrection, 133, 134, 141, 154, 156. *See also* End; Kingdom; Prophets and prophecy

Aramaic, 8, 19; and primitive Christian tradition, 3, 5, 19, 138–40, 179; Palestinian vernacular, 3, 13; and criteria of authenticity, 5–6

Astrology, 11–12

Baptism: in mystery cults, 12; in John, 21, 24; in Paul, 57; and repentance, 97, 127

Bible. *See* Covenant; New Testament; Septuagint; Torah

Body: in Hellenism, 11, 12; resurrection of, 18n1, 171; redemption of, 57, 58, 59, 174–75; and celibacy, 58, 90, 99

Charismatics, 91–92

Christianity: early varieties of, 7, 210–11, 212, 214; and orthodoxy, 7, 212, 214; relation to own past, 7–8, 64, 135, 177–78, 184–85, 190, 197, 207, 208, 209, 214–15; and Hellenistic Judaism, 17, 211; and Hellenism, 18, 62–64, 213; relation to Judaism, 62, 64,

104–05, 110, 135, 210–14. *See also individual gospels*

Church (also *ekklēsia*): as New Israel, 17, 102, 211; as "true Israel," 43; body of Christ, 57, 61, 164; in Jerusalem, 134, 142–45, 146, 148, 156, 157, 212–13; within Diaspora synagogues, 142, 149–56 passim, 170, 173

Circumcision: required of Israel, 15, 78; covenant with Abraham, 71; not required of Gentiles, 107, 107n16, 145, 150, 166, 173; required for male converts to Judaism, 107, 107n16, 150, 166; and Paul, 145, 147, 151, 152–53, 166–70

Cosmos: and matter, 10; in Hellenism, 10–13, 225; relation to soul, 11; hostile powers within, 11, 12, 56, 60, 100, 163, 175, 221, 222, 224; and evil, 12, 56, 213; in John, 19, 20, 21, 22, 26, 199; in Paul, 56, 57, 59, 60, 63, 122, 163, 172–73, 175

Covenant, xi, 70–77; and Exile, xi, 17, 188; and apocalyptic eschatology, xi, 82; Abraham, 17, 71; irrevocable, 59, 73, 74, 74n3, 75, 77, 82, 171–76, 205; Noah, 70, 75; and circumcision, 71; and Land, 71, 72; new, 76, 101, 115. *See also* Land; Torah

Creation, xi, 70; and Christ, 19, 56, 60, 157, 159; as bond of covenant, 77; and Sabbath, 77

Crucifixion: of the messiah, x, 123; insurrectionists, 3, 35, 79, 80, 96, 116, 123–25, 148; of Jesus, 3, 50, 56, 96, 97, 109–10, 116, 123–25, 133; as Christ's exaltation, 22, 123, 203; in Paul, 56, 122, 147–48; and "curse," 147–48; of Pharisees, 148

Devil (also Satan), 29, 32, 44, 46–47, 55; father of Jews, 22, 23, 25; ruler of this world, 22, 25, 26, 57; defeated at Parousia, 57, 61; and Judas, 116

Disciples: followed Jesus, ix, 102, 133, 153; continued his mission, ix, 134, 135, 153, 154, 170; resurrection experience, xii, 133, 134, 148, 153, 175, 180; in gospels, 30, 32,

252